REVISED EDITION

MASTERING THE ART OF SELF-RENEWAL

ADULTHOOD AS CONTINUAL REVITALIZATION

This book has also been published
under the title *The Adult Years*

FREDERIC M. HUDSON

MJF BOOKS
NEW YORK

Published by MJF Books
Fine Communications
Two Lincoln Square
60 West 66th Street
New York, NY 10023

Mastering the Art of Self-Renewal
LC Control Number 2001119161
ISBN 1-56731-460-0

Copyright © 1999 by Jossey-Bass, Inc. Publishers, 350 Sansome Street,
San Francisco, California 94104

This edition published by arrangement with John Wiley & Sons, Inc., New
York

Jossey-Bass is a registered trademark of Jossey-Bass Inc., A Wiley Company.

This book has also been published under the title *The Adult Years*.

Excerpt from *The Phantom Toolbooth* by Norton Juster is reprinted by permission
of Random House, Inc. Copyright 1961. The poem "Not Exactly a Command
Performance" by Ric Masten is reprinted by permission.

Manufactured in the United States of America on acid-free paper ∞

MJF Books and the MJF colophon are trademarks of Fine Creative Media, Inc.

BG   10 9   8   7   6   5   4   3   2   1

Contents

Preface   vii

About the Author   xv

Prologue   1

Part One: The Emerging Adult   5

1.   **In Over Our Heads**   7
2.   **Finding Fulfillment in Cyclical Lives**   30

    Table 1. Linear and Cyclical Views   46

Part Two: The Renewal Cycle: Life Chapters and Life Transitions   51

3.   **An Overview of the Renewal Cycle**   53

    Diagram 1. The Renewal Cycle: Life Chapters and Life Transitions   57

    Diagram 2. Ten Life Skills for Sustaining Purpose and Passion in the Renewal Cycle   72

4.   **Life Chapters**   75

    Diagram 3. Phase 1—Dreaming, Planning, and Plateauing   77

    Diagram 4. Phase 2—Managing the Doldrums   92

5.   **Life Transitions**   99

    Diagram 5. Phase 3—Cocooning: Coming to Terms with Yourself   109

    Diagram 6. Phase 4—Getting Ready for the Next Chapter: A Time for Experimenting   117

Part Three: The Adult Life Cycle   125

6.   **Meaning and Mission Across the Life Cycle**   127

    Diagram 7. The Life Cycle   128

Diagram 8. The Adult Life Cycle: Eight Versions
of Human Purpose   139

Table 2. Decade Orientations in the Life Cycle   142

7. **The Twenties, Thirties, and Midlife Transition:
Breaking Out, Staking Out, and Making It**   145

8. **The Forties and Fifties: Taking Stock,
Individuating, and Enjoying Life**   163

9. **The Sixties, Seventies, Eighties, and Nineties:
The Longest and Least-Defined Life Phase**   178

10. **Getting from Here to There: Six Principles of
Developmental Change**   204

Table 3. Historical Values   209

Part Four: Adults and Global Change   **221**

11. **Valuing the Global Context: The Adult
Challenges of the Twenty-First Century**   223

12. **The Self-Renewing Adult, the Resilient Society:
Ten Qualities of Self-Renewing Persons**   234

13. **A New Profession of Adult Mentors and Coaches**   253

Notes   263

Reading List   289

Index   317

Preface

I hear one central question over and over again in my work with adults: What can I count on in a world where little is definite anymore? This book provides some answers. In the twenty-first century, few adults know how to chart their lives with confidence. The thesis of the book is that as adults learn to master the change process within their own lives they will find new ways to renew their families, workplaces, and culture. Personal mastery of change is critical to the renewal process that our entire society seeks.

The purpose of this book is to identify skills and competencies that can empower adults throughout the life cycle. The book maps out the vast adult territory and provides a framework for how adults can proceed vitally from age twenty to age one hundred in the twenty-first century. Through a careful reading of this material, readers should be able to locate where they are in the change process and which skills are critical for designing a fulfilling personal and social future.

Point of View

Most grown-ups know very little about the territory of their sixty to one hundred adult years. They often lack realistic expectations and get mired in their own disappointments. They run out of dreams and may lack the ability to envision new ones. Some feel trapped by their early adult decisions regarding life partners, education, and careers. Most lose their way on a long journey they are not trained to take. In the twenty-first century, personal lives will be more complex and more fragile—all the more reason to master the art of living consciously and deliberately, day by day, year by year.

Good intentions and hard work are no longer enough to ensure lasting happiness and success. Today's adults need maps for the journey, along with the required human competence. As a nation, we waste our most valuable human resource—adults—because we don't promote their continued learning, development, deployment, and utilization in a systematic way. The relatively young field of adult development has produced much information but little applied knowledge on how adults can sustain self-renewing lives. Abundant research describes and explores aspects of adult life but precious little wisdom for how adults can design and manage their own lives.

This book is an effort to provide both guidance and wisdom. We will explore ways an adult today can establish a life course, construct durable life chapters, manage life and career changes and transitions, engage in lifelong learning and training, live an anticipatory life rather than a reactive one, master the art of self-renewal, and contribute to planetary renewal.

A major theme is that today's adults can provide our society with an ongoing source of cohesion and renewal. No one has stated this better than John W. Gardner, whose writings on self-renewal have been a major inspiration for this book:

> If a society hopes to achieve renewal, it will have to be a hospitable environment for creative men and women. It will also have to produce men and women with the capacity for self-renewal. . . . We know that men and women need not fall into a stupor of mind and spirit by the time they are middle-aged. They need not relinquish as early as they do the resilience of youth and the capacity to learn and grow. Self-renewal is possible.[1]

Audience

This book is written for adults who want to examine their future potentials and possibilities, people seeking to master more of the adult journey through new learning and training. These are adults who typically work hard, live busy lives, maintain careers or volunteer roles, manage money, play often, and fear that the yellow brick road ends sometime soon.

These adults are increasingly a pluralistic group of men and women from many ethnic backgrounds, with varying amounts of formal education and career experience. They include single and married adults, those who are divorced or remarried, homemakers as well as careerists, leaders and followers, the wealthy and the not-so-wealthy, individuals from varied lifestyles, and twentysomethings through ninetysomethings. This diverse audience, which will soon become the dominant majority, is looking for ways to fulfill individual dreams while providing leadership to the struggling institutions of our society.

Included in the audience are *high-performing adults*—people who are outwardly successful but who have not developed autonomous, private lives. Also in this group are professionals who want to rearrange their lives and priorities but don't know how to do so, as well as midlife adults facing outplacement, job terminations, or new career directions.

Some who are searching may be *disappointed persons*—men and women who feel stuck, bored, or trapped by the routines of their lives. Or perhaps they want to find a new beginning, or their lives are unraveling and they are overwhelmed by change or tragedy.

And *professionals* may be seeking new ways to manage human and organizational change—managers and human resource directors, for example. Educators, career counselors, members of the clergy, physicians and nurses, psychologists, and social workers who work with adults and adult systems are included in this group.

Some in the audience may be *students* who are searching for both an overview of the adult journey and a basic grasp of the competencies required—undergraduate, graduate, and professional-degree students who want to understand the adult life process in the context of contemporary change and renewal.

Organization of the Book

Part One, which focuses on the emerging adult of our time, examines the paradox that, while accelerating change has unshackled adults from cultural constraints and provided many new opportunities for personal and professional development, it has also disoriented and disempowered them. Chapter One contrasts the new opportunities for adult living with the widespread negative belief that the best days for America are behind us. The chapter concludes with a challenge for personal and social renewal.

Chapter Two contrasts linear and cyclical frameworks for understanding adult life. A case is made in support of a cyclical pattern in which people experience stability in their lives for a period of time, followed by a period of transition and reevaluation, followed by more stability. Diagrams are provided to illustrate the fundamental differences for adult life between the modular process of cyclical living and linear portraits. Two kinds of cycles—the cycle of change and the adult life cycle—are identified as the critical notions for mastering adult empowerment.

Part Two, which interprets the ongoing cycle of change in our lives, describes the human skills that empower adult life chapters and transitions. Chapter Three presents the pattern of adult change, with four phases of change and ten life skills for facilitating adult renewal and empowerment. Diagrams illustrate how the cycle of change works. Chapter Four describes how to build strong adult life chapters and how to cooperate with their endings. The chapter explains how adults usually repair and renew troubled life chapters. Chapter Five interprets life transitions that occur when life chapters cannot be sustained, repaired, or renewed; it defines life transitions and their purpose. The intricate processes of disengagement and *cocooning*, during which adults heal and discover their own self-sufficiency, are interpreted.

Part Three portrays the life cycle changes that take place in adult life from about age twenty to age one hundred.[2] The dominant theme is how adults redefine their life purpose at different points in the life cycle. Chapter Six explains how adults define life meaning and mission across the life cycle, as basic values are reprioritized within human systems. A diagram of the adult life cycle is provided, along with a table of adult changes, by decade, in life purpose, values, systems, and tasks.

Chapter Seven describes today's twentysomethings and thirtysomethings, including case examples and interpretations of their central life issues. Chapter Eight examines how fortysomethings and fiftysomethings express their life purpose, as self-reliance and interdependence become important focal points in the adult life cycle. Chapter Nine looks at the continuities and changes in sixtysomethings, seventysomethings, eightysomethings, and ninetysomethings as adult life continues to find new orientations and integrity, even as the aging process becomes more noticeable.

Chapter Ten presents six principles of life-cycle change—how adults understand the change that they go through during the long adult years. Six very different points of view are described and explored.

Part Four applies the ideas of the book to the self-renewing process in people and society. Chapter Eleven investigates the connections between adult life and global chaos. Six human dimensions of chaos are identified as creative ways adults can move into leadership roles and participate in the world. Chapter Twelve outlines the qualities of self-renewing people and then presents an articulation of adult mastery skills. And finally, Chapter Thirteen shows how mature people who take on roles of mentor-coaches can contribute valuable expertise to communities and corporations.

Background

Robert Lifton, in *The Broken Connection,* says, "There is a special quality of life-power available only to those seasoned by struggles of four or more decades. . . . The life-power of this stage can be especially profound."[3] This book grows out of thirty years of teaching "adult development" and "human systems development," mostly at the graduate level, and training adults in the skills presented here in a variety of settings, including corporate, governmental, religious, educational, and national intensive seminars that I have sponsored. The major struggle in the field of adult development, as in most of the behavioral and social sciences, has been over methodology. How can adults be studied objectively? Examining adult phenomena is like studying a moving target—touching on genetics, personal life cycles, family and work systems, the aging process, political and economic issues, sociohistorical epochs, and environmental conditions. The study of adults is extremely complex, and the orientations of the various academic disciplines do not seem adequate for the interdisciplinary or transdisciplinary phenomena in this field.

Nevertheless, the professional researchers in this field are high on methodology and low on theory. They are more concerned with objective ways of knowing than with beliefs about the objects being studied—adults. They study the parts more than the whole. Biologists examine adults from a perspective of organicity, chemistry, and evolution. Psychologists study individual behavior moving through a life span. Sociologists see social forces and systems shaping roles and events that they call adult life.[4]

Describing how adult life proceeds is difficult. Today's introductory texts on adult development are litanies of research findings from hundreds of studies that do not lend themselves to generalizations or life applications. Students and laypeople often feel flooded with information and tidbits of knowledge but left with little wisdom they can apply to their own lives. There is no easy way out of this dilemma.[5] We need both more theory building *and* more quantitative research.

Carl G. Jung has had considerable influence on this field.[6] Although a psychiatrist by training, his orientation is basically spiritual and mythological. Unlike Freud, who viewed human life as shaped through psychosexual stages in the early years of life, Jung portrayed the second half of life as a time of immense growth and development, particularly for personal introspection, reevaluation, and spiritual discovery. Although many developmentalists are not attracted to his mythological and symbolic way of organizing human constructs, Jung has exerted considerable influence on Charlotte Buhler and Fred Massarik, David Gutmann, Daniel Levinson, Joseph Campbell, and Robert Bly.[7] I have found that much of the Jungian material speaks to people in midlife and beyond, particularly his theme of individuation, which he viewed as the ripening of the inner, adult self in the second half of life. Many Jungian themes will be endorsed and woven into the material in this book, but these themes need to be related to other theories and modified by research findings in the field.

Erik H. Erikson produced the first systematic scheme of adult development, which was based on a Freudian perspective as it had evolved into ego psychology.[8] Erikson's genius was to stretch the psychosexual stages of human development into psychosocial concepts, bridging psychological and social orientations. Erikson, who has written much more specific material about children and adolescents than he has about adults, pictured life as a series of sequential stages. Two more recent scholars, Roger Gould and George E. Vaillant, expand Erikson's perspective.[9] Gould identifies adult progressions in relation to gradual transformation of the infantile myth of absolute safety, whereas Vaillant views adult life as a gradual adaptation of defense mechanisms to the realities of aging. Robert Kegan, a stage theorist from a Piagetian orientation, offers a theoretical model of the stages of adult life based on an ongoing rhythm between a need for independence or separation and a need for inclusion or attachment.[10]

Although stage theory is popular today, this book will argue against specific stages during the adult years. We will talk about the *maturational process* across the life cycle, and we'll maintain an interaction between developmental events and the social forces that surround them. Social forces of change are now major sources of personal change and development and can be neither subordinated to normative age periods nor distilled into predictable events. Yet we all need some way of explaining the sequencing of our lives from birth to death, and this book will suggest that throughout the life cycle, adults keep rearranging the same basic life issues (such as identity, achievement, intimacy, play and creativity, search for meaning, and contribution) around changing perspectives that our personal development, aging, and social conditions evoke from us. In this book, adult development will be conveyed in the context of continuous personal cycles within ongoing social change.

Most of the current literature on adult development has been written with the assumption that adults live in a world in which order is predominant over change. This book assumes that we now live in a period in which change is predominant over order. Adult life from now on will proceed with multiple options, random opportunities, information overload, life-long learning, a global orientation, ongoing social upheavals, and a constant need for people to be responsible for themselves as they raft their way along the river of change.

The field of adult development is shaped by many scholars who weave together our understanding of the adult years. Take a look at the Notes section at the back of this book to get a sense of the breadth of the field and the diversity of points of view. Although the study of adults is barely sixty years old, the demographics of the first half of the twenty-first century are creating a social urgency to understand adult issues as they apply to ourselves and to impending changes in our society.

This book is meant to provide direct information to the reader, with notes that connect the main text with many further notions and references. The major contribution of this book is helping adults understand the contours of their lives within the world as it is experienced today. Each of us individually and all of us collectively must become responsible for the personal and social realities of our time. The future presents us with more freedom than we ever asked for and more complexity than we ever wanted. Yet it is all we have and more than enough for shaping life paths far beyond the destinations that most of us seek or settle for.

Acknowledgments

I wish to thank many people for their contributions to this book: my mentors and guides and the scholars who received my manuscript as it was taking shape. These include Richard Beckhard, Ted Berkman, William Bridges, Joyce Cohen, Robert Farnquist, Charlie Garfield, Robert and Mary Goulding, Joseph Handlon, Althea Horner, Morris Keeton, Elaine Kepner, Dorothy Largay, Malcolm Knowles, Judy Long, Jack Murphy, Sam Osherson, John Schuster, Edie Seashore, Deborah Simmons, Robert Tannenbaum, John Vasconcellos, Louise Vondran, and Jackie Zilbach. Also included are my wife, Pamela McLean Hudson, and my children Jeffrey Scott Hudson, John Marshall Hudson, Lisa Sue Hudson, Christopher McLean Hudson, Michael McLean Hudson, and Charles McLean Hudson, as well as the many adult clients with whom I have worked and my colleagues on the faculty of both the Fielding Institute and the Hudson Institute of Santa Barbara. In addition, I want to thank my former students, particularly my doctoral students who researched themes of adult life, and those who volunteered biographical material for this book—Marvin Banasky, Marilyn Mosley, Richard Haid, and Larry L. King.

Santa Barbara, California FREDERIC M. HUDSON
April 1999

About the Author

Frederic M. Hudson is president of the Hudson Institute of Santa Barbara, California. He received his B.A. degree (1956) in philosophy from Kalamazoo College, his M.Div. degree (1959) in social ethics from Colgate Rochester Divinity School, and his Ph.D. degree (1968), specializing in the history of consciousness, from Columbia University. Hudson is a Rockefeller Fellow and a Danforth Fellow.

For the past twenty years, Hudson has conducted seminars for adults wanting to exercise creative choices in planning their lives. Through consultation, coaching, leadership training, transition management, and life-design seminars in educational and corporate settings, he has worked with more than seventeen thousand adults. His training programs have been effective with executives and managers, as well as with adults who have neither a career nor wealth. He is most widely known for his work with individuals and organizations "in transition" and has worked with personnel from hundreds of corporations and governmental agencies. The Hudson Institute of Santa Barbara, which he founded in 1986, has hosted participants from a wide range of backgrounds, including political leaders, senior officers of major corporations, work teams, educators, entrepreneurs, public relations and advertising executives, scientists, strategic planners, physicians, religious leaders, and sales executives.

Hudson is a member of the Society for Values in Higher Education, the American Society for Training and Development, and the Organization Development Network. He has served as president of the National Association of Free-Standing Graduate Schools; he has served as a trustee of the California Family Studies Foundation and the San Francisco Consortium and has been an institutional representative at the Council of Graduate Schools in the United States (1979–1986), the American Council on Education (1974–1986), the American Association of Colleges (1975–1986), the Western Association of Schools and Colleges (1974–1986), the Council for Adults and Experiential Learning (1974–1986), and the National Council of Schools of Professional Psychology (1976–1982). He has contributed articles to such publications as *Innovations in Counseling Psychology* (1977), *Instant Relief: The Encyclopedia of Self-Help* (1979), *Guidance Bulletin of the Iowa Personnel and Guidance Association* (1979), *Rothman's World Symposium on Human Resources* (1983), the New Directions for Higher Education quarterly sourcebook from Jossey-Bass called *Meeting the New Demand for Standards* (1983), and *Redecision Therapy: Expanded Perspectives* (1985, volume 2). His books include *Careers in World Affairs* (1960), *The Reign of the New Humanity* (1968), *Planning Your Life Through 2004* (1979), *Poems from Midlife* (1982), *The Joy of Old—A Guide to Successful Elderhood* (1995), *LifeLaunch—A Passionate Guide to the Rest of Your Life* (1996), *The Handbook of Coaching—A Resource Guide to Effective Coaching with Individuals and Organizations* (1999).

Hudson's career has been devoted to leadership roles in experiential education for adults. He has designed learning programs at several collegiate institutes to help students grow and develop as persons and as innovative change agents. He has lectured widely at universities and professional associations on adult learning, social ethics, and the management of change. As a dean and teacher at Stephens College, Columbia, Missouri (1961–1964), he directed off-campus service projects and internships. As assistant professor of Colby College, Waterville, Maine (1964–1969), he engaged students in learning projects related to the civil rights movement, the antipoverty program, and the peace movement; he was a frequent lecturer at universities on human development through participation in social movements. In 1969, he was appointed academic dean of Lone Mountain College, San Francisco, now part of the University of San Francisco, where he developed an external master's degree program in clinical psychology.

In 1974, Hudson became the founding president of the Fielding Institute, a professional graduate school in psychology and organization development. Fielding is a freestanding external degree institution, with headquarters in Santa Barbara, California. Now regionally accredited and widely recognized, it is one of the few graduate schools in the nation designed exclusively to educate adult professional leaders with advanced degrees in developmental and clinical psychology as well as organizational development. At Fielding, Hudson applied his knowledge of adult development and social systems to the graduate training of midlife students.

In 1986, Hudson left the Fielding Institute to begin the Hudson Institute of Santa Barbara, which offers training programs for adult renewal, career development, and organizational change. With over three hundred trained coaches located throughout the United States and Canada, the Institute provides programs in life planning, life transition management, retirement planning, organizational development, and career.

Hudson can be contacted at The Hudson Institute of Santa Barbara, 3463 State Street, Suite 520, Santa Barbara, CA 93105, or by telephone at (805) 682-3883 or by e-mail: frederic@silcom.com or website: hudsoninstitute.com.

This book is dedicated to
my father, Albert F. Hudson, 1907–1990,
my mother, Clara McChesney Hudson, 1913–1998,
and
my father-in-law, Percy W. McLean, 1919–1990.

Prologue

In August 1943, when I was nine years old, I awakened one morning in silent terror. I was unable to move any part of my body except my eyes. My muscles seemed frozen, and my voice was silenced. Although I had gone to bed as a walking, talking, wiggling boy, I woke up the next day paralyzed with polio. Neither my legs nor my arms would respond to my desperate efforts to move, and my neck and jaw were rigid as rocks. My breathing was panicky. I hurt all over. In the 1940s, polio was a dreaded epidemic of unidentified origin for which there was no means of prevention and no real medical treatment. Many who contracted it died; others went through life in braces and wheelchairs.

The next thing I remember was lying on the back seat of my parents' old automobile as they drove me thirty miles from my home in upstate New York to a hospital in Syracuse. That journey was unbelievably painful. I was sicker than I had ever been in my life, and I knew the seriousness of the journey. I felt a helplessness and fear I had never experienced before. What would happen to me? Would I die soon? Would this be my final trip? Would I ever see my home or family again? Why can't somebody do something? How much worse can I get and still stand it? It isn't fair. . . . That day remains vivid in my mind, like a screeching siren or flashing red light. I felt I was leaving my family to live my entire remaining life in the next few days, weeks, months—who knew how long?

At the hospital, they placed me on a very hard bed (with no pillow) in a quarantined ward. I spent my waking moments staring upward at the ceiling—my only option—and feeling totally helpless. The main treatment I received was the "Sister Kenny" hot packs administered frequently throughout the day and night, so hot that they scorched my body and smelled like wet, burnt wool—a smell I will never forget.

A wise nurse named Susan spent lots of time with me. Susan was quiet and caring; she visited me frequently and told me many things. Her main message went like this: "Your future, Frederic, is hidden on the ceiling, and you can find it if you look very hard. Look for what you will be doing as you grow up. It's all up there. Will you be a track star, a tennis player, a scientist? Will you be going on trips to faraway places? Will you be making model airplanes and flying your kites? Will you be going to summer camps and swimming? Will you go to college and become someone special? Will you marry and have a family? Frederic, all you have to do is study the ceiling. When you see your future, it will start to happen!" I spent hours and then days and months searching for my future in the maze on the dirty ceiling above my immobile body. There were many designs discernible there, with cracks in the plaster, shadows, and abundant Rorschachs for me to identify. The first vision I saw had me running and playing and active again. After a while, I had only to lift up my eyes and I would see myself bouncing through the woods, like a gazelle, alive with movement. Then I saw myself having friends, laughing again, and climbing trees. After a few months of ceiling gazing, I pictured myself going to college and becoming a husband and father someday. I envisioned myself as a doctor.

My nurse Susan convinced me that if I would keep rehearsing my vision on the ceiling, sooner or later my body would begin to move again and make it all happen. I never doubted her. I let her coach me toward my highest self when my body was at its all-time low. Knowing my eyeballs were my only moving part, she brought a projector and flashed stories and pictures on the ceiling for me to consider as I pondered my future. She projected a checkerboard and taught me how to play checkers and chess as she learned to intuit my preferences. She would read me books while instructing me to find my life in the patterns overhead. She brought me music to listen to, and I began to feel the world of sound open up before me, as I had never heard it before. She obtained my fourth-grade through sixth-grade texts and homework assignments and tutored me without my even knowing I was doing schoolwork.

Before contracting polio, I had not been much of a student. My family was struggling to survive the Depression and World War II, and I was squeezed in between a brother a year older and a sister a year younger. Life was a constant scramble. But during my months in the hospital, in my desperate physical condition, time was all I had, second after second, and I wanted to learn everything I could. I wanted to become everything I could become. And I believed, magically, that what I envisioned on the ceiling would come to pass. Everything I imagined seemed possible, and what did I have to lose?

One day, as I was entranced in a forest walk along the cracks in the ceiling, I felt a wiggle in the toes of my left foot. It was not much—but it was *everything*. I could move my toes, a little. When Susan made her rounds, she assured me that this was the beginning of my future unfolding—not merely my getting well but my visions being realized. She said my strength would slowly return up my legs, my backbone and arms, and finally to my upper neck and chin. "You are now in training," she would say, "so practice moving your legs for the rest of this month, and soon you will walk and then you will run. We will prepare you to be an outstanding runner, okay? You will want to be in good shape for medical school." Susan attached strings to my toes so I could ring a bell if I wanted her, and I remember making so much noise that the other nurses complained royally.

When my legs became somewhat mobile, Susan found a way to have them open and close windows and doors, using ropes joining my legs to them through pulleys that she installed in various places. Pretty soon my room looked like a gymnasium, and I had no intention of ever leaving. This was my learning center, my opportunity to become all that I could be. The last thing to cooperate was my neck and upper chest and, although I still can't touch my chin to my chest, I have been eternally grateful for everything I learned and have become in my recovery. I now walk, run, play tennis, and live without any noticeable deficit.

The hardest thing I ever did was to leave that room. I cried in anguish as my wheelchair left the hospital for my uncle's farm, where I was quarantined to learn to walk again. My loneliness there was punctuated by the deadly, daily visits of an orthopedic nurse who made me exercise, without any of the mentoring that Susan provided. It was months before I could walk, but when I did, I reentered my family system and my schooling as someone with a vision of where I was going and how I would get there. I had a mission, a life purpose.

I did not fully grasp what Susan had taught me until midlife, when I was struggling mightily with my path and life course. By then I had completed a Ph.D. program at Columbia University, entered the professorial ranks of higher education, and become a husband and father. But in my late thirties, when my youth felt spent, I thought my life was over. I had run out of vision. After much soul searching, I returned to what I had learned from Susan—to be visionary and responsible for my own future. At midlife I learned, painfully, to gaze at the sky above me and begin again. I found a new world of possibilities.

Thank you, Susan. You taught me some powerful lessons: to listen to those who care about me, as you did; to see how I want my life to unfold; to trust my vision; to take responsibility for my life course; to learn how to learn, and unlearn, and relearn. This book is my effort to return the favor to those paralyzed by the experiences of life in our time.

Part One

The Emerging Adult

In Over Our Heads

*For many Americans the "revolution of rising
expectations" may be simply a desire for a larger house
and a second car, but for some it is a growing demand
for the fulfillment of needs which are not basically
material but are a search for a larger and more satisfying
life experience.*
ANGUS CAMPBELL, *THE SENSE OF WELL-BEING IN
AMERICA*[1]

For years, John and Monica have been comfortable and modestly
successful. They have two active children, good friends, and a home
that they've enjoyed for nine years. John, a manager for fifteen years
with AT&T, is deep into his career. Although he hasn't received all
the promotions he thinks he deserves, he knows he is an effective
leader with his work teams. His evaluations have been positive, and
he believes he is relatively secure. But at forty-four, John doesn't feel
comfortable with his life. He keeps reviewing the same questions in
his head: "I'm worried about me. I'm concerned about Monica and
my kids. How can I feel less scared and more secure, knowing how
fragile the entire world is right now? I know I'm more successful
financially than my parents, but am I better off? Why do I feel disappointed when I've really done very well? Here I am at my peak,
and I feel less than full. How can I spend more time with my wife
and children? When will I get time to enjoy the lifestyle I've worked
so hard to obtain? When does my own life begin?"

Monica, forty-one, worked her way up to her present position
as the director of marketing for a midrange computer firm. Like

John, Monica often finds herself pondering difficult questions: "I like everything I'm doing, but there's not enough of me to go around. I'm off to work each day, scrambling with the house chores, worrying about my kids, and jamming my weekends full of activities. I'm spread too thin, and I keep saying that it is only until the kids grow up, but what will I be like by then? I feel very challenged by my career, and I want to keep going. And that's my problem—I want to focus, but I don't want to give anything up. Should I accept my limitations or try to fulfill my promise? If I'm as wonderful and successful as everyone seems to think, why do I feel that part of me is drowning while another part just wants to break free?"

This book is for people who, like John and Monica, have run a few laps into the adult years and on the one hand feel they are getting somewhere but on the other hand feel they are not empowered. They are busy making life work but living only a little. They are gravely concerned about the state of the world and how it may affect their future but unsure what they can do about it.

Six New Adult Realities

Since the beginning of our country, the adult years have been predesigned and guided by our society. No longer. To master our fifty to sixty years as adults we must know how to navigate our own lives through the peaks and valleys of an ever-changing territory. Compared with previous generations, our adult prospects are freer from social pressures yet more complex, less predictable, and more turbulent. Consider the impact of six new realities on your life.

Our Entire Society Is Becoming an Adult Culture

What for centuries has been a youth-oriented culture is slowly being transformed by an aging America.[2] In 1984, the number of people sixty-five and over for the first time equaled the number of adolescents in our country. In fact, the number of Americans over sixty-five has more than doubled since 1950. In 1987, there were 25,000 people one hundred years old living in America; in the year 2000 there will be 100,000; in 2020 the number will be an astounding 160,000. During the past decade, the number of Americans between the ages of thirty-five and forty-four has increased by 42 percent, while the increase from forty-five to fifty-five is 47 percent. Today, the median age in the United States is forty; that is, half of all the people in our country are older than forty and half are younger. By the year 2025, the median will reach forty-seven. The twenty-first century begins with half of the nation in "midlife." The graying of America is our most significant demographic trend. Just as a youth culture characterized the 1960s, an "agequake" describes the turn into the twenty-first century. More older adults will remain in productive lifestyles because the meaning of retirement is changing rapidly from a sudden disconnection from work to a redefinition of work and other life interests.

How will this maturation affect American institutions? What new services and opportunities are required to support the needs of the growing ranks of middle-aged and elderly? Will there be age wars and internal conflicts, or will American leadership become more caring at home and diplomatic abroad? How will the consciousness of the country—its deep-seated values and dreams—change?

We Are Reinventing Adulthood

Our world is not the world our parents knew. Our parents found stability in the social containers of their lives—family, workplace, community, and nation. We find those containers to be in constant flux, sometimes pulling us apart but often allowing us to experience new roles and opportunities. Our parents moved passively through their maturity, believing that the rules and roles for getting older were definite and fixed. We assume that we have fewer rules and more choices for mapping our race through time. Our parents viewed the adult years as a time when the man worked, the woman raised the kids, and the rewards for both were becoming grandparents and reaching an adequate retirement. Invisible rules guided their lives, measured by predictable time points: when to marry, when to have children, when to retire. Cultural expectations were relatively uniform.

For us, the adult years are filled with volatile change and multiple options. We can design our lives more or less the way we want them without inviting cultural scorn. At the same time, the social forces that govern our lives are more turbulent, fostering strains on marriages and convulsions in the work world. Through the intensity of our television screens, our lives are related to the international scene as never before, a connection we vividly experience with every crisis. For us, life is more flexible but less definite, less secure but with more—and sometimes blurrier—options. We are altering the way we look at the grown-up years.

At forty-seven, Louise suffered a severe heart attack. In spite of her remarkable recovery, she wondered how many years she had left. Ever since her illness struck, she had been conducting a silent review of her life, and she was often anxious or depressed. What kind of future could she plan on? As a successful realtor, she reasoned, "If I'm going to be okay, then I want to stay in charge of my work and keep as active as ever. If I'm going downhill and into more heart surgery, I want to cut back and do some personal things with my life." Her husband and two teenage children were terrified by her brush with death and wanted her to work part-time or retire completely.

Louise decided to work out of an office in her home. She maintained a regular schedule of workouts at the local athletic club and adopted a diet for a healthy heart. Although it took her many weeks to get accustomed to being with the family most of the time, she enjoyed the projects she was doing with her children. Her work progressed satisfactorily, but she discovered that it wasn't as important to her as she had thought it would be. She was gradually rearranging the direction of her life and feeling good about it.

Today's Adults Are Living a Quarter Century Longer Than Adults in 1900

The life span of men and women has been extended significantly. In 1776, life expectancy was about 35, and the median age of our populace was 16. In 1886, life expectancy was 40 and the median age 21. In 1920, the typical woman lived to be 54; the life expectancy of women born in 1998 is 83; and for women born in the year 2040 it is projected to be 91.5. In 1920, life expectancy among men was 53; today it is 76, and by the year 2040 it will jump to 85.9.

Since 1920, we have added more than a quarter of a century of living. What do we do with it? Where do we turn when we run out of script? What do we do after the first or second plunge into adulthood has plateaued or peaked? How do we sustain passion and a sense of purpose for fifty or sixty adult years?

Mac was eighty-three and confused. His life was blessed with health, sufficient funds, and the ability to take care of most of his needs. But in the previous year his wife had died after a lengthy illness. Mac didn't like living alone, and he didn't have much to live for. He figured that he had pretty much done it all. But after participating in a support group for several months, Mac decided to begin a small mail-order business with two of his grandchildren. Using his financial resources for start-up funds, he taught them how to succeed at running a business—something that Mac had done all his adult life until he retired at seventy-five. As the business began to grow, Mac met Gertrude, a widow who had much in common with him. In time, Mac felt like his old self again, but with a future.

Adult Intimacy Comes in Many Forms from Many Sources

Today's adults get love and affection in their lives in many ways. Until now, adult intimacy in North America has been defined largely by unwritten cultural rules for marriage and family life. With the arrival of effective birth control in the second half of the twentieth century, social patterns of intimacy changed more dramatically than at any previous point in history. Adults now have choices not available to earlier generations—to marry or not to marry, to parent or not to parent, to divorce or not to divorce. Gay and lesbian relationships now openly provide patterns of love and affection that earlier generations denied or hid. Adult friendships are another important source of intimacy today, for both sexes. In today's world, intimacy is a series of bonds and attachments, not merely a significant other.

Leisure and Health Are Major Commitments

America has traditionally been a work-ethic culture, but a leisure ethic has recently evolved and is equally important to the new breed of adults. In the past two decades, a significant number of Americans have changed the way they think about food, calories, cholesterol, fat, dieting, smoking, exercise, participatory sports, and stress control. Smoking is in social disfavor, and sparkling water has replaced alcohol for many. Compared to adults in 1920, we have leaner bodies, more active lifestyles, and a will to manage the aging process instead of merely getting old. *Health* has become a watchword for self-esteem and longevity. Today's adults see the connection between taking care of their bodies continuously and extending the quality of life well into elderhood.

Adults Anticipate Several Careers in a Lifetime

We used to think of a career as a linear progression throughout the adult years, moving from an apprenticeship to a mentor phase. Now we understand that careers develop in a sea of changing lives and work opportunities. Through multiple careers or jobs, it is possible to explore more parts of the work world and to develop more parts of oneself.

One group that benefits from the new flexibility in career lines is those who reenter the workforce at midlife or perhaps begin to shape a career identity for the first time after the children leave home. At fifty-six, Donna felt she was at a turning point. Her husband, a businessperson in Atlanta, was absorbed in his career. The last of Donna's three children had just graduated from high school and was on her way to college. Donna felt that her world was being torn apart. Even though she was proud of her accomplishments as a wife and mother, she felt abandoned and stripped of her rank. "I say I'm not going to cry about it, but in fact I cry a lot. What's going on with me? I just don't feel complete without my kids in my home. Is that so bad?" The truth was that Donna didn't feel complete with herself. She needed a new agenda for her own life, apart from others. She talked about her options with her women friends and gradually created a plan. In a few years, Donna graduated from her local community college and began her career as an interior designer. She felt competent and challenged again. Her marriage, meanwhile, changed considerably, as her husband became more interested in travel and gardening.

Although most adults spend more of their lives at their workplace than they do anywhere else, a 1996 Roper poll reported that Americans view work as the eighth most important consideration in their lives. Rated higher than the benefits of work were children's education, family life, health, quality of life, friends and relatives, love life, and income and standard of living.[3]

For eighteen years, Donald had been a community leader. He had served on task forces, the city council, and the county administration. He was a dynamic leader who knew how to make strategic moves and empower others. He was often the recipient of generous praise and recognition. At forty-nine, however, he wanted a private life of his own where he could talk about and share something other than politics, crises, and deadlines. To enrich his personal life without endangering his professional success, Donald found a professional counselor who could help him make some fundamental changes. Because he had always wanted to sail, he rented a sailboat for a year and committed himself to weekly sailing ventures, usually by himself. He joined a men's group made up of men a lot like himself and found profound support there. Donald succeeded at growing Donald—the person—through travel, cooking, sailing, new friendships, and a rebirth of passion at home. He became interested in contributing to the Nature Conservancy as a volunteer, so he donated significant portions of time to its work. He felt more relaxed and humorous and less consumed by his public duties. He was the same Donald, yet a better one.

The Decline of Confidence and Hope

The rub is that many adults do not feel emergent. They love their newly acquired freedom but resent the loss of social protection and safety. A great many capable adults feel vulnerable instead of visionary, trapped instead of empowered. They feel that they are marking time or sliding downhill. The complexities of their lives confine them at the very time when new freedoms and options arrive. Just when personal options have expanded, making adult life work has become more problematic. Planning the future is more tenuous. Consider the following situations:

- Leah feels a double bind. "My government job provides me with benefits I simply can't or won't give up—retirement, health insurance, flextime, and frequent vacations. In seven years, my benefits will reach the highest level. I can't risk making a job change. My golden handcuffs control my future, and I hate that."

- Jim loves his engineering job, but his life at home is a disaster zone. Although people call him a workaholic, the truth is that Jim doesn't feel comfortable, challenged, or rewarded anywhere but at work.
- Susan feels that somehow she got off course. "I'm a savvy lawyer, but that's not enough for me anymore. I'm thirty-eight and should have thought more about marriage and children."
- Rodney lives in silent terror as AIDS takes away so many of his friends. "How can I plan my life when I may not have a future?"
- Ralph, a musician, remembers when he was bursting with energy. "Nothing could stop me back then. Now I've lost it, whatever 'it' was. What I need is passion again, a new adventure I can believe in. Maybe a trip to Bali?"

These situations are commonplace today, as more people who entered the adult years with a flurry some time ago now find themselves mired down by changes and complexities that they hadn't anticipated. There are at least five reasons for this.

Lost in Yesterday's Decisions

We are all ushered into the adult years with great hoopla, but few are prepared for the long haul. "I like the freedom to be me," one midlifer blurted, "but I just don't know how to make me happen anymore." When you trade in your early years for adult ones, few trumpets blow; it feels more like an ending than an arrival. Adult lives are long strings of days and years, lacking demarcation. It's easy to get lost.

Adult life begins as a series of snapshots, which soon take the form of a rather long, repetitive movie. After young adults sort out their life options, they often feel trapped by their early decisions. Some get mired in the specialized roles that they create in career or home life. By the time you're twenty-seven or so, you're pretty much on your own and either accelerating ahead or caught in the undertow of your early adult decisions. Some people marry young, expecting love and parenthood to make their lives sing. Parenting lasts a very long time. At forty-five, Katie, who has never complained about just being a housewife and mother, wonders what she can really do outside the home that can make a real difference and give her a life of her own. Others shape their early adult lives around career decisions, which may not make sense ten years later, when they may be difficult to change. As one dentist put it, "How could I have known at eighteen when I decided to become a dentist that at thirty-eight I would be spending 98 percent of my time repeating simple routines in which I lost interest long ago? How could that eighteen-year-old boy do this to me?" Laurie, a beautician, remembers when going to work made her life complete. "Now it's a real drag, but I'm so far into it that I don't know how to jump ship and still have the money and lifestyle I've got now."

Some doors in life can be entered but can't be opened from the other side; some places in adult life seem to have no exits. Choices have consequences, and even though time is on the side of the young adult, if the youthful dreams are extinguished in one's twenties or thirties, life may proceed as little more than stale routines and bankrupt habits. Creative adult life requires the birth of many new dreams, the possibilities of many new adventures, and the excitement of risk taking.

Betrayed by Our Expectations

Although adults today are increasing their expectations for life options, they often experience a wide gap between dream and reality. There are more options but fewer real choices. By thirty-five or so, a great many feel that what they wanted isn't what they got, and what they got is a world they didn't ask for and don't understand. Although the end isn't in sight, the end of the beginning has arrived, and it often feels as though the future cannot and will not fill the void. The expectations of youth are seldom matched by the experience of later life. No wonder so many hardworking, well-intending adults often say that they feel lost, deprived, or out of synch with their expectations. Should they try harder or lower their expectations? Are there other alternatives?

- At forty-two, Don, a fitness addict, confesses, "Although my body is still in great shape, the prospects ahead aren't. I don't see much except a boring downhill ride."
- Mary, who is up to her ears in supporting her family and getting somewhere at work, wonders, "Where am I, with my own life? I'm busy all the time, but I don't feel like I'm going anywhere."
- Sandy has tried her best to make her life work, but she hasn't found the key. "I'm divorced, raising a kid alone, still scrambling for a career that fits me, and hurting for money. I am thirty-five and mad."

A significant number of Americans are pondering ways to balance the security achieved in their early adult years with their unfulfilled dreams that linger. The disjunction between expectations and realized experience cannot remain extreme for very long in adult life without a crisis occurring. If we are to enjoy our mature years, our hopes and our common experience need to be ordinary friends. If we experience grandiose expectations alongside ordinary reality, we get *EXPECTATIONS/reality*—a formula for chronic disappointment. Equally disappointing is the opposite equation, which is experienced by a growing number of young and disfranchised adults—*expectations/REALITY;* motivation is low while survival issues are overwhelming. The best formula for creative living is *expectations/reality,* in which adults find available resources for their dreams and available dreams for their resources.

Unprotected by Our Social Systems

The social conditions that have provided us new permission and pathways for our adult lives have also provided us with reduced social stability, predictability, and safety. When the long adult years proceed within ambiguous social containers such as marriages, families, schools, careers, work organizations, communities, and nation, it takes strong, confident adults to guide the rudders—no easy requirement in today's world. Our cultural containers are themselves going through convulsive changes, setting many adults adrift on any odyssey not of their own choosing.

An even bigger surprise is the extent of global turmoil affecting our lives today. The social context of adult life in America is less stable than previously. Marriages are less secure; careers are in flux; financial security is difficult to manage; corporations are undergoing major upheavals; the future of the natural environment is tenuous; economic cycles are less predictable; and political turmoil is a never-ending global phenomenon. Americans are no longer assured a definite future of progress, prosperity, and predictability. Our assumptions about adult life are changing.

The world of my father was very different. In 1934, when I was born, my father went bankrupt, and the Depression detoured his life and mine into survival issues. It took him fifteen years and endless jobs to achieve economic stability for our family. Yet even during the nightmare of personal failure, he felt that he was riding the wave of an immutable promise of manifest destiny. And he was.

My father and his generation believed that our nation had a unique mission—to set a moral example for how life should be lived and how a society should be run. He believed that Americans should cooperate with whatever the president, Congress, and our military forces might decide was right. Although my father did not like President Roosevelt, he viewed the presidency as a sacred role, and he felt that we could depend on the moral and legal integrity of elected officials, judges, members of the professions, and the churches throughout the land. Guiding us all, he used to say, was the American dream of liberty, justice, and opportunity for all. Almost all the people I knew when I was growing up felt that they were part of an unstoppable progress. The social institutions of our democracy would provide safety, protection, and expanding opportunities for the development of personal life.

My dad was a pharmacist working in a pharmaceutical manufacturing plant. Even though he believed strongly in individual freedoms, he had no doubts whatsoever about the primacy of the basic organizations of society over all of his personal decisions. During World War II, he worked to fill a medical ship with supplies for the wounded. When the ship was sunk by enemy forces before it reached England, my father rolled up his sleeves and started over. His career as a pharmacist served as a linear container and definer for his entire adult life. All he wanted, throughout his adult years, was to live out the occupational, marital, parenting, and leadership roles that befell him. He assumed, like those before him, that he was building a better America and that progress toward some new world that his children would inherit was the grand design that would be carried out if he and others just did their best and trusted the cultural flow. His was an ordered world where heterogeneous people were bound together by common beliefs. Or so he thought.

Until the early 1960s, most Americans similarly constructed their lives in the shadows of our dominant institutions. Government, corporations, businesses, churches, and schools shaped the roles that we assumed and provided reasons for things being the way they were. If some change or crisis occurred forty years ago, the stable forces of our culture would interpret and assimilate it. Both conservative and liberal forces worked that way: tolerating dissonance while shaping consensus. That is how we rallied as a nation to face external threat in World War II and its aftermath. Today we have no consensus, and crisis is an everyday event.

In a world of chaotic change, what seemed linear in the past seems cyclical today. What felt stable is turbulent; the once permanent is transitory. What we know most of all is that the society around us doesn't seem as safe or dependable or honorable as it used to be. Our institutions are discordant and our global destiny is questionable. As Americans, we are adrift in a sea of change, without an indisputable cultural core. We remain nostalgic for an America that is no more, and we anticipate decline instead of gain.

Compared with my father's generation, the American people have gradually diminished in both self- and social confidence. My dad felt that there were permanent rules and principles; I experience fluctuating holding patterns. The containers of my life are no longer dependable repositories for defining my life; they are only temporary vehicles for evolving my future. Although I feel freed from the constraints that restricted my father's life options, I lack a dependable and predictable environment for the living of my days.

Inundated by Information and Random Choices

When our cultural containers do not measure our lives and filter change for us, the forces of change penetrate us directly as individuals. Individual adults now directly monitor more information, more consumer decisions, and more news than they can possibly want or use. The very forces that provide us new life options also flood us with a sea of imagined choices. If knowledge is power, then information is not knowledge—it is only data. How can adults wade through the flood of data that they receive constantly to get the knowledge they need for making wise decisions?

A large supermarket has more than 45,000 items to choose from. Cable TV may provide as many as 53 television channels. There are now 11,092 magazines and periodicals. Information invades our lives constantly, requiring us to sort out the kernels from the chaff. The information explosion confronts our lives at such a pace that it is difficult to maintain a distinction between trivial and important data. What purports to be news often focuses our attention on issues and events that we have no say over, leaving us feeling powerless as individuals, as with the voluminous reporting of the latest crisis in the Balkans or the Near East. How do we stay informed while not becoming overloaded and overwhelmed? How do we keep a balanced view of the world when the news is, by definition, alarming and crisis-laden?

Each person must now manage an increasing number of consumer variables. Cars are more complicated to drive, and managing traffic in urban areas takes constant vigilance. Warehouse stores provide us with extensive choices for tools, food, toys, furniture, and clothes, but making the right decisions is taxing and time consuming. Returning items is frustrating. Getting almost anything repaired is a long and complex process. The adult liberation from societal constraints is often accompanied by an overload of decision points on each individual. While the systems of our lives have loosened their grip on us, the direct decisions required of each individual to make life work have multiplied, leaving many people swamped and stressed.

Bewildered by Complex Change

Change has come in many forms throughout the course of history. Many people have had their lives transformed for the better or wrecked beyond repair by unanticipated change. If change opens doors to human betterment, it is viewed positively as a source of new opportunities. Without change, there would be no growth or development, no creative breakthroughs or discoveries, no becoming. If change diminishes human betterment already in hand, it is considered a threat to the quality of life. The pace and discontinuity of change seem to make experience obsolete. People then become defensive about the past and resistant to the future.

What is your experience with change, and how do you view your own human prospects in the twenty-first century? Is change your friend or foe? Consider five basic questions:

1. How has change affected the way you think and feel about your future? How has it affected your motivation and sense of purpose? As you experience more change in your daily experience, are you more optimistic or pessimistic about your life prospects today than you were ten years ago?
2. Have the forces of change increased or decreased your opportunities for living and working and reaching your goals?
3. Have the forces of change increased or decreased your financial security over the past ten years?
4. Have the forces of change increased or decreased your confidence in America's future? In your own future?
5. Has change freed you from the artificial constraints of the past, allowing you to find many new ways to find fulfillment? Or are you swamped by change—unable to maintain constancy and the quality of life you desire?

I have been asking these questions of audiences for more than fifteen years now. The most common answer is that while we feel that our past is less reliable than it used to be as a guide to the future that we deserve, the forces of change feel like part of the problem, not the solution. Most of us are not change masters; we resist it.

Change takes life away from us, and we don't want to lose the America that was. Like earlier Americans, we remain isolated from the world around us and think that the magic of America will somehow keep our past alive no matter how turbulent change becomes. We can take in the chaos of the world and make it over into an Americanized order. Or can we? Consider what has happened in the past forty years to our great factories, our automobile industry, our educational system, our control of the dollar, our space mission, our health care system, our influence abroad, our sense of purpose. As a culture, we are reacting to change and not learning very much about the change process itself.

Most of us continue to live as though change were an occasional intrusion, an irritant, in our otherwise organized lives. It is precisely our organized lives that complex change is altering, whether we like it or not. Today we get ruffled but not terribly surprised when change makes a new appearance. We expect random intrusions, more and more. We may kick and scream, but we know that it is "just another crisis," requiring us to "adapt" in some new way we wish we didn't have to. Take the occasional rise in gasoline prices. When the price of gas first soared as the oil cartel was getting under way, there was a public outcry. We grumbled and drove our cars a little less. Now we take it for granted that the cost of gas will rise again, along with almost everything else. Even after Iraq invaded Kuwait in 1990 and the gas prices leaped, the reaction was nothing compared to the first such crisis. Change is here to stay, accepted as an inevitable intruder that will bother us but not force us to alter how we live and work.

The sociologist C. Wright Mills once made a distinction between problems and issues. When four or five people in a social setting are jobless, that is a "problem," but when huge numbers of people suffer from unemployment, that is an "issue." We treat change as a problem, not an issue. Unfortunately, change is not only an issue; it is the dominant issue for our foreseeable future, and the empowerment of adults in our time depends on finding ways to be friends with change. We keep reacting to change; we have not learned to ride on its waves; we resist taking on a new consciousness anchored in the change process itself. Change brings with it its own kind of organization, like a river flowing, and we do not seem to be learning that. Change. We've grown accustomed to its face, but that's about all. Most of us are not on the inside of the change process, and it is not on the inside of us. Instead of viewing change as a challenge to live as global citizens with new ground rules, we feel angry and sad that our American privileges are being altered or diluted. We feel an intense loss, but we are not grieving and moving on.

America's Failure of Nerve

Our very resistance to change is fundamentally an inability to let go of a past that is now unworkable. Adults have reduced their dreams to personal concerns and acquisitions while finding infinite fault with social structures. We have lost track of the necessary connections between our well-being as persons and the well-being of the social environment around us.

According to Daniel Boorstin, author of *The Image or What Happened to the American Dream,* our dream has devolved from extravagant expectations in the founding years of our country to several types of shrinkage.[4] News gathering is now news making—a flood of pseudo-events. Heroes have become celebrities, and travelers are tourists. With that shrunken dream has come a pendulum swing from a naive endorsement of American ideals to a pervasive pessimism about our future. Consider the impact of Vietnam and the murders of John F. Kennedy, Martin Luther King, and Robert Kennedy. Consider the ignominy of Spiro Agnew and Richard Nixon and the drawn-out Watergate episode. Consider Jimmy Carter's reactive presidency, with runaway inflation, the oil embargo, the Iranian crisis, and endless unanticipated problems. Our temporary NASA success in outer space and our military blitzkrieg in the Persian Gulf served to ignite our hopes, momentarily. The late 1990s flight of a seventy-year-old John Glenn was momentarily uplifting only to be washed away by the murky waters of the Clinton impeachment hearings. Overall, we have moved from the end of our childlike innocence as an isolated nation to a superpower country marked by disappointment, guilt, and anger over our inability to lead in the old-fashioned way. Now, it seems, the world is leading us. So we cling to our shrinking dream as we back into the future with less and less sense of direction.

Motivation to make life work is disabled by a vicious circle: personal daring and adult empowerment are curtailed by social disillusionment and cynicism; social empowerment is curtailed by reduced personal vision, motivation, and leadership. In fifty short years, we have moved from a victorious superpower of dreamers and achievers to a society of whiners and cynics.

Recently, I consulted with the entire regional workforce of a Fortune 50 company about issues of low worker morale and poor customer service. When I asked hundreds of people to tell me what was wrong, I heard the usual corporate complaints about company leaders and bureaucracy, but the loudest concerns reflected a widespread loss of confidence in our social system itself. In various ways, the broad forces of change had invoked a failure of nerve within the company.

Robert Zinderman, a twenty-five-year employee serving as vice-president for service and sales, was concerned about the current changes in corporate ownership. "Controlling stockholders of major firms," he began, "are more interested in immediate profits through mergers, acquisitions, and buy-outs than they are in building excellent companies. Do you think my CEO cares about me and my future? I can tell you this: the loyalty of workers to this company has decreased remarkably in the past ten years. The company doesn't stand by us any more. We are all temporary, working at the whim of our investors, waiting for pink slips we don't deserve."

Michael Gideon, a district manager for thirty-six years, lamented that "the quality of life in America will never be as good as it used to be. We don't make things the way we used to. Our engineering, our equipment, our parts—they used to be the best, and today they are only so-so. We are no longer committed to being the best we can be. My workers are less committed to bottom-line results than they used to be. What is most depressing is that I don't know what we can do to change things."

Ann Brydon, the administrative manager who worked her way up the ladder from a secretarial position during the past twenty-two years, was more concerned with the quality-of-life issues: "The cost of living and the current tax structure have reduced the quality of life for everyone except the upper class, who must be in corporate headquarters or among the stockholders. Inflation simply wrecks the lifestyles of the administrative staff. Their raises and benefits don't compensate for the rising costs they face. My people are pretty discouraged."

Perry Bradshaw, a twenty-four-year veteran and a frontline supervisor, voiced his feelings: "The heart has gone out of people everywhere. We've lost our special thing, our belief in ourselves. We're going nowhere but downhill, reacting to change and to the advances of others. Americans have lost their game plan for leadership. Where are the great leaders, the heroes? They're gone, that's where. Both political parties follow media polls that they conduct, not some political system that they believe in. Nobody knows what to believe anymore."

The overwhelming concern throughout this company was that change was altering America so extensively that the operation of the company was undermined. The declining morale of the country was demoralizing the workplace. When the people of a society respond to complex change by diminishing their past beliefs and present expectations without an infusion of new vision and hope, that society becomes increasingly dysfunctional. Four ways in which this negativity is being expressed in the lives of American adults as we move into the twenty-first century are through cynicism, powerlessness, personal isolation, and hopelessness.

Cynicism

Whatever you may think of Ronald Reagan as a politician, he tapped this pervasive feeling of disillusionment with our society. "Are you better off than you were four years ago?" he asked us in his great debate with Jimmy Carter, and we knew we weren't. Not if economic stability and progress were our measures. We knew what felt wrong even though we didn't know how to make things right. As Peter Finch exclaimed in his final movie, capturing the feelings of many Americans, "I am mad as hell, and I'm not going to take it anymore"—but take it we do as we deepen our negative attitudes and feelings.

Powerlessness

If you experience your world as being out of control for very long, you assume that events surrounding your life are uncontrollable. If you feel powerless much of the time, you give up feeling that you can shape your destiny. "Organisms, when exposed to uncontrollable events, learn that responding is futile," concludes Martin Seligman, an expert on helplessness.[5] He goes on to say that people who feel helpless have increased fear and depression and reduced motivation to exert influence. Ever since 1960 or so, we have been a people in search of a soul, feeling powerless before the complex forces of the world—even though we are still the most powerful nation on earth.

Personal Isolationism

America has always both suffered and benefited from its geographical isolation. Today's isolation is more psychological. In the 1970s and 1980s, many upwardly mobile Americans responded to their weakening grip on the world with personal isolationism: "If we can't make our dream happen in the workplace, our society, and beyond, then we'll make it happen in our personal lives." They simplified our caring, expansive dream—"Give me your tired, your poor, your huddled masses yearning to breathe free"—into individualistic issues—acquiring things, capital, and fun. It is no secret that in the past twenty years we have neglected our communities, the world, and the dream itself.

Overall, our adult American response to change is a sense of loss followed by a reduction of our values to individual interests. We feel deflated, defeated by an enemy we neither understand nor have an opportunity to combat. Buying more things for ourselves is our ultimate weapon for feeling good. Federico Fellini, the Italian film director who created *La Dolce Vita*, suggests that we are experiencing a loss of psychological cohesion: "People are losing their faith in the future. Our education, unfortunately, molded us for a life that was always tensed toward a series of achievements—school, military service, a career and, as a grand finale, the encounter with the heavenly father. But now that our tomorrows no longer appear in that optimistic perspective, we are left with a feeling of impotence and fear. People who can no longer believe in a 'better tomorrow' logically tend to behave with a desperate egotism. They are preoccupied with protecting, brutally if necessary, those little sensual appetites. To me, this is the most dangerous feature."[6] Once a people reduce their dreams to acquisitions and status symbols, their appetites become voracious. Enough is never enough.

Hopelessness

People who cling to reduced privileges within a society in great turmoil lack hope—lack a belief that the future will fulfill their lives.

Without hope and a sense of the future, people lead lopsided, unrewarding lives, no matter how successful or wealthy they are. Without hope, both personal life and the social fabric disintegrate. Hope produces energy, motivation, courageous living. The absence of hope produces reminiscence and dying. At our worst, our lives yearn for the past, consume the present, and feel empty about the future. The greatest dilemma facing American adults is not the country's midlife crisis but a cultural failure of nerve. I remember when, as a professor of philosophy, I was questioning my class in the noble tradition of Socrates to lead them to doubt the current assumptions about life and a student came up to me, in tears, saying, "Dr. Hudson, I have been questioning my life for a long time. What I want from you is direction and an example to follow. I just want a sense of direction." I was visibly shaken, but I got the point. People today want and need role models and mentors with future-oriented scenarios, not more endorsements about the past or doubts about the present.

We live between eras, and we continue to trust the dying era without sufficiently exploring the new age being born. It takes courage to move away from our cultural moorings into the raging river of change and opportunity. In the past, the American dream thrived when our country faced external threats that tested our beliefs and unity. Today's external threats are legion but the major identifiable enemy is Saddam Hussein. Our gravest dilemmas as a people are not "out there" but rather "in here"—within each of us. Tomorrow's dream must come from within us, born from our inner beliefs. There are few precedents to guide us into the rebirth of our dream, only the possibility that as we leap into the unknown we will have the courage to create the lives and society we so desperately want. With that leap we may find the dreams and hope we deserve.

The New Adult Challenge

I believe that we have the courage to create new lives and a new society. As we press into the twenty-first century, many are making friends with the enormous changes taking place around us. They are looking for recurrent patterns within change that provide dependability and meaning, connecting our past to our present and future. The dream is ready to be restored to its twin core values of personal worth and social caring. For the most part, this new and vigorous leadership will come from adults who are ready to do more with their lives than merely succeed and consume. Many who are now seeking leadership will, among themselves, rekindle the American dream in the twenty-first century.

The transformation of our failure of nerve depends directly on our finding new personal comfort within the forces of change and chaos. What do we have to do to let go of what's not working in our lives, while taking on what may work in the context of the world we experience today? This book suggests ways to manage the forces of organization and disorganization in our lives, using change as a primary vehicle for constructing our future—from within us to the far reaches of our society. Two central issues embedded in our personal and cultural impasse are our emotional difficulty with loss and our difficulty in imagining a future for ourselves as glorious or more glorious than our past. If Americans learn how to process and to move through the profound loss that grips them, they will begin to discover immense capabilities for shaping the future. This book describes ways to begin this in the lives and settings of America's new dominant minority—adults.

The childlike version of the American dream was anchored in the notion that the containers of life would provide lasting happiness for those who exerted effort, sought education, and stayed committed. It was an outward-in vision. The adult version available to us today is that our fulfillment is grounded in our ability to live with all types of change without stable containers. The new dream is anchored in personal empowerment and social determination. It is an inward-out vision.

A central challenge for Americans today is for the adults in our society to create new continuities for their lives within the dimensions of change itself. For too long we have mourned the premature death of our dream. The time has come for a rebirth of an adult version of the same dream. It is not too late to revise our expectations and vast resources to fit the frontiers of today's world. These are the challenges:

- *The Internal Challenge.* We are being challenged by a new frontier so personal that it requires us to explore new personal depths within ourselves. If we can break the bonds of the myths that feed our powerlessness and at the same time discover vision-ary capacities for making our own lives work, we will be capable of resurrecting not only ourselves but our institutions and society. We have the human readiness to do so. As we learn to manage the structuring and destructuring of life in a world of change, we will invest in human destiny again and become renewed as leaders, careerists, parents, and spiritual beings.[7]

• *The External Challenge.* We are being challenged by a new frontier so vast that it spreads from our souls to the far reaches of the planet—and beyond. We need to extend the dream that we call American into the very worldwide forces that have kept us scared and powerless for the past thirty years. Before a world government can exist, this challenge requires a global consciousness, a rever-ence for the one environment shared by all, the presence of new forms of capitalistic cooperativeness, new solutions to glaring eco-nomic inequities, and experimentation with international teams and alliances. Cultural renewal requires a deep commitment to pluralism, diversity, and new opportunities for social contributions from women and men, the young and the old. The external chal-lenge is to release an American dream capable of inspiring new hope for people, organizations, society, and nations beyond our own. Any social agenda that falls short of this vision will fall into the jaws of our chronic cynicism and navel-gazing.[8]

The social resource that I believe to be most ready for this chal-lenge is the growing contingent of adults between the ages of thirty and seventy-five who are frustrated with their lives but ready for new beginnings. They are connected to the past, immersed in careers and families, experienced in democratic process, and determined to leave the planet in better shape than they found it. Instead of being orphans in the land of future shock, they are the new domi-nant minority in a land that is sick of feeling sorry for itself. "Where are the Jeffersons and Lincolns of today?" asks John Gardner, founder of Common Cause and now a professor at Stanford Uni-versity. "The answer, I am convinced, is that they are among us. Out there in the settings with which we are all familiar are the unawak-ened leaders, feeling no overpowering call to lead and hardly aware of the potential within. . . . How do you send out a call to the unawakened leaders? How do you make them aware of their leadership potential? How do you make leadership feasible and tolerable for leaders? . . . It is my belief that with some imagination and social inventiveness we could tap these hidden reserves—not just for government, not just for business, but for all the diverse leadership needs of a dynamic society."[9]

In the first half of the twenty-first century, adults will have the clout to effect personal and social transformation. Even though they must develop a new political consciousness, they already have links with power, the prerequisite moral restlessness, and a deep passion for transforming the American dream from its childlike versions into adult scenarios addressing today's needs. The power center for reversing our prevailing cynicism and atomistic behaviors into renewed leadership for the common good lies in the personal resilience of the mature contingents who will dominate American life for at least the next quarter century. They remember when America's excellence came from its unyielding hope. They have the capacities for self-renewal and the abilities to put the enormous resources of this nation to work for inventing a new future that we can believe in.

Adult empowerment in America today requires much more than psychotherapy, self-help, adult education, and human resource development. The primary context of our disempowerment is cultural, and each of us will gain most when we commit ourselves to the transformation of our common consciousness. Without that, our efforts at psychological and institutional renewal will be little more than Band-Aids on a wounded giant. When Richard Gephardt, a Democratic member of Congress from Missouri and House majority leader, completed a tour of foreign nations in the 1990s he expressed a frustration that many adults feel: "I'm embarrassed, almost ashamed when I see the sacrifices leaders from Mexico to Czechoslovakia are asking their people to make. They have so little, and are daring so much. We have so much and are asking so little of ourselves."[10]

Chapter Two

Finding Fulfillment
in Cyclical Lives

*All our lives long, every day and every hour we are
engaged in the process of accommodating our changed
and unchanged selves to changed and unchanged
surroundings; living, in fact, is nothing else than this
process of accommodation; when we fail in it a little we are
stupid, when we fail flagrantly we are mad, when we
suspend it temporarily we sleep, when we give up the
attempt altogether we die.*
SAMUEL BUTLER, *THE WAY OF ALL FLESH*[1]

Our world has changed but conventional wisdom has not. To make
sense of adult life today, we need a fundamental change of consciousness, from linear to cyclical notions of how life works.

Linear and Cyclical Ways of Thinking

Linear means "in a straight line," implying that our lives and society are supposed to get better, year by year, generation by generation. According to this point of view, adult lives progress through
predictable sequences: learning, loving, working, living, leading,
and succeeding. In linear thinking, adult life is viewed as an orderly
development following universal principles and rules. Life is lived
for future goals and results and is driven by perfectionism and
social constraints. *Cyclical* implies going in circles, with the repetition of familiar patterns—night and day, the four seasons, birth

and death. From this perspective, the purpose of life is to master the repetitive patterns in our ever-changing experience. Cyclical thinking looks for human meaning in the ongoing flow of daily experience, from world news to family events to personal concerns. It assumes that life can make sense in good times and in bad, in growth and decline, in beginnings and endings. Cyclical thinking tolerates high levels of ambiguity and finds pathways for living in dark and unseemly places, if necessary.

Ever since the industrial revolution, linear thinking has dominated our consciousness, with its basic notions of progress, perfectionism, success, happiness, and planned change. A linear perspective portrays life as a series of advances from simple to complex, from lower to higher, from good to better. Linear thinking aims at results that are seen as serial improvements; life is viewed as incremental, additive, purposive, and predictable. As we orient our lives to cyclical thinking, one major shift in our thinking is from progress to process.

From Progress to Process

The promise of progress was a great motivator for middle-class, eighteenth- and nineteenth-century Americans who sought increased security, power, and well-being in a nation insulated from the rest of the world. First we tamed the wilderness and then human culture evolved. But today's middle-class people are bogged down in that culture. They are more frustrated than fulfilled by the notion of progress, which seems like a promissory note that has been withdrawn. Because the conditions of today's world are often discordant, those who endorse a linear perspective feel that they are failing or going downhill when they experience a crisis or surprise in life. If they are unable to sustain progress and arrive at success, security, and happiness, they feel discouraged, disappointed, and upset. Many of the frustrations of adults today stem from the dysfunctions of the linear way of thinking, not from human incompetence. If we would alter the way we think instead of feeling bad and inadequate, our lives could be challenging and rewarding again. My grandfather expected my father to exceed him in educational and financial attainments. My father expected the same of me. I do not expect my six children to exceed me on these linear measures;

some of them may, but my main concern is that they live fully and well, day by day.

In a world where order predominates over change, the notion of lives unfolding as linear progressions is tenable. But where change keeps order in its shadows, finding meaning in life's peaks and valleys makes more sense. The expectation of progress is that order will triumph over chaos rather than that order and chaos will coexist. A world with frequent pockets of chaos requires a perspective that can find meaning in disturbing times as well as blissful times. Cyclical thinking seeks order within the change process itself. Life transitions, job losses, political surprises, and accidents are windows for learning rather than barriers to progress.

What we can know and master in our kind of world is the process of ongoing change, not progress toward ultimate results. As a process, our lives are a continuous, cyclical stream of continuities and changes. Orienting our lives around the changing patterns in our daily experience instead of around our presumed destinations permits us to enjoy the journeys we are on and to invest in learning, living, and leading.

From Acquiring Happiness to Mastering Change

Another linear notion in the American mind is the belief that happiness is a place or state of mind that we arrive at and sustain as a permanent acquisition. We think of happiness and security as items to be possessed. For example, in children's stories, the good man and woman marry and live happily ever after. In a world where change is a dominant force, there is no such permanence, and all acquisitions—material and otherwise—sooner or later dissolve into the river of change. Happiness and security are not exceptions. We can't possess, buy, or ensure them. We have no ultimate safety or security with our looks, bodies, money, marriages, children, education, career, achievements, possessions, investments, insurance, legacy, nation, or religion. What most of us have is limited protection, measured security, temporary safety. Yet the adult culture in industrialized nations overwhelmingly lives as if human destiny depended on the acquisition of happiness and security. Such a culture is bound to have a high level of disillusionment and despair, even if it is the greatest nation on earth.[2]

In our topsy-turvy world we can learn to live with both happy moments and unhappy ones without feeling derailed or impotent. Throughout our lives, we experience ever-changing proportions of blessings and curses, safety and danger, sureness and insecurity, ecstasy and misery. The challenge of the cyclical perspective is to develop human competence in both our up and our down times to facilitate a conscious mastery of the journey—wherever it takes us. When we learn that there are very few places in the human journey where we cannot find major resources for affirmation and fulfillment, we will have transcended the myth of happiness and security. There is a story about a Western man seeking enlightenment in India who, before dying in a cave, inscribed these words on the cave wall: "Oh boundless joy, there is no happiness." Feeling joy in the heights and depths of life's never-ending adventures is much more realistic and profound than expecting to arrive at a lasting state of happiness.

From Negative Aging to Positive Elderhood

The linear perspective portrayed the promise and energy of youth unfolding throughout the adult years. When the twentieth century arrived, it was heralded as "the century of the child," with hopes that the careful upbringing and education of children would sow the seeds of permanent progress. By 1900, the country was dotted with colleges and universities, all devoted to launching young people into reliable orbits of adult life and responsibility. While romanticizing the importance of youthful attributes, this perspective saw little value in old age. When you got old and had to stop working, you got out of the way so that someone younger could carry on. To be old in that way of thinking was to prepare to die.

This point of view fosters ageism in a society, characterizing old people as feeble, nonsexual, incapable of serious work, and lifeless. The myth of aging as steady, linear decline creates social prejudice against the old, and it keeps those in midlife and retirement reminiscing and looking backward, wanting younger bodies and dreams. Ageism robs thousands of people of enormous possibilities that they are capable of attaining as they get older. Elderly people who buy into these notions have low self-esteem, little motivation, and poor future prospects.

A cyclical perspective replaces this way of thinking with accurate information about the multiple dimensions of aging—some good news and some bad news. For example, with most of us, our interior awareness gets richer as we age while our physical abilities slowly lessen. The increasing sense of integrity is profound, while the physical losses are gradual. Sooner or later, we all experience decline and death. But the terminal phase of aging is, for most of us, a small and relatively short-term part of the total adult experience. Our ability to grow and to contribute continues throughout most of life. It's a matter of making the most of the trade-offs—a continuous process throughout the adult years. The cyclical perspective finds value and meaning in every life period, including elderhood.[3]

The Linear View

The linear view portrays the human journey as a gradual unfolding of human improvement, with fairly specific pictures of when and how the events of the adult years should unfold. There are specific times throughout the life cycle that are appropriate for adult decisions and actions—when to go to school, to marry, to have children, to go through a career, to retire.

Childhood through early adulthood is preparation for life:

- You grow up in a nuclear family in one geographical location, with intact parents, a mother at home full-time, regularly scheduled family meals, planned vacations, and a life together through the high school years.
- At eighteen or thereabouts, you leave your family of origin to finish your education, enter the military, or begin a career.
- In your twenties, you find a life partner, marry, and settle down to family life and a career.

The adult years are for sustaining love and work:

- During your twenties, you have children, and you assume the primary parent role if you are a woman or a secondary parent role if you are a man.

- If you are a man, you invest in your career; if you are a woman, you invest in home and family and secondarily in work, as needed.
- If you are a man, you sustain your career, which you envision not only as a ladder leading to your fulfillment but as your principal contribution to the happiness and success of your family needs. Your primary adult identity is with your career roles.
- If you are a woman, you envision your fulfillment through your marriage, family, education of children, maintenance of the home, and volunteer work or employment, all of which are supposed to contribute to your happiness. Your primary adult identity is with your nurturance and caring roles.
- You rent or, preferably, buy a house, provide for your family, and plan for your children to obtain a better education than you did.
- You provide leadership for schools, religious organizations, and civic groups; you support your country in any way that it asks you to in times of armed conflict; you contribute to the improvement of your world.

Elderhood is the time for completion and stepping aside:

- You leave your career behind and begin a life of retirement.
- You live a life of leisure activities, with travel and the development of hobbies and possibly some part-time or volunteer work.
- You cultivate new friendships with your peers and deepen your religious affiliation.
- You dedicate yourself in new ways to your children and your grandchildren.

In the adult years, the linear plan calls for constancy, stability, and leadership—with family development, vertical career climbing and cultural enhancement. Those who work hard and love well are supposed to succeed and be rewarded. Not only is individual life a linear progression, cultural life is supposed to be evolving as well. Science pushes back the boundaries of ignorance and, through applied research, industrial America achieves breakthroughs representing "progress." Businesses are supposed to prosper and grow; medical care will constantly improve; and the nation will evolve into a moral world power. The linear view, lived out as a dominant cultural pattern for adult life until about 1960, was deeply embedded in the teachings of religious groups, educational institutions, voluntary associations such as the Boy Scouts and YMCAs, the Kiwanis and Rotary, corporations, and the mass media.

There are four major characteristics of the linear way of thinking: First, it operates according to a normative and prescriptive picture of how the adult years *should* happen. It justifies different roles for men and for women, and for adults of different ages. It shapes personal destiny with a cultural design, which requires a socially cohesive, homogeneous culture. Second, the linear view portrays the adult years as a sequence of events within a social timetable with predictable outcomes. A linear life means a planned linkage of age- and gender-related roles at specific times in the life cycle—marrying, having children, developing careers, and retiring. Third, it assumes a simple equation that if an individual does what he or she is supposed to do to live well, then happiness and success will follow. From an individual point of view, the focus is on the rewards of personal life, not the complex life journey through ever-changing forces, options, and commitments. Fourth, the linear view assumes that control over change is possible. As long as change enhances the linear plan, it is positive. But change that slows or subverts the plan is negative, unnerving, and perhaps demonic. Living in a world that is out of control is unthinkable.

The linear view was an amazingly successful motivator for the early centuries of our country. It worked to keep Americans attuned to building character, families, communities, businesses, and a nation. But today, not only does it not work or motivate but in our kind of world it sustains the very dysfunctions described in Chapter One—people who are angry, disappointed, scared, reactive, disempowered, and cynical.

The Evolution of Adult Reality in the Twentieth Century

Winthrop D. Jordan observes that "The concept of adulthood . . . did not appear in America at all until after the Civil War and not really until the early twentieth century."[4] It wasn't until during and after World War II, when considerable attention focused on understanding adult behaviors and dysfunctions, that research on the adult years began in earnest. Bernice Neugarten, one of the pioneers of adult development, wrote in 1967 that "as yet we have no developmental psychology of adulthood; and psychology as a science has just begun to study the five or six decades that constitute the adult portion of the life span with something of the fascination that it has been studying the first two decades that constitute childhood and adolescence."[5]

Since about 1945, the public concepts of adult reality have evolved through three stages:

1. The adult years represent a steady state of being all grown up, stable, dependable, and, most of the time, bland. For centuries, it was the understanding that when people became adults, they stopped growing and became fixed as predictable, responsible persons for the rest of their lives. Growing was over. The adult years were shaped by the personality and experiences of the child. Adults were expected to be devoted to what the father of psychoanalysis, Sigmund Freud, said were their principal activities: love and work. To some, this sounded less than exciting, hence phrases like "over the hill," "put out to pasture," and "mellowed out." While adults were expected to be consistent and responsible, they were also portrayed as predictable, boring, and sexless. Someone said that middle age is the time between foolishness and wisdom, without much character of its own. "In over two thousand years," write Bernice and Morton Hunt, "very few people have ever written about middle age by way of either praise or condemnation, for in our culture it has not been seen as a separate and special time of life. There was only youth, and when that was gone, old age."[6] This point of view was coherent with linear thinking. Adults were the workforce for progress and the propagators of a better future.

2. Between 1950 and 1980, an alternative picture of adult life emerged: adult life contains periods of stability and crisis—turbulence in the young adult years, crisis in the thirties, a midlife upheaval at about age forty, and further convulsions in the fifties and sixties. Erik Erikson and Carl Jung set the stage for this concept in their seminal writings. A "crisis," as they pictured it, was a crossroad in life that evoked strong emotional turmoil but could result in

opportunities for new growth. "The crisis might lead one person to divorce his wife and marry his secretary, and another to quit her job and go sailing around the world. Still others might get depressed and take up drinking, or become angry and abusive. Others might seek to change careers, as Albert Schweitzer did when he retired as a concert organist and became a physician in Africa. The alleged 'crisis' often had to do with changes in the body, an awareness of the inevitability of death, feeling trapped in the decisions of early adulthood, an itch for roads not yet taken, and a sense that time is running out."[7]

Edmund Bergler's *The Revolt of the Middle-Aged Man*,[8] published in 1957, promoted this point of view, as did the writings of Elliot Jacques, Daniel Levinson, Roger Gould, Lois Tamir, and others. At a popular level, the midlife crisis was portrayed in poetry (T. S. Eliot's "The Cocktail Party"), novels (Philip Roth's *Portnoy's Complaint*), plays (Arthur Miller's *Death of a Salesman*), and films (*Shane* and *On the Waterfront*).

Although the concept of the midlife crisis was never universally accepted by adult researchers, it prevailed in the popular mind until about 1980 and still has widespread cultural support. Compared with the rosy picture of adults as steady-state performers, this one at least made the adult years look human, interesting, and filled with the possibility of growth. Although this perspective called into question a simplistic linear perspective, it was advocated by stage theorists who were modifying, not rejecting, a linear point of view.

3. The current popular view of the adult years portrays them as a Ferris wheel, or roller coaster, with up and down times that are repeated over and over again in a cycle of continuity and change. Throughout the adult years, we experience periods of stability followed by periods of transition. When the vast research between 1970 and 1990 affected mainstream America, we learned that adults are neither fixed robots locked into a permanent state of mechanical stability nor crisis-laden "middlescents" stuck in transitions. Adults are human beings who adventure through both stable and unstable times, with many peaks and valleys, and have capacities for managing both. Cyclical thinking gained momentum and began to make sense.[9] Today we view the adult years as a long period filled with positive life chapters and troublesome life

transitions. As Henri Bergson wrote at the turn of the twentieth century, "To exist is to change; to change is to mature; to mature is to create oneself endlessly."[10] This is the cyclical point of view, the view of this book.

The Cyclical View

Ecclesiastes expresses the cyclical view: "To every thing there is a season, and a time to every purpose under the heaven; a time to be born, and a time to die; a time to plant, and a time to pluck up that which is planted." Cyclical concepts are patterns that are repeated but have different meanings at different times in our lives. They are not better or worse than earlier forms, merely different from them. When I was twenty-four I bought a powerful hi-fi set and listened for months to Peter Tchaikovsky's *1812 Overture.* I had a recording of a performance that incorporated a real cannon whose sound shook the entire room. Listening gave me goose bumps. Today, when I listen to the very same recording, no longer one of my favorites, I turn the volume down so that I can hear the music, not the noise. It's still the same recording, but it means something entirely different to me today.

The cyclical view portrays childhood through adolescence as a time of preparation for many adult directions, along with opportunities to try some of them out:

- You grow up in a family network, probably with both parents working; your parents might be divorced and remarried, creating a stepfamily; you might be living with a single parent. In any case, you probably have irregular family meals and episodic rather than daily family gatherings.
- Through schooling, travel, and special camps or training opportunities, you develop basic skills in sports, hobbies, and intellectual interests.
- Through TV and computer technology, you acquire a global picture of events, technology, and human problems.
- You develop a variety of friendship networks, peer contacts, and media orientations. You gain familiarity and comfort with pluralism, world issues, and ongoing disagreements.

The early adult years are the time for establishing adult identities through lifestyles and work styles.

Personal Identity

- In your twenties, you seek to define your identity as a person apart from the roles you are playing—student, son or daughter, aspiring careerist, lover, friend.
- You look for ways to test your boundaries, to find out who you are and who you aren't. You are eager to prove that you are not a carbon copy of your parents. You look for your music, your kind of clothes, your type of automobile, your preference in friends, your limits.
- You move in and out of institutions and events that foster your sense of self.

Achievement or Work

- In your twenties or sooner, you leave home to become responsible for yourself, more or less. You may attend a college or university, take a job, enter the military, travel, or invest time in a sport or hobby. You do something with your life that will connect you to the values that you believe in.
- You acquire and maintain communication skills and use them by networking and succeeding in your emerging career possibilities.
- By your middle to late twenties, you identify a tentative career path and obtain sufficient work experience to warrant plunging in to see how far you can go, knowing that there are other options and that you can change careers.

Intimacy

- You discover that leaving home takes a long time, because throughout much of your twenties, your basic life bonds remain the ones that you have had all of your life—with your family of origin, even if you are rebelling against them. You work hard to stay attached but separate, caring but free, included but unique.
- You look for mentors and role models other than your

parents to validate your life direction and to endorse you as a person.
- Throughout most of your twenties, you spend time in young adult networks, practicing being a peer and looking for friends who share your basic values and interests.
- You practice managing a household with an intimate partner or partners.

Play and Creativity

- You continue an active leisure life and keep your body in shape by eating carefully and exercising regularly.
- You sustain whatever lifelong sports you began earlier and make recreation a high value in your lifestyle.
- You find ways to be creative.
- You enjoy parties or times when you and your peers can be spontaneous and alive.

Search for Meaning

- You may take stands on personal and social issues that matter to you.
- You may remain active in the religious preference that you grew up in or in a new one.
- You may espouse a utopian expression of spirituality, seeking a higher road than your parents chose.
- You may keep this theme in low profile, for development later in life.

Compassion and Contribution

- You look for ways in which your career can contribute to the world beyond yourself.
- You may elect to volunteer or work for a cause that you believe in, anywhere in the world.
- If your parents are well-to-do, you may choose to devote your life to contributing to the well-being of the planet rather than to making money.
- You may decide to postpone contribution until you have arrived at your own brand of success later in life.

During midlife, you rearrange your commitments to these same values or themes:

Personal Identity

- You tend to overidentify with your major roles, such as work or parenting.
- You pursue continued training for professional and personal development throughout midlife. You may want to reenter some formal educational program to provide a setting for your own growth and development as both a person and a professional.
- You learn how to reevaluate your life commitments and values. You seek therapy, coaching, and personal training as needed.

Intimacy

- You marry, remain single, get divorced, choose an alternative lifestyle, or live as a single parent; you may marry someone younger or older than yourself or someone in your own cohort group; as divorce occurs among your friends you realize that divorce, being single, and remarriage are possible—but not necessary—realities for your life.
- Over a long term, you manage a household with a partner or partners and negotiate shared responsibilities and financial investments.
- You decide whether or not to have children. If you choose to and are able to conceive, you have children in a more-or-less planned way, probably during your early, middle, or late thirties, and negotiate household and parenting roles.

Achievement or Work

- You sustain work roles that develop dual careers, incomes, and professional identities.
- You invest primary time in work advancement, anticipate career changes and geographical moves, and look for horizontal career enrichment as well as vertical moves.

Play and Creativity

- You have a leisure life with interests in health, nutrition, exercise, art events, traveling, and sports.
- You invest primary time in your leisure life and consider it to be an important part of your lifestyle.

Search for Meaning

- You find your concern for integrity and spirituality increasing. You examine your beliefs about human destiny, beauty, and spirit.
- You take more time for solitude, contact with nature, and even trips alone. You contemplate the mystery of life.

Compassion and Contribution

- Your interest increases in providing leadership in community, professional, or national organizations.
- You find grandparenting to be a fulfilling role.
- You devote time to projects and causes that protect the environment and ameliorate social ills. You are more willing than ever to live your beliefs.

A cyclical view of adult life includes five major characteristics. First, it portrays life as a complex, pluralistic, multivariate flow, with ongoing cycles in nature, societies, and people. Families, corporations, and nations are all part of a larger, often chaotic flow that can be influenced and shaped but not completely controlled. People with cyclical perspectives view adult development as adaptation to change—change within themselves and within their environment. They also know how to seize new opportunities provided by change. Living with a cyclical view takes faith in the larger swim of things and trust in the daily flow. People with a cyclical view of world process view the world as an organic whole; they respect social realities, environmental conditions, and community concerns because everything affects everything else and shares the same universe. This view is both personal and planetary.[11]

Second, the cyclical picture assumes that life "develops" through cycles of change and continuity rather than in progressive, linear, straight lines. It concentrates on understanding both what persists throughout our lives and what necessarily changes. The cyclical view portrays how the same basic themes are repeated throughout the adult years—themes such as love, achievement, and search for meaning. The life themes are rearranged as adults experience change from social forces, the aging process, and the internal dynamics of human development. The cyclical view focuses on repeatable life tasks that people perform in different ways at different times in the life cycle—coupling, work, play, care. What dictates human development throughout the life cycle is less one's stage in life than changing commitments to fundamental human values that we all share to one degree or another. Jane, at seventy-two, still maintains a full-time private practice as a psychologist, but she works not for money, as she used to, but for the human contact and the sense of being useful to others. Her leisure life, which used to be tennis singles, is now tennis doubles, and she belongs to a tennis club more for the recreational connections with friends than for anything else. Although widowed, Jane has many close friends. She is more active in her church than she used to be, and she feels more strongly about world peace.

Third, the cyclical picture honors both the ups and the downs of life, the blessings and the curses. Conflict and loss are part of everyday life, as are joy and ecstasy. Both are incorporated into the way we live and interact with one another. The cyclical understanding of life pictures society as forces and resources that sometimes form creative options for adult life and at other times become obstacles to be faced.

Fourth, the cyclical view portrays our human systems as modular, flexible, interactive, conflictual, and resilient, permitting continuous adaptations. It looks on all systems as cycles, so that couples' development, family systems, work systems, social systems, and the natural environment are all complex systems interacting with one another. All systems have up and down times, and beginnings and endings. Adults learn to shape and adapt to these systems in different ways at different times and places—designing scenarios and making them happen and, when they don't work, disassembling them and creating new ones. There is no cultural master plan, no human prescription for fulfillment. Cultural diversity is considered an asset rather than a liability.

Fifth, continuous learning is essential to the constant retooling of adult competence. Adults need not only knowledge and training to make the changing external world work but self-knowledge and training to make the internal world effective. As they age, adults need to unlearn old habits and learn new ways to live effectively. Some adults seek learning in order to gain personal and professional competence; others pursue learning in order to develop undiscovered parts of themselves; still others seek mastery in the realm of consciousness and spiritual oneness.

The differences between the linear and cyclical views can be summed up as in Table 1.

Tom, Mary, John, and Linda

One summer not long ago, Tom, Linda, John, and Mary got together for a month's vacation, during which each wanted to make plans for the future. At fifty-three, Tom lived and breathed the linear life. As the owner of his own company, Tom had devoted twenty-two years to growing his company into a winner. However, he had become bored and restless during the past year. Then recession had eaten away at the profits, and Tom was looking for something new to do with his life. Tom was married but increasingly aware that his only personal identity was in his work, and he felt angry and upset about that.

Linda was fifty-three, a secretary, and contemplating retirement. She enjoyed living alone and had never married. During the past two months, Linda had had breast cancer surgery and treatment, which left her distressed and worried. "How should I proceed?" she wondered. "Should I retire and start some projects I've waited to do all my life, or keep working so I can stay close to my friends and benefits?"

John, who was working in human resources at Motorola, came to discuss his personal life. At forty-six, he had been divorced for five years and wanted to gain custody of his two young boys. Although his former wife was willing to try it for a year, he wasn't sure that he could manage being a single father and still do his job. Actually, John was ambivalent about what he wanted.

Mary was thirty-eight, married, childless, and a district manager for the publishing company McGraw-Hill. She worked very hard and was proud of her career attainments. However, the alarm in her biological clock was ringing. Should she have a baby? Was her marriage mature enough for parenthood? Could she and her husband live on a reduced income?

Table 1. Linear and Cyclical Views.

	Linear View	Cyclical View
The World	The world is more stable than chaotic. Order is separate from chaos, and chaos can be cordoned off by order. Social institutions sustain stability so individuals can succeed and prosper	The world is more chaotic than stable. Order is a temporary holding pattern within our chaotic experience, and chaos cannot be avoided or cordoned off. Institutions and individuals seek to monitor change together so that acceptable levels of the quality of life can be experienced by as many people as possible.
Society	Development in personal life, family systems, work, and society is serial. Each serial point (marriage, having children, career, and so on) is something that we do in order to move on to some goal or result.	Development is continuous reprioritization and renewal of the same issues—identity, achievement, intimacy, play, search for meaning, and social compassion. These issues provoke life tasks that we do over and over again in different ways throughout the adult years.
Personal Life	The larger society governs and guides individual and family plans.	Adults and their networks are responsible for life designs and social stability.
	Life fits into a social master plan with defined roles, timing of events, and constraints. Personal life is a series of goals and objectives requiring long-term commitment, personal discipline, and postponed gratification.	Life is modular, flexible, interactive, chaotic, and resilient. Personal life is lived among many conflicting plans and social forces, requiring the abilities to tolerate ambiguity and adapt to new situations.
	The goal of life is to attain, acquire, and obtain results—a progressive quest that holds the promise of success and happiness.	Life is flow, an adventure into the unknown that holds the promise of continuous learning through the highs and lows of life.

Table 1. Linear and Cyclical Views, Cont'd.

	Linear View	Cyclical View
	Adult life is a long period of stability in which personal strengths, intimacy bonds, career development, and responsibility work toward personal fulfillment and social progress. Transitions are not viewed positively.	Adult life is a process that moves from periods of stability to periods of instability and transition to new periods of stability, and so on. Adults need to know how to build life structures and how to manage life transitions.
Family	The family is a traditional, nuclear one, with the wife as the primary caretaker of the home, being responsible for friendships, social life, child rearing, and schooling matters.	The family is an extended one, with an intimate couple sharing the caretaking of the home, including the maintenance of friendships, social life, child rearing, and schooling matters with continual negotiation of these issues.
Careers	The husband has a full-time career at all times. The wife is the full-time homemaker and parent and possibly has a part-time job or career.	Both the wife and the husband have careers or job options throughout the adult years, with economic interdependence.
Education	Education is youth oriented, to prepare for the grown-up years.	Education is a life-long process for reeducation, renewal, and redirection.

By the end of their time together, Tom had designed a personal life apart from his company. He reduced his hours at work, delegated more of his duties to subordinates, and decided eventually to sell the company. He chose to spend most of his time at home, figuring out how to live his life without his career routines. Tom was excited about the possibility of creating a private life for himself, for the first time ever. He and Felicia, his wife, have spent more time together since the month's vacation than in the past five years. Although Tom doesn't know what lies ahead, he believes that he has found the right direction for his life at this turning point.

Linda chose to remain with her career and work. She was able to reduce her time, however, to a four-day week and to begin some of her long-waiting projects on weekends. She also became a volunteer in a hospice and feels good about the way she is balancing her life. Although she has had periodic bouts of depression, she keeps close track of her health and friends and lives each day as fully as she can.

John, it turned out, wanted a new career. He was very unhappy in his ser-vice-oriented job and figured out how he could safely manage a transition into accounting, the area of his professional master's degree. That's the way it worked out, three months later. He changed careers and felt he was "on course" again and in better spirits. Although he felt guilty about his parent role, he was able to arrange for two weekends a month with his children, and next year his older boy will live with him.

Mary discovered that her real issue was not having a baby but dealing with a marriage that never was. She decided to get into counseling with her husband to see whether the marriage could be saved. If it couldn't be, she was now ready to end it and live alone. Mary is very happy with her work, friends, and life in general. Her primary intimacy issues need reevaluation and renewal, and the baby question is still unanswered but less demanding.

All four of these people have learned how to redesign, renew, balance, and manage their complex lives for a while—competencies required when we live within a cyclical view of adult life.

The Two Cycles in Adult Life

Two primary cycles affect adult life—the change cycle and the life cycle. Each cycle maps out a different section of the adult territory, and together they provide a basis for the development of adult mastery and leadership in a world of change. Adults who learn the importance of these cycles in their lives will see the world of the twenty-first century as familiar and challenging.

The cycle of change represents the ongoing change process within adult life. Within this cycle, adults move through periods of life chapters and periods of transition, which then repeat them-selves. This is the most important cycle for contemporary adults to master because it requires living creatively with the flow of inter-nal and external change and stability. The life chapter/life transition process and specific skills for facilitating it are described in detail in Part Two.

The life cycle is the birth-to-death journey that every human being experiences. In the adult years, the life cycle represents changing patterns of a person's sense of purpose, from about age twenty on. Throughout a person's life cycle, this sense of purpose shifts, with changes resulting from aging, social forces, and self-development. There are patterns to the life cycle as it proceeds throughout the adult years from twentysomething to ninetysomething, and these are presented in Part Three.

The Renewal Cycle
Life Chapters and Life Transitions

An Overview of the Renewal Cycle

> *If one's destiny is shaped from within, then one has become*
> *more of a creator, has gained freedom. This self-*
> *transcendence, a process of change that originates in*
> *one's heart and expands outward, always within the*
> *purview and direction of a knowing consciousness, begins*
> *with a vision of freedom, an 'I want to become . . .,' with a*
> *sense of the potentiality to become what one is not. One*
> *gropes toward this vision in the dark, with no guide,*
> *no map, and no guarantee. Here one acts as subject,*
> *author, creator.*
> ALLEN WHEELIS, *HOW PEOPLE CHANGE*[1]

You Are Your Story

The way you describe your life and portray yourself is directly related to how you live on a day-to-day basis. When you were born, your parents, community, and culture generated the themes, plot, and main characters in the "story" you came to call yours. When you become a mature adult, however, you have an opportunity to become the author of your own script and to take charge of the direction of your life. As a matter of fact, you are constantly making conscious or unconscious revisions in your story. When you are in a "life transition" you are making major revisions, whereas when you are in a "life chapter" you are making minor revisions.

It's important to ask yourself: Am I living my own story or someone else's? Am I consciously (or unconsciously) engaged in shaping the next chapter of my story? The more you can consciously construct the dramatic patterns of your daily-weekly-yearly existence through deliberation and choosing, the more you are *yourself*—determining plot, bringing in new characters, and allowing familiar characters to change and grow.

Take a moment to ask yourself the following questions:

- What is my current *plot* (the principles and reasons that explain why I am the way I am)?
- What is the larger *story* within which the plot functions (the interlocking narratives that hold my plots together)? What are the dominant patterns or themes of my story?
- What am I (the main character in my story) about? How would I describe myself? How do I feel in the different *roles* that I play in my story?
- Who is included in my *cast of characters*?
- What are the chapters of my life, up until now, and how would I describe the transitions I had between each of those chapters?
- What are the major *turning points* of my story and how did I change?
- What would be the title of my life story if I wrote it out as an autobiography?
- What do I like best about my life today? What do I like least?

Life Chapters and Life Transitions

We are all the time putting our lives together and taking them apart. But when we are mainly putting ourselves together we are in a *chapter*—an era of relative stability, predictability, and challenge. When we are mainly dismantling our roles and story lines, we are in *transition*—an era of instability, shedding, and new discovery.

Life chapters are about accomplishing something important with your life —having a career, raising a family, reaching a goal—that knits your life together in a meaningful way. For example, four years in college might be a chapter, or ten years working at IBM, or a divorce and being single again, or moving from full-time work to retirement. Life chapters vary in time spans. Some are long and others are not.

On the one hand, life chapters are externalizations of the self, doings, happenings, with explicit goals and objectives. Life transitions, on the other hand, are a pulling away from a chapter and an opportunity to turn inward, to soul search, to find a new sense of self—to discover spiritual vitality and meaning, to envision new ways to be you in the years ahead. Some life transitions are triggered by an external event, such as being terminated from a job or divorced from a spouse, moving to a new location, returning to school, being in an accident, or contracting a serious disease. Other life transitions are triggered from within—boredom, emotional distress, bodily changes, or powerful new callings. Life transitions are about letting go of roles, unraveling your identity, and discovering new dimensions of yourself from the inside out. They produce renewal, vitality, and resilience. Although few people want a transition to last long, they are seldom short. It takes time to process the metamorphosis from who you were to who you're becoming. It is largely an emotional and reflective process taking many months or years. People in transition are not sick. They can usually work and remain moderately active. Their inner work, however, requires most of their energy and attention, so they often appear to be preoccupied or moody.[2]

The Four Phases of Change

The twenty-first century backdrop for everyone's story is never-ending whitewater. We feel today like we're on rafts floating down a commanding river, with each raft having only a small mast and sail, a rudder, and some poles. Sometimes when it's calm, our journey is fairly effortless; we can moor our rafts in an eddy near a meadow and camp for a while. At other times the whitewater tests every skill we have, as we slide over rocks and rapids and swirl about in unforeseen directions.

The image of a river captures two qualities central to our experience of change: a sense of chaotic power beyond our control and a sense of never-ending adventure requiring our continual vigilance and readiness. The river is not merely external to us; it is internal as well. When people feel at home on this river, they cooperate with the flow, learn to navigate, and anticipate the forthcoming ports-of-call. They learn to manage constancy and change. The river journey of our lives flows in a cycle, with recurring patterns of events and life tasks. The renewal cycle of change moves from relatively stable periods—life chapters—to unstable periods—life transitions—and on to new life chapters. This cycle, which continues without stopping throughout our lives, is shown in Diagram 1.

The cycle of change has four phases or time periods. Each phase has an organizing principle that defines it, along with tasks or activities to make it happen. Each phase proceeds in a clockwise direction, quickly or slowly moving through the change process around the cycle. The description of each phase to follow begins with a quotation from the *I Ching,* the ancient Chinese "Book of Changes."

Phase 1: Go for It

"Assuming your cause is just, planning is needed to achieve success. . . . Do what is right and you will be rewarded. Move forward and you will get support. . . . As you succeed, continue with self-discipline and self-restraint. . . . You will be accepted and entrusted with leadership. You will have good fortune without seeking it. . . . There is no obstacle in your path."[3]

In Phase 1, you are consciously and unconsciously inventing a life chapter: You begin to structure your future when you become captivated and inspired by a vision or dream of the next chapter of your life. A dream is like a brainstorm, an imaginal picture of how you want your future to be. When you light upon the right dream, you feel energized and determined to make it happen. Your dream is how you really want to be. You are on course.

You distill from your dream a dramatic sequence of how your future will unfold. You create (or borrow) a story line for how it will happen, keeping the story focused on the central events and life themes that you want to happen in the final act (career success, financial independence, marriage and family, caring for others, being at one with the universe). When the story line is a sequence of imagined happenings, you have a dramatic form, with you as the author, the main character and hero, the designer of the scenes, and the director. You personally endorse the drama and enter it. You are at your best. You get others to believe in your story and to

Diagram 1. The Renewal Cycle:
Life Chapters and Life Transitions.

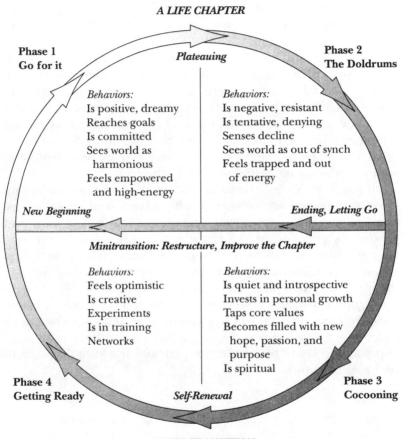

A LIFE CHAPTER

Phase 1
Go for it

Plateauing

Phase 2
The Doldrums

Behaviors:
Is positive, dreamy
Reaches goals
Is committed
Sees world as
   harmonious
Feels empowered
   and high-energy

Behaviors:
Is negative, resistant
Is tentative, denying
Senses decline
Sees world as out of synch
Feels trapped and out
   of energy

New Beginning

Ending, Letting Go

Minitransition: Restructure, Improve the Chapter

Behaviors:
Feels optimistic
Is creative
Experiments
Is in training
Networks

Behaviors:
Is quiet and introspective
Invests in personal growth
Taps core values
Becomes filled with new
   hope, passion, and
   purpose
Is spiritual

Phase 4
Getting Ready

Self-Renewal

Phase 3
Cocooning

A LIFE TRANSITION

play roles in your drama. You place the scenery where you want it on the stage and create the context for your next life chapter. The play begins! You enter stage left, and Phase 1 is under way. As the scenes unfold, you weave together the dramatic development of your achievements, adventures, happiness, and success. You feel like a hero in the making!

Soon idealistic dreaming leads to realistic planning, as you launch your plan with action steps, time lines, and endless revisions. It may take many years to turn the dream into reality, and that seems all right, because this is your personal mission. You feel on course. During launching, you embed yourself in system after system, and for the most part they seem to support one another—relationships, family, career, causes, sports. You are very focused on your agenda and measured with your time.

If you stay committed to your dream-plan and keep adapting it to your life, you are likely to reach a plateau eventually, where much of your dream is realized. The plateau may be a blessing and a curse. As a blessing, it may represent your success, your victory, your ability to make the world work. As a curse, it may mean that motivation declines with the attainment of the vision. And altering the life course in a plateau is difficult; you are all wrapped up in the complex systems of your commitments and can't make changes easily. You may feel that you would rather be taking up a new challenge than managing this one, which has peaked. But you also feel that you deserve to remain in this plateau for a long time and to find ways to improve it.

Anne Bradley

Anne Bradley was ready to make something of her life. For over a year, she had been trying to forget how her employment was terminated when Touche Ross merged with Deloitte Haskins & Sells. She felt betrayed by a company that she had been devoted to for twenty-five years of her life. Three years later, she invented her own future: "What I finally came to realize is that I've always wanted to have a business of my own—you know, a small accounting firm that specializes in working with small, family businesses. Those guys are really neglected by the Big Eight. So I've got this dream about relocating in Portland, Oregon, where I have some friends, starting my business, living in a condo on a river, and taking up whitewater rafting on the side. What do you think?"

Clearly, Anne had a dream, and because she was good with details, she soon had a plan. Two years later, Anne let me hear how she was doing. "In all honesty," she said, "it's not easy starting your first business in your fifties, but I love it. I feel free and challenged again. Although I'm not as far along in my business plan as I thought I would be, I am on my way and happy to be charting my own path." There was quite a lapse of time before I received an announcement of her victory: "To Whom it May Concern: Be it known that Anne Bradley, former subservient in a Big Eight accounting firm, has now succeeded as the owner of her own accounting firm: THE MONEY WORKS."

Phase 2: The Doldrums

"Know that all things reach their peak, then wane. Success, too, comes by degrees, moderately, reaches a peak, and does not last forever. . . . Be realistic and take a good look at yourself, not so much as an individual who stands alone, but as a person who reacts to and with others. Knowing how and where you fit into society and life is the object. . . . If the situation seems hopeless, it is because you have become accustomed to the wrong way of doing things. You are lost. The more you try, the more lost you become. . . . You are in a situation much like fighting a rear-guard action. . . . Withdraw quietly and gracefully. There isn't much choice. . . . The need for withdrawal must be so obvious there can be no doubt as to its need. When the situation looks hopeless, that is the time to stand by your convictions, true to yourself above all else. Do this and it will end well."[4]

In Phase 2, you continue to manage your dramatic chapter, but you feel yourself distancing from it, so you search for ways to keep it thriving. An organizing principle for this phase is "holding on and letting go," as you sort out the essential qualities of your life chapter from those that need to be changed. Throughout this phase you feel your life chapter slip-sliding away. You are in the doldrums. You feel less possessed by your dream and less enchanted by your attainment. You have a sensation that you are looking in on your life instead of living it. You see yourself getting mired down, diminishing your own story. Unhappy with the prospects, you look for ways to eliminate your ambivalence so that you can soar again with clarity and unconditional resolve.

You obsess over ways to reinflate your balloon; you evaluate, tinker, and reevaluate. As you brood, you become critical of yourself and others. You look for something to fix, repair, change, or blame. You look for ways to salvage your chapter, to make it better than ever. You notice, however, that as your mind works harder to reclaim the alignment of your life chapter, your feelings are electric with outrage. You feel angry, scared, sad, and trapped. You are stuck in a reactive mode and don't know how to get out of it.

Unanticipated events enter the drama. Other actors produce scripts, lines, and decisions that you did not write or authorize. Even though you feel somewhat jaded and distanced from your own life chapter, you refuse to give up control of the story line. It's your human right to own it! Others, however, are beginning to direct the drama, and you feel trapped in a state of affairs that you did not anticipate. You find your roles increasingly confusing, and your acts are perceived as defensive. The glorious ending you had in mind for your success is being eclipsed by a chorus of dissonant voices. You are in a tailspin. Your self-esteem is diminishing. Someone absurdly suggests that you are having an identity crisis, which you immediately deny. You refuse to let others rain on your parade, even as the clouds burst. You feel yourself holding on, yet letting go. A popular song by The Guess Who says it all: "She's come undone, she's lost the sun."[5]

In the last scene of this phase, you are making a momentous decision, as if you had reached a fork in the routes available to you. If you take the route to the right, named "Restructuring: Mini-transition" (see Diagram 1), you can repair the structure and end up in Phase 1 with the same vision and overall plan. If you take the route into a full-fledged life transition, you can exit your chapter and find resources for constructing new directions. At last, a proactive choice!

The "restructuring" route rather quickly refurbishes and rejuvenates the chapter you are in, with some strategic changes—a change of geographical location, a change of employer, changes in marriage or family, a new work team, or a new career. Unless you are overwhelmed and surprised by events that seem outside your control—such as a death in the family, an accident or illness, a lottery pay-off, or a business disaster—this is the route you will probably choose. Evaluation leading to the reconstruction of a life chapter usually feels preferable to exiting into a life transition. The sense of trouble in Phase 2 may actually produce new determination to make the life chapter better than ever. So you work hard to repair, heal, and upgrade the life chapter that you have been living. (Successful adults often recycle themselves through Phase 1 and Phase 2—the upper half of the cycle—several times, until the life chapter itself becomes permanently stale, dysfunctional, or unavailable.)

The life "transition" route, which usually becomes attractive only after you have exhausted your efforts to rebuild your chapter, leads you to disengage from your out-of-synch chapter and to enter a transition involving cocooning, renewal, and experimentation. When you take this path—or get thrown into it by events beyond your control—you feel like you are indeed slip-sliding away, for all kinds of reasons, and none of them matter much. There doesn't have to be a worthy option. You are leaving, ending, disengaging, exiting—that's all.

The drama may turn to character analysis or an analysis of your chapter—and the stage may be flooded with emotional turmoil. Others may be after your roles—the scriptwriting, the directing—and you may feel paranoid and angry. Your wonderful drama may seem tragic, or you may be greatly relieved that it is about to be over. Your exit is clear and imminent, even to you. Sooner or later, every life chapter fades and becomes unworkable. Then, either it gets improved through refurbishing or you (or others) dismantle it. Even if you choose the first route and make positive adjustments in your existing life chapter and continue successfully a hundred times through Phases 1 and 2, the second route to complete disengagement from the structure will eventually belong to you. Sooner or later in every life chapter, the doldrums leads to a small door with big writing on it: EXIT HERE.

Why do life transitions happen? Maybe the salt loses its flavor. Maybe you lose your taste for salt! More realistically, your dreams may dim; your routines become boring. Maybe your relationships are losing energy and commitment. Perhaps your job is in a tailspin after you have given years of loyal and successful service. Maybe your job never evolved into a career and that is what the "departure" is about. Perhaps you have been a soldier in an overseas skirmish, and you know that your life will never be the same.

62

Maybe you are older, and your values have changed, making the roles that you were playing in your life chapter a burden. Maybe a close friend has died, or you have contracted a life-threatening disease or had an accident. Maybe you are just dreadfully unhappy, and that is the driving force.

Perhaps there is nothing intrinsically wrong with you or the chapter, but you are being challenged by a new dream that calls you to leave so that you can explore a road less traveled. Maybe you received an unexpected inheritance, received a promotion that you always wanted, had a religious experience, or adopted triplets. You also may find yourself rethinking the questions that you thought you had successfully answered and discovering new questions that you hadn't asked before. As the mythologist Joseph Campbell often said, "Sometimes we get to the top of our ladder and find it's against the wrong wall."

Almost always we resist endings. Most people would rather hang on to a life chapter reeking with immense distress than to find an honorable exit. They would rather seek to improve a dysfunctional chapter they are in than to enter a transition filled with the unknown. However, the unknown has a way of knocking on the doors of our lives from time to time, requiring our full attention. "The truth of the matter," declares Stanley Keleman, "is that making an ending forces us to start being more self-reliant, or at least offers that opportunity."[6] So you prepare to leave the chapter that has defined your life for the past several years and contained your identity, your hopes, and your unfulfilled self. You feel that entering the unknown ahead is now preferable—or necessary—to drowning in the incessant echoes, pain, and traps of your inoperative life chapter. One way or another, you depart, and by saying good-bye you say hello to a new journey.

Martin

At fifty-seven, Martin was a burned-out college professor looking for a future that he could believe in. Although his wife, Leia, a nurse, wanted to understand what Martin was going through, she was extremely eager for him to get through his depression and on with life. With two college-age children now away from home, she had become impatient with Martin's impasse. "I work with patients at the hospital eight hours a day and then come home to my full-time patient!" she blurted with exasperation. And Martin felt rushed by

Leia. "I lost interest in my work years ago," he confessed, "but what else can I do? I've never really left school. Besides, I have tenure. My dean wants me to take early retirement, but what would I do then? Rot at home instead of at school?"

Martin was feeling trapped, and while he wanted to change, he didn't know how to do it without losing what he thought was his major attainment in life—professorial tenure. It wasn't until the last day of the seminar that he was ready to rehearse an exit plan. "Maybe the dean would grant me a leave of absence," he pondered out loud. "I mean, they owe it to me, and if I could get it, I would take my family to France for the year and plan my retirement. I really would. My sister has a place in southern France that I know I could rent. It would be a wonderful change, and it might lead somewhere. I'm sick of staying stuck."

The dean granted the leave, and during his renewing year in France, Martin discovered many new dreams within him. His energy returned, and his sex life improved. As he felt his residual strength, it became easier to imagine himself leaving the college. In fact, he didn't even want to return home! He decided to resign his teaching position, remain in the same geographic location, and become a part-time realtor. His wife and family rejoiced. In a recent letter, he admitted that "while it was a wrenching decision to leave my college and my professorial career, I feel now that a thousand tons have been lifted from me."

Jeff

At forty-four, Jeff was successful as an M.D. but unsuccessful as a husband and father. As he saw it, his profession required his primary attention, but his wife and child felt that he just didn't care enough for them. "You simply aren't available for me or for little Peter," his wife blurted out one day, "and you aren't ever going to make us your best friends. I am very sorry, Jeff, but I can't stay married to a workaholic. I want a husband who is a lover, father, and friend!"

After the divorce, Jeff continued his life as a physician but was unable to find a successful intimate relationship. For two years, he lived alone and organized his life around his work, which was easy to do. In his solitude at home, he learned new ways to reflect on his life course and to make peace with the path that he had chosen. Then he met Bertha, who worked in the marketing division of a pharmaceutical firm. Bertha was every bit as busy as he was. They both loved their brief but intense intimate times, as well as their demanding jobs. They decided to marry; afterwards, they led separate lives most of the time, with occasional excursions to interesting places. Although they knew that other couples felt that theirs was less than a complete marriage, Bertha and Jeff felt good about the balance they had created between their work and their life together.

Renette

At midlife, Renette seemed to have much of what she wanted—a good marriage, employment in a small research firm, and two children. Yet she hated her fat body. For a long time, she got down on herself, and her depression diminished her effectiveness at work and at home. Gradually, she withdrew from all of her social connections. She quit her job, refused sex, and became a minimal mother. Filled with personal disgust, she joined a Weight Watchers group, began an exercise program, and very gradually reclaimed her attractive body and self-esteem. Renette continued on the same life journey, but she had a new sense of purpose. Now she initiated activities with her husband and went on trips alone with the children.

Sam

Sam was sick and tired of his situation at PNN, an electronics firm where he was an area manager in Texas. Having grown up in Maine, Sam wanted PNN to relocate him in the Northeast and, of course, he wanted a promotion as well. But PNN had flattened the corporation, eliminating middle managers and leaving little opportunity for anyone to rise within the firm. At forty-eight, Sam felt that he had peaked, and he felt trapped. He found an hourly engineering position with AT&T in Boston and decided to switch companies, even though it meant a demotion and less salary. "When I exchanged companies and geographical locations," Sam explained, "my wife and three kids liked life a whole lot better. They liked me better, too. I actually find my current work very challenging, but my main challenge is to lead a balanced life, and I'm doing that. It feels right."

Phase 3: Cocooning

"There will be misfortune, but no serious harm. The real, natural you is resilient and strong. Be your natural self and you can do no harm. When misfortune comes, let nature take its course. The situation improves by itself, without the need for any action on your part. . . . Reexamine and rededicate yourself to your motives and values. . . . Inactivity should not disturb you, for you can use the time to contemplate who and where you are. Be yourself, but rise above selfishness to achieve a selfless serenity. . . . Do these things and you will achieve union with the universe."[7]

In Phase 3, you exit the extended stage and turn inward for the continuing drama, to rely on your inner resources. Your game plan is twofold: to shed the onion skins of your former life chapter and to become self-reliant. At first you have no lines, no roles, no recognition, nothing. You may even feel like a nothing, a nonbeing, an actor without a role or a play. You have left the outer world of action and have entered the inner world of soul searching. There you gradually recognize a different stage for the metamorphosis of the self.

You grieve the loss of your chapter and feel as if your own life had ended. Your sense of a future is very bleak and your energy level low. Although you began the cocooning process in Phase 2, you feel very burdened with yourself now that you are in Phase 3, cocooning full-time. Your lamentation and mourning have gone on much longer than you want: "The bottom has fallen out of my world," "Nothing matters now," "The meaning has gone out of my life," "I'm not there anymore." Ever so gradually, you let go of the external chapter as it clings to your mind—lost dreams, lost roles, lost beauty, lost muscles, lost parents, lost careers, lost children, lost marriages, lost income, lost hope—and you live for a while in a neutral zone where you are, psychologically speaking, by yourself, in suspension, in limbo, and more aware of who you are not than who you are becoming.[8]

Typically, but not necessarily, you feel a hollow loneliness that doesn't go away, and you fear that you've been abandoned not only by your past but by your future as well. You wander around, looking in on your life, as if you were a ghost or spirit from a Dickens novel. The ghosts from your past confront you, and the ghosts from your future taunt you, but eventually they have less and less impact as you grow stronger and find new life within. In time, you feel not merely healed but vital and alive. It is a quiet fire, within, and it brings warmth and new confidence. Your eyes mirror the resilience that you have found. You want little but feel much, and most of all you feel in touch with the deep murmurs of your own heart. Your deep-seated values arise to shape your new human agenda, and you get ready to journey again.

The big surprise is that the attunement that you feel in your life at this time has more contentment and fulfillment than the "success" and "identity" that you wanted so desperately to hold on to in your former life chapter. As your self-renewal deepens, you are overwhelmed by gratitude and joy. You are ready to launch a new adventure, much better fitted than the old one to your present life and destiny.

Disengagement is a time for "being," not "doing." In time, people who are devoted to working through loss find resources within them that they didn't realize they had. With healing and renewal, reintegration with the external world begins again. This time, new external extensions of the self will be chosen, like new clothes, to fit current dreams and values and competencies and to accommodate current social conditions and opportunities. The dark night of the soul fades into morning's sunrise, and the cocoon breaks open for the butterfly to begin its skyward journey.

Frank and Helen

Frank and Helen were profoundly shaken when their two children were killed in an automobile accident two years ago. It doesn't matter now just how it happened. What matters is that Frank and Helen were thrown into a total reevaluation of their lives such as they had never experienced before. They didn't want to talk much to anyone, and they felt embarrassed at their fragile emotions. On the living room piano, they made an altar of pictures of how Marie and Joe had looked in their all-too-brief years of life. At one point, Helen decided to take a trip to Vienna, alone, just to think things through. Frank said that he understood. But while she was gone, he cried more than ever.

Frank said that he wanted to "plan his life," but clearly he needed first to find some inner strength; he blamed himself for the accident, even though he hadn't even been near the automobile. He was neglecting his work to such a degree that he had received a negative job review, with a three-month notice to shape up or ship out. Frank was not able to shape up. "What should I do?" he asked. "What really matters, now?" he pondered, without finding an answer. When Frank recognized that he had to get a break from his work, he obtained a leave and later returned successfully. But during his leave of absence, Frank and Helen made some momentous discoveries. Helen put it this way: "I fell in love with Frank all over again. He became so human and tender." Frank said, "I learned that there is more of me than I knew. I have become more sensitive and more determined to live now, and to love now, and to put my life where my beliefs are." For months, they hibernated in their home and talked about everything they were thinking and feeling, as they had done before they were married. Both of them talked about how lonely the grieving period was and how dreadfully long it took and continues to take. "But in the end," Helen said, "we are more connected to what is important to our lives. In a strange way, we are the living legacy of our own children."

Phase 4: Getting Ready for the Next Chapter

"Be simple, free, and uncomplicated. . . . Develop virtues based on inner strength and signify them by outward self-restraint. Be yourself; do not emulate others. . . . Solve minor problems now while the solutions are still simple. . . . Remain somewhat aloof from the world and quietly improve yourself. In this way you will make of yourself something which will endure. . . . Do not take action prematurely. You must be ready, seasoned, with mature judgment, if you are to succeed. . . . You cannot succeed without the help of others. . . . Eventually an experienced person will come to help you and success follows."[9]

In Phase 4, you expand your self-renewal space to include the world around you. This is a time of rebirth, play, and experimentation. The inner self and the outer world find new ways to dance together. The organizing principles are exploration, creativity, and networking. Feelings are predominantly positive and expressive, and the world seems safe again. You slowly begin to link your renewed self with the possible scenarios for your life in the world that surrounds you. You are fresh and dreamy again. You feel creative and filled with energy, like a child: unencumbered, free, willing to try new ideas. You experiment with options, network with new kinds of friends, and play with possibilities without making many commitments. You engage in new learning projects and yearn to travel. You feel no need to rush and every reason to savor these moments of discovery. Sooner or later, you discover some path that feels right for a new life structure, and the cycle begins again. You become heady, optimistic, refreshed, ready, and prepared.

Jim

When I first met him, Jim, at forty-seven, had just been fired as the executive director of a prestigious YMCA in Chicago. Although he dressed like an executive and smoked big cigars, he talked like a man in distress. His voice was fragile, his humor raw, and it was obvious that he had been shaken to his roots. At first, he was not able to admit that he had been fired from his job. He was not prepared to face the transition he was already in.

Jim entered Y work when he graduated from Springfield College and became an executive director at age twenty-seven. In fact, the only type of job that Jim had ever had was as a CEO of one Y or another as he worked his way up from small to large operations. Jim was Mr. YMCA; he thought, breathed, and lived the Y world. When the board of directors at the Chicago YMCA decided to fire Jim, he declared war on his board and sought to reclaim his job. He was angry, depressed, and confused. He felt that his life was at stake. Within a week, he was deeply into a life transition without knowing it.

Who was Jim without his career identity—his YMCA roles, experiences, and accomplishments? To himself, Jim was a nobody, and his self-esteem and confidence were on the rocks. He had no identity apart from his work role, even though others found him affectionate, thoughtful, playful, and interesting—as a person. As Jim gradually accepted the transition territory that he was traversing, he realized that he was losing everything he had spent his life gaining. Although others offered him comfort and concern, he stayed armored in his grief.

People in transition need plans that help them discover their inner resources and faith in forces beyond themselves. Jim was low in trust and had an equally low awareness of his own interiority. Nevertheless, his pride required him to demand a new job with a YMCA as a CEO, immediately. He did not realize that he was, for now, unemployable. In time, Jim made it clear that he was burned out with his executive roles and that he wanted to renew his life and discover who he was as a person apart from career roles and status; to renew his marriage, which he'd ignored for years; to renew the fathering of his three teenage children, who were school dropouts in considerable rebellion; and to change his career direction to an entrepreneurial occupation that he could run on his own.

Jim mapped out a year's "sabbatical" that would serve as a twelve-month period of soul searching, renewal, and new beginnings. He held a big sabbatical party where he announced his plans and thanked his friends for their support for his new direction. That party was like a rite of passage for Jim, distinguishing his past from his future and providing him a dignified way to publicly let go and move on. During this grieving-healing period, Jim did fix-it projects around the house and even added a room for his teenage daughter. He went on daily walks with his wife, Rosemary, and they grew closer together than they had ever been since their honeymoon ended. Jim maintained a daily journal to keep track of his inner thoughts, and he spent two hours a day at a health center where he swam and worked out.

Several months later, Jim left for Europe, to drift about with his oldest son, whom he knew the least of all his children. The son was responsible for the planning, while Jim practiced the art of listening and following. It worked for both of them. After six weeks together abroad, they returned, filled with stories of adventure and love for one another. This sojourn exceeded the expectations of both father and son and prepared Jim for reentry. By the end of the year, Jim had discovered new inner resources and confidence. He was clearly into exploring the world again and was beginning to experiment with new career ideas and friendships. He had the makings of a consulting business with nonprofit organizations and a financial planning business for people like himself. In a message I received from him, he remarked, "I should have left years ago. I'm embarrassed to say that after all these years, I'm learning how to live, but it's true. I feel like a different person. Although my life is full of loose ends, I know I'm doing the right thing. After all these years, I am ready to build my future the old-fashioned way—upon my character."

How the Cycle of Change Works

Now reflect upon the excursion we have just taken through the cycle of change. What are the critical issues to grasp, in order to use these concepts in your own life? To begin with, you need to be able to locate where you are in the cycle, at this moment in time, and which life tasks are central for your future empowerment. You will probably find yourself at various places in the cycle if you think about your various adult roles—spouse, parent, worker. Your marriage may be in the doldrums, while your parenting is going well in a launching phase. Meanwhile, your career or work role may be undergoing a transition. However, as a person, beneath the roles—the inner self who talks to all the parts and tries to monitor cohesion and joy—you are at approximately one place in the circle. It is that residual self or core that guides a person, with all his or her roles and parts, on a "life course" throughout the life cycle.[10] The two basic alternatives are to be in a chapter or in a transition. A life chapter represents a cohesive period of your life; a transition is an opportunity to renew and retool your inner self. A life chapter embeds you in the human systems around you; a life transition frees you to discover more of your inner self. Neither is better than the other, and both are necessary places in the flow of adult life. But as a person, you are engaged, at any given time, either in building a life structure or in redefining your life purpose through a transition process. To be a successful human being, you need excellence in mastering both, and most of us have many opportunities to do so during the course of our lives.

Adult life flows around the cycle, clockwise, slowly or quickly, like a river. A life chapter happens when adults are able to align their inner strengths with resources in their surrounding environment, resulting in a plan that works. This could be the inspired artist ready to compose, paint, or sculpt. It could be a newly married couple establishing their careers and home around a shared dream. It could be a fifty-year-old ready to try a new pathway.

Transitions happen when life chapters are unavailable, painful, or out of alignment. A transition is a journey into your inner strengths, resulting in your renewal as a person. Some transitions represent fairly rapid restructurings of the same life chapter, such as a job change, a move, or a promotion. Other transitions are slow and transformative, leading to new and different life chapters, such as personal changes following the death of a spouse or child, being fired from a job, or a divorce.

Both life chapters and transitions are dramatic forms. You lead your life into stories that you find believable. You inspire, imagine, create the script, convince the players, learn the lines, act out the parts, direct the drama, and defend the actions. You take care of yourself, heal, and become self-sufficient. Of course, you are guided and constrained by a multitude of factors beyond your control, but the bottom line is that *you are ultimately responsible for your own life chapters and transitions.* Even if tragedy befalls you, you are the only one who can decide how to continue your story. As long as you can choose to live differently and extend your story chronologically, you are authoring your own story. This is the way you explain your life to yourself and others. You are a person, with a story, on a journey, weaving your way through the scenes of your life. If you do not write the script, someone else will, and you will learn about your lifeline through symbiotic relationships and roles. But if you write the script, it will be a "life design," an intentional plot to make your world work—the world of your own experience and imagination.

Ten Life Skills for Managing the Renewal Cycle

Adults experience the cycle of change as a renewal cycle. As you proceed around the cycle you will experience change as "growth and development, renewal, evolving." The very movement around the circle keeps you on your learning edge. No place on the cycle is better or worse than anywhere else. Each has its time, place, and lesson. Each place challenges us to extend ourselves as we move toward our completion.

At least ten basic life skills represent the most important abilities you need to grow and develop as a person within the change cycle, to succeed at creating life chapters and at producing significant self-renewal during life transitions. These are human competencies that assume strategic importance at specific times in your life. The ten skills (see Diagram 2 and list to follow) are approximate notions. People require many other competencies for making their lives work, but these ten are the generic, human tasks in which adults today need basic proficiency for the weaving and unraveling of their lives.

Although each life skill has a time in the cycle when it performs a critical function, all ten abilities are important at all times, because to some degree parts of our lives are simultaneously at various places in the cycle. During a life chapter, there will be many times when minor transitions must be managed, and during transitions it is necessary to maintain a minimal life structure in order to take care of oneself. Each of the ten skills represents a strategic activity for a particular time and place in the cycle. Each ability has a unique time in the cycle when it has special power for keeping life proactive and moving forward; each functions like a Zeitgeist and then needs to give way to the next, keeping you on course with optimal choices for your development at different places on the

Diagram 2. Ten Life Skills for Sustaining Purpose and Passion in the Renewal Cycle.

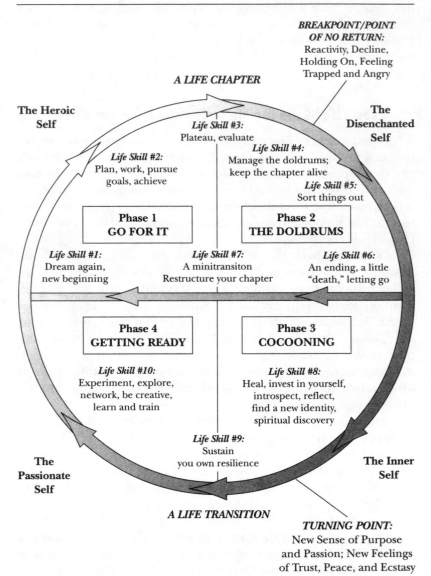

BREAKPOINT/POINT OF NO RETURN:
Reactivity, Decline, Holding On, Feeling Trapped and Angry

A LIFE CHAPTER

The Heroic Self

The Disenchanted Self

Life Skill #3:
Plateau, evaluate

Life Skill #2:
Plan, work, pursue goals, achieve

Life Skill #4:
Manage the doldrums; keep the chapter alive

Life Skill #5:
Sort things out

Phase 1
GO FOR IT

Phase 2
THE DOLDRUMS

Life Skill #1:
Dream again, new beginning

Life Skill #7:
A minitransiton Restructure your chapter

Life Skill #6:
An ending, a little "death," letting go

Phase 4
GETTING READY

Phase 3
COCOONING

Life Skill #10:
Experiment, explore, network, be creative, learn and train

Life Skill #8:
Heal, invest in yourself, introspect, reflect, find a new identity, spiritual discovery

Life Skill #9:
Sustain you own resilience

The Passionate Self

The Inner Self

A LIFE TRANSITION

TURNING POINT:
New Sense of Purpose and Passion; New Feelings of Trust, Peace, and Ecstasy

river. Each life skill leverages you through a particular portion of the cycle of change and prepares you for the next leg of the journey. Knowing which competencies to favor at various points of your personal cycle is the wisdom of adult life.

Phase 1—Go for It. The Heroic Self—Outer Work

1. *A dream or vision* provides conviction, inspiration, and energy for constructing a life chapter. A *plan* schedules the dream with available resources and possibilities.

2. *Launching* requires personal commitment, perseverance, and adaptations—and social and economic alignment.

3. *Plateauing* sustains and deepens a successful, functional life chapter.

Phase 2—The Doldrums. The Disenchanted Self—Out of Synch

4. *Managing the doldrums* comes to terms with decline, negative emotions, and feeling trapped in an increasingly dysfunctional life chapter.

5. *Sorting things out* results in a personal plan: what to keep, what to eliminate or change, what to add, and how to proceed into a revitalized life chapter.

6. *Ending* a life chapter with dignity and care requires an ability to say farewell with gratitude and clarity, leaving you free to consider your next options. There are two possibilities at this point: restructuring or making a life transition.

The Minitransition: Restructuring the Same Chapter

7. *Restructuring,* which conducts a minitransition back into a refurbished life chapter, can be used to move across the center of the cycle if the life chapter can be improved with some specific changes. Restructuring is like minor surgery, with a strategic plan to make the life chapter work better—a new location, a new job, a new home, or a new partner. The same basic values and goals prevail, but the action steps, setting, and/or players in the drama are altered.

Phase 3—Cocooning. The Inner Self—
Transformation from the Inside-Out

8. *Cocooning* is the first activity of a life transition—turning inward to take stock, to find your own basic values, and to disengage emotionally and mentally from the life chapter. If the life chapter cannot be redeemed, or if the optimal choice is to leave it in order to find a new and different one, the first step is to exit into a life transition where this skill is required. A life transition is like major surgery, usually resulting in personal development, new life options, and even transformation.

Phase 4—Getting Ready. The Passionate Self—
Preparing for the Next Chapter

9. *Self-renewal* follows from successful cocooning. It is the ability to be self-sustaining, producing confidence, energy, purpose, and hope. Self-renewal also involves a reevaluation of core issues and beliefs.

10. *Experimenting,* the final and tenth skill of the cycle, engages you in being creative, learning, exploring, risk-taking, and networking. When the self is ready to venture back into a life chapter, it takes on this skill.

As the self gains strength in its own sense of purpose, it feels alive and playful and begins to link up with new social support and new information about life options. The self, now feeling anchored and purposive again, spends its time exploring new external possibilities for a life chapter. Sooner or later, a new and compelling dream takes over and a new life chapter begins. Chapters Four through Six will explore the cycle of change and its ten empowerment skills in detail and with examples.

Chapter Four

Life Chapters

> *Freedom and captivity coexist. We cannot escape from our
> structures; we are condemned to structuring our worlds
> since this is the form of life in which we exist. But
> although we are imprisoned, we are free to choose what
> form our prison should take. . . . If we accept that our
> constructions are structures and not reality itself, and
> that each person has his own construction of reality, then
> we have to live with uncertainty. But we can choose to
> define that uncertainty as either prison or freedom. I
> prefer freedom.*
> DOROTHY ROWE, *THE CONSTRUCTION
> OF LIFE AND DEATH*[1]

Phase 1—Go for It: Dreaming, Planning, and Plateauing

A life chapter is not born in a vacuum. The social environment
must provide sufficient stability, resources, and freedom for the
drama of a life structure to unfold. A life chapter requires a dependable financial base and social opportunities. A life chapter
springs from a healthy self, brimming with creative energy, honed
skills, and inner determination. People beginning life chapters
have often just completed training programs, extensive travel, or
learning experiences that prepared them for a leap into the future.

People ready to create life chapters experience a shifting of
gears, out of the inward orientation of transition space into the
social expansiveness of constructing a chapter. This is the time for
moving from simple to complex, from inner to outer, from self to
systems, from separation to interdependence, from short-term

innovation to long-term embeddedness. Adults who are prepared for a life chapter see the world as fair and friendly, ready to fulfill their life needs and goals. Structurers are single-minded—to create a future by weaving all the expanding parts of their lives together around a central purpose or mission. Starting with visionary possibilities, a person beginning a life chapter devises plans and then manages them on a daily basis. If the long haul of launching is successful, a plateau is reached. Otherwise, the ending comes sooner than expected (see Diagram 3).

The Dream-Plan

The first renewal cycle skill that a structurer requires is the ability to evolve a new dream-plan. The new *dream* is the driving force for the life structure, a source of passion and values. The *plan* is the plot for making the dream happen—the methodical details for manipulating the everyday world.

The Dream

Your dream is a vision of yourself in the near future. What is the future? Not something waiting for you but something you create through your imagination. The future is possibility waiting for form, the "not yet" waiting to be programmed. Dreamers can taste their visions and feel compelled by them, as if they were self-evident truths. "We hold these truths to be self-evident," said our founding fathers, as they laid out the American dream that has guided us for more than two hundred years. "I have a dream," yearned Martin Luther King more recently in Washington, D.C., as he painted a picture of equality and fairness in America. John Lennon's song "Imagine" is a dreamer's commitment to human transformation, shared by a generation now in midlife or beyond. The dream comes first. Then reality chases after the dream to make it happen.

Dreams have the following qualities:

- A dream is a compelling picture of a desirable future. It is a poetic picture, not a literal statement. Once invented by

Diagram 3. Phase 1—Dreaming, Planning, and Plateauing.

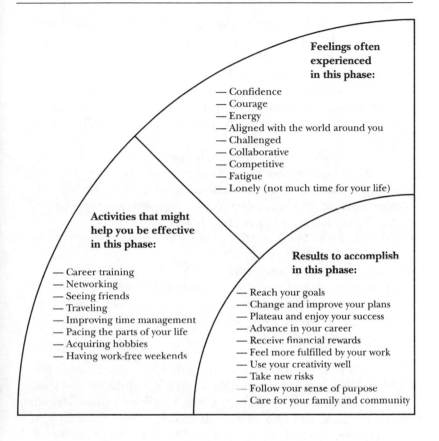

Feelings often
experienced
in this phase:

— Confidence
— Courage
— Energy
— Aligned with the world around you
— Challenged
— Collaborative
— Competitive
— Fatigue
— Lonely (not much time for your life)

Activities that might
help you be effective
in this phase:

— Career training
— Networking
— Seeing friends
— Traveling
— Improving time management
— Pacing the parts of your life
— Acquiring hobbies
— Having work-free weekends

Results to accomplish
in this phase:

— Reach your goals
— Change and improve your plans
— Plateau and enjoy your success
— Advance in your career
— Receive financial rewards
— Feel more fulfilled by your work
— Use your creativity well
— Take new risks
— Follow your sense of purpose
— Care for your family and community

the imagination, it hovers over a person as a lure toward the future.

- A good dream is simple, clear; it is easily recalled and rehearsed.
- A dream is a promise that is self-evident and convincing, an idea whose time has come. To think it is to go for it. It feels right, and it's going to happen.
- A dream is a visceral yearning, not a prediction or wish list. It taps a deep inner sense of personal destiny and provides pictures and voices for your inner sense of purpose. It is a picture of what you most deeply want your life to count for. A

dream provides a total picture for how you want your life to become.

- A dream is a pull toward higher ground, an inspiration for becoming. It is not a dream to want a new car, an exotic vacation, or even a new career. A valid dream is comprehensive, anchored in the courage to be.
- A dream is a spiritual promise of a new quality of life, a deeper sense of being, a promise for human betterment that is just beyond your reach but worth reaching for and possible to approximate.
- A dream inspires and motivates; it doesn't order people around. When you live as a visionary adult, you have a dream, even if the dream doesn't translate into marching orders for every hour of the day. A dream is energy; whenever you think of it, you get a burst of personal power.
- A dream works like a rudder guiding you toward your chosen destination, keeping you on course.
- A dream is like a haunting refrain. You know that you have one when it won't let you go and others are attracted to it within you. You know that you have a vision when it seems already to be guiding you toward its reality, and you don't have to explain it to yourself.

Much if not most of the dreaming that humans do takes place in childhood and adolescence. We encourage children and young adults to dream and to launch plans to achieve those dreams: "What do you want to do when you grow up?" In the adult years, however, when life is more complicated by many commitments and entrenched responsibilities, dreaming tends to be limited and episodic—a trip to Hawaii, moving into a new house, having an affair. Yet in truth, we never "grow up"; we just keep growing, and our human need for holistic dreaming pervades all of our life and never ends.

As far as we know, human beings are the only creatures on earth capable of envisioning a future and then setting about to make it happen. We dream and imagine; we expect and plan; we invent and create. This is how new companies get born, poems get conceived, Olympic races get won, music gets written, and new things get invented. Our greatest human power is our capacity to imagine, vision, and dream, over and over again. It is an essential part of the lifestyle of the self-renewing adult and the first step in empowering a satisfying life structure.

The Plan

Visioning and planning are very different. Dreams are imaginative, softheaded, motivating, and energy releasing. Planning is logical, hardheaded, factual, and realistic. Without a purposeful dream, planning is reduced to mechanical busyness. Without a realistic plan, dreams are random wishes—daydreams at best. Dreams impregnate new directions; plans help new directions develop and happen.

Few dreamers are good planners; few planners follow a dream. The two often war with each other, like hearts and heads, leaders and managers. To empower your life today, however, you need to be both a dreamer and a planner. When you plan, you take the visionary pictures of a dream and connect them to sympathetic worldly forces. A good planner protects the dream in two ways— by looking for environmental forces working against the plan and by adapting the dream to available resources.

Planning is more than a bunch of skills; it is an inner force, a felt competence, a strength within us. Planning is how our integrity gets the world to cooperate with the dream, and the dream with the world. The planner pushes forward with logical steps, like choosing reliable stepping stones to cross a stream. Through strategic thinking, the planner embroiders the dreamer's vision with the complexity of the world, weaving together technical and human resources required to bring the life structure into reality. In the life of any successful structurer, the possible dream becomes a probable plan.

A competent life planner follows four principles. First, he or she keeps the dream central to the plan. The plan is merely the instrument of the dream, never the raison d'être of a life structure. The dream stirs up awe and excitement for the journey, while the plan commits a person to an explicit course of action. A good planner implements good dreams; he or she is value-driven.

An incompetent planner becomes addicted to the mechanical details of management and short-term results—and gets lost in the process.

Second, a competent life planner constructs plans that draw on proven strengths that have worked well in previous life structures. If you are a forty-five-year-old just beginning a new life structure, you need to know what has worked for you in previous life structures. A primary advantage of aging is the reservoir of experience you accumulate. Use that store of knowledge—or lose it. People are full of transferable skills. Competence gained from career can be used in family life, and vice versa. "When I ask middle-aged people to tell me what they do well," writes Judith Bardwick, "they say:

> I have an ability to make things happen and I enjoy that.
> I'm a good husband.
> I'm a good listener.
> I think I get along with people.
> I communicate.
> I'm very proud of my children and they love me and I love them.
> I'm a good manager.
> I organize things well.
> I have a sense of humor.
> I'm very good at helping people I care about.
> I'm a good friend.
> I find creative ways to solve problems.
> I feel good about my perspective on life.
> I'm honest and ethical.
> I can create an atmosphere of cooperation.
> I bring common sense to a situation.
> I demonstrate leadership.
> I'm aware of myself for the first time.
> I'm a good tactician.
> I have good judgment.
> I am a responsible person.
> I have a very good relationship with my wife.

I am a very good wife and now I'm comfortable in that role.
I have maintained my integrity and have not sold out.

Middle age is value-added."[2]

What earlier were parenting skills may evolve as management talent, and leisure skills of the past may shape an entrepreneurial direction in tomorrow's life. Sales ability may now become redirected as diplomatic skills, and the peak performer who liked to "win" may evolve into a person who likes to "be." The most important human resources for the life planner are the virtues that have worked in the past. Almost anyone who has survived forty years of life has developed advanced personal skills that can create new paths and opportunities.

Third, a competent life planner faces squarely his or her limits and undeveloped abilities. By early midlife, virtually all adults are lopsided human beings. By then, you have almost always specialized in something—a career, parenting, profiteering, housekeeping, serving, or a leisure life—and as your unique abilities consume you, your undeveloped self and your deficits become more and more obvious. As you specialize you forget basic skills in other areas, and you further neglect your already neglected parts. By the time you are forty or so, you are bound to feel that your life is out of synch, merely because you have overaccentuated some of your abilities, neglected others, and become dependent on other people for significant segments of your life.

Carl Jung said that the real planner in the second half of life is our "Undiscovered Self," which yearns to get born in our forties and fifties. As we age, the voices of our neglected parts get louder, demanding a say in our (and their!) destiny. What were our so-called weaknesses may now seek to become our strengths. They need training, education, and opportunity. Some adults feel trapped in their own success, where they feel bored as their specialized competence continues to encapsulate them. The planner in us seeks to understand our weaknesses—to protect us from them or to turn them into assets.

Case Examples

Delores is a computer analyst wanting to become a manager. What skills does she already have? She may need training in leadership and interpersonal skills. Is she trainable and educable in those skills? How might she find out whether she is or not? Where would she get the training? What kinds of job openings would exist for her at salary levels that she can accept? Those are key planning questions.

George is a CEO wanting to retire and start a nursery, but he doesn't know how to stop thinking, talking, and behaving like a CEO. He panics at having to do all the chores himself, without an orchestration of helpers. What does it take to alter his management style, his personal needs, and the roles he wants to leave behind?

Pamela is a full-time parent who now wants a career as a lawyer. Although she had a brief career as a lab technician in her twenties, she will need to enter law school and establish herself in that career. How can she draw from her wealth of experience to leverage herself ahead? How will schooling mesh with her existing lifestyle and commitments? Has she already worked with lawyers to be sure that this direction is part of her dream?

Maurice was addicted to his work, and he yearned to break his habit and begin again. When he met Marie, an investment broker fifteen years younger than he, he wondered what it would be like to be a househusband, with some volunteer activities and perhaps some children in the future. They married, and seven years later, he had quit his job and conquered his workaholism. He also was the full-time father of two small children and active in the docent programs in the local art museum and botanical gardens.

Fourth, a competent planner keeps adapting his or her dream to the changing realities of the social environment. The planner does not turn chaos into planned change, as so many say. Rather, the planner swims in the sea of change as cooperatively as possible, searching for available ways to a preferred destination. The planner constructs a relatively short-term game plan, with evaluative principles built in, so that the turbulent waters can be tested in an inductive, ad hoc way, little by little. The planner is an adapter, determined to shape a chapter but not sure of every move to make. A plan is a living document, not a stone etching. Few dream-plans turn out the way they began. They take shape and get reshaped along the way. As new opportunities arise, the planner shifts gears to take advantage of them, if they serve the dream. When new obstacles appear, the planner creates new strategies to stay on course. At times, the planner may have to negotiate with the dreamer to modify the dimensions of the life structure in order to proceed. A capable planner is definite and flexible, committed and adaptable, centered and learning, loyal and clever.

Launching

The second renewal cycle skill for making a life chapter succeed is launching, which puts the dream-plan to work. With launching, the imaginal dream and the realistic plan get projected into the systems of the world to see whether they are congruent and stay in orbit. The launching process represents the months and years that it takes to bring the full life chapter into reality. It is birthing time, a time for working and waiting, an expectant but busy phase in the construction of the future.

Launching requires each of us to develop "executive" functions for making life work. You become the CEO of your life.[3] The launcher's job is to get the systems of the world to cooperate with the dream-plan and to modify the dream-plan so that it can fit the systems around it. The launcher aims at a successful completion in a plateauing orbit—a victory that can be sustained. But sometimes he or she chooses to abandon the life chapter. Perhaps the mountain is too high, or resources for the climb have been expended. Perhaps the importance of the destination has changed, and the trip is called off. Although launchers aim at plateauing and winning, the good ones are prepared to abort if they have to. And if a launcher has to exit, he or she will decide either to renew the same life chapter under different circumstances (restructuring) or to engage in a life transition and start all over again in new directions. The launching ability has two essential components—commitment and personal mission.

Commitment

To have a life chapter, a person needs commitment, which means much more than compliance with the plan. Commitment is persistence, dedication, interaction, and an intention to win. Commitment begins with adherence to one's own integrity. It is a steady covenant to be true to yourself and to those who share your path.

Commitment is lived values. "A value is only a value if it is life-preserving and life-enhancing," writes Allan Bloom. "Commitment values the values and makes them valuable. . . . The hallmark of the *authentic self* is consulting one's oracle while facing up to what one is and what one experiences. *Decisions,* not deliberations, are the movers of deeds. One cannot know or plan the future. One must will it. There is no program."[4] True commitment is inner-driven and anchored to the dream within. Henry David Thoreau said, "A man must find his occasions in himself. . . . If one advances confidently in the direction of his dreams, and endeavors to live the life which he has imagined, he will meet with a success unexpected in common hours. . . . If a man does not keep pace with his companions, perhaps it is because he hears a different drummer. Let him step to the music which he hears, however measured or far away."[5]

Although commitment is an inner decision to be definite, it is a learned behavior. Commitment requires faith, trust, hope, and patience—all inner capacities. Commitment requires risk taking, teamwork, and long-distance management—all outer capacities. Many adults in our society have not yet learned how to make their lives work; they lack the prerequisites of commitment, so they fall short of achieving a life chapter. They need training in basic life skills that will help them effectively combine their intentionality with the resources of the world around them. They need training in two primary areas of true commitment: attachment and achievement. The ability to attach stems from emotional bonding and inner comfort with others and with adult roles. The ability to achieve stems from clear thinking and actions that make the external world approximate the dream. Both attachment and achievement are necessary skills for creating successful life chapters. Both can be learned.

Commitment is more than inner determination; it requires worldly savvy and risk taking. Plans are merely blueprints for action. Launching requires leadership, collaboration, use of a network, adaptation, incorporation of new opportunities, safeguards against new threats, and timing. Commitment often requires the careful scheduling of time through the use of time management systems. Successful launchers have internal gyroscopes, keeping them balanced and moving toward their dreams; they also have radar, keeping them apprised of worldly conditions. Sorting out the signals, launchers make their moves.

Personal Mission

When you have a dream and a plan working together in the construction of a life chapter, you have a "mission," a circumscribed purpose that defines your use of time and space for the duration of this particular life chapter. People with a mission know where they want to go. A person with a mission is clear about what he or she will and won't do to serve the priorities of the plan. The boundaries for taking action are relatively crisp and definite. Life is a challenge, and the singular focus is to reach the goal line of a successful plateau. This is the all-American place to be: aimed at winning. "Winning," said A. Bartlett Giamatti in a speech when he was president of Yale University, "has a joy and discrete purity to it that cannot be replaced by anything else. Winning is important to any man's or woman's sense of satisfaction and well-being. Winning is not everything, but it is something powerful, indeed beautiful, in itself, something as necessary to the strong spirit as striving is necessary to the healthy character."

To win, you must grow your dreams in the structures of the world around you. That is not easy. Every social system has its own rules and prerogatives, and they do not easily cooperate with individual priorities. A successful launcher convinces whatever systems that he or she needs to cooperate with a dream-plan. In that exchange, however, a trick is played: once the dream is embedded in the world, it begins to be entrapped; it begins to die, and the external structures begin to control the person. Sustaining your personal mission means staying on the path that belongs to you, and this requires continuous evaluation and renewal of the journey. The ability to evaluate your journey is critical to staying on course. "Am I on course or off course?" the launcher asks, and if he is off course, corrective measures are taken. The launcher wants to win but loves the challenge of winning almost as much. She wants to be a peak performer with optimal performance. If the plan is not working or the dream is judged to be outdated, the healthy launcher aborts the mission and moves the chapter as rapidly as possible to disengagement, where a decision is made.

either to take the minitransition for restructuring the life chapter or to begin a life transition in search of new directions.

Plateauing

The third renewal cycle skill is plateauing, the art of sustaining a successful life structure. Oscar Wilde once remarked, "In this world there are only two tragedies. One is not getting what one wants, and the other is getting it."[6] Plateauing is knowing how to stay at the top of your realized dream and to keep enriching the dream-plan for as long as it makes sense to do so. People who succeed in achieving their life chapters discover that making a plateau work is a new ball game. Some people like it and thrive on it. They bask in the recognition and rewards and strive to enhance their position. Others experience themselves slipping into a pensive reevaluation and a loss of motivation.

There tend to be two distinct periods of plateauing—early and late. The first few months and years of plateauing serve to sort out the long-distance runners from the discomforted. The discomforted lack the capacity to enjoy their own success. They don't really want to succeed; they just want to prove that they can win. For them, being there is not as exciting as getting there. Some people who arrive at a plateau feel an absence of challenge, and they move toward disengagement and exit. They may have a fear of success that keeps them from settling into the plateau. These are often loners who move from job to job, from relationship to relationship, and from city to city, repeating their pursuit of success without achieving sustained success. They are pursuers of a plateau, not plateauers. They have not learned how to love success and to thrive on it.

The long-distance runners are positive plateauers who become their finest selves in their plateauing roles. This is their victory, and they want to invest in it. They renew their vision within the plateau so they can keep growing within the chapter. They learn to mentor others, to shape policies, to serve as ambassadors for their organizations, and to leave a legacy. They have staying power. They maintain their success by pursuing new levels of attainment, influence, growth, discovery, and contribution. Or, if parenting was the core of the dream-plan, they grow with their children to find more of themselves. Long-distance runners function with what Abraham Maslow called "unconscious competence," the effortless, masterful capabilities of high-performing people. They thrive on constancy, loyalty, honest criticism, curiosity, and a zest for life. Although they enjoy the security and safety of their successful life chapters, they keep growing within their plateaus and do not see themselves as having arrived at the top of their climb.

Instead of climbing another mountain, long-distance runners can sit and enjoy the one they are on and find new adventures there. Instead of having to prove themselves again, they can improve who they already are. Instead of being bored and finding that they need a new, unknown road to explore, they find fresh and fulfilling destinations on the road they have already mastered. A plateau is meant to be a dynamic and ongoing celebration of a successful life chapter, a time of considerable stability, creativity, and recognition. If the world cooperates with more order than chaos, healthy plateauers tend to their knitting.

Phase 2—Managing the Doldrums, Being Out of Synch

The Random House Dictionary of the English Language defines "doldrums" as "1. a state of inactivity or stagnation; 2. a dull, listless depressed mood; low spirits." In Norman Juster's children's classic, *The Phantom Tollbooth,* a boy named Milo who is on a wild journey arrives one day in a place called "The Doldrums." Those living there call it "a land beyond expectations," and they explain it to Milo: "The Doldrums, my young friend, are where nothing ever happens and nothing ever changes. . . . The main thing to do is to kill time. . . . No one's allowed to think in the Doldrums. . . . In the Doldrums, laughter is frowned upon and smiling is permitted only on alternate Thursdays. . . . [What we do] is brooding, lagging, plodding, and procrastinating."[7]

Adults also arrive in the doldrums from time to time, feeling that the accomplishments of the life chapter they are in are pretty much complete, and they can rest on their oars for a spell. The driving sense of purpose that inspired them to succeed in the chapter has diffused into a frantic kind of energy aimed at holding on to yesterday's dreams. It's a time when the success you thought would fulfill you has now become a hiding place, a trap for not moving on into new possibilities. Nostalgia replaces dreaming, and denial and resistance dominate thought patterns. Emotions drift to fear, sadness, and anger. It is not a pleasant place to be, and people don't have to remain here long. The problem is, most people would rather remain stuck in a familiar world that is declining in enchantment than risk moving ahead into unknown conditions to find a new life challenge.

Phase 2 in a life chapter is feeling out of synch, as if the plateau and even the life chapter were slipping away. During even the most successful of plateaus, gremlins invade to disturb the peace. With the flattening of your personal mission in the plateau, there is a tendency to lose momentum, to rest on your oars, and to defend the status quo. As your motivation fades, forces inside and outside of your life chapter invade to challenge your halcyon days. Sooner or later, you begin to look in on your life chapter to question it, as if part of you were already living outside it. You want to improve it, you think, but your questions penetrate your inner confidence. The comfort, optimism, naiveté, and unconditional determination are blunted by a growing chorus of discontent, pessimism, and worries. Out of your own success have come forces that are now working against you, and you begin to question whether the "success and happiness" that you have achieved are lasting friends. Instead of enjoying your plateau as the success you deserve, you feel like you are treading water to avoid drowning.

"Managing the doldrums" is a threefold sequence. It begins with sensing decline ("Why isn't my life as alive and challenging as it used to be?"), which evolves to feeling trapped ("I'm mad/depressed/scared as hell, and I'm not going to take it any more") and ends up as resisting change ("Life used to work wonderfully, so I'm going to keep things the way they were"). The job of the doldrums manager is to sort out what is working from what isn't so that a realistic and proactive plan of action—rather than a reactive one—can be followed.

Sensing Decline

There comes a time when the dream of the life chapter loses its luster, even though you continue to pretend that the life chapter is alive and well. Usually, in the plateau of a life chapter, the demise begins. Restlessness, defensiveness, inflexibility, or some acting-out behaviors reveal that the plateau has led to a downward slide. You may be thoroughly bored with your plateau, but since it is the only environment that you can imagine for your life, you deny the boredom and complain, reminisce, and pretend that all is well. Pushed to the margins of your plateau, where your rewards and recognition are minimal, you yearn to make the life chapter work again, but already the seeds of a transition have been sown, and you have begun to disengage from the life chapter. Decliners have a sense of living in the past without a clear future. They go through their days looking in on their lives, knowing that they are living on borrowed time. They have low energy, are easily tempted by addictions, and have a high level of denial that anything is wrong. The out-of-synch process for a decliner is an inner dialogue of dissonance and conflict.

Once you "succeed" and receive the rewards of money, prestige, recognition, and status—or whatever you mean by success—you will probably want to "freeze" your life chapter to keep it safe and available forever. You assume that your marriage and family will be happy from now on. You talk about "security," "financial independence," "tenure," "stock options," partnership," "benefit packages," or other ways to corral your success as a permanent acquisition. You become protective of number one and a bit paranoid about the intentions of others around you. The minute you shift gears to contain your success, you blur your original dream and mission. Secondary gains replace your primary passion. It is not just that your life chapter has lost the air in its balloon but the various parts of your life are conflicting with one another. Perhaps your spouse wants you to be different from the way you are. Or you may be working harder at your work than ever before but receiving negative criticism for your efforts. Or perhaps the value of the dollar has declined, and your economic position is in jeopardy.

Instead of living within a proactive dream-plan, you are now defensive and reactive. Instead of adventuring within your chapter as a charismatic leader, you are retreating into past achievements as a mechanical manager, and you don't know where you are going. And, as the old adage goes, "If you don't know where you're going, any road will get you there." Your main intent at this time is to hold on to your gains, at all costs. Those around you who are now vital to your life chapter may think that you have sold out and abandoned your right to be in charge. The screw has turned, and your place in the life chapter may have become, in the minds of others, a liability to their own life chapters. They say that you are having an identity crisis, while you feel that a power struggle is going on among them. The dissonance and conflict sap your energy and confuse you. "Sensing decline" is the thinking process of an out-of-synch person; the feeling side can be described as "feeling trapped."

Feeling Trapped

At this point, you feel very confused. Your emotions are like a roller coaster. Throughout the building of your life chapter, you had down times when you felt discouraged, sad, or angry. The difference now is that your bad feelings dominate your space and time as if they were part of your character. You feel outraged by the surge of negative emotions. You thought that you had earned the right to a life of positive emotions, with happiness and cooperation lasting forever. You feel betrayed by your own success, undermined by people you trusted (including yourself), lost in confusion, and unable to sort things out. Sometimes you feel angry, at other times sad. Frequently you feel scared that you will lose your life chapter. Drained by the complexities of this navel gazing, you now feel as if you were a caretaker of someone else's home—the someone you used to be. As the song by Harry Chapin goes, "There's no tick-tock on your electric clock, but still your life runs down."[8]

Some people accuse you of being stressed out. Others say that you are burned out or in a midlife crisis. You keep waiting for the feelings of stagnation to go away, but they get worse and worse. You try to reassess your options but decide that it's better to feel bad about the decline of your life chapter than to feel the loss of it altogether. As someone once said, "The only difference between a rut and a grave is the depth of the excavation." Judith Bardwick has captured the predicament of the out-of-synch person who has already succeeded in achieving a plateau: "When we are plateaued, we are not so much actively unhappy as we are just not happy. We could continue to live as we are, because usually it's not awful. But it is also not joyous. If we are truly unhappy, change is easier than when we are just not happy. When the negative is powerful, the need to change is obvious. Most of us do not make changes in our lives until the pain in the present eclipses our fear of the future."[9]

People who succeed in a life chapter usually expend their energy in Phase 1—Go for It. They are seldom trained to manage Phase 2—The Doldrums, which is an implosion of feelings within themselves. Indeed, they are seldom trained to manage their feelings at all, and this is one reason the out-of-synch Phase 2 is so badly managed by so many adults. "Sensing decline" and "feeling trapped" lead to "resisting change" (see Diagram 4).

Resisting Change

When you sense decline and feel trapped, you resist change. Somebody is raining on your parade, trying to take your life chapter away, trying to evict you! The decision here is to hold on and keep things the way they are, even if you are bored, unhappy, ineffective, and destructive. Resisters are reactive and often masochistic. In high denial, they back into their future, looking backwards. They tough it out and endure whatever happens as they live within a double bind: They don't know how to enjoy continuing in the life chapter, but they can't or won't leave.

Robert Tannenbaum and Robert W. Hanna explain that "1. Change is loss. . . . 2. Change is uncertainty. . . . 3. Change dissolves meaning. . . . 4. Change violates scripts. . . . In sum, whenever a new situation or our own evolving growth prompts us to make a change in the construction of reality (identity, world view, philosophy of life), there is a need to hold on."[10] John Gardner says, "Human beings have always employed an enormous variety of clever devices for running away from themselves. . . . [We] can keep ourselves so busy, fill our lives with so many diversions, stuff our heads with so much knowledge, involve ourselves with so many people and cover so much ground that we never have time to probe the fearful and wonderful world within. . . . By middle life, most of us are accomplished fugitives from ourselves."[11]

Diagram 4. Phase 2—Managing the Doldrums.

**Feelings often
experienced
in this phase:**

— Disappointment
— Stuck
— Resistant
— Pain and suffering
— Mad
— Sad
— Trapped
— Defeated

**Activities that might
help you be effective
in this phase:**

— Create an exit plan
— Look for new job
— Spend time with friends
— Take up hobbies
— Take evening courses
— Seek therapy
— Get marital counseling
— Get a physical
— Prepare for divorce
— Join professional organizations
— Take a sabbatical or leave of
  absence
— Others:

**Results to accomplish
in this phase:**

— Successful departure for a Minitransition
— Successful departure for a Life Transition

The doldrums manager looks for ways either to restore confidence and commitment to the dream-plan or to end the life chapter. Either you recapture the inspiration and commitment that you had for your life chapter as your personal mission, or you give up the life chapter and seek a new one before circumstance wrenches it away from you. The less time you are in the doldrums, the better, because they tend to become a bitter prison for the helpless and the enraged. Instead of sensing decline, you need future vision. Instead of feeling trapped, you need positive feelings of empowerment. Instead of resisting change, you need to choose a path that will be developmentally challenging.

Sorting Things Out

The ultimate job of the doldrums manager is to help you decide what to do and who to be. You must move beyond merely repeating the past. You figure out what to hold on to and what to let go of. You conduct a thorough inventory of your life, asking only one question of each assumption, possession, relationship, activity, and chapter: "Does this add meaning to my life?" If it does, you keep it; if it doesn't, you prepare for improvements or surgery. You identify necessary alterations in your life chapter that you believe will improve your life. You consider the possible advantages of moving on.

Sorting things out is like a game of keepers and leavers. The keepers are the continuing aspects that work and empower the life chapter—the roles, tasks, relationships, opportunities, challenges. The leavers are those items that detour you from purposive activity within your chapter. Sort them out: delegate what doesn't belong to you; eliminate parts of the structure that have led you astray; alter your roles to comply with your current inner strengths at this phase of the structuring process. Stay true to your passionate values, and rearrange your life structure accordingly.

Some of the sorting out has to do with external issues. As your life chapter evolved through its plateau, it probably became more complex, with more people and systems involved, deepening your embeddedness. How do you now sustain your accomplishments without being burdened by them? How do you maintain the routines of your chapter without losing your sense of mission? How do you continue indefinitely to feel visionary and committed to your life chapter? How do you let others gain ownership of parts of your life chapter? How do you let go of roles and functions that were profoundly rewarding to you earlier in the life chapter? How do you take advantage of new opportunities when you are so wrapped up in your current situation? Ric Masten, a contemporary poet, calls it "Not Exactly a Command Performance":

> have you ever sat back
> and looked at the life you were living
> and saw that it was playing
> like a really bad B movie?

appalled and taken back
by the inane lines you were saying
and the restrained way you were weeping
and weaving your arms about
over acting
but what really burns
is the knowledge
that someone of your reputed good taste
would sit through such silly hogwash
unable to leave till you learn
how the damn thing comes out.[12]

Sorting things out is a process of evaluating how to proceed when a life chapter gets blurry and dysfunctional and your role becomes less and less clear. If you are successful at sorting, you will make four piles: things to hold on to, things to let go of, new things or skills to take on, and a game plan for when to move on to either restructuring or cocooning.

Typically, but not necessarily, a life chapter lasts several years and ends when something slowly or suddenly, internally or externally, triggers an ending. A trigger upsets the tenuous balance of an out-of-synch life and provokes a person to let go and move on. Some typical internal triggers of a life transition are boredom, loss, panic, stress, or a yearning to try out a new self. Some typical external triggers of a life transition are an accident or illness, loss of a job, a new baby, sudden changes in the financial market, separation or divorce, change of geographical location, a new grandchild, death of a family member or friend, an inheritance, an empty nest, a promotion, new friendships, a career change, a return to school, travel, and retirement.

Each person has life chapters of varying lengths, and each sequential life chapter differs from previous ones in duration. When you disengage from a life chapter, you have two choices (and only two choices): either take a minitransition and restructure your life or engage in a life transition that involves you in new growth and future possibilities. The prevailing preference until midlife or later is to restructure through a minitransition. Perhaps you move to a new location to start over. Perhaps you change career positions or companies. Maybe you alter relationships in your personal life or face medical treatments that you had been postponing. In any case, you are ready to say goodbye to the doldrums and to your life chapter the way it has been. Your eyes are riveted on the future.

Saying Goodbye and Farewell

The change cycle skill of saying good-bye and disengaging from a life chapter is an essential adult ability that is possessed by few. Most adults are not trained to exit or depart from their heroic space and time; they would rather stay distressed. Letting go is hard. When they do leave, they often demean themselves or attack those around them (or hire a lawyer). However, the self-renewing adult designs exits that honor both those remaining and those leaving—a win-win strategy. Good endings are marker events—turning points that deserve rituals for celebrating the importance of life lived and life ahead.

Endings are symbolically the acceptance of death as reality, yet most of us spend our lifetimes denying the many little deaths that we experience in the form of losses. Our endings, more than our beginnings, keep us committed to living as fully as we can. Letting go of what is not working in your life creates the opportunities for making improvements and new beginnings. "If you can begin to see death as an invisible, but friendly, companion on your life's journey," writes Erich Lindemann, "gently reminding you not to wait till tomorrow to do what you mean to do—then you can learn to *live* your life rather than simply passing through it."[13] Perhaps Elisabeth Kübler-Ross has said this as powerfully as anyone: "It is the denial of death that is partially responsible for people living empty, purposeless lives; for when you live as if you'll live forever, it becomes too easy to postpone the things you know that you must do. You live your life in preparation for tomorrow or in remembrance of yesterday, and meanwhile, each today is lost."[14] There is no way to progress deeply into the future without taking leave of the past—making a leap of faith into an unknown future. The pain of loss becomes motivation to look ahead instead of backward. "Letting go" is usually experienced as a loss, but it also is a liberation, a graduation, a commencement.

Restructuring Your Chapter: The Minitransition

The seventh change cycle skill, managing a minitransition, leads back to Phase 1, with a revised plan attached to a renewed dream. A minitransition is repairing and updating the same life chapter, making it stronger and better. It is enacting the plans that have been made to improve the life chapter and to begin again. A minitransition is a fairly rapid return to reenact the same dream with a slightly different plan. A minitransition feels like you are crossing a bridge to familiar territory. This produces a catharsis, with renewed energy, confidence, and determination. You feel on course, following your path again. You have restored a sense of purpose and mission in your life. You are on your way.

A minitransition makes sense when the chapter you are in is basically healthy but requires some minor changes to work effectively under current conditions. For example, if your career is a central theme of your chapter, you can move to a different location, change career roles, change companies, but keep the career you are in. Or you can join a religious organization, enter personal therapy, take an intensive seminar training program, begin dieting, or schedule time in a health spa. The minitransition is a restructuring of the parts of your chapter. It is an effort to correct the personal tensions and larger system problems causing distress in Phase 2 and to introduce new stabilizing features. It's aimed at recovering the fire in your belly and feeling challenged again in the known areas of your own competence and values. In effect, the old dream and life chapter are rejuvenated and extended, and this actually goes on throughout the entire lives of some people who have high stability in their lives to provide continuous cohesion. During the adult years, a person may repeat the upper half of the circle several times, maintaining a life chapter by reconstructing it over and over.

A minitransition is like a personal strategic plan that extends the old plan by reformulating it.[15] The deep places of the self do not have to be searched and transformed. However, if a minitransition fails or proves futile, a person ends up, naturally, cocooning and then proceeds through the life transition route on the bottom of the cycle described in Diagram 1 (Chapter Three). *A minitransition is a purging of the life chapter, whereas a life transition is a purging of the self.* One is the way of strategic planning for structural reform; the other is the way of personal transformation. One is to repair and to upgrade what is; the other is to metamorphose toward new possibilities. A minitransition is like getting an automobile repaired; a life transition is like acquiring a new car. Virtually everyone elects the way of minitransitions—over and over—until leaving the life chapter itself is either a worldly necessity or less painful than remaining. At some point in the life cycle, everyone finds the path into a life transition to be necessary or preferable to the minitransition route. A competent adult needs to master both minitransitions and life transitions at different times in the life course. Neither is intrinsically better, and both are necessary and inevitable.

The route through a life transition takes much longer than the minitransition but provides profound personal renewal and leads to a new and usually different life chapter. The choice of routes is not always an option. If you experience a trigger event with sufficient emotional force and reality information as to require an immediate exit from the chapter—as with the death of a spouse—cocooning will begin; efforts to minitransition will be futile. However, for a great many people and organizations, the minitransition is the only acceptable social format for dealing with intense change. They dread the thought of entering a full-fledged transition, which they perceive as a waste of time, a loss of status, expensive, and pure terror. So they repeat the same patterns of achievement and decline from their past, often with decreasing passion and vision. Better they had gone the other way, into a life transition.

"Doing" and "achieving" cannot endure forever without powerful renewal of the inner "being." This is the primary work of a life transition. When you are overwhelmed by change and faced with losses beyond your ability to contain, you choose or accept the path that leads through a life transition. As you approach it, it feels like an impossibility, yet most everyone emerges from one with new life and perspective. Mircea Eliade, an outstanding teacher on myths and rituals, has written: "In no rite or myth do we find the initiatory death as something *final,* but always as the condition *sine qua non* of a transition to another mode of being, a trial indispensable to regeneration; that is, to the beginning of a new life."[16]

In 1908, the Dutch anthropologist Arnold Van Gennep published *The Rites of Passage,* describing the life events that constitute human turning points: separation from the group or society; transition or revision of the personal agenda; and incorporation back into the group with new roles and functions.[17] The next four personal skills that guide the cycle of change through a life transition—disengaging, cocooning, self-renewing, and exploring—perform the functions of separation, transition, and incorporation.

Chapter Five

Life Transitions

> *Any real change implies the break up of the world as one*
> *has always known it, the loss of all that gave one identity,*
> *the end of safety. And at such a moment, unable to see*
> *and not daring to imagine what the future will now bring*
> *forth, one clings to what one knew, or thought one knew;*
> *to what one possessed or dreamed that one possessed. Yet it*
> *is only when man is able, without bitterness or self pity, to*
> *surrender a dream he has long cherished, or a privilege he*
> *has long possessed, that he is set free—that he has set*
> *himself free—for higher dreams, for greater privileges.*
> JAMES BALDWIN, *NOBODY KNOWS MY NAME*[1]

Phase 3—Cocooning: Finding New Passion and Purpose

In November 1980, when Jimmy and Rosalynn Carter left the
White House, they plunged into a disturbing life transition. Their
lives were at a dead end—the former president had suffered a
crushing defeat by Ronald Reagan, his peanut business was $1 mil-
lion in debt, and the Iran hostage crisis remained unresolved. Rosalynn felt as dejected and rejected as Jimmy did, perhaps more.
After they returned to their home in Plains, Georgia, each wrote
separate accounts:

> *Jimmy:* Many people have to accept the same shocking
> changes in their lives as we did that winter: the invol-
> untary end of a career and an uncertain future; the
> realization that "retirement" age is approaching; the
> return to a home without the children we had raised

there; new family relationships, for which there had been no preparation. And in our case, all this was exacerbated by the embarrassment about what was to us an incomprehensible political defeat and also by some serious financial problems that we had been reluctant to confront. . . . Although my disappointment was great, I kept it bottled up for a long time.

Rosalynn: There was no way I could understand our defeat. . . . Would we ever look back on this election and say losing was for the best? . . . Not long after we came home, Amy went off to boarding school in Atlanta, our last child to leave home. We were lonely without her. . . . There was another adjustment that we had to make. For the first time we were both at home together all day every day, and as much as we care for each other this sometimes proved difficult. . . . There was still the longer-term question of how we could make our work more meaningful.

Jimmy: We became confident that we would find significant outside activities while living in the quiet environs of our youth. We especially enjoyed the luxury of walking through the woods and fields for miles without seeing a single house. . . . What we had done was to seek out, in our chosen home community, those things that were the most meaningful to us. . . . There is no doubt that the healing period after the political defeat was also a learning process for both of us, sometimes together and at other times a slowly evolving understanding deep within us individually.

Rosalynn: One night I woke up and Jimmy was sitting straight up in bed. He always sleeps so soundly that I thought he must be sick. "What's the matter?" I asked. "I know what we can do at the library," he said. "We can develop a place to help people who want to resolve disputes. There is no place like that now." . . . He talked on enthusiastically about other areas where negotiation might help—in domestic disputes and in dealing with civil laws. A center to settle disputes. For the first time since our return to Plains, I saw Jimmy really excited about possible plans for the future.

Jimmy: Since leaving the White House we have had a chance to revive a number of our old interests and pursue some new ones, a process that we hope will continue for the rest of our lives. There is no way to know how many years we will have to spend together, and we want to make the most of them. In addition to having a good time, we have taken on some challenging projects, but our tendency has been to move toward the simpler activities that we can share with each other and our friends—and enjoy now and for a long time to come.[2]

Now, over twenty years later, Jimmy Carter appears all over the globe, as an ordinary man with a heart, mediating disputes from Ethiopia to Nicaragua. Although his presidency seemed to end in personal disaster, and his brothers and sisters have since died, Jimmy's current life and work now symbolize—perhaps better than the presidency did—his deep beliefs in universal human rights and world peace. The crisis of his transition became an opportunity for finding new ways to connect this personal integrity to social reality. His most recent book, *The Virtues of Aging*, is a remarkable statement of his understanding of adult life.

Transitions Are Normal

Life transitions happen. They happen to presidents and to ordinary people. They happen to rich and poor, to men and women of all ages. They are a part of life. They represent down times during which new personal resources are created or discovered. Just as every automobile sooner or later needs a major overhaul, so do we. Life transitions are normal and inevitable parts of adult life; they clarify life issues and life direction. They are retreats into the deep recesses of our real selves. Successful transitions simplify, purify, center, and empower a person's life course. Like pruning a rosebush, they purge the past and prepare for the future.

Transitions often happen because of circumstances that we don't control, so we end up in some transitions not of our choosing, as with many who survived such disasters as earthquakes, forest fires, floods, high school shootings, wars, and domestic violence. Or they happen because we get older or our values change or our jobs end. In a time of rapid change, transitions occur more frequently in our lives. Many things trigger change that we cannot control. Yet sometimes they happen just because we choose them.

Transitions follow a predictable pattern—from loss to rebirth—whether they are personal transitions or transitions within marriages, families, organizations, or nations. Adults can be trained to anticipate and facilitate them. There are specific abilities that we can cultivate for enhancing the process. However, we first must recognize and accept the positive functions of transitions. A great many people think of transitions as a penalty box, a place for losers, quitters, and weaklings—people who can't take the heat, victims who thrive on self-pity and helplessness. "It sounds so negative," reported a doldrums person in considerable distress. "Why would I want to have one?" The acceptance of an ending sounds like termination, humiliation, resignation, and defeat. Many would say that it is better to do your best to make a worn-out, dysfunctional life chapter work and to tough it out than to face a life transition. That very attitude, erroneous as it is, keeps thousands of people locked into life chapters that have died and into routines that are lifeless.

Such high denial and devaluation of transitions come at a very high price in stress, relationship damage, financial losses, time wasted, and the reduction of future options. Refusal to process an ending creates a storage pile of barnacles from your past that clutter all your future life options. The gradual disablement of so many adults in midlife occurs because they lack the ability and courage to let go of the exhausted or toxic structures of their lives. The truth is that saying good-bye is not cowardly when it is spoken by the voice of the courage to be. Transitions, however disorienting and painful they may be at first, are almost always pathways for growth and discovery. Your personal transitions are as important as your life chapters in the construction of your life course, because transitions cleanse, center, and connect you to the deeper currents of your life. The basic issue is this: Denying the value of the transition territory is a major cultural deficit, keeping us from knowing how to manage the inevitable losses of our own lives, which in turn keeps us from being free agents for living into the future.

What Is a Life Transition?

- A life transition is a natural process of renewal of the inner self, which leads to renewal of the outer self.
- A life transition is a transformative experience that occurs from the inside out. It is the discovery of inner resources that contain immense value and direction for how to live.
- A life transition takes place within a "holding environment" providing acceptance, nurturance, patience, and "guides" who facilitate the transition process.
- A life transition affects all aspects of a person's life—personal confidence, intimate bonds, family interaction, jobs and careers, social commitments, and ultimate concerns.
- Life transitions proceed gradually and sporadically. Grieving, healing, and renewal are organic and take time. There is no shortcut, no quick fix. Adult life transitions typically take one to three years. However, most adults do not have to stop their usual routines and work to process a transition.

In my house, where three young boys live, we have some animals that remind us of this process. Our pet snake, for example, loses its skin every few months as it grows. Although we are so amazed at the beauty of the skin that is shed that we display it for everyone to see, we don't mourn the death; we marvel at the life. The pollywogs that we catch at a local pond grow into tiny frogs in time; the fish-form stops living as the amphibian takes on the life. A few weeks ago at a picnic, the boys picked several stalks of fennel that had caterpillars in them. We placed the fennel and the caterpillars in a covered bowl, where the caterpillars made cocoons. Today they opened to release several silent, magnificent, yellow butterflies, all born within an hour of one another. Like snakes and pollywogs and butterflies, adults sometimes lose their previous orientations and retreat into what looks like oblivion in order to incubate new life orientations and lifestyles that fit them better for moving into the future. The transition model presented here begins with disengagement from a life chapter and concludes with reintegration with social forces.

Disengagement

Three change cycle skills facilitate this phase, each of which is an ability to regenerate the self: *letting go of the life chapter* in its dysfunctional form, *cocooning* (grieving and healing), and *self-renewing* (tapping core values and inner resources). Self-renewal leads to personal reintegration. It is a new grounding, a new anchoring of the self, a new experience of "being," characterized by self-sufficiency, peacefulness, purpose, and energy. Like fresh clay hitting the potter's wheel, the self-renewing self becomes centered, balanced, and formed around the residual self with its inner strength, vitality, and esteem. Although self-renewal at first feels like a gift, it quickly becomes a conscious skill for defining personal boundaries and creating a new future.

Reintegration

In time, the renewed self will interact again with external resources, primarily through three skills: experimenting, being creative, and networking—skills leading eventually to a new dream-plan and new life chapter. The reintegration phase is a hopeful, optimistic, awakening period that often involves training, travel, and new behaviors. Being and doing begin a new dance, as inner joy projects itself into the world around it.

Ending: Letting Go

When talking about entering a life transition, I often use an eight-word chant that goes like this: "Hold on, let go, take on, move on" (repeat over and over). A transition is a time to *hold on* to what is working in your life, *let go* of what is not working, *take on* new learning and exploration of options, and *move on* to new commitments.[3] All four of these are normal and necessary for growth and development. As you depart from a life chapter, however, letting go seems like all there is, because you are much more aware of what you are leaving than where you are going. Only later do you discover the importance of the other three abilities. The first task, and the hardest one to manage, in our culture at least, is letting go. Why? More than one hundred years ago, de Tocqueville observed that Americans "are externalizers, doers, achievers." These are essential virtues for building life chapters, but other virtues make life work well—particularly well for making transitions succeed. They all begin with letting go.

Doers like to move from one activity to another, from one mountain to another. They like achievement and results. Doers receive recognition and prestige in our culture. But an accumulation of doings will actually disempower you if you don't renew your being in between doings. You will achieve less and get poorer results as you try harder and harder unless you continue to renew and update yourself. You can't run a car on an empty tank. A transition renews your being and prepares you for new doings. Most of all, a transition rekindles hope—a sense of a preferred future. Just as a life chapter is an externalizing development of your self, a transition is an internalizing development of your self in which new meeting points are devised for connecting your past, present, and future. A transition is a turning point, from the conscious to the unconscious, toward resources and perspectives that you don't know you have. Although there are few cultural rewards or recognitions for successful transitioning, there is personal awareness at the conclusion of a life transition that you are more in charge of your life and destiny than you have ever been before.

Hugh Prather says, "When you find yourself in a battle with life, lose. There are no triumphs over truth."[4] Mary Baker Eddy often remarked, "When it ceases to bless, it ceases to be." You have to sustain congruence with all the parts of your life to sustain self-esteem, productivity, love, and joy. If you insist on lugging your bruised, band-aided, dysfunctional life structure into your future and pasting it onto a new scenario, you are bound to be filled with hesitation and conflict, not a new beginning. You will probably feel condemned to spend the rest of your life in the doldrums. Better that you refurbish the vessel that takes you on all your journeys throughout your entire life: your self, that inner creature who monitors your life space, your many roles, your private moments, your fire.

Letting go of your old chapter is a change cycle skill that promotes proactive exiting, a "hero's farewell" from a successful life structure. To help you disengage, you can declare a sabbatical, take a leave of absence, negotiate a withdrawal, or design a graduation or commencement. You can create a succession plan that is fair to you and to the structure so that others can take care of the life chapter that you are leaving behind. You can ask for whatever blessings and benefits you feel you deserve, but exit with style, dignity, and caring.

In his book *Loss and Change,* Peter Marris takes bereavement as a model for understanding all profound change, personal and social. He states, "The fundamental crisis of bereavement arises not from the loss of others but from the loss of self—the loss of purpose, of interest, and above all, of meaning."[5] Psychologist Ellen Y. Siegelman relates the story of Beth, a talented young jeweler, who reported: "Being stuck, being depressed is awful. But it's safe. It's—well—it's like walking around in the dark in a room you hate. . . . You can tell in the dark where every table, every nicked chair is, every picture, every ashtray. You could walk it blindfolded without bumping or scraping. It may be an ugly room, a drab room, but it's *familiar.* But when you change—when you take a risk or do something that's way out of character for you—it's different. It's like being thrust in the dark into a furnished room that is unfamiliar. This is probably a more interesting room, one you may get to like because it's going to be all yours. But the furniture is strange. You don't know where anything is yet. You might bump into something knobby and hard, you might trip and fall."[6]

Exiting is often a lonely act, even if there are friends and loved ones supporting you. The ending strips you of roles, routines, and relationships that used to seem permanent and essential to your being. As you exit from the life chapter within which you spun the living of your days and years, you have only two attitudes to choose from: either you feel evicted and abandoned by the best days of your life or you feel grateful that you lived fully in that life chapter and now have an opportunity to journey on. In either case, you feel the loss. Ann Kaiser Stearns writes:

> Recovery from loss is like having to get off the main highway every
> so many miles because the direct route is under reconstruction.
> The road signs reroute you through little towns you hadn't
> expected to visit and over bumpy roads you hadn't wanted to

bounce around on. You are basically traveling in the appropriate direction. On the map, however, the course you are following has the look of shark's teeth instead of a straight line. Although you are gradually getting there, you sometimes doubt that you will ever again meet up with the finished highway.[7]

Fortunately, transitions almost always lead to renewal. As you disengage from the external life chapter, you turn inward to heal. Healing is fundamentally human and normal, not medical. It involves preparing all of you for a livable future. Healing takes time, a lot of time. There is no way to rush a transition, and hurrying will only sabotage the renewal and impede the success of a new life chapter. Healing not only binds the wounds; it opens new doors and windows within you. You gain access to more of your personal abilities. You find strength that you didn't know was there. You discover that by letting go of unworkable parts of your external life, you are holding on to profound continuities deep within you. As you heal, you feel free to take on new possibilities for your life and to move on into a new life chapter that fits you the way you are today, driven by the deeper currents of your own heart and soul.

Cocooning

When the dream dies and you depart your former life chapter, you may encounter what feels like a room with no exits. You are an empty soul with no sense of a future. You may feel an intense loss without much awareness of any gain or hope or promise for improvement. If you are not sad and depressed, something is wrong with you!

When a life transition begins, your life loses its reference points, its anchors in your life chapter. You may feel like an abandoned orphan, a betrayed person, a mistake, a lost soul. You live in unordinary space and time, suspended in a nonscript that floats heavily through days and nights. You may well have felt this way for a long time, but now the terror of your aloneness reaches full force. Your energy dissipates, and the routines and relationships in your life seem strange and distant. You feel like a nobody, a hollow vessel looking backward on the life that you have no more. As your familiar territory becomes unavailable to you, you feel lost, alienated, and alone. Cocooning feels like a death experience—all endings and no beginnings. Typically, you go through some or all of the stages of dealing with dying: denial, bargaining, anger, fear, grieving the loss, and finally finding acceptance and moving forward. Arnold R. Beisser, paralyzed by polio since age twenty-five, wrote at thirty-six: "Years ago, I realized that being afraid of dying was really a cover for being afraid to live. . . . There are advantages to an ever-present awareness of death, if it makes you realize how precious life is and that each moment should be savored."[8] The loss of the life chapter is finally experienced as relief so that the vital, emerging self can construct a new chapter that fits your current condition and emergent future (see Diagram 5).

Living with Loss

Managing intense loss is virtually un-American. We hospitalize it, medicate it, therapize it, and attempt to eliminate it. Yet loss is a natural part of the normal development of a human system, and it persists in our human experience. Robert Greenleaf expresses this with simple elegance:

> To be on with the journey one must have an attitude toward loss and being lost, a view of oneself in which powerful symbols like *burned, dissolved, broken off*—however painful their impact is seen to be—do not appear as senseless or destructive. Rather the losses they suggest are seen as opening the way for new creative acts, for the receiving of priceless gifts. Loss, *every loss one's mind can conceive of,* creates a vacuum into which will come (if allowed) something new and fresh and beautiful, something unforeseen—and the greatest of these is *love.* The source of this attitude toward loss and being lost is *faith:* faith in the validity of one's own inward experience; faith in the wisdom of the great events of one's history, events in which one's potential for nobility has been tested and refined; faith in doubt, in inquiry, and in the rebirth of wisdom; faith in the possibility of achieving a measure of sainthood on this earth from which flow concerns and responsibility and a sense of rightness in all things. By these means mortals are raised above the possibility of hurt. They will suffer, but they will not be hurt because each loss grants them the opportunity to be greater than before. Loss, by

**Diagram 5. Phase 3—Cocooning:
Coming to Terms with Yourself.**

**Results to accomplish
in this phase:**

— A sabbatical
— Personal resilience
— Spiritual renewal
— New friends
— Positive solitude
— Personal confidence
— New sense of purpose

**Feelings often experienced
in this phase:**

— Anger
— Grief and sadness
— Fear
— Loneliness
— Relief
— Quiet excitement
— Inner confidence
— Liberation
— Trust in the future

**Activities that might
help you be effective
in this phase:**

— New training
— Therapy
— Friends
— Traveling
— Time management
— Transition job or part-time work
— Journaling
— Art classes
— Hobbies
— Meditating or praying

itself, is not tragic. What *is* tragic is the failure to grasp the opportunity which loss presents.[9]

Unfortunately, few of us have skills that will empower us through transitions, and even if we did, we would remain bewildered by the disorientation of personal loss. The approved cultural solution is to turn loss over to "professionals" who are experts at "dysfunctions," when what we need most is to heal and renew ourselves as normal human beings.

Of course, for some people life transitions trigger regressive issues that express themselves through social maladaptation or mental illness; these people need medical and psychological attention when loss strikes deeply. However, most adults in life transitions do not require medication or treatments aimed at relieving their "distress," which is actually a vehicle for normal growth and development. Rather, they need to learn how to grieve and to move on through the transition territory and into new life directions. What was wrong, sick, or dysfunctional was wrapped up in the social setting of the old life chapter, and the possibility for new strength is maximal as transitions succeed. It is competency in transition management that we all need, to find new directions in our own disorientations.[10]

Just as each life chapter has ongoing, minor transitions, each developmental transition has beneath it a sufficient life structure to provide the basic continuities and necessities of life. A developmental transition is a normal process in which we shed some or much of our previous identity as we discover new possibilities in our undiscovered selves. It is precisely in the gradual act of shedding, bereaving, and letting go we gradually discover our emerging values, priorities, excitement, and dream of creating a new life structure. Stanley Keleman captures it with these words: "When we step out of our social roles, when we disengage ourselves from our programmed fears, when we immerse ourselves in the river of self-experiencing, we are bathed, merged in the non-verbal, non-conceptual, non-visual, non-idealistic world. We are indeed in the sea of creation. We are the sea from which we create our own lives. When you find your own answers, it is you."[11]

Cocooning takes place almost entirely on the inside of the person experiencing the loss of a life chapter. The loss of a burdensome life chapter is the full-time gain of the healthy inner self. Activists may see cocooning as cowardly withdrawal, but it is actually the courageous regeneration of the person. In *A Study of History,* Arnold Toynbee identifies a basic principle of cultural renewal as "withdrawal and return" by leaders and creative minorities; sensitive leaders disengage and withdraw temporarily from their social milieu, and then return with new convictions and powers.[12]

Arnold Van Gennep describes cocooning as a "neutral zone"— a temporary structure apart from the beaten path, a safe place for grieving and incubation, for testing the soul and renewing the self. Feelings surface, and doubts are raised. "Do I have the capacity to get through this? How do I proceed? Do I have sufficient trust and love?" People in the neutral zone lead lives that are in suspension, in parentheses, in temporary environments with transition objects. Their thoughts take the form of attentive inactivity; their lives function with simple ritualized routines; their interactions are filled with ambiguity. Cocooning is a withdrawal from external structures in the service of getting new inner perspective for a vital return. The cocoon itself is a separation from the outside world with sufficient protection and safety to allow the inner process of recuperation its full power. The three parts of cocooning are grieving, loneliness, and healing.

Grieving

Robert Tannenbaum and Robert W. Hanna declare:

> There is the need to mourn, to work through the dying and death of attachments to elements of personal identity, to aspects of one's view of the reality outside of one's self, to ways of being to which we have clung but that are often dysfunctional for us in the present. To mourn means to face death—little deaths, to be sure, but death, nevertheless—in order to make a rebirth possible. Each of us is ultimately vulnerable, yet most of us typically blind ourselves to this truth.[13]

Cocooning typically begins with grieving, where the emphasis moves from "doing" to "being" tasks—activities having to do with healing. You measure yourself by who you have been in the chapter you are leaving—your only reference at this point in the cycle. You feel empty, without life or direction, looking in on a world that is no more. Looking ahead is bleak and virtually impossible. You are in the *DIS*'s of the self:

Disengaged—having left the familiar life structure
Disenchanted—having negative emotional moods
Discouraged—experiencing a loss of motivation
Disappointed—feeling sad and dejected
Disoriented—feeling confused, lost, and at bay

Disillusioned—feeling cynical about the past and doubtful
about the future

Disidentified—experiencing the absence of many familiar roles
and happenings

Disgusted—feeling angry or upset

Dislocated—being lost or disrupted

Disrespected—experiencing loss of self-respect and fear of
rejection by others[14]

During grieving, you simplify your life, stripping away the complex lifestyle that you were immersed in during the life chapter. Grieving is a move toward simplicity and quietude. Grieving is shedding the unworkable past, mourning the loss, and saying good-bye. Grieving is letting go. Grieving is an emotional competence conducted by the self within you, when you minimize your ego functions and allow yourself to feel your feelings and thoughts that go with them.

Because grieving involves compounded losses at many levels within us, it cannot be rushed. Grieving people do not respond to "Why don't you just get a new job?" or "Join us at the party tonight." Healing must first take place. As with the healing of a deep wound, time must pass, and new personal resources must be found. Grieving takes us (or our organizations or families or nations when they are in cocooning) into our archaic fears and our primordial powers, where we discover new resources, insights, and energy for beginning again. As Mircea Eliade has written, "One does not *repair* a worn-out organism, it must be re-made; the patient needs to be born again; he needs, as it were, to recover the whole energy and potency that a being has at the moment of its birth."[15]

I suggest that cocooners create a "cocooning room" in their home, a room devoted to enhancing the process of letting go and moving on. The cocooning room should be a very private, quiet place, with no radio, TV, telephone, or beeper. Have a futon if you wish, a CD player, a pile of post-its for putting ideas on the walls, and a journal for writing down your thoughts. Spend time every day in your cocooning room, and wait patiently for insight, energy, and new purpose. It will arrive, for you, providing you spend your time introspecting instead of "being busy." While cocooning, avoid alcohol and drugs not prescribed by your doctor. Cocooning is a natural, developmental place to be, not a clinical, dysfunctional event. Invest yourself in the inward task of finding your new identity and direction.

Loneliness

During cocooning, it is normal for intense feelings of loneliness to occur. Few people seek to be lonely, but it is a state that we all pass through whenever we are cast off from our life chapter. Loneliness is a natural part of the human condition. Knowing how to manage loneliness is a survival skill for a life transition. Loneliness does not mean "being alone" but rather being cut off from the personal meaning that was conveyed through the beliefs, roles, relationships, and reference points in the previous life chapter. Loneliness is a feeling of estrangement from past and future. People in this place in the change cycle have lost their moorings and not yet found replacements. Clark Moustakas, who has written widely on loneliness in human experience, says this:

> In loneliness, some compelling, essential aspect of life is suddenly challenged, threatened, altered, denied. At such times only by entering into loneliness, by steeping oneself in the experience and allowing it to take its course and to reveal itself is there hope that one's world will achieve harmony and unity. Then the person can begin again, born as a new self, with openness, spontaneity, and trust. What I experience within myself, and what I yearn for from other persons is an acceptance and valuing, a tacit agreement to let the loneliness be.[16]

Healing

Healing is where regeneration begins. The slings and arrows suffered during the adult years—and earlier—may leave festering wounds from having been neglected, betrayed, abandoned, abused, wasted, rejected, or shamed. The wounds may stem from personal attitudes as well as the actions of others—overweight, low self-esteem, addiction to chemical substances, fears. Cocooning is a time to heal these and to get them behind you. While the healing may not be complete, it can be more than sufficient for empowering the next phase of your life. We think of healing as the physical repair of a wound or the psychological recovery from a betrayal or abandonment. The body must heal: nutrition and exercise are important aspects of the self-repairing cocooner. The mind must heal: finding ways to make your own inner voice the primary caretaker of your life feeds the healing process. Learning to forgive those who have violated your integrity is the only way you can heal and ultimately be free of them. "Heal thyself" is the cocooner's injunction. Pay full attention to the many ways in which you need to care for yourself. Healing is the foundation for self-renewal and the rebirth of hope. When you are healed enough to look ahead, you move on along the cycle of change. And the mystery is that the healing has not merely bound the wounds; it has transformed the cocooner into a new person.

Solitude

The lonely griever becomes a person with a confident solitude. "There is a place," writes Hugh Prather, "where you are not alone, where your voice sings with every voice that has ever sung, or ever will sing."[17] In contrast to loneliness, which mourns the loss, solitude is positive aloneness, a confident presence of self-sufficiency. Solitude begins when the grieving self gives way to the real self—a deep and caring reservoir of abilities, resources, and affirmation. The positive forces of the self now break through to remind you of the depth and breadth of your being. You are awed, amazed, and joyful with a quiet peace. The poet Wordsworth phrased it this way:

> When from our better selves we have too long
> Been parted by the hurrying world, and droop,
> Sick of its business, of its pleasures tired,
> How gracious, how benign, is Solitude.[18]

Solitude is a quiet, deep, inner experience. Albert Einstein called solitude "the teacher of personality." Through the experience of solitude, you tap your inner sensibilities and current values. Often overlooked in our culture, managing solitude is an essential human competence. The British scholar Anthony Storr portrays the value of solitude with these words: "Removing oneself voluntarily from one's habitual environment promotes self-understanding and contact with those inner depths of being which elude one in the hurly-burly of day-to-day life. . . . *The capacity to be alone thus becomes linked with self-discovery and self-realization; with becoming aware of one's deepest needs, feelings, and impulses. . . .* The capacity to be alone is a valuable resource when changes of mental attitude are required. After major alterations in circumstances, fundamental reappraisal of the significance and meaning of existence may be needed. In a culture in which interpersonal relationships are generally considered to provide the answer to every form of distress, it is sometimes difficult to persuade well-meaning helpers that solitude can be as therapeutic as emotional support."[19]

Phase 4—Getting Ready for a New Chapter

When cocoons fulfill their functions, butterflies emerge. With people, renewal begins within the self. The point in the cycle of change when self renewal is the central phenomenon of life is when you are as far removed from structural embeddedness as you can get, after you have shed layer after layer of attachments to your past way of being and doing and thinking. It is this very distance from your past life chapter that permits a receptiveness to new life that you didn't know you had within you. The positive result of disengagement, cocooning, and loneliness is the rebirth of the self. You are "getting ready," which is a process that has four distinct parts: revising core values, exploring the world again, finding new hope and purpose, and creating an exiting ritual.

Revising Core Values

Like cocooning, getting ready cannot be rushed. Whereas the outer events of your life can change your human prospects in an instant, the reconstruction of inner resilience and perspective takes time. In your solitude, you discover a well of life that connects to an abundance of unused resources. You learn that there is more than enough life, beauty, and strength within you for moving ahead, and this confidence generates energy, hope, and courage. Four years after Admiral Byrd returned from his winter alone in Antarctica, he wrote, "I did take away something that I had not fully possessed before: appreciation of the sheer beauty and miracle of being alive, and a humble set of values. . . . Civilization has not altered my ideas. I live more simply now, and with more peace."[20] When Franklin Delano Roosevelt was asked how he could possibly be a good president with his body partially paralyzed by polio, he responded, "It's not what you lose but what you have left and what you do with it." That is the attitude of a person who has experienced the reconstruction of the self.

Throughout your adult years, you have opportunities to make significant revisions in the assumptions that have guided you since childhood. It is at moments like this in the change cycle that you have an opportunity to seize your script and become its author in a more self-determining way, on the basis of information and experience that you have accumulated during your adult years. The transcendent perspective of a transition is a powerful base for revising your raison d'être (see Diagram 6).

When your conscious reflections take place in the comfort of your own interiority, you can draw on more of yourself and claim who you are and want to become. As the inner reaches of your mind are reviewed, a rare opportunity comes to recalibrate the values and beliefs guiding your life. This secret place, filled with emotional fire as well as mental awareness, can be found by the self when it has distanced from external structures and renewed itself from within. This is the time and place to acquire more of your own human imprint and shape your next life chapter accordingly. You are still who you were, only a little more so and with considerably more awareness. But it feels like a metamorphosis, a new beginning, and that is what makes it so important in the cycle. You are able to revise some of your fundamental assumptions about who you are and what is important for you, leading to profound redecisions for how you want to live and be in the future. Now you can confront the polarities of adult life and arrive at new ways to balance them. There are several perennial polarities, most of which

Diagram 6. Phase 4—Getting Ready for the Next Chapter: A Time for Experimenting.

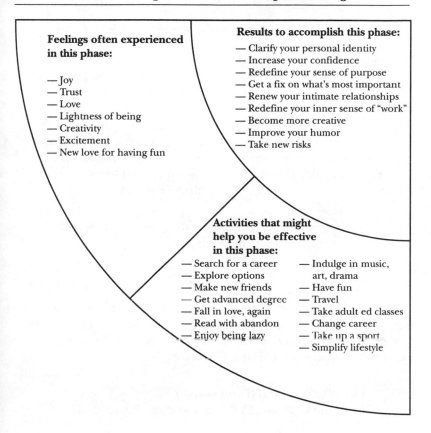

Feelings often experienced in this phase:

— Joy
— Trust
— Love
— Lightness of being
— Creativity
— Excitement
— New love for having fun

Results to accomplish this phase:

— Clarify your personal identity
— Increase your confidence
— Redefine your sense of purpose
— Get a fix on what's most important
— Renew your intimate relationships
— Redefine your inner sense of "work"
— Become more creative
— Improve your humor
— Take new risks

Activities that might help you be effective in this phase:

— Search for a career
— Explore options
— Make new friends
— Get advanced degree
— Fall in love, again
— Read with abandon
— Enjoy being lazy
— Indulge in music, art, drama
— Have fun
— Travel
— Take adult ed classes
— Change career
— Take up a sport
— Simplify lifestyle

are versions of a basic struggle between wanting to develop yourself as completely as possible and wanting to demonstrate your human competence in the best way you can.[21]

1. New Self Versus Former Self

What are the basic beliefs of my new self—the values, the assumptions, the purpose of my life?

What are the residual values of my former self, and how do I integrate them with my new sense of self?

How can I merge the new into the former, and the former into the new so that I have both continuity and change?

2. Connection to Others Versus Separateness from Others

To what degree am I wanting to be connected, attached, and included? How capable am I at bonding and at sustaining intimacy with others? How important are nurturance, caring, inclusion, and interdependence at this time in my life?

To what degree am I wanting to be distinct, independent, and autonomous? How capable am I of managing my separateness? How important are autonomy, assertiveness, achievement, independence, and my need to win at this time in my life?

How can I balance my self-sufficiency with my interdependence with others?

3. Young Versus Old

How might I value the "young" in me? What "young" virtues might I sustain and increase in my life at this time? How might I value the "old" in me? What virtues of being "old" might I incorporate into my life at this time?

How can I grow old and sustain both the wisdom of my years and my inner child?

4. Creativity Versus Destructiveness

How am I creative and life-affirming? How do I want to express my will to live at this time of my life?

How am I destructive and abusive? How will I manage the rage, violence, and unhealed wounds within me?

What changes in my lifestyle are needed to diminish my life-denying forces and to increase my affirmation and creativity?

5. Caring Beyond the Self Versus Self-Indulgence

In what ways am I complete? How might I contribute to the next generation through mentoring, benevolence, volunteerism, political involvement, professional leadership, community leadership, or leisure?

In what ways do I need to fulfill myself and reach a new level of completeness? What do I need more of to be me: money, career success, recognition, friends, love, sex, children, grandchildren?

How can I continue to grow while contributing to the world?

The activity here is to receive the life that is waiting for you, not to do anything in particular. You are beginning to look out of the windows of your mind into the external world again, and you feel at home. Your future is beginning to happen; it is grounded in the depths of your experience.

Cocooners who are just emerging from their cocoon are gaining new confidence. They usually lead simple lives. They are not needy. They are very awake. They listen. They feel. They use few words. Their thoughts seem linked to a deep well beneath them and to the skies above, and they are ready to live the truth as they know it, and no less. They choose to be their own persons and to march to their own drums.

The renewed self feels free, alive, and beginning, not living out the last days of the last chapter but starting the first days of the next chapter, emanating from the virtues of the heart and believing again in a livable future. The symbolic encounter with death has led to a resurrection of life, with a simple formula for how to live in harmony with the world. The consciousness that comes from self-renewal reflects awe and reverence for renewal everywhere, and hope opens its doors to new scenarios for living.

Exploring the World Again

When a person in a life transition develops sufficient self-esteem and confidence to poke around in the external world, reintegration begins. Internal life weaves itself into external structures. Whereas *the revision of core values* represents the rediscovery of inner resources beyond healing, *exploring* represents the rebirth of the self-in-the-world. People experiencing this phase are typically curious, daring, eager, venturesome, positive, risk-taking, sexual, and not yet ready for long-term commitments.

The healthy internal forces seek compatible external opportunities for projecting confidence, competence, and a new future. This phase is very much like late adolescence, and we need to invent terms such as *middlescence* and *elderescence* for validating this recurring experience of vitality, learning, and growing.

Exploring the world again involves three change cycle skills that together prepare a person to structure again: creating, experimenting, and networking.

Creating is the playful exploring of new ideas and possibilities. It is untethered imagining. It is a bubbling spirit that wants to try new ways of thinking and doing. It is uncensored brainstorming, the discovery and pursuit of novelty, a willingness to express yourself in unconventional ways. Out of the disorderly universe of a profound transition comes a life force in search of new symbols, forms, and stories. Renewed selves like to play, invent, and celebrate. They like to have fun. Adults at this point in the cycle are like children again, filled with energy, whether it be channeled into the arts or science or some practical field. Often they write poetry or songs, take up dancing, begin to draw or paint, join political groups, build something, expand the garden, or travel. They like to touch and be touched. According to Silvano Arieti, an authority on creativity, the creative process springs from solitude, aloneness, and inactivity. The transitional self is now daydreaming, brainstorming, taking risks, experimenting and networking. "The creative process," suggests Arieti, "is a way of fulfilling the longing or search for a new object or state of experience or existence that is not easily found or attained." Creativity is a symbolic expression of new life taking form within the person in transition, and the transition itself is the process of giving birth to creativity. People at this place in the change cycle often feel a transcendence over limits that before had constrained them. Anchored in personal energy, creativity emerges as art, science, play, and quest.[22]

Experimenting is trying out new ideas and projects without making them permanent. It is risking discovery and risking failure. The Berkeley psychologist Ellen Siegelman writes, "The urge to risk reflects the urge for competence; rightly approached, it can enhance that sense of competence, which is so intimately connected with self-esteem."[23] Experimenting is looking for new ways to do things, new ways to be you. Experimenting means having fun and learning how to learn. Experimenting is the infusion of energy into future possibilities. With new social support and information, a person begins to experiment with life options. Like a new college graduate, a midlife person in transition experiments with relationships, jobs, leisure ventures, hobbies, travel, lifestyle, social causes, and environmental concerns. Such a person is often "creatively unstable," and experimenting with options helps to sort out the paths that will lead to a new life chapter. Experimenting has energy for effervescing, wherever it may lead. This energy serves not only the reconstruction of personal lives but it reaches out to touch far-reaching places. In the words of sociologist Louis A. Zurcher, Jr., the self becomes "mutable," comfortable with and oriented toward "process, change, flexibility, autonomy, tolerance, and openness"— all natural outcomes of a life transition. Mihaly Csikszentmihalyi describes this as "flow" stemming from a person's ability to exhibit joy and meaning in everything that he or she does.[24]

Networking is a major vehicle for testing out life options during the final phase of a transition. Networking links you to new resources: exploring friendships, finding new ways to do things, gathering information, and pursuing new learning. A common environment for adults emerging from a transition is new training or reentry into formal learning. When you feel anchored in yourself, you search for new friends who are also alive and curious. You seek friends who know more than you do about the territory that you want to investigate for your next life chapter. Instead of looking to friends for approval and admiration, you look for mentors and role models to guide you into your preferred future. People who are beginning to evolve out of a life transition are usually hungry for new information and learning. They absorb new ways of thinking, and they entertain many possibilities for their future. Like young people going to college, they seek new learning, education, and information about their future options. Sometimes they return to school for advanced degrees or for certificates in professional training programs. When they complete adult certificate and degree programs, midlifers managing a transition and preparing for new life chapters are performing an important rite of passage.

An Exiting Ritual: Choosing New Priorities

During the final phase of a life transition, adults build the future on the vitality within themselves. They scan the horizon for external settings that are congruent with their renewed lives. If you are at this point in the change cycle, ask yourself these questions: What are the passionate preferences of my life, now that I have retooled myself? What is my purpose—my compelling reason for being alive at this time in my life? What gives me energy, direction, and boundaries? What are my talents and gifts? What goals and rewards am I seeking? The deliberate selection of preferred values becomes urgent at this point in the cycle, because you are on the edge of making a commitment to a new life chapter.

Life chapters are powered by value commitments embedded in a dream-plan—a story of how you want your life to proceed, at its best. The dream is a time capsule of life yet to be lived, hope bottled up in a simple story with empowering values ready to shape the plan and fuel the launching. At different times in the cycle of change these values have different degrees of importance. It is during the final phase of a life transition that you have the greatest freedom to choose new core values for your life. Your choice of values inspires you with a sense of purpose sufficient for shaping the themes of your new life chapter, such as these:

- Political determination to improve society in some way
- Artistic expression, wherever it leads you
- Love, marriage, children, friends, and a nice home
- Wealth, pure and simple, with economic independence
- A career or job that validates you, along with a healthy marriage
- A commitment to defend our nation and serve the country
- Parenting roles along with volunteer activities that support causes that you believe in
- Individuation, to become more of yourself, and more self-driven
- Living as a researcher to find a cure for the AIDS virus

- Golf, tennis, sailing, friends, and a life of leisure
- A spiritual passion for oneness, peace, and service

The move from the final days of a transition to the beginning days of a new life chapter usually happens fairly quickly. Like a whack on the side of the head comes the realization of what you want and how to proceed. You feel filled, confident, ready, and focused. Your dream for the future is helping you identify the course to follow, and you feel ready to pour your life into what seems like a very friendly world. You are alive, clear, self-motivated, and unstoppable. Charles Garfield puts it this way:

> To keep alive and effective, you anticipate difficulties and opportunities. You adapt, changing and growing as the individuals and the world around you change, and you periodically recommit yourself to your mission. You act to preserve what is best and discard the rest. . . . Developing a mission means seeing a pattern in the things and thoughts that get you moving; assessing your resources; then formulating your feelings into words.[25]

The Adult Life Cycle

Meaning and Mission Across the Life Cycle

*Our lives are a series of births and deaths: we die to one
period and must be born to another. We die to childhood
and are born to adolescence; to our high-school selves and
(if we are fortunate) to our college selves; we die to our
college selves and are born into the "real" world; to our
unmarried selves and into our married. To become a
parent is birth to a new self for the mother and father as
well as for the baby. . . . I must never lose sight of those
other deaths which precede the final, physical death, the
deaths over which we have some freedom; the death of self-
will, self-indulgence, self-deception, all those self-devices
which, instead of making us more fully alive, make us less.*
MADELEINE L'ENGLE, THE SUMMER OF
THE GREAT-GRANDMOTHER[1]

Life proceeds like a series of snapshots—infancy, childhood, adolescence. But over the years the string of cycles seems more like an
ongoing movie, with pervasive themes, turning points, and changing characters. The repetitive cycles form chapters in a continuous
story, which is the human life cycle from birth to death.

How the Life Cycle Works

Every time you go around the renewal cycle, you go around the
same circle of change, but it seems like a new ball game. Each subsequent life chapter has a somewhat (or considerably) different

value base, cast of characters, and social agenda. Each redefines your sense of purpose. Yet each sequence is an extension of what came before and has as many commonalities as differences.

Adult life is something like a large slinky, with cycles that go on and on (see Diagram 7). Each new life period is different from, yet similar to, the last one. The focus changes but life goes on. With each serial life chapter, there are new, temporary answers to the perennial human questions: Who am I? Where am I going? What am I up to? Who is going with me? How will I get there? The answers that seem acceptable at thirty seldom satisfy at fifty or seventy. Throughout your years, you keep reworking these basic questions, which leads you into life chapters serving different purposes throughout your life cycle.

As you move through midlife and elderhood, your sense of purpose is likely to shift from ego-driven issues to more spiritual ones, from competence and attainments to consciousness and caring. You experience a gradual decline in physical prowess along with an increase in self-clarity. However, if you experience unbearable losses and lack sufficient funds and health to enjoy life, you may become self-absorbed as you view your life cycle as a downhill ride.

At different times in your life, you have different visceral sensations about what you are up to and should be pursuing—your raison d'être, priorities, expectations. These are not all prompted

Diagram 7. The Life Cycle.

| *Young Adulthood* | *Midlife* | *Elderhood* |
| Chapter | Chapter | Chapter |

Transition Transition Transition

by aging and developmental issues alone. If you experience unanticipated social crisis—an accident, a big win in the lottery, disease, divorce, loss of job—your sense of life purpose will be profoundly affected. The life cycle is like a kaleidoscope turning—while there are predictable features to the changing patterns, there are also random and never-ending surprises, some pleasant, some not so pleasant. Yet when looking back on our lives, all of us can discern chapters that make up our life cycles. Each chapter is defined by a shift in priorities, values, and purpose. When these chapters are told as a "life story," adult life has duration, a flow through time from young to old, from beginning to end. The chapters of your own lifeline represent the windows in your mind through which you view your past, present, and future. The more you can be aware of this life cycle process in yourself, the more you can shape your sequencing and take responsibility for your life.

This chapter suggests five major ways adults can understand and influence their life cycle:

- Knowing the key concepts of the life cycle
- Employing the appropriate core values at different times in the adult journey
- Evaluating the best use of human systems in the various periods of adult life
- Viewing the life cycle through the changing perspectives of the decades of adult life
- Practicing the principles of longevity.

Key Concepts of the Life Cycle

A life cycle is what takes place between birth and death; it spans infancy, childhood, adolescence, young adulthood, middle adulthood, and elderhood. Life cycles are understood as personal stories or histories, with unique and universal characteristics. Our life cycle stories form a kind of personal mythology about our lives, profoundly shaped by the myths and rituals of our families, communities, work settings, and culture. At least eleven concepts form an overview for understanding the adult life cycle. These notions represent generalizations found acceptable by most scholars of adult development, although there is always healthy disagreement.

Nevertheless, the following are dependable concepts for understanding the pervasive characteristics of the adult life cycle today.

1. *The childhood years shape, limit, and enrich the adult years.* Most adults know that they are anchored in their childhood experience. The more they can learn from reevaluating their own childhood years, the better they can build fulfilling lives. The human agenda is to rework the same issues of the younger years in new environments and to add new issues as well.[2]

2. *Healthy adults adapt and grow throughout the adult years.* Adults are constantly adapting to changes within themselves and their environment. Successful adaptation occurs when adults alter their perceptions of how the world works, in a constant process of learning and relearning congruent with personal experience.[3]

3. *The adult years are a process of ongoing change and continuity.* Each of us weaves a different but similar tapestry, taking on individual hues and designs, as we make sense out of our experience through the loom of time. Adult life is a natural unfolding of the maturation process and a series of responses to surprise events and opportunities, all of which together shape a "life course" around the evolving interaction of biological, psychological, and social processes. It is more like a series of adventures or an ongoing journey than an arrival. Adult change is best understood as the reworking of perennial issues within different settings and age periods.[4]

4. *Social status is a major determinant of adult developmental issues and directions.* Educational background, income level, occupation, status recognition, organizational memberships, cultural orientation, religious participation, geographical location, sports affiliations, and other social factors have a heavy hand in shaping adult values, commitments, expectations, reflective capacities, and aging patterns.[5]

5. *There are dramatic differences between the styles and priorities of men and women during the adult life cycle.* Men who invest highly in their careers in the early adult years may become more nurturing

and less self-absorbed during midlife. Other men are so indelibly formed by their first life structure that they spend their adult years repeating the roles and patterns of their early adult behavior, which usually includes a primary identification with career and dependency on a spouse and others for emotional nurture and care. Women who invest highly in caretaking roles (often in addition to their jobs or careers) in the early adult years may become more assertive in their middle years. During midlife, women who have not been in careers often push beyond caretaking roles into tasks involving external challenges and financial independence. However, there are many variations in the developmental patterns of adult men and women.[6]

6. *Careers and work environments have considerable influence on adult lives.* A majority of adults, male and female, now work throughout most of the adult life cycle. Dual-career marriages are now normative for those who are married. Most adults spend more time in their work settings than they do at home, or with any other commitment. Their roles at work affect their behaviors in all the other parts of their lives. Many adults organize their lives around their work, and critics of this phenomenon call this "workaholism" or "work addiction." Others argue that the work organization is the primary social system in which today's adults learn and achieve personal empowerment. In any case, the work culture—with its stress and challenge—affects the lives of most adults today. As adults age, the meaning of work changes, and most adults seek to alter their career roles. Careers and corporate structures are more fragile and malleable than they used to be, and it is normal now for adults to expect career crises and career changes throughout the life cycle. When adults retire, they often have difficulty creating life plans if their former work identity was their primary sense of self.[7]

7. *Adults in midlife and elderhood often become preoccupied with their mortal limits, death, and time left to live.* While this may sound morbid, it often functions to inspire them to live fully now and to follow their deepest values. They experience shifts in perspective, from quantity time to quality time, from grandiosity to realistic attainments, from casual friends to lifelong friends, from procrastination to action. Midlife adults learn that their time is measured,

and they pursue new ways to find greater depth in their more limited sense of destiny as they race against time.[8]

8. *Adults in midlife often experience an increase in individuation and introspection.* As middle-class young adults move further into the adult years, they usually move from external injunctions and constraints to internal ones, from pleasing others to pleasing themselves; status comes more from internal rewards than from external recognition. Through introspection, self-evaluation, and reflection, midlife adults develop a sense of self that provides resilience and constancy. Mature adults learn how to restructure their lives, tending toward self-direction and individuation. Observable signs may include a greater sense of humor, new ability to compromise and engage in teamwork, new hobbies or interests, and a desire for solitude.[9]

9. *During the adult years, leisure—or, more fundamentally, play— takes on new meaning, as a vehicle for living rather than as a vacation from working.* Adults learn much about their own lives from reading, traveling, going to movies and plays, playing golf or tennis, watching TV, weekending with recreation vehicles, engaging in crafts or art classes, joining an orchestra, volunteering in a museum, or trekking in the Himalayas.[10]

10. *A major trend in midlife is the pursuit of personal integrity.* This is manifest through increased interest in deep-seated values, wholeness, a capacity for mentoring future generations, the mastery of life itself, and the presence of seminal wisdom. This increased sense of personal integrity often joins with an outer sense of being connected with life everywhere, through nature, friendships, political activities, and spiritual intuition. Integrity fosters a personal sense of purpose, a passion for being, a mission in life. These same qualities of adult life continue to develop in their fullest during the elder years of adult life.[11]

11. *From midlife on, adults frequently become more invested in leadership roles and social contribution.* With the strengthening of the self, many mature adults feel empowered to contribute new leadership to their lives, families, jobs, and society. They want to make a dif-

ference, to be role models, and to contribute to the next generation. They want to improve some aspects of the earth, to be good
stewards of the future. The trend toward personal leadership grows
with age in many lives and draws on a deepening well of life experience. The importance of this theme is underlined by the increasing numbers of adults in midlife who are extending their midlife
behaviors into their elder years. Through nutrition and exercise
programs, they maintain healthy bodies; through relationship nurturance, they sustain love and sex; through continued work and
financial planning, they sustain an economic means for travel and
living; and by taking on positive attitudes about being "old," they
seek leadership and mentoring roles.[12]

Today's adults have available to them more knowledge about
their lives and human prospects than ever before in history. Not
only do we have more information on more aspects of adulthood
but we have better concepts for understanding how lives get constructed and creatively altered. How to use this profound reservoir
for adult empowerment is the central concern of the next section,
in which the inner workings of the adult life cycle are explored.

The Six Core Human Values

At least six fundamental human values compete for your loyalty
throughout the adult years to shape your sense of purpose. Each
represents a basic human capacity that you can choose and organize your life activities around. I conducted a study of autobiog-
raphies and biographical material on heroes or highly recognized
persons who lived in the twentieth century—persons like Thomas
Edison, Mother Teresa, Eleanor Roosevelt, Woodrow Wilson,
W. H. Auden, James Agee, Carl Jung, Simone de Beauvoir, Ingmar
Bergman, Albert Schweitzer, Bertolt Brecht, Benjamin Britten,
Martin Buber, Mary Cassatt, César Chavez, Winston Churchill,
John Foster Dulles, Buckminster Fuller, and many others. In each
case I searched for the driving sense of purpose in the person's
life—the values that provided passion and motivation. I found that
six values were basic to all of these people: personal identity or a
sense of self, achievement, intimacy, play and creativity, search for
meaning, and compassion and contribution. Each of the persons·

I studied combined one to three of these core values to reach their life goals. All their other values could be placed in subsets under these six.

So I began to examine my clients and myself. Are there core values that all human beings have access to, unlike any other animal? Although I don't have an absolute answer to that question, I do believe that these six are attractive and persuasive sources of fulfillment for a great many people. These values are emotional themes that generate energy and life purpose. They are primal feelings and beliefs—visceral forces, often at an unconscious level. They are often difficult to talk about, but once they are infused into a life chapter, they provide internal reference points for continuity and stability. More important, they produce motivational energy that can last for many years.

The six core human values are the primal incentives of adult life—deep sources of passion and commitment. In various combinations at different times throughout the adult years, you draw on them to design and redesign your expectations. The selection and balance of core human values makes each sequential adult life chapter different from the previous ones, giving each a different sense of purpose and meaning.

The six abiding core values of adult life are:

1. *A sense of self:* identity, self-esteem, confidence, self-reliance, autonomy, personal boundaries, self-responsible behavior. This value pursues a satisfactory answer to the question, Who Am I? Clarifying your personal identity is a lifelong process, but there are particular points in a life when this value becomes central. Young adults work hard to sort out their personal mission from that of their parents and peers. During life transitions, adults clarify their sense of self and use that as a basis for a subsequent life structure. In the first half of life, this life core value typically sponsors the quest for personal ego clarification and empowerment. For many adults in the second half of life, this same core value pursues a connection of the inner self with universal meaning and mystery.[13]

2. *Achievement:* reaching goals, conducting projects, working, winning, playing in organized sports, having ambition (for recog-

nition from others, money, and results), being purposive, getting results. Achievement represents successful goal attainment and for most adults is most dramatically displayed in their work and career roles, although it is also important in sports, military, and volunteer activities. Achievement is usually a dominant core value for young adults who make their careers central to their life chapters and for women rejoining the workforce again in their forties and fifties. Men tend to favor achievement as a dominant form of human expression throughout their life cycles, even after they learn the importance of the other values. Women who sustain full-time careers during their early adult lives often feel a lifelong bond to this core value. Achievement is also important for older adults who often discover a renewal of purpose through projects, work, and activities.[14]

3. *Intimacy:* loving, bonding, attaching, caring, nurturing, being intimate, making relationships work, nesting, coupling, parenting, being a friend. Intimacy forms and maintains affective bonds and is essential for long-term attachments in adult life. In early adulthood, women often serve as the nurturing, emotional gate-keepers of the intimate bonds they form, making intimacy an important core value in their lives. Young men often seek women who will manage their intimacy and friendship needs for them. In midlife and elderhood, men often increase their capacities for giving and receiving intimacy, through friendships, mentoring roles, hobbies, and grandparenting.[15]

4. *Creativity and play:* being imaginative, playful, spontaneous, original, expressive, humorous, artistic, celebrative, innovative, funny, joyful, and nonpurposive. Creativity and play are an expression of spontaneity and joy, which are particularly plentiful in the last half of a transition. Creativity and play are sources of positive energy, full of optimism and promise. They tap a powerful life force that seeks new forms of human expression. This is a core value that children know best. Spontaneous play and creativity are regenerative forces in our bodies and lives and important to our ongoing resilience and vitality. Few adults have enough genuine play in their lives. Many treat play as an achievement rather than as an opportunity for spontaneous and imaginative expression.[16]

5. *Search for meaning:* integrity, the experience of joy and rapture, an inner connection in oneself to order and meaning in the universe, inner peace, contemplation, a sense of transcendence, ultimate concern. Search for meaning is usually a central core value during a life transition but can be a spiritual motivator in a life chapter as well, particularly in the second half of life. Victor Frankl says that at some point in the human life cycle, each person "is questioned by life; and he can only answer to life by answering for his own life; to life he can only respond by being responsible."[17]

6. *Compassion and contribution:* caring, giving, helping, mentoring, leading, improving, reforming, supporting, being grateful, leaving the world a better place, bequeathing a legacy. Compassion leads you beyond your needs to help others or to contribute to the community. Compassion and contribution are particularly powerful core values in the life chapters of people over forty. They represent an attitude as much as a result, a desire to return something of what one has received in life.[18] Sister Teresa, a hero in our time, finds her life meaning through serving others. So did Albert Schweitzer, who after spending the first half of his adult years as a master musician, spent the rest of his life as a medical missionary in Africa.

Each core value has its negative as well as positive side. Too much emphasis on "sense of self" leads to narcissism and self-absorption. Too much emphasis on "achievement" results in workaholism in which a person's life is a projection of his or her work role. Too much emphasis on "intimacy" results in symbiosis and codependency. Too much emphasis on "play and creativity" keeps adults infantalized. Too much emphasis on "sense of meaning" leads to a fusion delusion with some ideal state of being. Too much "compassion and contribution" leads to neglect of a private life. *What makes these values important to adults is the personal appropriation of the right ones at the right time in the right proportion or balance.*

Healthy life chapters are powered by about three core values that supplement and balance one another. These values become embedded in a dream-plan, providing each life structure with a different sense of purpose and mission. The dream is a time capsule of life yet to be lived, hope bottled up in a simple story with empowering values ready to shape a plan and fuel a launching. Your choice of core values shapes your choice of human activities, friends, and lifestyle throughout a life structure. Then, during transitions between life structures, you choose a different arrangement of core values as you move on through the life cycle.

Human Systems, Activities, and Roles

We employ our values to direct our decisions within system commitments. The systems of adult life shape our lives as much or more than our professed core values (see Diagram 8). Too often, adults think they can individually change their lives, irrespective of the human systems in which they are embedded. At a basic level, we are anchored in economic, political, and spiritual systems. More concretely, we manage our adult lives in family, occupational, and leisure systems. Monitoring our connection to these human systems is a unique challenge for each adult.

On the one hand, how much fulfillment do you get from each system of your life—marriage, family, work, leisure, friendships, social networks? To what degree is your embeddedness in each system an opportunity for you to grow in the direction of your personal goals? On the other hand, how much of you is consumed or wasted by the systems you are in? To what degree do your family and work systems impede your personal goals and diminish your freedom to be you? Your embeddedness in systems can be a wonderful fulfillment or it can be a form of bondage. How can you create a fair balance with these two concerns?

Systems are the social or environmental containers of our lives. By *systems,* we mean orderly structures and functions that engage our commitment and time and provide us with meaning. Consider these eight basic human systems and their social roles:

1. *Personal System* (the maintenance of personal space, the use of personal time, health, and physical maintenance, self-care and nurturing, spirituality, lifelong learning and training)[19]
2. *Couple's System* (primary intimacy, sharing, touching, sex, social occasions, leisure activities, householding)[20]

3. *Family System* (mothering and fathering, cooking and eating, TV, chores, education for children, medical care, vacations and some leisure activities, care for parents)[21]
4. *Friendship System* (work friends, leisure friends, couple and family friends, lifelong friends, same-sex friends, opposite-sex friends)[22]
5. *Work and Career System* (work roles and rewards, professional persona, ongoing training, commuting, benefits, career expectations)[23]
6. *Leisure System* (play, travel, hobbies, artistic expression, gardening, sports, and games)[24]
7. *Social Systems* (for example, participation in and meaning derived from community organizations, professional organizations, religious groups, networks, the Internet, social causes, political groups)[25]
8. *Environmental Systems* (human influence on climates, weather, natural disasters, oil spills, and other conditions of nature and the cosmos; experience of wonder, awe, and spirituality)[26]

Systems provide us with arenas for our own fulfillment, and they program us with roles and expectations that are not always fulfilling. As you change throughout the life cycle, your connection with your human systems changes, just as when those human systems change, you change. That is how embeddedness works. It is like push-pull. At its best, it's an ongoing, lively dialogue between you and your systems, where you are experiencing your competence, finding colleagues, and gaining rewards; at its worst it's feeling trapped and diminished by impersonal systems that make seemingly random changes that affect your life far more than you expect or want.

Just as a fish cannot live without water to swim in, we cannot live without human systems. Most of the time we live within our human systems and don't grasp what they are doing to us and for us. But it is possible, particularly during adult transitions, to transcend our human systems, temporarily, in our minds, to get perspective on how our systems fit our lives and on how we can choose a preferred balance of system commitments. Throughout the life cycle, we contour our human space and time with core values within human systems.

Diagram 8. The Adult Life Cycle: Eight Versions of Human Purpose.

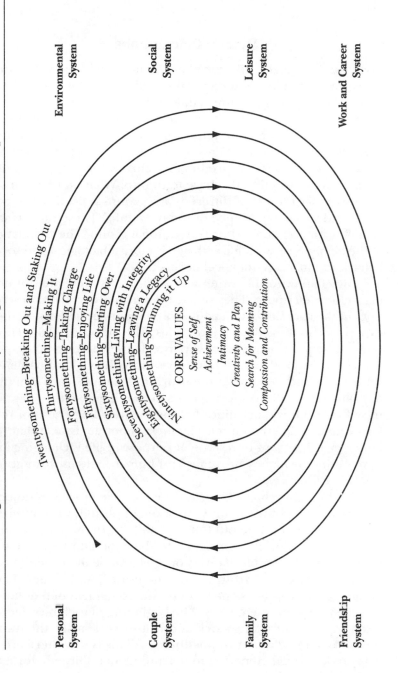

Personal System

Couple System

Family System

Friendship System

Environmental System

Social System

Leisure System

Work and Career System

Twentysomething–Breaking Out and Staking Out
Thirtysomething–Making It
Fortysomething–Taking Charge
Fiftysomething–Enjoying Life
Sixtysomething–Starting Over
Seventysomething–Living with Integrity
Eightysomething–Leaving a Legacy
Ninetysomething–Summing it Up

CORE VALUES
Sense of Self
Achievement
Intimacy
Creativity and Play
Search for Meaning
Compassion and Contribution

Decade Orientations

Approximately eight different chapters in adult life serve as reference points for most of today's educated Americans between the ages of twenty and one-hundred. Adulthood is a very long period of time, with few socially demarcated places along the way. In my assessment of adult lives and the literature about them, I conclude that there are no adult stages, no necessary phases that you inevitably experience, no predictable chronology that you must adapt to, no boxes that you have to fit into. What we have are relatively similar reports of different age groups reflecting the personal and social experience of today's adults. These reports will change with every cohort or generational group. The correlation of the chapters of adult life with age is more a biological and social behavior than a psychological necessity.

The chapters or life orientations suggested here are not normative or prescriptive. They represent personal and social descriptions of the core values that adults today report as the focus of their experience in these different decades. The purpose of Part Three is not to help you adapt to these particular perspectives but to portray convincingly that each of us does move through fundamental value shifts and system changes during the adult years. You may find altogether different focal points in your life from the ones portrayed here. Or you may find that the identifiable periods of your life occur in a different order. The most important issue is that you understand how your own sense of purpose in life is changing and developing through your values and human systems throughout your life cycle.

The following chapters portray the life cycle process by describing the decades of the adult years as eight periods with different versions of the purpose of life (see Table 2). In our current society, there is a popular tendency to describe adult experience through decade identification. People who share the same age also share marker events from youth, memories, and values. Each decade, they share the same anxiety and excitement of redefining that life period for themselves. The beginning of each new decade often triggers our taking stock of our lives as we make the transition into a new chapter of possibilities. This is why there are so many special ritual events for adults hitting their thirtieth, fortieth, fiftieth, sixtieth, seventieth, eightieth, ninetieth, and one hundredth birthdays. Throughout adult life, each decade symbolizes a somewhat different orientation on life purpose.

The themes of these life periods are not restricted to one decade; they are all present throughout the adult years and often cherished at various times throughout the life cycle, as are the core human values and preferred human systems. But in certain decade periods, specific values come close to defining the life purpose of a great many adults of similar ages and developmental interests. At this time in our society, they form social identification and provide psychological and spiritual meaning.

Table 2. Decade Orientations in the Life Cycle.

Age	Sense of Purpose	Human Systems	Core Values	Life Challenges
Twentysomething	Breaking out of family of origin and staking out adult territory	Personal, couple, peers, work and career, leisure	Intimacy, achievement, creativity and play, sense of self	Experimenting; making tentative attachments, working; gaining comfort and competence with money, love, and sex; establishing habits of self-responsible behavior; maintaining a leisure life
Thirtysomething	Making it: achieving success in career, coupling, family (if chosen), recognition, and acquisitions	Couple, family, work and career, leisure, social	Intimacy, achievement, sociability, creativity and play, sense of self; search for meaning, compassion, and contribution	Reaching the top of a career; creating a home; parenting (if chosen); managing financial obligations; sustaining a social life; participating in children's (or one's own continued) schooling; maintaining a leisure life; caring for parents; facing possible losses such as divorce, loss of partner, or loss of career; postponed ego development
Fortysomething	Individuation, being in charge of one's own life, developing a spiritual awareness (some people move from indi-	Personal, couple, family, work and career, friendships, leisure, social, environmental	Sense of self, achievement, intimacy, play and creativity, compassion and contribution, search for meaning	Reevaluating one's life; establishing clear ego boundaries; cultivating the self; becoming one person in all roles; clarifying career and marriage; ex-

	viduation to interdependence, while others reverse this order)			amining roads not taken; measuring decisions by time left; facing the possibilities of divorce, career change, geographical moves, and addictions
Fiftysomething	Enjoying life through interdependence; feeling most oneself in the presence of nature, co-workers, spiritual awareness	Couple, family, leisure, personal, work and career; friendships, environmental, social	Intimacy, play and, creativity; search for meaning; compassion and contribution	Enjoying being with others; traveling and indulging in leisure activities; deepening intimacy; favoring passive mastery at work; enjoying postparental roles; assuming new leadership roles; displaying increased social caring; preparing for increased losses
Sixtysomething	Starting over: redesigning life, work, and leisure, investing in family and friends; mentoring; racing against time	Personal, social, environmental, leisure, friendship, couple, family, work	Play and creativity, search for meaning, sense of self, compassion and contribution	Sharing knowledge and competence with younger people, grandparenting, renewing intimacy, seeking new leadership roles, creating a new beginning

(cont.)

Table 2. Decade Orientations in the Life Cycle, Cont.

Age	Sense of Purpose	Human Systems	Core Values	Life Challenges
Seventysomething	Living with integrity, celebrating the fullness of life, contributing beyond personal needs	Personal, couple, social, friendship, leisure, environmental, work	Search for meaning, compassion and contribution, intimacy, play and creativity, focused work	Managing physical decline, sustaining hope and trust, blessing and appreciating others
Eightysomething	Focus on legacy, caring for favorite causes, social mentoring; stewardship	Couple, family, social, community, leisure, work; environmental	Generativity, blessing, spirituality, gratitude	Managing physical decline, staying engaged, simplifying
Ninetysomething	Embracing mortality, staying focused; having grace and style; turning inward	Personal, couple, family, community	Compassion and contribution; search for meaning, peacefulness	Candor, generosity, managing health issues, summing up
One-hundred-something	To be written by the oldest readers of this book for a future edition			

Note: About each decade, adults reorganize their lives around a different prioritization of six core human values (sense of self, achievement or work, intimacy, creativity and play, search for meaning, and compassion and contribution) within the human systems of adult life (personal, couple, family, friendship, work and career, leisure, social, and environmental), following the renewal cycle as a continuous adventure and journey.

Chapter Seven

The Twenties, Thirties, and Midlife Transition

Breaking Out, Staking Out, and Making It

The young adult is at the height of his physical and mental vigor as he launches upon making his way and establishing his place in the world. . . . Now, more than ever, alternative ways of life must be renounced to permit the singleness of purpose required for success and to consolidate his identity; and his intimacy becomes reserved for a single person to make possible meaningful sharing with a spouse. . . . Vocational choice and marital choice are two of the most significant decisions of a lifetime. . . . The novice learns a way of life along with the knowledge and skills of the occupation. . . . The arrival of the first child transforms spouses into parents and turns a marriage into a family. . . . The parents need to be persons in their own right with lives and satisfactions of their own, firmly related in marriage and gaining satisfaction from it, rather than having their individuality and the marriage become subordinated to their being parents.
THEODORE LIDZ, *THE PERSON*[1]

During their twenties and thirties, adults leave their families of origin and design the first chapter of their adult years. Although few are prepared for the responsibilities and loneliness of adult life, most are eager to design their own lives.

Twentysomethings: Breaking Out and Staking Out

The adult years begin when adolescents break out of their family of origin and stake out the adult territory of love, work, and play. The primary goals are personal identity, sustained intimacy, career mastery, and individuation from family of origin. The twenties represent a period marked by audacity and grandiosity, self-doubt and emotional instability, playfulness and risk taking, intense learning and mental rigidity. For most, it is a scary, wonderful time.

The Experience of Frances Horn

During college at the University of California, I found a place in which I could be a star with an ever-widening stage. One of the campus activities was the student YWCA, a liberal group with national and international affiliations. I made my way up that ladder and became chairman of the western region and then of the National Student Council. . . . But I developed pernicious anemia and was effectively flattened for months. I missed the last semester of my senior year and could not graduate with my class.

As I lay on a couch listening to music and looking out of the window that spring, I was forced to do some reshuffling of my values, and the quiet time was not wasted. For years I had been goal-oriented; I had "busted a gut" to achieve, and to prove how capable I was. I had used willpower and a bright mind to push things through in the way I wanted them to go.

Then in May I was asked to be one of six people, three men and three women, to go from the United States to an international student meeting in India in the fall. . . . Shortly before I was to leave for Europe on the first segment of the trip around the world, one of the staff members of the student YWCA at Berkeley, who had lived for some years in China, said to me, "Frances, when you are in the Orient I think you are going to find that superficial cleverness will not be enough. The people you will meet will see through that because they know the meaning of real wisdom." I was angry and resentful at what I sensed as her critical tone, but I pretended not to be. However, her words stayed with me and came back to me as truth during the journey. In particular, I recall an instance in China when I was giving a talk which had to be translated. I became painfully aware that personality-level charm and charisma fell flat in translation, and that only solid, honest communication reached such an audience.

As I look back now at the young woman I was, I am struck by the contrasts between parts of myself which were so different, out of touch with one another, and so unconscious. I see the bright, capable, independent leader who can and does manage and manipulate groups of people to suit her goals, who needs to be first and who selects people and circumstances where she can be first. And I see the little girl, unsure of herself, unacceptable to herself, perilously dependent on the opinion of others for self-validation. I see a young woman, sophisticated and naive, worldly and unworldly, facing outward and facing inward. . . .

For me, the pattern that dogged my footsteps on the new path was the deep self-rejection behind the superficial appearance of capability. I lived with the unrecognized belief that I had been found inadequate, unsatisfactory, "less than." To compensate, I needed to be not only "more than" but *the* best, *the* first. Instead of maintaining myself consistently at a relatively balanced level, something would seem to attack my vulnerable ego and I would plunge down to minus 100. Then, instead of moving back up to a centered level, I often shot on up to plus 100, or if possible to plus 1,000, to overcome the sense of lack and of being "less than."[2]

The Up Side

When sufficiently on their own to stake out this chapter of their lives, twentysomethings try on adulthood as if it were an infinite wardrobe of possibilities. They attach themselves like Velcro to relationships, jobs, new ideas, songs, and financial obligations. They also detach themselves whenever they feel like it and look at life as an experiment that they are not yet fully within, even though their security needs require the appearance of commitment.

The twenties are a time for experimentation, uncensored fun, and adventure. If you are healthy and lucky, the foreign territory of adult life becomes a staging ground for "the new generation." This is a time when freedom and dreams and friendships contain the culture, and love and sex are bigger than life itself. Twentysomethings proceed as though they can and will create the life they want, with or without help from the rest of the universe. They will make their dreams happen, no matter what. They don't think that the constraints of previous generations apply to them. Theirs is a new generation, a new age, with new rules and magic. Siegfried Sassoon once made a remark that speaks for this decade: "At the age of twenty-two I believed myself to be unextinguishable." This dreamy optimism sometimes expresses itself through increased empathy with others, particularly the poor, the oppressed, or people in mental or physical pain.

Although twentysomethings experiment with moral decisions, they seldom have sufficient experience to calculate the price they may pay for the choices they make, nor do they believe their choices are irreversible. Their innocence and arrogance allow them to try their dreams, take a chance, and try something new; but in time they discover that they have altered their life course with the choices they have made.

When they were adolescents testing the boundaries of the adult world, twentysomethings had the protection, support, and guidance of parents and parent figures. Now there is vulnerability to twentysomethings' strong-mindedness; they want total freedom and access to the adult world, along with assurances, guidance, and approval. They are not sure how to ask for or get a safe passage into the adult roles they are seizing. Mentors are pursued for models of the way toward success and safety. But it is difficult to trust a mentor if you haven't resolved your trust with your own parents. Peers are pursued for reassurance and approval. Compromises with big dreams are often made to find security and jobs with adequate salaries. Twentysomethings often settle for immediate rewards and recognition, and their larger dreams get downsized.

After years of education, training, and preparing, it is finally launching time. But when schooling ends, a whole new ball game begins, for which they are not prepared. Up until now in their lives, their schooling experience has kept them oriented toward behaviors appropriate for their age group, but from now on, their primary orientation will be toward their work environment, with its diverse adult populations. In their private life, they must learn how to love beyond courtship—to sustain and nurture couple, sexual, and friendship commitments. They must now master the management of time and money and a leisure life. The challenges are wonderful, but the responsibilities often seem overwhelming. Few twentysomethings feel as prepared as they want everyone to believe they are.

Today's young adults often live together before marrying. Many adults marry in their twenties, but more and more who are college graduates are marrying in their thirties. The majority of these are now dual-career marriages, in which both the husband and the wife are full-time wage earners. This is a relatively new phenomenon in American life, and one that is transforming marital roles and family life. Some young adults—an increasing number— choose not to marry, while others seek same-sex, intimate partners. In today's world, both intimate partners work, participate in household chores, play, dream, seek a full adult script, and are determined to transcend their families of origin. Couples in their twenties have much in common as they join together to find successful paths into the full adult world. They share a common subculture, lofty expectations, sexual pleasure, and a hunger for affirmation. Leisure is increasingly important to twentysomethings, who find considerable meaning in play, physical prowess, health, creativity, music, travel, and time with friends. When successful twentysomethings hit thirty, they feel proud of their experimentation with life and view themselves as on their way.

Mature twentysomethings are open to experience, eager to adventure, and self-accepting. They take responsibility for their own lives, stay committed to continued learning, and maintain a philosophy of life—an internalized set of beliefs and values that are both unifying and directing.

The Down Side

No matter how prepared twentysomethings are to leave home or how angry they are with their parents, breaking out of a family of origin is almost always more difficult than expected. This represents the first predictable, major transition in adult life, usually filled with cocooning behaviors, self-renewal, and lots of experimentation. Family systems experts judge that this transition takes several years to work through, not merely for the young adult but for all the members of the family system. Few manage this transition knowingly or easily.

Twentysomethings are so devoted to leaving their family of origin that they seldom give sufficient thought to the qualities of the adult life they want to arrive at. They think that those qualities,.

along with careers, financial security, and mates, will be bestowed upon them automatically, now that they have arrived at the gates of adulthood. It seldom occurs to them that they have to learn how to master the adult years. For about twenty years, they have been the children of their parents and monitored by school systems. Now, with the flick of a switch, they are supposed to be "on their own," "grown up," and "responsible." Meanwhile, beneath the veneer of sleek muscular boldness lies a childlike fear. Twentysomethings and thirtysomethings spend their decades sorting out who they are from who they were. When ideas and emotions are still on loan from the family of origin, it is hard to own them. Throughout this first life chapter, even though they are driven by the conflicting messages of parents, mentors, and peers, twentysomethings want to believe that they are in charge of their lives.

Some twentysomethings are early peakers who reach or surpass their personal goals during their twenties. They get thrown into social recognition for some role that they perform—a musical or acting career, sports success, possession of inherited money. The person behind the role usually doesn't have a clear identity, so the role dominates for a while. Unfortunately, people who build their life chapters around their physical prowess or beauty often find that their lives peak in the twenties and thirties. After the peak, life is a downhill slide. Early peakers who decline behave much like old people who have only the past in which to live. Early peaking is an increasing problem among some upwardly mobile twentysomethings.

Every generation of twentysomethings is slightly different. Times change and people change. For example, there is less difference between male and female roles among twentysomethings today than there was a generation ago. Today's men and women in their twenties share in education, careers, intimacy, and leisure interest. Both sexes ask the same questions: How much intimacy and commitment do I want? and How much independence and freedom do I need? How important are achievement, success, and money in relationship to quality time with friends, family, and causes that I believe in? How can I keep fit and maintain an active leisure life? The difference between the sexes is much more dramatic for thirtysomethings than for twentysomethings in today's world.

Our society used to have buffer zones that provided transitional environments for youths as they moved from adolescent rebellion to adult identities. Colleges, universities, the military, the Peace Corps, and apprenticeship roles in careers used to acculturate young people gradually into the adult years. Young people could take a "psychosocial moratorium" during which they could experiment with various roles, values, and belief systems. They could travel, participate in religious or political groups, enter the work world for survival money, and live together. This "youth culture" gave American twentysomethings extended time to know who they were and how they wanted to live.

Today, it is not so easy. The undergraduate years have lost much of their general education function, and college cultures now reflect the society rather than provide incubation laboratories for maturation and socialization. The buffer for "practicing" adult personal and social behaviors has worn thin. Few schools are left that facilitate a rite of passage into adulthood. Colleges used to grow people; now they more often grow majors. College majors do not always link with today's careers, and the anxiety over financial matters has led many to shortchange learning for training so that they can launch careers and find some security in the adult world. That is why so many twentysomethings are becoming instant adults, jumping into jobs and relationships, postponing much of their emotional and inner turmoil until later in life. The adolescent transition into the adult years—the only culturally approved transition in all adulthood—has been shortened and shortchanged by a society lost in its own identity crisis.

The new twentysomethings have more cultural diversity than ever before, representing a variety of national, ethnic, and socioeconomic backgrounds. Today's twentysomethings face troubling social dilemmas. They enter the adult years at a time when the society struggles reactively with an AIDS epidemic, drugs, an economic recession or depression, wars, environmental scares, political disillusionment, and widespread terrorism. Where is the welcome mat? If this is their inheritance, what are the future prospects? What can they hope for? What should they work for? Is it any wonder that many in the current generation of twentysomethings report that they feel abandoned and neglected by their own culture? Alienated, some get locked into survival and subculture roles before knowing who they are as adult persons.[3]

Twentysomethings tend to believe that they have all the time in the world to shape their lives. They often settle for immediate rewards and recognition, and their larger dreams get trapped within their smaller advances. They assume that their mistakes can be reversed. But in reality, some of the gates that young adults walk through close behind them and can be reopened only with great difficulty, if at all: career decisions, geographical choices, intimacy selections, parenthood, bank loans, and lifestyle preferences. Even those twentysomethings enraged by the apparent waning of our society will eventually learn that not to decide to do something with their lives is a decision that affects their own future options. The barely formed adult in us makes many decisions that have to be lived with for the rest of our lives or altered with considerable pain.[4]

The three greatest challenges facing twentysomethings are achieving an adult identity, sustaining intimate bonds with others, and developing a distinct career or work identity. Because the acculturation forces are increasingly weak and diverse, more and more twentysomethings are failing to achieve one or more of these three developmental goals of the twenties. A lack of one or more of these can lead to intense loneliness, and anyone who works with twentysomethings knows how lonely they often are. This is an age group increasingly prone to accidents and suicide.

As they approach thirty, twentysomethings begin conducting an audit to see whether they are on course with their dream and with their peers. This zero-year transition is very common; it produces a rigorous evaluation of the decisions of the past decade, leading to new decisions to either deepen existing commitments or to alter them significantly. In a newspaper column, Dan Brown called his evaluation "Thirtynothing":

> Waking up the morning of my 30th birthday with my three-year-old snoring in my ear and the cat trying to gnaw my foot through the blanket, nothing seemed different. GTE still hadn't rehooked my phone. The rent was still past due. My main source of income was still a job digging ditches and bending nails, which, glancing at the clock, I was again late for. I lay there for a while, waiting for my well-earned wisdom to kick in. Nothing came. . . .

Why, I thought lying there, is it the dawn of my 30th year and I am still in the dark? Turning 30, I figured, meant crossing the invisible line from promising phenom to wily veteran. Or at least it would be the year I quit considering myself in terms of an athlete, make a compromise with my dreams. But noooo. When shooting hoops or taking Sunday batting practice with friends, I'll still be scanning the sidelines for some old codger who will shuffle up to me and say I'm just what the Lakers or Dodgers are looking for. Hell, I'm not 30, I'm simply 10 for the third time. . . . There doesn't seem to be a lot of progress.

Cindy, my wife, didn't say anything until I was pushing the car out of the driveway. "Hey, speedster," she shouted from the front door, "bull your neck, don't sweat the small stuff, and remember, progress is highly overrated." After pop-starting the car, I took the first corner like Mario Andretti.[5]

Thirtysomethings: Making It

From the late twenties throughout their thirties, most adults spend their time "making it." They want to "arrive" fully, to feel the comfort of life beyond waiting and receive the rewards and recognition of having arrived. No longer initiates into adult life, thirtysomethings are committed to making the world work for them, which means investing in long-term issues: careers, marriages, parenting, and social leadership roles. Feeling that they have made valuable corrections in their life course on the basis of what they learned in their twenties, thirtysomethings plunge into a race for first-class citizenship in the adult world.

Consider this conversation between Mary and Derek—two thirtysomethings.

Mary: I was thirty-four when Cheree was born. Nothing has changed my life more than becoming a mother. I felt so close to Cheree, and I reorganized my life around her needs. I changed many of my friends to other mothers of infants. I decided not to return to work for at least six months. Derek began to work extra hours so that we could maintain our income level, and he really liked being home on weekends, when he could have special time with Cheree.

Derek: My law firm asked me to become a partner when I was thirty-seven, and I couldn't say no, even though I knew it would mean longer hours and more work. It also meant a permanent position, recognition, and higher salary.

Mary: Everything was easy with Cheree until she could walk, and then we had to rearrange the house. Although I loved to be with her, she was a full-time job. I went through several "mother's helpers," but I still felt the need to be around Cheree during those years. I was more tired than when I worked at the hospital. After talking it over with Derek, I decided to have another child to complete our family, so that by the time I reached forty the kids would be in school and I could return to work. Little Christopher was born when I was thirty-five.

Derek: By the time I was thirty-nine, I was fairly well recognized for my legal specialty. I was talking frequently at conferences and regional meetings. I felt good about my attainments.

Mary: By the time I reached thirty-nine, my life was in a tailspin. My relationship with Derek had all but disappeared, and I was very angry with him. At the very time the children needed him most as a father, he increased his busyness at work and spent less time at home. I was desperately trying to return part-time to my career to supplement my parenting chores; I needed a life of my own. Our social life, which I managed, was almost entirely with parents of kids the ages of ours, and while on paper everything was coming out the way we wanted it, I was bitter and unhappy.

Derek: The guys at the office all hear the same story from their wives: "You're working too much and not coming home early enough in the evenings. I need you to be my partner with the family!" I don't know why Mary doesn't realize the predicament I'm in. In order to maintain my position in the firm, I have to be a leader, and that means long hours—and more pay. On the other hand, my closest friends are my work buddies. They're the greatest—

but Mary doesn't know them much at all. When I go home these days, I feel like a stranger. Even the kids know better than I do where things are and what's going to happen. And I must admit, my sex life isn't the greatest. But we'll catch up after the kids get older. Right?[6]

The Up Side

Thirtysomethings want their piece of the rock, and they feel an urgency about reaching their goals. Forty is an approximate deadline that many young adults unconsciously set for reaching the goals that so often constitute "making it": career recognition, financial attainment, marriage and having babies, friendships, status, acquisitions, lifestyle, leisure life, travel, and social leadership roles. There are many variations, some excluding marriage, others including marriage without children, and still others creating alternative lifestyles. The pressure is the same: make life happen to its fullest in this decade. Thirtysomething has a large agenda and a clock that is constantly ticking.

The two major developmental issues for thirtysomethings are achievement (work, money, recognition) and intimacy (coupling, family, parenting). As children arrive, the division of labor between mother and father increases exponentially. Mothering, in particular, is a transformative experience, and women who have waited until their thirties to bear children usually are highly devoted to the mothering roles. However, those roles usually strain the mother's ability to follow her established career path. Strains also appear between the husband and wife as the two gradually evolve two virtually separate worlds of experience, joined primarily by parenting roles. Typically, he plunges deeper into career and financial responsibility as she immerses herself in building a family unit. However, fathering has gained interest among men as a primary identifier, and it is not unusual now to find men choosing to reduce their work hours or alter their careers in order to be active in parenting roles. Likewise, mothers today usually have careers to return to, and shared parenting and wage earning is common among thirtysomethings.

Thirtysomethings want to achieve authority, independence, and respect. They are basically tired of being apprentices, and they want responsibility and rewards. For many, this is an exhilarating decade, filled with opportunity and challenge. These thirtysomethings get what they asked for and feel as if they are in a permanent orbit as the forties begin. Many thirtysomethings, however, find this decade to be a time when expectations and reality thrash about in a civil war of inner and outer conflict, leading to midlife transition and a major life evaluation at the end of the thirties tunnel.

America has experienced an agequake among its thirtysomethings. The baby boomers have moved out of this decade, and a small cohort with a more cautious outlook on life has replaced them. How this will affect the profile of future thirtysomethings is difficult to say. Will the process of adult development work to bring the new group into line with what is written about thirtysomethings here (which is based heavily on the baby-boomer group)? Or will social and economic differences require a rewriting of this chapter?

The Down Side

The thirties may well be the most complex adult decade to manage. It is driven by a pressure-cooker agenda formed in the family of origin and modified by the experience of the twenties. This is the major adult period of expansive mastery based largely on blueprints obtained from parents, peers, mentors, or society itself. The internal drive is to reach external expectations. And the expectations are not really negotiable because they are mostly unconscious imperatives and injunctions.

This is the decade when young adults feel driven to reach too many goals at superlative levels too fast. Not only is there a huge agenda to complete but it usually must be completed "perfectly." The thirties are years of role overload as the clock ticks toward self-imposed deadlines for realizing dreams and game plans. By roughly forty, at the latest, they want to arrive at the fulfillment of their early adult dreams—success, happiness, financial security, and a lifestyle filled with trips, friends, children, and recognition.

Thirtysomethings want and expect permanent acquisitions in the adult world. They want to get beyond "preparing" and "waiting." They want to arrive. Men typically focus in on their jobs as their special assignment for achieving and producing financial results. Women find it difficult to balance all the life roles that they feel they should have, usually including jobs or careers, husbands or lovers, children, household design and maintenance, friendships, care of aging parents, and a social life. Houses must be bought and furnished, status symbols acquired, and financial equity stored away.

Intimacy is now in its long-haul phase, and routines have settled into well-recognized and anticipated conversations, touching, and sex. If thirtysomethings are in conventional marriages, family life is oriented around the growing needs of the kids, and this displaces the ego needs of mom and dad as they slide through their multiple roles as taxi driver, sports promoter, school monitor, disciplinarian, and food provider. For careerists, there are the daily routines of work: commuting, settling into the work space, plunging into the tasks at hand, taking a break, working some more, lunch, edging back into work, conversing through the late afternoon, commuting, and reentering home space and time. Thirtysomethings typically work long hours with great intensity in pursuit of quality living, which they postpone because their lives are driven by high expectations for external attainments. Quantity issues overpower quality ones.

There is an undertow as well. For most thirtysomethings, the great decisions of life have been made, and they are waiting for the results. However, they are enmeshed in commitments from which they cannot easily extricate themselves; this is unlike their twenties, which were characterized by newly felt freedom and adventure. Now they are lodged in complex, routine intimate relationships, work agreements, financial commitments, and maintenance functions.

When you're a thirtysomething, you develop an increased ability to reflect on your life. Through introspection you begin to reevaluate your life decisions. You are still challenged to reach your goals, but you also wonder, "Is this all there is? Is this what my life is all about?" You supplement your routines with adventuresome weekends, visits to exotic places, intensive seminars on self-help themes, and a fanciful use of public holidays. Still, 94 percent of your time is invested in routine activities aimed at sustaining your life, leaving only 6 percent for celebrating your gains. You are goal-rich but time-poor—not exactly what you had in mind when you started out.

Whereas twentysomethings are generalists determined to get their acts together, thirtysomethings tend to specialize in specific tasks for making it. This often leads to lopsided personalities, with pigeonholed roles, advanced expertise, and enormous areas of undeveloped abilities. What was fun in your twenties may become an addiction in your thirties. On the one hand, if you work full-time and are moving up in your career, you may become called a workaholic, getting ready to live, but not yet living very much. After a decade or so of spending more time at work than at home, you may feel like an outsider when you visit the kids' schools or answer the phone at home.

On the other hand, if you raise children, your orientation toward parenting may force a trade-off with your spouse: "I'll be the primary resource for family and home even though I, too, work—and you be the primary resource for money since you have the greater earning power," the wife often says. After a few years, his world revolves around his career and hers revolves around many things, with the home, family, and her work often being the most important. He expends his energy at work and comes home to be cared for. She expends her energy at work and at home and expects an active partner in the evenings and on weekends. His passivity at home is matched by her anger at his psychological absence, and trouble often follows. The dream that was supposed to fulfill their lives seems now to be separating them. Instead of a primary relationship, the marriage becomes an extracurricular activity. Trouble brews in Camelot.

The Midlife Transition

By your late thirties you may feel misguided by your earlier dreams, exhausted by your frenetic activities, and trapped by your career and intimate relationships. You wonder whether you should get into personal therapy, change careers, or what? The closer you get to your early adult dream's deadline, which is often sometime between thirty-five and forty-five, the less sure you are that the ladder you have been climbing is up against the right wall. Even if you reach your dream, you may feel disappointed that so much of your life has been consumed in that pursuit, at the expense of other activities that now seem important to you. Carl Jung describes this transition succinctly:

> Middle life is the moment of greatest unfolding, when a man still gives himself to his work with his whole strength and his whole will. But in this very moment evening is born, and the second half of life begins. Passion now changes her face and is called duty; I want becomes the inexorable I must and the turnings of the pathway that once brought surprise and discovery become dulled by custom. The wine has fermented and begins to settle and clear. Conservative tendencies develop if all goes well; instead of looking forward one looks backward, most of the time involuntarily, and one begins to take stock, to see how one's life has developed up to this point. The real motivations are sought and real discoveries are made.[7]

Some people call the transition that often comes a little before or after age forty a "midlife transition" or a "midlife crisis" because it separates the first half of adult life from the second half. Most life transitions separate the decades or chapters of our lives, but this one serves a larger purpose. Like the fulcrum under a teeter-totter, it represents the midpoint in a person's life—a major shift in perspective, values, and purpose. This transition represents a shift from external expansiveness toward internal clarity. It separates your sense of endless time from limited time left, infinite options from limited choices, a denial of death from its personal certitude, expecting life to happen from accepting life as it happens, and parental or social scripts from personal ones. Sometimes these shifts are natural evolutions; at other times they are convulsive, producing disorientation and disillusionment with life as it has been lived, as for the thirty-five-year-old character Ivan in Anton Chekhov's play *Ivanov:*

> I go about with a heavy head, with a lazy soul, tired and broken, without faith, without love, without aim; I wander about among my friends like a shadow and I don't know who I am, or why I live, or what I want. Already it seems to me that love is silly, that caresses and endearments are sugary nonsense, that there isn't any meaning in work, that song and impassioned words are trivial and old fashioned. And wherever I go I bring misery, blank boredom, discontent, disgust with life.[8]

At least six issues contribute to the midlife transition:

1. Biological changes in the body may trigger a reevaluation of self, through such events as crow's-feet around the eyes, a double chin, increased weight, thinning hair, or diminished sexual energy.
2. The gap between expectations and reality may induce a sense of failure and futility, particularly if the early adult dream was grandiose and unrealistic.
3. Job satisfaction and career advancements may hit a plateau or actually decline at about this time in life, fostering a reevaluation about work in particular and life in general. Or career goals may not be met, resulting in boredom or restlessness.
4. It is common for adults to restructure marital and family commitments at this time in life, which can trigger a deep personal reevaluation as well. In midlife, men tend to become less aggressive and more interested in love, relationships, and simple pleasures; women, on the other hand, become less comfortable in nurturing and submissive roles and more interested in external challenges, assertive roles, and their own personal development. Those women who are defined by their careers further complicate the mix. These changes affect marital and family roles.
5. Issues regarding social recognition and status may trigger new stock taking by, for example, a woman who is "only a housewife" or a man whose low-level job and moderate salary seem destined to keep the family in a small housing unit in the wrong part of town.
6. There is often an increased awareness of the limits of life, such as financial constraints, reduced ambition, the amount of time left, and the inevitability of death.

These are some of the issues that come to a head during the midlife transition, requiring minor or major adjustments to the life course in order to make it acceptable. The goal of the midlife transition is to unite life, not divide it. It connects time already lived with time left, being young with becoming old, feeling unique with feeling connected, and being in control with being nurtured by forces greater than ourselves. The central theme of the midlife transition is to get clearer than you have ever been before about who is running your life and to let it be you. In his book, *A Year in the Life,* William Bridges offers a useful description of a person going through a midlife transition:

> I have recently and reluctantly come to the conclusion that I am lost. Not just unsure that this is the right trail, but off any trail whatsoever. I find myself, figuratively, looking for footprints, broken twigs, any sign that someone has been over this ground ahead of me. . . . This is a time of transition for me, and I long for a little of the god's understanding. I am in that in-between state in my life, having left behind an outgrown but still perfectly serviceable past, and moving toward a future that resists all my efforts to bring it into focus. . . . What I long for this morning is some way of extricating myself from *who I have been.* I need some way to break the bonds of enchantment holding me to a self-image that needs to be cast off, now, like an outgrown shell. I assume that whatever natural process it is that causes us to burst old shells leads us to grow new ones. That's what I hope this morning, anyway. I'm not in a mood to scuttle around the floor of the universe bare. . . . One thing is sure: You have to give up on the idea of getting some one stable view of things. It's where you are in the journey that determines the view.[9]

Adults who deny this transition continue to live "as if they were young," according to their early dream about acquisitions, security, and proving themselves. These people deny the realities and opportunities of the second half of life—particularly aging issues having to do with the decline of the body and the growth of the human spirit. At sixty, they still talk about the same concerns they prized at thirty; typically, they are wrapped up in one or two adult roles—careerist, spouse, parent, leisure activity—and are untrained at introspection, self-nurture, and adult development. A great many adults—particularly those who believe they are succeeding—die psychologically at the beginning of the midlife years as they lock themselves out of the incremental gains available in the second half of life. Although their bodies continue to age, their behaviors do not. They remain arrested as persons and do not evolve their stories, plots, and scripts.

Fortunately, the midlife transition is not chronologically restricted to thirty-five- to forty-five-year-olds. Equally powerful transitions can and do occur whenever adults come to terms with the major changes in their lives—at thirty-five, forty-five, fifty-five, sixty-five, seventy-five, eighty-five, or ninety-five.

If you have been making these adaptations gradually throughout your twenties and thirties, you may not even be aware of a midlife transition, which does not need to be a traumatic crisis. But if you have clung to a static, youthful picture of your adult years, you may experience a jolting turning point that will prompt a change of perspective, feelings, and priorities—a natural transition from early adulthood to midlife for many adults today.[10]

The Forties and Fifties
Taking Stock, Individuating, and Enjoying Life

> *The mass of men lead lives of quiet desperation. What is*
> *called resignation is confirmed desperation. . . . A*
> *stereotyped but unconscious despair is concealed even*
> *under what are called the games and amusements*
> *of mankind.*
>
> *I went to the woods because I wished to live*
> *deliberately, to front only the essential facts of life, and see*
> *if I could not learn what it had to teach, and not, when I*
> *came to die, discover that I had not lived. I did not wish to*
> *live what was not life, living is so dear; nor did I wish to*
> *practise resignation, unless it was quite necessary. I*
> *wanted to live deep and suck out all the marrow of life, to*
> *live so sturdily and Spartan-like as to put to rout all that*
> *was not life, to cut a broad swath and shave close, to drive*
> *life into a corner, and reduce it to its lowest terms.*
> HENRY DAVID THOREAU, *WALDEN*[1]

Adult life in the forties and fifties continues most of the activities and commitments of the early adult years, but with new perspectives and concerns. Fortysomethings are often preoccupied with self-analysis and taking stock. They know they have reached the midpoint of their lives, but they are not sure how to address both the unfinished business of their twenties and thirties and the inevitable realities of getting older. Fiftysomethings have generally come to terms with midlife and have found positive ways to enjoy it. Many fiftysomethings report this decade to be one of increasing self-esteem, deepening intimacy, expanding leisure, reduced economic pressures, and improved sense of perspective on life.

Fortysomethings: Self-Reliance and Individuation

As adults move into their late thirties and early forties, many of them feel driven to be in charge of their own lives. Tired of waiting in line for first-class adult citizenship, they want to control their own destiny. That is what self-reliance—the dominant pursuit of today's fortysomethings—is all about. However, others in their forties have unfinished business left over from their twenties and thirties. They want to finish that before devoting themselves fully to their own personal issues, so they choose to master interdependence, the art of achieving win-win relationships with others with whom one lives and works. The critical question is, Which is your dominant concern at this time in your life—self-reliance (to get more clarity about you and your personal agenda) or interdependence (to find new and better ways to relate to children, friends, career, spouse, and others)?

Self-reliance arrives as a decade orientation for those fortysomethings who have peaked in some major life role, such as parenting or career. Whenever you feel that you have "done your duty" to some major role in your life, you begin to look for a way to make space for your own personal agenda.

A number of scholars on female development argue that there is a fundamental difference between the way men and women develop during the adult years. Men develop by being different, separate, autonomous, self-reliant, independent, boundaried, self-sufficient, and self-actualized. Women develop by being similar, connected, related to, caring, attached, and interdependent. Carol Gilligan described the woman's way with these words: "We know ourselves as separate only insofar as we live in connection with others and that we experience relationship only insofar as we differentiate other from self."[2] Men and women often display this difference by the midlife years, with men attached primarily to their work, where they can be self-reliant and achieving, and women with more complex attachments to families, friends, and work settings centered around nurturing, caring, and achieving roles. It is natural, then, to expect men to want to individuate when their careers no longer fulfill them or their intimate relationships stifle their autonomy and for women to individuate through their commitments to children, intimate relationships, and careers. However, the argument isn't so simple. These two tendencies are more male and female forces within all of us than gender distinctions per se. Some women, for example, follow the "male" line of reasoning and end up stressing self-reliance first, just as some men follow the "female" line and move from interdependence to self-reliance. With the options available to today's adults and the multiple roles that we can all have access to throughout adulthood, each person must choose the decade orientation that fits his or her own lifeline.

Sometime between thirty-five and fifty, most adults become the authors of their lives. They differentiate themselves, individually, more than they had done previously. They look back to their youth and ahead to their elder years, as if standing at the center of the see-saw of their lives.

Fortysomethings are usually embedded in commitments—intimate relationships, work roles, friendships, sports, and financial plans. They yearn to simplify their lives so they can spend more time living. Although this is a time in life for reevaluation, it is also a time for feeling good about life. A ten-year study of nearly eight thousand Americans by the MacArthur Foundation Research Network on Successful Midlife Development stated in its first report issued in February 1999 that "midlife is the best place to be." Adults in their forties and fifties report increased feelings of well-being and a greater sense of control over many parts of their lives.[3]

Marvin Banasky

For me, the forties have been a series of wake-up calls. These signals for impending change appeared gradually, yet they were inescapable. During my thirties, my life was filled with symbols of stability and success, and simultaneously the cracks in my inner security were ever widening.

My first wake-up call alerted me to a profound restlessness within me. As I reflected back on my life, I lacked an understanding of what I was about. I felt as if I had been radar-locked onto achievement goals and had channeled my high energy to attain those goals for the past twenty years. At about age forty, I realized how unprepared I had been for being a husband and a father and how confused I was with my wife and family. In my business, I felt I was succeeding at someone else's business interest, not my own.

Then my wake-up signals began to give me some direction. I began to reevaluate my entire life. In my marriage, I wanted more partnership and equal sharing from my wife. In parenting, I wanted to relate out of love rather than as the disciplinarian. In my career, I wanted to start all over in some new field. It was time for me to speak up and be myself.

The next twelve months were the most disrupting period of my life. I was not ready for all the changes that would rush at me and out of me. At about the same time that the divorce was finalized, I closed down my fourteen-year-old business. My son moved in with me, and within five months my two daughters joined me, too. I felt lacking, like a glass half empty instead of a glass half filled. Little by little, self-discovery deepened.

I am now forty-five, and I believe that I am more vital and alive now than at any other time of my life. As I look back over my odyssey, I realize that my transitions were more useful to my journey than I had wanted to believe while I was in the midst of them. Each year, I feel that I am achieving deepening satisfaction, and even though I do not know my ultimate goals, I trust I will find them—or, more likely, create them.[4]

Marilyn Mosley

At forty-one, I am a single parent, the sole provider for my household, and the director of a private high school. My three children are between the ages of fourteen and eighteen, and the eldest will be going to Bennington College this fall. My relationship with my children is evolving into one of friend and confidant, and I am very pleased about that.

My twenties and thirties were a vulnerable and confusing period for me. My expectations and my realities were in different worlds, and I felt fragmented much of the time. The thirties were traumatic for me, as I moved from Baltimore to California with three children, a troubled marriage, parental strife, and a return to school.

I am now freer to work on my own issues and to focus on my career. I am interested in making an impact on the world around me, whatever that may mean. I want to leave a legacy of a better earth-nation-state-city-home-family—whatever I can do. I think to myself, "I have forty years of life left, and I will commit them to making a difference."

I used to think that I was immortal, that life would go on forever. I had so much to contribute and all the time in the world to do it. That has changed for me. I am more aware of the ticking of the clock. I am beginning to think smart, to create strategies for my life. It's no longer appropriate for me to be a ship afloat without a rudder. I am now interested in financial plans, health policies, wills, life insurance, and other "reality issues." After all, sixty-five is twenty-four years away. It's time to think and create for my future.

My quest for marriage has ended, but I do hope for a fulfilling relationship with a life companion. I am interested in creating a partnership with intimacy and friendship. My identity is not as tied up in my body as it used to be or in using my body as a sexual tool. I am looking for a different quality of relationship: communication, creativity, and spiritual aspirations are my primary concerns. I am not seeking to rescue a man or to be rescued.

I know I am far too busy. I keep postponing my own development and interests in order to raise my children, which I thoroughly enjoy. I am also providing my parents with emotional support. But I long to be alone, to visit my friends, and to travel. I often ask myself, "How do I shift gears and place more emphasis on my personal interests?"

I am preparing to become a fifty-year-old woman. I want to know what it will be like. At thirty, forty was ten years and a lifetime away. Aging was not a process that I was interested in knowing more about. Now I am ready to acknowledge my age and to learn from it. I am a woman and no longer a girl, and I like the woman in me. Planning for the future, with intimacy, contribution to the world, and nurturing strong family ties, is the heart of my tasks at this time in my life. Being forty brings with it a certain intensity and pensiveness. I feel that I am a woman with her own life slowly emerging.[5]

The Up Side

The forties are a time for inward reflection, reevaluation, simplification of the life course, and deepening of the human journey. The goals are to chart your own path, to be your own person, and to possess your life. The shift toward self-reliance may be part of a life transition, since the changes in behavior and values are often enormous. Commitments sometimes change dramatically, as do marriages and careers. With a keen sense of racing against time, people in midline shift from quantity to quality activities, from external acquisitions to internal satisfactions, from pleasing others to pleasing themselves.

Adults pursuing self-reliance have two goals, one developmental and one transformational. The developmental goal aims at a completion of the first half of life: to evoke a complete human being capable of shaping his or her own destiny. In this context, self-reliance means the assumption of responsibility for your own thoughts, feelings, and decisions—to write your script and be accountable to yourself for your joy and sorrow. It means to take over the dream and to pull it into the here and now, to be lived daily. The developmental impetus is toward becoming a self-responsible person ready to live more deeply and more simply, driven from within and not by parental voices or external forces. Some of the developmental commitments of fortysomethings are

- Renewing the self
- Evaluating and renewing the couple relationship
- Learning to parent adolescent and young adult children
- Caring for aging parents
- Investing in leisure time
- Obtaining training in new personal and professional skills
- Reevaluating career options and paths

Self-reliance means becoming accountable for your thoughts, feelings, relationships, and commitments. It is an inner decision to be in the world differently than before by not pretending to be who you aren't and not waiting for impossible dreams to happen. Arriving at self-reliance, fortysomethings gradually withdraw from superficial activities, invest in personal growth and development, and begin to live by their own conscious intentionality. They move beyond organizing their lives around their roles in jobs, marriage, and parenting. Without reducing their external effectiveness, they seek ways to invest in themselves. More than anything, fortysomethings want a "private" life—a place within themselves they can always retreat to. In work settings, this may mean getting off the fast track of upward mobility. At home, the postparenting years often arrive during the forties or fifties, making it possible for new projects, education, and relationships. The result is a shift of perspective, from external compliance to internal motivation. Forty-somethings attend to their own interiority with the same intensity that has already been expended on the external world. After interviewing many middle-aged men and women, developmentalist Bernice Neugarten drew this conclusion:

> Most of this group, as anticipated, were highly introspective and highly verbal persons who evidenced considerable insight into the changes that had taken place in their careers, their families, their status, and in the ways in which they dealt with both their inner and outer words. . . .
>
> We are impressed, too, with reflection as a striking characteristic of the mental life of middle-aged persons: the stock-taking, the heightened introspection, and above all, the structuring and restructuring of experience—that is, the conscious processing of new information in the light of what one has already learned; and turning one's proficiency to the achievement of desired ends.
>
> These people feel that they effectively manipulate their social environments on the basis of prestige and expertise; and that they create many of their own rules and norms. There is a sense of increased control over impulse life. The successful middle-aged person often describes himself as no longer "driven," but as now the "driver"—in short, "in command."[6]

The transformational goal in pursuing self-reliance is to prepare for the second half of life, moving beyond "ego" concerns into the life of the "self," a spiritual aspect of mature life. By "spiritual" I mean increased participation in universal truths through gratitude, love, and laughter. This transformation might be called "the psychological birth of the adult," because it opens the doors of the mind and heart to respect the past, to live in the present, and to anticipate the future. You feel as if for the first time you were in the presence of all the puzzle pieces that your life represents. Carl Jung, who called self-reliance "individuation," said that its aim is "completeness" with yourself, so that you live not to project yourself but to be yourself. You move from living out of your ego needs to living with your "self." Instead of striving out of your incompleteness to find life, security, and safety, you enter a receptor mode and accept the life deep within and around you. In *Modern Man in Search of a Soul,* Jung describes this process with moving words:

> We are all thoroughly familiar with the sources of the problems which arise in the period of youth. . . . It is often a question of exaggerated expectations, of under-estimation of difficulties, of unjustified optimism or of a negative attitude. One could compile quite a list of the false presuppositions which give rise to the earliest, conscious problems. . . . Thoroughly unprepared we take the step into the afternoon of life; worse still, we take this step with the false presupposition that our truths and ideals will serve us as hitherto. But we cannot live the afternoon of life according to the programme of life's morning—for what was great in the morning will be of little use at evening, and what in the morning was true will at evening have become a lie. . . . Expansion of life, usefulness, efficiency, the cutting of a figure in social life, the shrewd steering of offspring into suitable marriages and good positions—are not these purposes enough? . . . Ageing people should know that their lives are not mounting and unfolding, but that an inexorable inner process forces the contraction of life.[7]

Through the conscious development of an inner self, we discover connections to universal qualities of life everywhere. This spiritual awareness transforms our sense of purpose, and we begin to pursue a higher consciousness characterized by wholeness, reflection, and trust—investing our energy in forms of life and work that will outlive us. A popular view of spiritual people is that they are weak, emasculated, and otherworldly. In the context of this book, *spiritual* means just the opposite—strong, bold, and profoundly present. Spiritual awareness creates what Robert Bly calls "the inner warrior," a person who chooses to heed the voice within and to follow it. Spirit gives birth to integrity, depth, risk-taking, and the courage to be.[8] Spirituality is empowerment of human resources that exist in their most complete form in the lives of mature adults. Anchored in trust, experienced in gratitude, this spiritual force reaches for human meaning beyond (not in place of) mere pleasure, power, and possessions. It searches for abiding values and lasting contributions. It promotes the highest level of risk taking—human caring. It generates profound compassion.

The Down Side

Fortysomethings are typically evolving from being specialists in some external role to being generalists in themselves. It is common for young fortysomethings to feel lopsided. When they were young adults, they applied themselves and became fairly good at something—selling, managing, raising babies, teaching, playing basketball—and their friends and mentors agreed: "You're really good at that. You should get more training and move further into your specialty." So they did, and as they perfected their specialties, they found less and less time for all the other parts of their lives, so that by their forties, they are very good at a few things and remarkably undeveloped in the rest of their human capacities. So we find fortysomethings wondering how to develop their undeveloped parts. For women who have spent their twenties and thirties as homemakers, wives, and mothers, this may mean reentering school to prepare for a career, economic self-sufficiency, and leadership responsibility. For those who have spent their twenties and thirties in full-time careers, it may mean having children and nesting. For most men, who typically overidentify with their careers, it means getting in touch with the universe within them—the land of interiority, feelings, and spirituality.

Picture, if you can, a room full of lopsided fortysomethings feeling an urgency to develop the parts of their lives that until now have been handled through symbiosis, dependency, neglect, or repression. If they have shaped their lives around their careers, they may now feel remorse about the intimacy that they neglected—the achiever who didn't get married, the absent father who wasn't emotionally available to his children, the woman who forgot to have children, the gay man or woman who stayed in the closet. If they have shaped their lives around caring for and nurturing others, they may now feel a sense of failure at unreached personal goals—career paths uncharted, financial independence not secured, private life undeveloped, leisure goals lost, bodies neglected. Fortysomethings seek well-rounded lives with overall human competence. They seek balance and completion.

Fortysomethings are sometimes called middlescents when they behave like grown-up adolescents thrashing about to test their boundaries. They often use anger, depression, and other emotions to break away from what isn't working in their lives. What makes middlescents different from adolescents is their extensive commitments: to marriages, children, jobs, civic roles, financial obligations. Repossessing your soul without wrecking your life is not always easy. Although being true to yourself requires a rigorous inner honesty, it seldom requires trashing all that you have been. This is a time for sorting things out, simplifying, and choosing stepping stones that lead to the future that you truly want.

Fortysomethings want to be their own persons and diminish their dependencies. How do you do this when your career has brought you to an advanced position or to a reputation as the best internist in town? How do couples with twenty years of dependency in their marital relationship transform their marriage to a model based on equity, mutuality, and passion? How does a fortysomething change his or her parenting style when the children are quite accustomed to manipulating the old style and to resisting change? How can fortysomethings change habits of deprivation, indulgence, and addiction? Do you continue to aspire to all that you can be, or should you reduce your goals and choose a simpler life? The internal dreams of fortysomethings are usually very different from the external dreams of twentysomethings. Typically, fortysomethings lower their expansive expectations while increasing their expectations for quality in their lives.

Fiftysomethings: Interdependence

Sometime before the fifties arrive, it is not uncommon for fortysomethings to tire of self-reliance. Although taking charge of your own destiny is essential to your development as a person, self-reliance leads beyond itself, to interdependence with others. Autonomy is a stepping stone, not an end point; it prepares people for relationships and leadership roles that have deeper integrity than they have had in their earlier years. The fifties are usually filled with successful efforts at interdependence: deepening intimacy bonds, forming new friendships, investing in increased leisure activities, accepting leadership roles in community and professional organizations.

For most people, the fifties are a comfortable decade devoted to the art of living. Fiftysomethings are generally more at home in the world than at any previous time. They celebrate all the parts of their lives with joy, humor, and less hurry.

Herant Katchadourian, M.D.

Turning fifty. The "Big Five-O." Wonderful like the dawn of a new age, brimming with promise of fulfillment? Or ominous like a tanker coming at you through the fog? Which is it? What happens at age fifty?

I approached my fiftieth birthday with great expectations. There were no major crises in my professional or personal life. But there were many loose ends on all fronts, and I firmly believed that as I turned fifty, those loose ends would get tied up; I would get closure on issues that for years had drained and distracted me like so many dripping faucets.

My expectations of turning fifty were entangled with my sense of being fully adult. Mind you, this had nothing to do with external evidence of being adult. I acted mature enough as an adolescent to pass for an adult when I turned twenty. The issue did not involve objective accomplishments or the perception of others but had to do with my own perception of what it meant to be adult. And to me that meant doing what I thought I ought to do with my life.

The day finally came when I turned fifty. For a short while there was the illusion that the long-awaited closure had been attained. But then I could hear the faucets dripping again, and I realized with some amusement that no magical transformation had taken place. I continued to change ever so slightly— sometimes for the better, sometimes for the worse—but most of the time into someone merely a little different.[9]

Richard L. Haid

For some twenty years I have hoped that there might be another career within me where I might do something of educational and social significance. For thirty years I had been part of my father's insurance agency, which I ultimately inherited and successfully managed, located in a small city in southern Ohio.

I have always had a quest for meaning and purpose in my life, and I was not fulfilled as a businessman in recent years. Was there another career that would offer more satisfaction than what I had been doing for over thirty years? I didn't like paperwork and detail. I did like taking charge of my learning, creating something new, being in new surroundings, taking risks, and developing the potential of people and organizations.

During my fifties, all four children left for college, and my wife, Leslie, and I had an empty nest. Although she had occasionally worked part-time during her adult years, her primary devotion had been to the family and home. A new sense of intimacy developed between Leslie and me. She went back to school for a year of paralegal training, and so I did much of the cooking and cleaning and laundry. I had a sense of immediate completion from the domestic chores, and Leslie found that my doing the chores was a bit threatening.

In my business, I found it harder and harder to keep myself motivated. I was very bored with my work. Then I attended a last-half-of-life workshop at a retreat center, and when I returned home, I knew I was starting a new chapter in my life.

I became aware of my long term interest in people and their careers, and as I learned to use more of my potential, I was able to coach others to do the same. I became energized and became the first intern ever to train at a nearby outplacement firm, where I was able to help unemployed businessmen start again, as I was doing. With grief and pain, I sold my insurance agency and entered a Ph.D. program where I could design my own study in career transitions. I also started consulting and leading seminars.

People tell me that my face glows when I talk about my new career and the fascinating experiences that I am having. I now have the freedom and energy to be part of this change. My theme is "What Are You Going To Do With The Rest of Your Life?" From my experience I believe that most persons have the capacity to achieve more satisfying lives than they think, especially in the second half of life. My experience as a businessman is invaluable in my new career, and my increasing maturity as a scholar is helping me move rapidly through my studies, although I like what I am learning so much that I am in no hurry to graduate. My passion is coaching persons as they take charge of their lives by renewing their learning and make career transitions.[10]

The Up Side

Fiftysomethings view life as a social process of sharing, negotiating, celebrating, accepting, and living. Interdependence promotes a decade orientation of interaction, mutual affirmation, multiple friendships, and shared enjoyment. Interdependence is an androgenous experience, occurring at a time when our masculinity and our femininity are more or less in balance and "sex" is not so much a determiner of relationships and activities. Quality-of-life issues increase, along with an openness to be in the world as it is— connected to nature, life, and the flow of things. Interdependence is like a dance with life wherever it can be found, with mutual participation, rejoicing, and sharing. The "I" of self-reliance becomes the "we" of interdependence.

Fiftysomethings typically have lowered defense mechanisms, deal with conflict directly, and have increased trust in others. Fiftysomethings do not see the present as an improvement on the past or the future as a happier time; they view the present time— now—as the only time dimension that matters. They live to live. At fifty, it is time to stop preparing and to start living. The lure of leisure matches the lure of working.

Fiftysomethings often see their world as an extended family. For many, travel has a profound appeal as an invitation to learn more about life everywhere. This is a time when marriages can deepen and spirituality can flourish. With their children often off to college or somewhere else, peer networks of friends take their place. The importance of work and external issues often lessens while the development of close relationships increases. Marie Dressler writes, "By the time we hit fifty, we have learned our hardest lessons. We have found out that only a few things are really important. We have learned to take life seriously, but never ourselves."[11] For the most part, fiftysomethings are preoccupied with living, not with themselves. "Perhaps middle-age is, or should be, a period of shedding shells," states Anne Morrow Lindbergh, "the shell of ambition, the shell of material accumulations and possessions and the shell of the ego."[12] Germaine Greer expands on this: "You care about yourself less and less. Your vanity and pride stop getting in your way. You begin to develop a sense of proportion. . . . You stop squandering emotion on foolish things . . . or waste time on fatuities. You can escape from the dominion of your own passions and enter into a calm wherein you can fix your eye upon a worthy objective and pursue it wholeheartedly."[13]

Fiftysomethings are less inclined than they used to be to use immature defense mechanisms. They are more inclined to say what they think, express their feelings directly, be forgiving, and suppress whatever they don't know how to deal with. They isolate what they find unacceptable in themselves and either work on it or keep it in check. Fiftysomethings usually have a capacity to integrate and become at one with their experience. The marriages of fiftysomethings often take on a spiritual dimension, with each partner serving as a facilitator of the other's life journey. At this point in life, marriage can become a central vehicle for the life course process, facilitating his life, her life, and our life. It can be the warm glow of two best friends celebrating profound companionship, including love, sex, and growing old together. It can also be a livable truce that will be either revitalized or terminated, although there are always some who would rather endure the misery of marriage than improve or give up the attachment. There are increasing numbers of fiftysomethings who are divorced, single, widowed, or living alternative lifestyles. In fact, from fifty on, adults live and love in all sorts of arrangements to give and get affection, support, and fun. Diversity of options for living and working will continue to expand in the twenty-first century.

In the career and work world, fiftysomethings who have been in careers since their twenties are usually coasting on what Abraham Maslow called "unconscious competence." They don't have to prepare very much or think about their tasks; they know how to get their jobs done at high levels of excellence. Although motor skills have begun to slow and accuracy may not be as good as it once was, the value of fiftysomethings' experience is usually more important. They bring stability and perspective to the workforce, provided that they are not bored with their work or angry with their companies. Fiftysomethings are less interested in active mastery in the workplace, where they have to be present to get results; they prefer passive mastery where they can monitor results through leadership roles, policy formation, or monetary control.[14]

A significant number of fiftysomethings might be called late bloomers. They reach their peak in their careers, sports, or hobbies later than most of their peers. This group includes a significant number of women who had to postpone their own development as they married, raised families, and got out of synch with their careers but were able to achieve well in later years. In all probability, an even larger number of late bloomers would emerge if sexism and ageism were reduced in our society and welcome mats extended. The American Association of Retired Persons is hard at work on this, and given the relatively low numbers of young adults, it is likely that older Americans will have increasing opportunities for achievement and leadership in the twenty-first century.

The Down Side

The bodies of fiftysomethings are slowing down. Mirrors are less friendly; the formation of the pear shape of old age is well under way. Nutrition and exercise are more important than ever. Sexual drive diminishes somewhat, but the most notable physiological happening is female menopause (which need not be an impasse to creative living and loving). However, you are bound to hear about friends who experience strokes, heart attacks, cancer, or diabetes. You will have acquaintances who suffer early disabilities, and each incident rings bells in your head—time is running out. Energy for most fiftysomethings, however, depends more on motivation than body issues. Are you feeling bored, cynical, and hopeless about the future? Or are you eager to make your future the best years of your life? That is the fundamental choice, and your answer determines your destiny—to view your life as continuing challenge and growth or as continuing decline. The smart answer is to choose continuing challenge and growth *for your life,* while managing the inevitable declines *of your body.*

Chapter Nine

The Sixties, Seventies, Eighties, and Nineties
The Longest and Least-Defined Life Phase

> *To be young is to be fresh, lively, eager, quick to learn; to be mature is to be done, complete, sedate, tired. From this point of view, only the distraught young would think positively about growing up, and most of the mature would think longingly about being young. But what if we consider a different perspective? To be young is to be unripe, unfinished, raw, awkward, unskilled, inept; to be mature is to be ready, whole, adept, wise. How valid are our glorification of youth and our shame about having lived many years?*
> LILLIAN E. TROLL, *EARLY AND MIDDLE ADULTHOOD*[1]

The sixties, seventies, eighties, and nineties are extensions of the previous adult years, with a continued emphasis on work, leisure, and relationships, and they are decades in which adults come to terms with their lives. These years can include continued mastery and unanticipated difficulties, often depending on issues like health, status, money, self-motivation, and friendships.

During the twentieth century the life span of Americans increased by about thirty years, all at the end of our lives, and those years have not yet been defined by our society, the American Association of Retired Persons, Gerontologists, or the American Society on Aging. This chapter is an effort to examine the range of human possibilities in this, the longest period of the adult years, which we shall call "elderhood." The journey from sixty on—typically a twenty-five to forty year period, is the least defined adult phase in the life cycle. We are accustomed to thinking that "retirement" provides the definition for these years, but retirement is a rite of passage from full-time working to a cafeteria choice of options, not a master plan for the rest of your life. "Full-time living" means options.

Retirement no longer means to disengage from work, but to begin again, with "living" as the centerpiece. I call it "protirement," meaning to move ahead into those activities that will contribute to a continuance of "the best years of your life." This chapter has immediate relevance to our society, since the number of adults moving toward the last third of their lives is the largest cohort in our country, and in other industrialized nations as well. During the next thirty years the human realities of elderhood will be articulated and developed as social expectations by those who are passing through them.

The Sixties: Redesigning Life, Work, and Leisure

The developmental and aging changes that take place in adults during their fifties and sixties is a very gradual process of continuities and changes. Just as fiftysomethings find the world to be challenging and fulfilling, so do sixtysomethings. For the most part, both decade groups are fairly healthy, fairly well-funded, active, and increasingly concerned with social mentoring. There is not that much difference between the two age groups. In fact, the main difference is that fifty-year-olds tend to measure their lives in relation to improvements made beyond their forties, whereas sixty-year-olds tend to view their decade as a passage into the uncertainties of their remaining years. People in this decade often feel they are "racing against time," as they try to combine their current plans with the unknown realities ahead of them.

Nevertheless, few sixtysomethings today sit around feeling old and impaired, waiting for a bell to announce their demise. Rather, they seek vintage living and quality choices. The drumbeat for sixtysomethings is retirement, which is about two things: financial planning and increased free time for living. Some people retire in their fifties or even their forties; others never retire. But everyone gets older year by year, requiring some scenario for moving ahead. Like twentysomethings, people in their sixties want to begin again—take time building upon life experience, acquired financial resources, and social networks.

Although people retiring usually have a rosy picture of what life beyond work will be like, few have life plans guiding them intentionally into the future. What sixtysomethings need most is "script" for the years ahead—concrete stories about to unfold. Society does not have social scripts or expectations beyond age sixty, only infinite options. Sixtysomethings have to tap their own dreams and formulate their own plans or else they will disengage from work and life and accelerate their aging processes. Here's a list of life areas that elders explore and redefine for themselves throughout the elder years:

• *Work.* If work has been a central source of meaning in life up to now, build it into your scenario for your sixties and seventies. It doesn't have to be full-time work or even work in the same career field, but it should be a source of deep meaning and personal fulfillment, not just a way to be busy. Stopping work "cold turkey" can be a shock to many people who have defined their lives for many, many years through their work roles. Just because you are sixty doesn't mean you *should* stop working. It's up to you. Think it over. It's a big decision, because once you have extracted yourself from a work identity, it will be more difficult to return to the work world. According to current projections, there will be employment opportunities for elders for the next thirty years.

The secret is knowing what you want and how to make it happen. There are many ways to write this script. First, you can find ways to continue the work you have been doing, either full-time or part-time. Second, you can retrain for a new career or work role, to take on new challenges or to make new contributions through new employment opportunities. Third, you can become a volunteer and work hard at making a difference in your community. Fourth, you can start a business from your home, such as consulting, or a service offered over the Internet, or writing and public speaking. Be conscious of the positive work roles you have had previously, and use them as clues to what to seek at this time in your life. You can and will make several reevaluations of work roles in the next twenty to thirty years. Fifth, you can develop a portfolio of all the parts of your personal-professional "work," including activities with your intimate other, time with children and grandchildren, engagements with hobbies and leisure interests, community service, training commitments, and so on. A portfolio approach honors all the parts of your "work" as important to the whole of your life.

• *Family and Friends.* Family and friends have increased importance for sixtysomethings. They typically want to stay connected to kin, to sports friends, to neighbors, to social connections. Not that they want to sit around in rocking chairs. Rather, they want active, engaging relationships with those they care for. They look for episodic events for reunions, projects, sports activities, and professional associations.

• *Adventure and Leisure.* Sixtysomethings often seek fulfillment through adventure and leisure activities. They are not unlike forty- and fiftysomethings except that they have less resistance to saying "yes" to this mode of spending time. Travel is often a high priority, along with socializing with other people their age. Sixtysomethings usually love fun, parties, dancing, and informal socializing.

• *Mentoring and Volunteering.* People in their sixties usually want to "make a difference" in their communities, professions, Habitat for Humanity, and other contexts. The reward they want is that they have contributed, personally, to something greater than themselves.

• *Search for Meaning.* There is a strong spiritual theme in the lives of most sixty-year-olds, to find deep meaning in their experience. The thirst for solitude increases, along with a yearning for inner peace and connectedness to all things.

• *Learning.* Although there are no colleges exclusively for elders (yet!), elders are inexhaustible learners. They are eager to move beyond the specialized arenas of midlife and to discover more about life in general. They prefer experiential, hands-on environments with dialogue and group participation. Learning experiences often increase their zest for life and help them discover new friends, and future directions.

- *Bodily Care*. This includes being intentional about eating and exercising; being savvy about vitamins, minerals, and other food supplements; and seeking holistic and traditional medical attention as needed.

Rachel Rosenthal

I feel so much happier now than I ever did, because I spent so many decades in conflict with myself, having feelings of guilt and angst and regret and misery and self-deprecation and dumping on myself all the time. It's only in the last few years—I don't know exactly when it happened—that this has been lifted from me. Suddenly one day I realized, It's gone. When did that happen? It was kind of a strange discovery. . . . So I don't even know what it is to feel my age, what that means, or how other people are experiencing this, you see. To me, time stands still. I'm in the middle of this raging river, but I'm in my little boat and I just move along. I just try to stay afloat and do what I need to do day by day because there's so much to do. . . . If I ever reach the point where I need to retire and stop what I'm doing—which doesn't seem likely for a while—I think I would go someplace where the living is inexpensive. I would hope that my eyes hold out so I can read a lot of books, and I would probably go back to painting, to the visual arts. . . . I would keep doing what I'm doing, only do it differently. I don't worry; I'm not a worry bird at all.[2]

Larry L. King

Long ago—though not as long ago as I once thought—I decided that "old age" began at 60. "Old age" was self-defining; it meant, simply, that life for all practical purposes was over and done. Those who had attained it could look forward to nothing but solitary thumb-twiddling, warm mush, and the folds of the shroud. This harsh edict was handed down when I was a cocksure 20 and, seemingly, light years away from its personal consequences.

This year I turned 60, an accomplishment causing many reassessments. It is much clearer than formerly that 60-year-olds are vigorous entries in life's race. . . . Age begins sneaking up on us in soft, quiet shoes long before we are aware of its shadow. Even when it begins rattling our door, we are reluctant to bid it come in. We call it "maturity" so long as the mirror or our medical charts permit, the American culture teaching that youth is all and that youth must be served. When was the last time you saw a television grandmother, or even a matron, perched on the hood of a new automobile or *old* cowhands celebrating the end of the workday and the arrival of beer time?

Athletic events, beauty pageants, talent contests, soap operas: All accentuate youth and identify it with glamour. . . . The fear of being excluded from life's "mainstream"—as our culture perceives it—probably accounts for those traumas attending entry into each new personal decade. . . . Fifty was the age that made me snarl and throw things. I was throwing them at a television commercial telling me that those in my "age group of 50 to 80" could now buy a certain product without having to submit our ancient bones to the risk of embarrassing physical examinations. . . .

I realize that I am more fortunate than most as I face the aging process. My health is far better than I deserve, considering my body's prior rough treatments, and would be even better if I could whip a long addiction to cigarettes. As a freelance writer, I have no job subject to mandatory retirement regulations but can work so long as I have the will and faculties to perform. Thanks to luck in the marketplace, I am unlikely to face financial deprivations in my final years. Three of my offspring are adults long past old-parent-progeny conflicts, so that we may comfortably share our time together. I have the additional benefit of a young second family—a good wife with her own successful career, and children 10 and 7 who benefit not only from their mother's intelligence and stability but also, one hopes, from an older and more experienced father taking care not to repeat the youthful mistakes he made in raising his first family.

These factors give me reasons to face each new day not with despair but with hope and with purpose. I do not mean I am always as sunny as Mary Poppins; indeed, there are days when I wake tired and grumpy and exhibit old vestiges of my alcoholic personality unless I remind myself—or my wife reminds me—that the evidence of my daily life simply does not support periodic bouts of sullen self-pity. Nine times out of ten, my morose mornings are tied to troubles with a writing project and disappear after a few good hours at the typewriter.

I will not pretend that I *like* the notion of growing old or the prospect of increasingly accommodating to old age. I remember, and now better appreciate, the pain of my father in having to make personal surrenders: no longer driving a car or climbing trees for pruning purposes or smoking cigarettes, all of which he continued into his 80th year. I do, however, *accept* the notion of impending old age in realistic terms. It requires no genius to recognize that one is not as supple or as tireless as formerly; that one expends more energies to accomplish the same amount of work and requires longer to recover. One knows that at age 60 a heart attack and other sneak debilitations are possible, and thus postpones mowing the grass on the hottest summer day or seeks help in carrying a heavy item of furniture up two flights of stairs. . . . The aging man discovers that it is prudent to keep his life insurance paid up and his legal papers current, that he will wake earlier than when younger, that his bones may creak a bit more en route to his morning shower, that chili or peanut butter do not taste as good as they once did, that 26-year-old blondes are not as interested in him as they once might have been. . . .

Thankfully, there are compensatory rewards. Our memories grow richer, and what once appeared to be random events assume logical patterns with causes and consequences—a realization most helpful to one in my business and, I would think, at least interesting and comforting to those who are not. One is likely to become more happily ruthless in avoiding what once seemed to be obligatory social waltzes. This has less to do with choosing the hermit's life than with reserving more of one's time for what one truly *wants* to do— whether it is reading a book or going to a ballgame or simply avoiding the torture of neckties and tedious dinner-party chitchat. There is a freeing liberation in discovering our true priorities and then shoving aside hindrances to those priorities without fearing harm to one's career or being marked off some hostess's "A" list. My priorities these days are work and family and a bit of time to leisurely observe, analyze, and take stock.

There is a sense of urgency about accomplishing work one feels compelled to do—yes, a sense of limited time—but there is no frenzy in it, no hanging cloud raining dark thoughts of approaching infirmities or death. One simply knows what one wants to *do* with the remaining good years and plans the doing as efficiently as circumstances permit. . . . I am gratified that life has taught even a slow learner that it is far better to hang in there, mixing it up, than to quit on one's corner stool in the early or middle rounds.[3]

The Up Side

In 1990, there were more than sixty million sixtysomethings in the United States, most in good health and many in sound financial condition. Although there are pockets of poor elders in both urban and rural areas, poverty is at the lowest level in this century for sixtysomethings, and financial planning along with Social Security has made the economic prospects excellent for building quality lives.[4]

The American society is increasingly open to having sixty-somethings live, learn, work, travel, whatever. Now that retirement is an elective rather than a requirement, people are having to ask themselves, "What do I want to do with the rest of my life?"—because they probably can do it. Many will go on working, begin new careers, or enter entrepreneurial ventures. Some will go back to school to learn something that their curiosity seeks to understand or their consciousness wants to explore. Others will join the leisure life and invest in their friendships. Still others will concentrate on travel and adventure, while some will retreat to private settings to enjoy nesting. People in this decade can decide several times how they want their lives to be; they are not stuck with their first choice. The sixties are a vital chapter in the adult journey—another opportunity to rearrange priorities.

A basic rumbling in the lives of many sixtysomethings is the wish to mentor—to guide, model, shape, transform, help, serve. They want to extend their talent to the next generation, to contribute what they can to the future. It is quite normal for mentoring to begin in the forties or fifties, but it often becomes the central theme in the lives of many sixtysomethings who want to invest in supporting, challenging, and providing vision to others. A mentor is someone who not only is competent at doing something but is competent at being human as well—a mensch, a complete person.[5] Some mentors have something to teach; they look for learners seeking their knowledge and wisdom. Some mentors are senior careerists who model the way for younger workers, conveying the mystique of high performance and joy. They may sponsor specific younger men and women to ensure they get whatever can be learned from being around experienced masters. Some mentors tell stories about how the world works to feed the consciousness of those who listen, to provide memories and dreams. Other mentors seek avenues such as the Peace Corps or the social-service agencies of religious groups where they can contribute some of their expertise to those who want it. Grandparenting is a mentoring role that is available and fulfilling to many sixtysomethings, as well as to many in their fifties and seventies. Older fathers such as Larry L. King are increasingly common, and their style of parenting is very likely to follow the mentoring process. Leadership is the form that mentoring most often takes—leadership at work, leadership in the community, leadership in leisure life. The urge to mentor may well have begun when sixtysomethings were in their forties or fifties, but now they view their lives as at their peak, and they want to make a difference in the world around them.

The Down Side

The sixties can be a decade of too many dreams that don't exactly come true. First, retirement is a major transition, particularly for those who have built their lives around their work. It requires more adjustment than those entering retirement typically anticipate—loss of role recognition, work friends, routines, salary, and work habits.

Second, although sixtysomethings are not typically feeling or acting like they are "old," they are often treated as if they were old. They experience increasing amounts of ageism, discrimination against people who are perceived as old. Ageism reflects a negative response to "old people," usually based upon a lack of facts and associating growing old with feebleness, disease, disability, uselessness, and death. Sixtysomethings begin to experience doors closing on their lives: work opportunities, social roles, and other mainstream connections. They begin to feel they are being shoved into the margins of the social flow. Part of this is their own ageism, expecting this to happen, and part of it is age discrimination by the society around them. Although their bodies are not changing dramatically, the mirror reflects the aging taking place, and only people with positive future vision can absorb the message of the mirror.

Third, people entering retirement often charge into a full agenda of leisure activities, travel schedules, and a busy lifestyle. But by age seventy or so, many sixtysomethings have completed their lists of busy projects and have become relatively passive with their lives, taking in more television, food and drink, and other behaviors that pull them away from engaged, forward-looking behaviors.

Fourth, there is often a slowdown in physical performance during the sixties, noted by increased short-windedness, a quicker tendency to fatigue, irregularity in sexual performance, and a slowing of mental recall. Although each of these can be countered through physical exercise, mental activity, supplements, and physician prescriptions, the bell still sounds an alarm that "the old gray mare ain't what she used to be."

Sixtysomethings know that the drum is beating. The bodies of sixtysomethings work a little less well. Problems with seeing, hearing, controlling the bladder, and losing short-term memory may develop during our sixties, unless we inherited superlative genes and immune systems and have kept our bodies in excellent condition. Everything slows down, and for every organ and function, the rule is: If you don't use it, you'll lose it! For the most part, sixtysomethings are active in leisure activities and attentive to new information on nutrition and health care. Still, aging progresses incrementally and inevitably, and the sixtysomething who can adapt effectively to whatever happens is most likely to have a positive feeling of life development.

A healthy sixty-year-old might live forty more years, and living *into the possibilities* of those years is the challenge rather than living in reminiscence. These forty years are largely uncharted by our society. We make a big fuss about retiring in our sixties but have little sense of our development as human beings during our seventies, eighties, and nineties. One way to approach the final forty years of your life is to make a forty-year plan. It is one of the longest time periods in most people's lives, and if you plan it out and stay engaged with the themes and functions of younger life, you will evolve and mature at the same time you get older and decline. View your elder years as moving again and again around the renewal cycle. It's not that different from when you were younger. Do not take yourself to the margins of a full life, or you may age quickly or miss the challenge of elderhood. The two features of positive aging during the elder years are (1) to tap the challenges of this life period through the mentor's role, generativity, friendships, legacy, leadership, leisure, and work, and (2) to manage the inevitable deficits of aging—coping and adaptation mechanisms.

When I'm working with clients who are struggling with retirement issues, I recommend protirement, throwing yourself ahead into a new blend of work and other activities. Protirement is a positive plan for a new chapter in life, emphasizing possible options and personal renewal. It might include a new career, but more often it has to do with an unfinished life agenda that successful people have put off long enough. Protirement is a great time for shifting gears into a new life chapter that enriches and fulfills. Why not?

Friends are very important to most sixtysomethings. Many men discover new ways to be friends with others and enjoy their relationships; other men, who never learned to sustain friendships, retreat from social contact, expecting their spouses to remain their social monitors. Women are more typically accustomed to having many kinds of friends, and these relationships often flourish during the retirement years: convenience friends, geographical friends, historical friends, leisure friends, special-interest friends, cross-generational friends, mentor friends.

From this point on, up to a hundred years of age or so, there is no informed guide to understand the optimal choices for human development. In the next thirty years, these scripts will be constructed, with role models and public relations campaigns, because (1) there will be a large number of adults who are seventy or older, (2) society will want and need these elders to be active participants in productive social roles, and (3) elders will constitute a major new "market" group. The gates are opening to new opportunities and callings for elders.

The seventies, eighties, and nineties are new frontiers. These decades have few guidelines. Currently, society as a whole "tolerates" the engagement of competent elders, in work, politics, and leadership roles, but lacks "inclusion" of these age groups in the culture as a whole. Although elders represent an enormous resource of human capital for the society, at the present time a majority of these three age groups are invisible Americans living in their own retirement subcultures. In the near future, society itself will find ways to include them (if they wish to be included!) in productive and challenging functions in the mainstream of the culture. Colleges and professional training centers will offer learning opportunities for elders to find meaningful ways both to continue to contribute their talents and to be financially rewarded. Corporations will discover important roles for older workers to perform, such as mentoring, consulting, and training.

Since the elderhood decades currently lack form and definition, they resemble a thirty-year flow more than three distinct segments. Elders themselves develop and age in many different ways and within different time frames. Some seventysomethings are indistinguishable from sixtysomethings in their energy, acuity, and overall competence. Others are crippled with arthritis or suffering from some other degenerative disease. There are, today, centenarians who are healthier and more active than some sixtysomethings who struggle with the aftermath of strokes, heart attacks, and other disabilities. Life is not fair. However, there are many ways elders can prepare for longevity. These ways are discussed in Chapter Ten.

The Seventies: Integrity, Celebration, and Contribution

Active seventysomethings have three missions: to live their integrity, to celebrate their fullness, and to contribute beyond personal needs. These three themes begin taking shape during midlife, and continue to grow in importance, but in the seventies or later, they are centrally compelling. Living your integrity has to do with core values. What matters most to you, and how can you contribute to it? Currently, this decade includes Dick Clark, Jules Feiffer, Liz Claiborne, Jimmy and Rosalynn Carter, Bob Newhart, Andre Previn, Ed Asner, and Arnold Palmer.

People in their seventies know that this is a decade in which many elders will die. The mortality charts stare them in the face. They want to be good stewards with their talents, wealth, and possessions—while they are still alive. It is natural for elders to be generative and concerned about the future, and benevolence, volunteering, and social leadership are ways they often choose to manifest their values.

The hearts of most (but not all) elders increase in compassion for others. Elders often appoint themselves as stewards of the future, out of a deep concern that those younger than them are consuming the earth recklessly and unconsciously. Even in primitive societies, elders represented a resource for perspective, conscience, and policies. A significant proportion of the volunteers of the nonprofit corporations of our country come from older people who want to make a personal difference in the social landscape. Here are four stellar examples who are currently in their seventies.

- Elisabeth Kübler-Ross, born 1926, is a psychiatrist and pioneering author on death and dying. "My understanding of the human being in this world is simply that we are all children of the same God. We are in the most literal sense of the word brothers and sisters. The ultimate lesson all of us have to learn is UNCONDITIONAL LOVE, which includes not only others but ourselves as well. . . . Generosity, compassion, understanding, and love will plant seeds of the same kind and will, in times of need, return to us. . . . We can change the world, but only by changing ourselves—by being aware of our actions in everyday life, by becoming masters of our spoken words, and being in control of our thoughts."[6]

• Elliot Richardson, born 1920, is former Attorney General, Secretary of Defense, Secretary of Health Education and Welfare, and Secretary of Commerce. "Our obligations, not just to refrain from harming others but to help those in need, should—and do—run most strongly to those who are closest to us and grow weaker in proportion to emotional distance. A widening series of concentric circles starts with the family and goes on to the neighborhood, the larger community, and the nation. At its farthest reach, whether of distance or time, the moral bond is most attenuated, but still there. It embraces the whole world. Every other human being, including those not yet born, has some claim on me—and I on them."[7]

• Edward O. Wilson, born 1929, is author, professor, and entomologist. "Every person constructs his life around a belief system. Mine has led me increasingly to environmentalism, which I try to promote by means of writing, by service on committees and boards devoted to environmental issues, and, as much as an introverted personality allows, by activism on behalf of particular threatened species and habitats. . . . The native fauna and flora of each country are part of its national heritage, as important as its art and history. I am convinced that they will come to be valued far more by our descendants than they are by us, and that we will someday be blessed for every species we save as we pass through the current bottleneck of environmental impoverishment."[8]

• Jimmy Carter, born 1924, is former President of the United States, Governor of Georgia, and founder of the Carter Center in Atlanta. "We should consider our life as expanding, not contracting, and modern technology can help to make this ambition easier to realize. . . . We not only have longer to live, but in some ways each year now equals several years in olden times. We are exposed to fifteen times as much knowledge as Aristotle was; many of us travel as much in a year as Marco Polo did in a lifetime. . . . None of us can afford to let ourselves become societal dependents, seduced into dormancy or inactivity by the same technology that offers expanded access to knowledge. As anyone who visits a nursing home could deduce, the average older person now watches television forty-three hours each week. There is a great world away from a soft chair and a flickering screen. There's no need for most of us to be so passive. We can still explore some of the more active pleasures of the 'good old days.' . . . What is good health? It's not just the absence of a physical illness or something like a long vacation without pain. I would say that good health, more than being able-bodied, involves self-regard, control over our own affairs, strong ties with other people, and a purpose in life. These things don't just evolve automatically, but have to be sought and maintained. . . . (Retirement age) is a time when we can, by default, live a passive and inactive life. But there is a wonderful, if riskier alternative. We can take advantage of our newfound freedom and embark on new and exciting adventures. We now have time to fulfill some earlier ambitions. If we make a mistake, there are plenty of fallbacks. We need not be too cautious. . . . Retirement years are a time to define, or redefine, a successful life, both in respect and for our remaining years—a definition likely to be quite different from that of our younger years. . . . You are old when regrets take the place of dreams."[9]

Robert E. Lee

Vast reaches lie out there to be touched, explored, interpreted, reinterpreted. The world has acquired more new information in the years of my lifetime than all mankind has assembled throughout the millennia since the first Ice Age. And we're only starting.

I'm not a young man. So? Should I disqualify myself because I have fewer hours to see and breathe and think than my daughter has? Or my son? My wife's father, well past eighty, was working in his backyard the week before his heart stopped. Pointing to a row of fruit trees he had just planted, he said: "In twenty years, these will yield more than we can possibly eat!" He was right. Those trees now give magnificent pears and peaches and apples. Though he's not here to savor the taste, others do. Or perhaps he's enjoying vicariously through the tingle of a latter-day tongue. Can anyone say that planting those trees wasn't a thousand times more useful than dwelling on his age and infirmities? Emerson says everything has its compensations. Salty-saccharine Lord Tennyson swears, "Though much is taken, much abides. It is not too late to seek a newer world!" . . . I caught a glimpse of myself in the mirror a few days ago. I don't do it often, because I don't believe what I see. I feel about twenty-two—and I think there's more truth in my feelings than in my reflections.[10]

Sarah McClendon

I never think of myself as an old lady, although I am seventy-eight years old. I keep looking at older people and thinking that they are "old," not I. . . . How does one face the realization that he or she is growing old? It does not require courage as much as it requires adjustments. Since I thrive on work, my greatest problem is coming to terms with the fact that I cannot work as much or as hard as I formerly did. . . . So I think we need to invent jobs for the elderly or suggest ways for them to work either for fun or profit—or both. The great need is to have society using their talents so that nothing of value goes to waste.

I would start such a program by registering all the elderly in the United States under the guidance of the government. In this way we would know where they lived, how to get in touch with them, what they could contribute, what their physical limitations were, and what they would like to do. Along with this we could have a register of needs for talented elderly volunteers. They could check with this register to seek jobs and opportunities for productive living in late life.

Given what I've said, I believe that it is tremendously important for the elderly to organize for political power and clout. We need to sign petitions to pass new laws, to improve existing legislation, and to check on current regulations in the health field. We need to keep watch on congressmen and other public officials and must make our desires known.

The elderly could and should serve as mentors and guides to oncoming generations. We should guide young people to think always about how to improve life in this country, both political and private. We must ask them to reflect upon the heartbreaking scene of the homeless elderly sleeping on grates near government buildings; we must alert them to the discrimination against women which is prevalent in our society and which hits so hard on elderly women; and we must make them aware of the fact that increasing homelessness results largely from the inflation of home mortgages, caused by governmental policy.

During my life I saw poverty on the farm near my home, the biggest oil boom in history with its attendant rags-to-riches stories, much progress in health care, and considerable improvements in communications. I have seen the nation go in cycles only to return, it seems, to the place where we started. What I perceive is the need for improvement, and this is what us [sic] talented oldsters must help bring about.[11]

Malcolm Muggeridge

The hardest thing of all to explain is that death's nearness in some mysterious way makes what is being left behind—I mean our earth itself, its shapes and smells and colors and creatures, all that one has known and loved and lived with—the more entrancing; as the end of a bright June day somehow encapsulates all the beauty of the daylight hours now drawing to a close; or as the last notes of a Beethoven symphony manage to convey the splendor of the whole piece. Checking out of St. Theresa's second-class hotel, as the revolving doors take one into the street outside one casts a backward look at the old place, overcome with affection for it, almost to the point of tears.

So, like a prisoner awaiting his release, like a schoolboy when the end of term is near, like a migrant bird ready to fly south, like a patient in hospital anxiously scanning the doctor's face to see whether a discharge may be expected, I long to be gone. Extricating myself from the flesh I have too long inhabited, hearing the key turn in the lock of Time so that the great doors of Eternity swing open, disengaging my tired mind from its interminable conundrums, and my tired ego from its wearisome insistencies. Such is the prospect of death.[12]

The Up Side

Although personal integrity is something that adults strive to obtain throughout their lives, it becomes the preoccupation of seventysomethings. At this point in the life cycle, integrity refers to the state of being complete and whole with all that is. Seventysomethings live in the space and time of "elderhood," which is the territory of sages—the wise ones whose experience and memories encompass more living than all who are younger. "One of the possible payoffs of living a long and varied life," states seventy-five-year-old Robert Tannenbaum, "is that one gains a certain amount of wisdom. I think that depends on how open the individual is to new inputs. It seems to me that the kind of perspective that one gets from having lived through a wide spectrum of experiences—prosperity and depression; war and peace; a full range of personal crises that not only involve one's self, but people close to one—provides a backdrop against which to understand deeply and meaningfully any given problem that confronts one in the here-and-now."[13] The value of wisdom in elderhood is captured in the words of one of America's leading developmentalists, Erik Erikson, in his book, *Identity: Youth and Crisis:*

> A meaningful old age, then . . . serves the need for that integrated heritage which gives indispensable perspective to the life cycle. Strength here takes the form of that detached yet active concern with life bounded by death, which we call *wisdom* in its many connotations from ripened "wits" to accumulated knowledge, mature judgment, and inclusive understanding. Not that each man can evolve wisdom for himself. For most, a living *tradition* provides the essence of it. But the end of the cycle also evokes "ultimate concerns" for what change may have to transcend the limitations of his identity and his often tragic or bitterly tragic comic engagement in his one and only life cycle within the sequence of generations . . . a civilization can be measured by the meaning which it gives to the full cycle of life, for such meaning, or the lack of it, cannot fail to reach into the beginnings of the next generation and push into the changes of others to meet ultimate questions with some clarity and strength.

> To whatever abyss ultimate concerns may lead individual men, man as a psychosocial creature will face, toward the end of his life, a new edition of an identity crisis which we may state in the words, "I am what survives me."[14]

In the film *Gigi,* Maurice Chevalier sang "I'm Glad I'm Not Young Anymore," suggesting that older people transcend many of the anxieties and social pressures of youth and the middle-aged. Elders, he sings, can be more free to say, to be, and to do *exactly* what they believe in. Seventysomethings who feel fulfilled by their past, active in their present, and reaching for new goals in their future are the mentors that younger adults want to learn from and emulate. Seventysomethings who extend middle age by being purposive and self-sufficient also extend a blessing to those younger than they who harbor mostly negative images of being old. Our society needs creative contact with its sages. To grow old well, young people need to learn from and revere those who have aged and developed wisely.

The Down Side

Much of our society still sees people in their elder years as old, worthless, dying creatures. Seventysomethings project characteristics of being old that we do not want to face in ourselves—stooped posture, wrinkled face, shuffling gait, wider-waisted body shape, slower response time, inability to hear and see, and fragile, age-spotted skin. Many of us do not want to look at people in this age group because we do not know how to see their sagacity behind their physical presence. Many elderly do not know how to see this in themselves.[15]

Ageism shapes the destinies of many elders (and even fifty- and sixty-year-olds) far more than their inner plans do. Who will employ them at salaries commensurate with their proven competencies? Will federal laws permit them to accept those salaries, or will they be denied Social Security and other available benefits? What leadership roles are available for them to mentor and model the way? Seventysomethings want to make their remaining days count for something. But when they search for ways to do so this, they often discover that the mainstream is not interested in what elders have to say, even though they carry, within their memories, several generations of human experience. An African motto says, "When an old person dies, a library burns down."

Elders are not so much afraid of death as they are afraid of becoming dependent on others and on life-support systems. They fear that they will lose their faculties before they die or lose their savings and become dependent on people and institutions about whom they have no choice. They mourn not merely their own passing but the future events they are sure to miss. They don't want to miss out on how the scenes of their lives, and particularly their family and friends, will evolve over the years.

These are the elders who often look back on their life experience and reflect on it, reaffirm it, and then look ahead, to offer advice and blessing for a world that they may never experience. They share one thing: being closer to the end of life than to the beginning or the middle. There is no one breed of elder in this stage of life. There is great diversity of conditions, lifestyles, and prospects. Some seventysomethings are thriving and continuing life as usual—no big deal. Others are in special places of creativity and contribution—something special is happening. Many are suffering from physical pain, degeneration, or diseases—the terminal phase is beginning; for others it is ending. Coping with physical problems and developing a point of view about death are preoccupations of this life period, but many elder adults who can sustain health, relationships, visions of the future, and financial resources continue to live full and active lives devoted to extending their beliefs and purpose into their eighties and nineties. What contributes to successful aging and living at this period of life? Mostly, it is sustaining enthusiasm instead of apathy and accepting personal responsibility for your own life instead of blaming yourself or others for problems; it is maintaining a close proximity between what you want and what you get, a positive self-concept, and a predominance of positive emotions over negative ones.

The Eighties: Legacy

Currently, our society has not defined the purpose and mission of people in their eighties and nineties. Gerontologists used to label them "late old age," but I predict that future scholars will find words to describe their élan vital and social importance. They are becoming a large cohort that is healthier than previous eightysomethings, and more inclined to staying engaged with social roles and functions. They reject the "waiting to die" agenda that society has long maintained for them. During the first third of the twenty-first century, more and more eightysomethings will become commonplace in the workplace, elected offices, and community leadership positions. Even though as many or more eightysomethings struggle with maintaining independent living, and others suffer major setbacks to their health, a new breed is emerging in increasing numbers. "During the past twenty-five years the number of people over the age of eighty-five grew almost six times more rapidly than the overall population. The fastest-growing group of all, however, is those over a hundred; in 1956 there were 2,500 centenarians, 25,000 in 1986, and in 2000 there will be 268,000!"[16]

I spoke to about five hundred eighty-year-olds this year, who had assembled for inspiration, free medical examinations, and a day of social contact with one another. Most of these people had been getting together at this annual event for years; this is an important event for them. Many came as couples, others alone or in groups. The room contained quite a few wheelchairs, hearing devices, and medical equipment. I talked for a half-hour on "How to Live to Be One Hundred," after which I responded to questions. The talk promoted ways to sustain hope, manage stress, stay active with mind and body, keep learning, invest in family/friends, maintain a broad portfolio of skills and activities, and keep up with the rapidly increasing findings of longevity research.

The room felt something like a twentysomething meeting in the late '60s—a social movement was taking place. Although these people did not all have equal abilities to hear, speak, or take action, they shared common concerns: to have a voice in how they lived, to remain active, to care for one another, to interact with the larger community, and to prepare as a group for exerting influence in the next elections.

If you had been there, you might have asked me "How can these people get around and stay as spirited as they seem to be?" The answer was simple: although the bodies of many of these eightysomethings were "impaired" in some way, they themselves were amazingly active, enthusiastic, and supportive of one another. People with physical difficulties are often able to make good use of their time and efforts. Sometimes younger people think that chronic physical ailments mean the end of life, but most often they mean using what's working well a little differently. I felt that I was the one who benefited most from being at their rally. I will never again assume that people in their eighties are doing little more than getting ready to die, even if their bodies suggest to an untrained eye that there is no way to go but down.

Three months after that meeting of eightysomethings, my own mother, at eighty-five, experienced a stroke, followed by another, leaving her unconscious for weeks. She finally regained consciousness, temporarily, before she died. Her terminal phase, which was painful to watch, took less than three months. And while more and more adults are living into their nineties and beyond, a great many conclude their lives in their eighties.

Over the years, I have watched hundreds of people successfully move through their eighties and into their nineties. They are almost always as amazed as the people around them. They often say "Doesn't feel any different than any other time in my life," or "I've been granted more time to live for a purpose, and I'm going to follow that purpose." The American culture tends to think of people this old as burdens to the society. Contrary to general belief, most of the elderly are relatively self-sufficient. Only 5 percent live in nursing homes (a number that is decreasing), while just 15 percent receive any financial help from their families.

The truth is that while some eightysomethings require social support and health services, our society has never tapped elders as "human capital" for adding value to the society as a whole. During the years ahead, eightysomethings will themselves generate social roles that will benefit the larger society and provide them with inner meaning and purpose. It will happen before 2030. They will develop stories of successful elders as part of the American culture—life stories of normal people who were extraordinarily alive in their elder years. Some examples of such elders follow:

- William Barrett, born 1913, was associate editor of *The Partisan Review* for many years. He is an author and former professor of philosophy at New York University. "I was raised as a Catholic. But very early on—about the time of my confirmation, somewhere around twelve—I had become a precocious doubter, though I kept the doubts from my family. . . . I have become aware more and more over the years that I personally cannot be godless. . . . So I have returned to the Church. . . . I do not know why I am going to church. Every now and then, however, I seem to catch a glimmer of what one part of that goal might be: to awaken to joy in the sheer fact, the wondrous miracle, of life itself. I am not there yet, I have to keep going on."[17]

- Madeleine L'Engle, born 1918, is a prolific author of children's stories and a devoted mother and grandmother. "I believe in an open universe, still being created, and that this is a purpose-ful, not an accidental universe. . . . The writing of fiction is about connections, connections between people who break the connec-tions, fragment themselves and others, and (it is hoped) remake connections. I look at what is happening on our planet, and I see the breaking of connections, nation setting itself against nation, race against race, religion against religion, but I still feel hope that at least on an individual basis connections can be remade, must be remade if we are to survive as a planet."[18]

• Hugh Downs, born 1921, is a well-known television person-ality and has written books, assembled his own telescope, com-posed an orchestral suite, sailed a ketch across the Pacific Ocean, and chaired the U.S. Committee for UNICEF. "I believe that the mind is greater than its scaffolding of reason. The realm of feel-ing, ranging from esthetics to genuine caring for others, tran-scends reason, even though reason is an indispensable tool to be recruited in the service of important life issues. . . . If I see that I have done no harm and that some positive results have come about because I was given a role here, I will be content."[19]

• Steve Allen, born 1921, is comedian, musician, and author. "I believe in mystery, not in any dark-shadows-and-incense way, but as a matter of fact. The world seems to me absolutely based on mys-tery. . . . My own belief in God, then, is just that—a matter of belief, not of knowledge. . . . I can, nevertheless, refer to a few instances when I have practiced what I preached. One was the creation of the twenty-four programs of the Meeting of Minds television series, which a critic has called the ultimate TV talk show, whose guests were such as Thomas Aquinas, St. Augustine, Martin Luther, Socrates, Plato, Aristotle, Francis Bacon, Adam Smith, Mohandas Gandhi, Susan B. Anthony, Florence Nightingale, and Thomas Jef-ferson. Such individuals' ideas and labors have greatly influenced our world. I thought that by expressing their views in conversa-tional form I could provide an example of the sort of rational and informed dialogue that is in lamentably short supply in the mod-ern world, except among scholars. Even though these visitors from the past were misguided in many of their views—as in the cases of Karl Marx, Machiavelli, the Marquis de Sade, or Attila the Hun—I felt it was necessary to become familiar with their teachings simply because they are still so influential in the world. . . . I recommend that from an early point our schools, churches, and other social institutions provide instruction on personal human relationships. They ought to teach how to love, as well as how to reason. Just as there are millions who do not think very well, so there are millions who do not love well. They may well constitute a majority. . . . Love's a magic force that knows no laws, a well without a bottom, a purse that's never empty. Use your own cliché just so you get the point. And one point more remains to make: that like the other faculties, the physical, the musical, the social and the rest, love swells in action. Will sets it aflame; it grows in height, direction, depth, and kind. It is the wise and wholly just investment."[20]

The Up Side

Many eightysomethings are not much different from how they were in their seventies. They remain active, healthy, involved, and contributive. They enjoy good social occasions and celebrations. They are often willing to do menial or manual work and don't have to be rewarded. Serving others has its own reward. Elders are a valuable social resource for community development and maintenance, and you will find many of them in leadership roles throughout the society. Seventysomethings and eightysomethings continue to enjoy leisure activities, travel, and sports. The exercise room at my tennis club in Santa Barbara has more people—on most days— in their seventies and eighties than any other age. The good news is that increasing numbers of men and women in their eighties are resilient, active, and enjoying life. They may be aging (aren't we all?), but they aren't behaving "old." Some are "late bloomers" with new careers, hobbies, and adventures.

The Down Side

In a recent random survey I conducted with eighty-year-olds in various locations, they cited these complaints in this order: First, too many people and social groups treat them as if they were fragile, sick, or about to die. On too many occasions, they do not feel welcomed or encouraged to be themselves, much less invited to lead. Second, they feel the workplace is closed to them. People in their eighties believe that if they have the "competencies" required for a work position, they deserve to be considered for the job. Because of social discrimination, a considerable number of elders become entrepreneurs, often working out of their homes. Third, elders report that they get discouraged by the number of infirmed and dying people their age. Fourth, they experience physical problems: trouble hearing, seeing, maintaining balance; memory lapses, muscle reduction, decreased sexual activity; broken bones, operations. The list goes on. Fifth, they feel the need for more social contact. Eightysomethings often feel themselves distancing from others, even when they seek contact and sharing. They need to feel genuinely appreciated, without being patronized.

It is important to remember that from an early point on elders experience a wide spectrum of aging patterns. Some experience minor or serious impairments in their fifties or sixties, while others in their nineties have little to complain about. Having stated this, I want to reiterate that "old is not a progressive disease," so you shouldn't expect eighty-year-olds to be worse off than seventy-year-olds. Expect elders to be a lot alike and a lot different.

A major theme of this book is to understand that every age has tradeoffs based upon assets and deficits. Most eightysomethings are eager to transcend themselves through efforts that compose a "legacy," knowing full well that their bodies are slowly betraying them and that the limited time they have left calls for timely actions. Their legacy may be their grandchildren, their personal volunteering, or financial contributions to causes they believe in. They often experience a spiritual freedom to speak and act with greater clarity than they have ever had. As they experience the passing of peers, they recommit to their own determination to celebrate life and to add value to the lives of others.

The Nineties and Beyond: Summing It Up

The nineties is a period that few people expect to experience. Yet more and more elders are moving into it. The same is true for centenarians—those over a hundred. The numbers of older seniors are rapidly expanding. Few of us can imagine it as a decade of developmental challenges, fulfillment, and social contributions. But to be fair, we have to challenge our assumptions and negative expectations about these age groups, and learn how to promote purposive living, healthy relationships, and inclusion in the social life of the broader society.

With increased awareness of sound eating practices, coupled with active exercise, more elders are sustaining healthier lifestyles and living beyond their expectations. It is no longer a rare "miracle" to meet someone who is ninety, and it is often difficult to know that the person is in his or her nineties. Of course, while the increase in healthy elders in this age group is astounding, it is also true that because the cohorts of older elders is steadily increasing, the number of adults needing special medical or home care, or are dying, is also increasing.

My wife has a grandmother who turned one hundred last year. Grandma is amazingly healthy, active, and forward looking. She has lived for about fifteen years in subsidized housing units for the elderly in her small, midwestern city. She has her own apartment, where she cooks her own food, cares for others, and maintains an active life in the community, where she is a weekly volunteer. Although her husband died over fifty years ago, she did not remarry. In fact, she likes living alone. She says she gets plenty of social contact in the housing units. She rises early, "works" most of the day, has a close network of friends, and few physical complaints. On Sundays she is active in her church and does not indulge in self-pity or worry about the future. We find her absolutely amazing, and an example to us all. According to the statistics, there are, today, about 268,000 Americans like her—mostly mobile and engaged, over the age of one hundred. That's a significant number of people on the forefront of the adult revolution, inventing new scripts with roles and senarios that connect them meaningfully to family, friends, work, and community.

Death and Dying

Dying is part of living. It is, for most of us, a long process throughout the life cycle. Every life transition is a "little death," a letting go of part of life that will no longer be the same. When you have managed many transitions throughout your life, you have learned to some extent to trust the unknown, to find peace and hope through resignation, and to search for new paths in darkness. Metaphorically, we experience "dying" in many parts of our lives, and have a sense of what our final dying will be about.

Death, however, is a turning point that is absolute. It is not merely a process like dying, but also a black and white event. The finality of death introduces the fear of nonbeing, the possibility that our very identity will be eliminated. During the "dying" process we either make our peace with our final good-bye, or we refuse to do so. Mature people normally seek a conscious dying, in which they can work through the process of letting go, both internally and with those they love.[21]

The crisis of death is that the body, which until the moment of death has been the chief vehicle of life expression, must cease functioning. It no longer can be a vehicle for the self who dwells within it, wondering what will become of it when the body ceases to function. There is no sure answer to this. But older adults have seen the face of death in every life transition they have traversed. They have lived with the unknown, the sense of helplessness, the futility of loneliness, the lack of a future. And each time, they arrived at new strength, fresh vision, and hope. Perhaps our transition experiences throughout our lives are rehearsals for our dying—our greatest resources for living with our ultimate unknown, over which we have no control.

Chapter Ten

Getting from Here to There
Six Principles of Developmental Change

And one man in his time plays many parts,
His acts being seven ages. At first the infant,
Mewling and puking in the nurse's arms.
Then the whining schoolboy, with his satchel
And shining morning face, creeping like snail
Unwillingly to school. And then the lover,
Sighing like furnace, with a woeful ballad
Made to his mistress' eyebrow. Then a soldier,
Full of strange oaths and bearded like the bard,
Jealous in honor, sudden and quick in quarrel,
Seeking the bubble reputation
Even in the cannon's mouth. And then the justice,
In fair round belly with good capon lined,
With eyes severe and beard of formal cut,
Full of wise saws and modern instances,
And so he plays his part. The sixth age shifts
Into the lean and slippered Pantaloon
With spectacles on nose and pouch on side,
His youthful hose, well saved, a world too wide
For his shrunk shank, and his big manly voice,
Turning around toward childish treble, pipes
And whistles in his sound. Last scene of all
That ends this strange eventful history,
Is second childishness and mere oblivion,
Sans teeth, sans eyes, sans taste, sans everything.
WILLIAM SHAKESPEARE, *AS YOU LIKE IT*, 2.7

There are at least six principles that adults adopt—unconsciously or consciously, in varying combinations and proportions—to weave a story line throughout their lives and thereby make sense out of their life cycle. These principles guide our thinking as we shift our commitments during the life course. We draw on these principles to try to make sense out of our continuous and discontinuous biological, psychological, and sociological conditions—how our inner and outer lives fit together meaningfully, even as our bodies, minds, and settings keep changing. All six principles contain some information combined with some rationalization.

1. Internal Gyroscope

The most powerful principle that guides our thoughts and feelings throughout the adult years comes from the decisions made as a child about how the world works. As adults, we often "see" the world through mental assumptions and emotional responses formed very early and modified continuously throughout the life cycle. We proceed through life with an internal gyroscope in our heads, monitoring our lives. "Is the world safe and available to me or dangerous and unavailable? Am I supposed to live by strict rules or figure things out as I grow up? Do I trust myself and others? Am I comfortable with my feelings? When things go wrong, what do I do and say? What is my favorite 'bad' feeling?" When we are young, the gyroscope is programmed by our parents and society; when we are fully adult, we learn to program our own gyroscope. To what degree is your childhood consciousness directing your adult behaviors, and what can you do about it?

According to such authorities as Sigmund Freud, Carl Jung, and Donald Winnicott, adults are driven by primitive thought processes serving their basic impulses. When you are young or not yet grown up, the internal gyroscope functions as if a committee held meetings in your head fairly frequently to decide what you will do and think and feel. This committee, made up of parents, siblings, and early mentors, forms a long-lasting internal dialogue that decides what you should and shouldn't do, think, and feel— and assigns blame when you go astray. It is primarily concerned with keeping your life within the boundaries of what worked, in terms of emotional responses, thoughts, and decisions, in the early years. The early thought patterns of a child are more mythological than logical and lack information about how the adult world works. You understand your life course through the various voices of persons who have influenced your life. Much of the time, the primitive internal gyroscope is unconscious, but as you mature, you are more and more aware of it. As you become familiar with these voices, which at first are parents' voices and later those of teachers, mentors, and peers, you become an active participant in the dialogue. Unless you learn to reprogram it, the committee in your head will be the central monitor of personal development until your death.

When you decide to program your own life, you assume control of your gyroscope to direct your own life to the best of your ability. More than a conscience, your internal gyroscope monitors your thoughts; it oversees your feelings and influences your decision making. It is a powerful shaper of how you proceed from twentysomething through seventysomething—and beyond. Adults have the capacity to replace much of their early programming with more accurate and caring information and attitudes. The mythic structure is always there, but self-conscious adults can dominate the gyroscope's functions. Learning from your own life transitions is the most natural way to reshape your mythic consciousness and reframe it around the positive features of your real self. Psychotherapy is one approach for increasing adult consciousness and power over the mental and emotional distortions of the childhood years. Group psychotherapy is often very effective at accelerating individual work. Any life experience that gets you to reflect on your freely flowing thoughts and feelings provides a basis for self-transcendence and liberation from the committee in your head so that you can direct your own life course through internal dialogue that honors your values, current information, and future goals.[1]

2. Future Blindness

Another unconscious principle is the inability to imagine how we will think, feel, and choose to live in the future. Particularly when we are young, we project our youthful assumptions, believing that we have sufficient knowledge and power to make the future happen. We believe that our current perspective will suffice to guide us throughout our years; we haven't yet learned that our life orientation changes every decade or so. We have great difficulty antic-ipating future consequences and necessary changes. So we move ahead while looking backward. Who can imagine how they will change their perspective on life as they age and gain experience? Who can anticipate the impact on their life that natural and social catastrophes will impose? How can people in their twenties have a positive picture of being in their fifties? They are most likely to believe that when they get to be fifty, they'll be very different from the fifty-year-olds of today. They'll defy aging, statistics, evidence, and all the rest—that is future blindness. How can a fifty-year-old have a realistic picture of being seventy? At fifty, most people aren't prepared to see that much value in seventy. And today, the life cycle is extending itself for many adults into their eighties, nineties, and beyond one hundred. How can we prepare for those ages with informed expectations?

Future blindness serves positive as well as negative functions. It provides a justification for heroic acts that later in life we would probably not undertake with the same degree of certitude and abandon—decisions such as choosing a mate, marrying young, hav-ing children, not having children, choosing a career at age twenty-one, changing careers at thirty-seven, moving from New York to San Francisco, having an affair, traveling around the world alone, or choosing to divorce. It makes us willing to forgo consequences for intentionality and action and to indulge in risk taking and bold decisions. It helps people "just do it," "wing it," and "get on with life." But even at its best, future blindness is a form of positive denial about the future. It keeps people motivated to break out of the way they were but without a rational outline of future options and their likely consequences. It is more of an adolescent princi-ple than an adult one, yet it is often useful to young and middles-cent adults.

3. Generation Identity

Your identification with those who were born at the same time you were and grew up in the same world may contain residual values that shape the continuities you seek in your adult experience. Cohorts share the same marker events in their memories—the Depression, World War II, the postwar boom, the death of the

Kennedys and Martin Luther King, Vietnam, Richard Nixon, Middle East conflicts, the break-up of the Soviet Union, the emergence of China, the Clinton presidency, and the booming U.S. economy in the 1990s. People born in the same decade often share common cultural reference points—from political events to popular music to favorite movie stars to economic conditions to messages about how life really works. Critical historical events that occur during your childhood may shape your values and those of your peers throughout the life cycle (see Table 3).

Those who were young during the Depression of the 1930s see the world as having limited goods, so they tend to live like survivors. They also are strong believers that the American way is the best way and that we can all work together through any hardship to help our country fulfill its mission. Those of the post–World War II generation find the world to be full of abundance; expansion and growth are normal expectations of this generation of optimism, rock music, parties, and good times. This postwar generation has been called the "baby boomers" because of its enormous size—seventy-five million people, the largest single generation America has ever experienced. Its first splash as a trend-setting wave came in the 1960s with its music, lifestyle changes, and activism. This was the age of marches, causes, and very high expectations. By 1970, the American experience of the Vietnam War, along with rising inflation and international conflicts, led this generation toward security, money, and conventional happiness.

Now in midlife, the members of this generation are leading the wave of adult redefinition with their own historical values. Growing up with the new medium of television as their window to life, they believed that they were connected to the world as their land of opportunity. In their teens and twenties, they may have championed free love, drugs, and freedom. Many were involved in social causes. Most are familiar with psychotherapy, group incentives, and spirituality. But as they move up the career ladders, they discover fewer and fewer openings and challenges. So they look to other areas for accomplishment—to lifestyle issues, family life, entrepreneurial projects, social leadership, and leisure pursuits. All this is reinforced by the gradual blurring of gender roles, as women move into challenging careers and men share in parenting and household roles.

	1900–1929	1930–1959	1960–1980	1980–2005
Communications	Face-to-face, newspaper, radio, phonograph	Movies, telephone, radio, newspaper, hi-fi	Television, movies, radio, newspapers, stereos, cassette tapes	Computers, Internet, cell phones, beepers, faxes, videos, TV, newspapers, radio, stereos, cassette tapes, CDs, movies
Marker events	World War I, Depression	Depression, World War II, H-bomb, postwar boom	Social upheavals, deaths of JFK, RFK & MLK, Vietnam, the pill, lifestyle	Reagan, deficit, ongoing global crises, Persian Gulf war
Culture	Good guys, bad guys, pro-American	Nationalistic, work-oriented, values, conservative, naive	More leisure, travel, human potential, sex, drugs, divorce	Environmental disasters, more rich, more poor, fewer middle-class, recession, terrorism
Heroes	Sergeant York, Woodrow Wilson	FDR, John Wayne	Neil Armstrong, MLK, JFK	Anti-heroes, Mother Teresa, Princess Diana, celebrities
Mood	Idealistic, optimistic	Optimistic, realistic	Optimistic, anti-authorities, and challenged	Less optimistic, more cynical, and overwhelmed
Worst disease	Tuberculosis	Polio	Herpes, cancer	AIDS, cancer
Generation labels	Flappers, new wealthy	Survivors, boomers	Activists, New Age, Yippies, Yuppies	Punks, DINKS, busters, GenExers
Favorite music and dance	Charleston, tango	Jazz, big bands, fox trot, Bing Crosby, Kate Smith	Beatles, rock, twist, disco, Paul Simon, Elton John, Judy Collins	Madonna, Prince, heavy metal, rap music

As they move into midlife, they ask, "What are our best options for making life soar as we move through our forties and fifties?" "How can we blend parenting and social concerns to make our environment better?" "What do we need to know about the years ahead of us?" While they are fascinated with materialism and money, they are also moved by spirituality and continual transformation. They are the first generation to view old age in a positive way, as they experience the newly old as active, healthy, and affluent. They experiment with new options and believe that they can find answers to the problems they encounter.[2] The big question is whether the boomers will follow their generational values into their midlife and elderhood years. Will they use their enormous influence to provide new leadership for social renewal?

People who came of age in the 1970s behave differently from the boomers—they are more conservative and worried that the world is running out of steam. Their central concerns are jobs, security, money, and survival issues such as safe sex. Whereas earlier cohorts seemed sure of some kind of future and "progress," this is the first American generation in the twentieth century to be unsure that the land of opportunity exists for them. What they see is a downhill slide into a world in which they won't be able to afford a house or to surpass their parents. This generation has begun to play a tune that subsequent young adults are likely to enlarge upon: orphans of the society, born too late to enjoy the benefits, and destined to struggle throughout their lives with declining natural and social resources, with ever-changing careers, runaway inflation, and a nation without leaders.[3]

Generation identity has considerable impact on how we see our lives and world, which leads to how we age and develop as human beings. To a considerable degree, every generation reinvents the meanings given to *aging* and *development*. Even so, as the early marker events wash away with time, their ability to provide continuity to our lives lessens. With the speed of complex change, generations are getting shorter, and with the need to keep abreast of new technology and other developments, generation identity may weaken and the emerging identification come to be with change itself.

A distinct disadvantage of generation identity is that rigid adherence to the values of the past makes adaptation to change difficult. Generational values are merely marker events, part of your long-term memory bank. Although they are predictably influential, every transition that you experience will transform much of your memory bank into current beliefs and purpose. In fact, we need to move beyond generational identification as we mature beyond age fifty, when we begin to identify with all humanity.

4. Trade-Offs

One principle of trade-offs functions throughout the life cycle: trade-offs are exchanges. Something old that is outmoded or dysfunctional is exchanged for something new that works better. As we age or watch our social conditions change, some aspects of our lives seem to get better while others get worse. Our bodies slow down, so we switch from playing baseball to managing the team, or from running the mile to playing chess. Our earning power may decrease, so we budget more carefully. Our kids leave home, so we develop new friends and projects. We lose our total devotion to our jobs, but we gain balanced lives with more leisure. We trade off a negative for a positive and feel good about the process. Instead of merely getting older, we get older and smarter.

Trade-offs are exchanges between minuses and pluses, decrements and increments, losses and gains. You trade off one attitude, value, commitment, attachment for some other, preferred one. Perhaps you find you've declined as a basketball player, but as a coach you are experienced and competent. Or maybe your love of work shifts from aggressive achievement to enjoying the friendships in the worker setting. If you experience aging as gradual but inevitable physical decline and development as the evolution of a profoundly deepening and empowering consciousness, you will justify the loss by accepting a gain. Not a bad deal.

Other trade-offs have to do with changing external opportunities and threats. A friend of mine who smashed her knee in a skiing accident a few years ago has never walked without crutches or canes since. She could have spent the rest of her life feeling sorry for herself, but instead she seized the moment to begin a career at home as an author, and she has produced three novels and a blazing trail—on her typewriter.

There is no list of right and wrong trade-offs for adult life. Each person must decide what to diminish and what to add. Habits?

Some adults make a conscious decision to eliminate booze from their lives and to take up nutritious food and sensible exercise instead. Relationships? Some midlifers choose to be single: they trade off one kind of relationship for another, which leads to other trade-offs later in life. Some couples choose not to have children in order to do other things with their lives. That is a trade-off; you gain experience in one direction and lose it in another. Careers? Career people in midlife often struggle with the decision of whether to stay on in their corporate positions or become entrepreneurs on their own. Retirement? Many seventy-year-olds feel fairly complete with their lives, while others are beginning new business ventures or political careers. What is important in a trade-off is to know on the one hand whether it reduces a concern you've been having and, on the other hand, whether it adds meaning to your life.

Trade-offs encourage choices that serve both our developmental needs and our aging realities. They also promote adaptation to change, a basic principle for successful adult development. A disadvantage of trade-offs is that they tend to be short-term adjustments, not long-term principles. They are not sufficient in themselves to construct a long-term plan or a life structure. They are more reactive than proactive.[4]

5. Events Beyond Your Control

The principle of events beyond your control is an external principle for understanding the changes in our lives. Sometimes it is described as being in the right place at the right time or the wrong place at the wrong time. Some doors get opened or closed for us. Some doors we never get to. We experience many social and natural events, such as earthquakes, fires, accidents, wars, diseases, stress, addictions, loss of job, an inheritance, divorce, or we meet an interesting person on an airplane. The more unstable our society becomes, the more influence this principle will have in our lives.

The timing of events triggers an immediate altering of our assumed stability, usually followed by changes that can have long-lasting consequences. We alter our plans and our life course. Whenever any internal or external factor upsets business as usual in a person's life, a transition of some sort is likely to ensue, leading to new assumptions, coping strategies, value shifts, and next steps. Life proceeds differently. When a spouse dies, his or her mate is often thrown into a profound identity crisis compounded by grief. It is not unusual for the reconstruction of life to take several years.

Intruding events can also be positive, such as winning the lottery, but even then they shake up our lives in ways that we can't anticipate. With every sudden unbalancing of your life, you tend to initiate changes that you are not trained for or ready to manage. When I had polio as a child, I thought that I was in the wrong place at the wrong time. The pain and paralysis were overwhelming, and there was no real medical treatment available. But after more than a year in a hospital and recuperation setting, which served as a "transition environment" away from my family of origin where I could learn new ways to think and to plan my life, I emerged with profound personal dreams and determination to follow them, which I did. Looking backward from today's vantage point, I see my experience with polio as a major turning point in my life, motivating me to design my own future at an early age.[5]

The advantage of this principle is that it promotes an understanding of adult life as a complex interaction of factors, many of which can't be controlled or even anticipated. This principle requires an appreciation of human systems, environments, forces, and nations. It also helps us to deal with death, a predictable event that often arrives as a giant surprise. Although we are not in charge of a great many of the critical events that affect our lives, we are responsible for the decisions we make in light of those events.[6]

6. Visioning

Visioning the future is another principle for making sense out of the life cycle—to imagine a desirable future releases your energy and commitment to work toward your goals. Development, as opposed to aging, occurs when you are goal-oriented and living into a future that you believe in and can make happen. Without a positive sense of a livable future, you will either idealize your past and back into your future or resign yourself to decline and darkness.

With the speed at which our lives are affected by change today, the past is less reliable than it used to be as a resource for models and information. We need models that work well in a world of change, discontinuity, and chaos. Twenty-first-century living will be on a fast-moving wave linking the present to the future. We must all be futurists, creating imaginative scenarios and sorting out options. With the principle of visioning we are led to invent the future by imagining, planning, designing, and enacting it. We anticipate possibilities and then we rehearse the scenarios and make them happen. We create purpose and let our deep human values guide our lives.

Visioning takes visioners. Behind every dream there is a dreamer. Visions do not pop out of nowhere; they burst out of the minds of men and women who have profound memories and understand the critical issues of today. Visioning requires a holy alliance among the three tenses of human time: past, present, and future.

Past

The present can't exist by itself; it is the product of a collective memory, social evolution, and a set of beliefs about the world. When you become an adult, you are a collective memory. Your mind has been programmed by those around you, by the past experience of others. You can transcend the past, but you can never repudiate it, nor can you ever afford to stop learning from it. The past is your infinite memory or database—a resource for everything that evolves from you. If you are ever around someone who has lost his or her memory, you will discover that without a memory, there is also an absence of a living present and a hopeful future. Memory is a necessary repository for your being human. Healthy, wise adults seek to understand their past and how it informs the present, for better and for worse.

From midlife on, many adults lose their dreams and lock themselves into their memories. As they see it, their best days are behind them. Their lives have peaked, so they reminisce, reflect, and view their current lives as diminished extensions of their memories. They can't imagine heroic possibilities as they grow old. Their stories of the past will evolve from historical vignettes to heroic and magical tales embellished by the desire for lasting self-importance. People who plan their future on the basis of their past are able to extend their lives, but only as shadows of who they were. They keep repeating the old ways of thinking and doing, and feeling more foreign in a world of rapid change. They have reduced themselves to a repetition compulsion. But adults who maintain a vision of their future along with their valued memories never peak, because they keep finding worthy new adventures when old ones end. Some features of our lives rise and fall, but our sense of purpose continuously finds importance and linkages in each of the time frames. Rooted in the past, the visioner has a history and a memory but is preparing for the future.

Present

Life is lived in the present, the here and now of our space and time. The present is the moment of consciousness, your present awareness, based on your immediate sensations, your reflective capacities, and your ability to make decisions. It is in the present that you may feel that time drags and that you have time on your hands; others may sigh because there isn't enough time to do everything they want to do. The present is where the future and past meet, as tomorrows become yesterdays. Those who confine their lives to their memories or their expectations choose to reject the joy and completeness they already have, in the here and now. It is in the present that we evaluate the past and construct the future—in our minds. The visioner is mindful of the past but anchored in the present—awake, alert, and informed.

Future

The future is a projection of the present and the past, a mental activity that anticipates desired events and occasions. The imagination that yearns and hopes for new meaning and joy is inevitably anchored in who you are and have been. The future is also the emergence of novelty. It is hope, promise, and new possibilities. It is not mere repetition of the past and not mere projection of the present. When we imagine the future, we project our notions of past and present into the not-yet, but we add new features. We build into our visions our human yearnings for completeness and fulfillment. We dream of a future that, for us, at this time in our lives, can be better than our past has been. Human dreams have a transcendent quality, and that is why all who dream have a positive sense of a future. They trust the total time process, not merely the present moment. Visioning a future is an act of creativity, invention, and ecstasy. Without a future vision, we shut ourselves down and begin to die, individually and collectively. Those who do vision generate the energy and motivation to construct plans for making the future happen in the present—the center of all human time—and celebrate the awe and wonder of it all.[7]

As our lives are always in motion between birth and death, our minds are forever trying to make sense out of the journey. Each person's life cycle is a long flow of time and space in which the principles reviewed in this chapter—along with others—are used to understand life's continuities and changes. Most of us use several of these principles as we seek to map out our future and understand our past. They all have advantages and disadvantages, and none is sufficient for understanding or empowering the human venture. Just as a goldfish cannot understand the significance of the bowl of water that contains its existence, we cannot get a final perspective on our life cycle. We see through a glass darkly. We all have a very brief slice of time to be on earth. Our lives are wrapped in limiting cognitive structures through which we maintain distorted visions of who we are and who we might become. Such is the human condition. We are mortals not gods. Yet the principles that we choose to explain our lives are absolutely crucial to our destiny, for they shape our thoughts, feelings, and actions. They link us to the world as we see it and define our boundaries. They express our beliefs and define our hopes. They are all we have to measure our lives. Through them we have an opportunity to honor our past, celebrate our present, and design our future. The next section discusses preparing for that future.

Longevity

Longevity means to be as well and active as you can, for as long as you can. (Read David Mahoney and Richard Restak, 1998, and John W. Rowe and Robert L. Kahn, 1998.) Longevity means to stay engaged with life, to take responsibility for designing the future you want, to stay vitally connected to friends and loved ones and to the society at large. The concept of longevity is something to be practiced during young and middle adulthood, so your body and mind are prepared for the long haul. Here are some of the key ideas:

- *The sooner you commit to living to one hundred, the sooner you commit to having a vision and a plan for the rest of your life.* Not everyone who aims at one hundred will get there, but more and more are, and the statistics point toward a marked increase in the numbers of centenarians during the next twenty years. Assume the odds are in your favor. Challenge all your stereotyped ideas about aging. Plan to get older and better, even as your body may get worse in many ways. Take a long view of your life, and pace yourself daily and weekly with shorter views. Live into a future vision, and your brain (frontal lobes) will actually be stimulated to help you reach your vision through daily actions. Take executive control of yourself and your journey.

- *There is a difference between aging and getting old.* Aging is finding ways to manage your life changes so you can be optimally alive, active, and engaged. Healthy aging includes a positive attitude toward life, good stress-coping skills, health-promoting behaviors, human skills to deal with everyday problems of living, and the good fortune to avoid infectious diseases and serious injuries. On the one hand, centenarians score high on optimism; they are rarely depressed. Getting old, on the other hand, means taking on the characteristics that our society expects old people to have, losing interest in life, accepting the notion that it's too late to change, believing that life doesn't matter anymore, failing to set goals and commitments, losing a sense of surprise, and giving in to passivity and boredom. Aging is not a spectator sport; step out of the stands and do something now to increase your chances for a long life and do your part to change our national attitudes toward aging. None of us can stop aging, but we don't have to grow old.

- *Don't blame your genes; invest in your best choices.* Heredity accounts for only one-fourth of the variation in human life spans. Gerontologists have found that nutrition, exercise, and social relationships are more important than genetic structures.

- *Keep up, mentally, with your fields of expertise, with new knowledge and skills, with areas of emerging interest.* If you neglect your talents and skills that have been essential to your life, they begin to wane, and then you begin to wane. If you are interested in new skills rather than the ones you've been performing, that will work fine. Learning is a central feature of creative aging. Practice keeping all of your neurons active in the networks you wish to maintain. Resilience will be sustained best if you make small, consistently applied efforts at sustaining your competence and skills. Your brain is the most important organ to invest in for positive aging. Tweak the high-performing parts of your brain through reading and reflecting, and through discussions with others of all ages. Relax about normal slips and slowings of brain functions as you get older. The reservoir is huge from all the experience you have had, so respect the slower speed of your internal operating system. Give your brain smaller assignments as you age, but keep it on duty at all times. Understand the degenerative diseases of the brain and what you can do to stay healthy and able to avoid Alzheimer's, Parkinson's, schizophrenia, depression, cancer, heart attacks, and strokes.

• *Maintain as high a level of physical fitness as you can:* muscle strength, agility, and endurance to sustain vigorous exercise. If you neglect your body, keeping it from being the best it can be, you will not age as well. The object is not to appear to be young but to manage your body effectively at the age you are. If you can, follow the Rule of Ten. Each month for the next six months, introduce a 10 percent *increase* in the following areas of your life: physical activity, dietary complex carbohydrates, fiber intake, sleep or naps, reading and other mind-expanding, intellectually stimulating activities. Each month, *decrease* by 10 percent the following areas of your life: calories, fat, alcohol (no more than 2–3 ounces per day, maximum), and stress. Eliminate all smoking, including breathing second-hand smoke; eliminate or reduce TV-watching and other passive pastimes. The most important decision is the decision to change.

• *Develop mental attitudes that promote positive aging:* basic optimism, healthy self-esteem, a willingness to adapt to new situations, a sense of personal power and readiness to take responsibility, self-motivation for continued resilience and staying power, involvement in meaningful projects and relationships.

• *Longevity depends on how well you handle stress.* When your brain is healthy, your body does a better job of resisting illness. When your body is functioning at its best, your brain is stimulated and your feelings are more positive. It is essential to manage information overload so you are not overwhelmed by media invasion and its consequent feelings of helplessness. Let go of things that are outside of your control or influence. The opposite of feeling stressed is a feeling of well-being. Stay connected to friends, networks, and other people. Don't withdraw into yourself or into your marriage. Lack of trust has great mental health consequences. Practice trustful optimism along with self-talk. Sustain a healthy sense of humor.

- *Continuous learning tops the list of factors that scientists have found to promote longevity and the retention of mental acuity.* Stay curious about something, preferably something that evokes a sense of purpose in you. Pursue enthusiasm and zest as you learn.

- *Invest in your relationships with family and friends.* Frame your life around the concerns of your extended family or friends. Appoint yourself a mentor to them. If you don't have a family, create one and then nurture it to make it your highest priority. The goal here is to be an intimate player to the very end, investing in your family as your most precious asset and legacy.

- *Maintain several task areas in parallel—areas of commitment and rewards for your life.* Some may be work. Others may be avocations, but schedule yourself into multiple areas of interest, through training, consultation, leisure engagement, and leadership roles.

- *Live on the edge of your possibilities, but be able to lose and adapt.* As you age, you become freer and freer to have your own voice, your own projects, your own impact. Spice up your life with risk. Know how to cut back if you have to.

- *Keep up with longevity research.* The twenty-first century will be the century of increasing numbers of elders. Scientific research that is relevant to longevity is appearing daily. It may well apply to you. The idea is not to live forever but to live fully as long as you can, or, as one person put it, to help you die young, as late as possible.

Part Four

Adults and Global Change

Valuing the Global Context
The Adult Challenges of
the Twenty-First Century

*Think about the life record of humanity as one "animal."
Like an individual person, developing from infancy to
adulthood, humanity gradually widened its world,
increased its power and its control. It originally lived, like
all animals, in its natural ecological niche. And then
something special happened; it moved farther and farther
from its home and began to create an artificial world, the
world of civilizations.*

*It began to take control of all life, and its actions had
overwhelming consequences. It created, then had to adapt
to, medical wonders, the synthesis of pesticides, the
existence of nuclear weapons. As humanity grew, its
ability to dominate challenged its ability to adapt. And in
the twentieth century its size and power, at least for a time,
have overwhelmed it. If we can teach this understanding
of our history and capabilities, both students and adults
must begin to channel the development of humanity in
new directions. . . .*

*A new conservatism—true conservatism—would be
dedicated to organizing a human society that can persist
for millennia without degrading the life-support systems of
its only home; that can avoid large-scale conflict; and
that, we hope, can enjoy not only freedom from want but
the political freedom that is necessary if the minds of all
are to cooperate in maintaining society. . . .*

*For the first time humanity has the knowledge to
destroy itself quickly, and for the first time humanity also*

*has the knowledge to take its own evolution into its hands
and change now, change the way people comprehend and
think. . . . Can we learn to become conscious of the problems
that face us collectively? Can humanity win through to a
new conservatism and a better world? We think so.*
ROBERT ORNSTEIN AND PAUL EHRLICH, *NEW WORLD
NEW MIND*[1]

Adults who manage change knowingly in their own lives are usually able and willing to face the cycles of change beyond them.
Instead of shrinking the American dream into private issues, they
are prepared to expand the dream into broader issues of life.

Making Friends with Society Again

The healthy self is a fluid, interacting participant in the wider
world.[2] John Vasconcellos of the California State Assembly writes,
"We owe it to ourselves to seek to unlock the secrets of healthy
human development. It is time to plumb the reaches and mysteries of inner space and discover effective strategies that could serve
to improve our communities, our personal lives, and the lives of
those around us."[3]

The imperative is to believe again in ourselves *and* our social systems, to make them both as life-sustaining as we can. The goal is to
see ourselves and our world as one organism, requiring cooperation
and compromise so that the whole earth wins. The poet Rilke asks:
"Earth, isn't this what you want: an invisible re-arising in us? . . . What
is your urgent command, if not transformation?"[4] How can we, as a
society, develop the required learning and leadership for empowering the systems of our lives—our families, the neighborhoods where
we live, our places of work, the air we breathe, the hospitals we use,
the governments we endorse—and beyond?

Living with Chaos

The ripples of change we feel in our lives today increasingly origi-
nate with the tidal waves of global chaos. Living with chaos is a
metaphor for our time, which requires adventurers akin to artists,

scientists, and athletes seeking new levels of performance. The founders of our country had this very spirit, as they pushed into the wilderness of a new land to create pockets of order for their lives. Throughout the whole westward movement across the United States, living with chaos was required, and those pioneers were drawn to it, not repulsed. Except for the global scale and omnipresence of chaos, it is not a new phenomenon. Americans with a memory will recall the ways their ancestors lived creatively with chaos; most of history has been strongly influenced by turbulence, surprises, and the unknown.

Often in the evening, my wife and I take our family to the nearby Pacific Ocean, where our three boys "body board" on the waves. Riding the waves on a body board or surfboard is the closest picture in my mind of what living with chaos is like. Join me on a brief ride:

> We approach the beach watching the waves like hunters studying the paths of a well known prey. The swell arrives from the north, building slowly, lining up in long, even rows. . . . Many of the breaks are unmanageable and more than once I am pushed back by a cascading waterfall of angry ocean. As the big wave approaches I am pulsing with a combination of fear and elation. There is time only to act and turn, and paddle with it. Suddenly I am aware of movement, a motion that is ever accelerating, and I am up. I am moving at an angle down the face of the wave and without thinking I know I've had a perfect take-off. Exhilaration.

> Suddenly everything stops and I see myself on a steep face of green, wet, silky water. In the next frame the wave folds over me and I am in the mid-point of a long tunnel. . . . My movement is in all directions, and at the same time not at all. The light is at the end of the tunnel and that is the direction of the flow.[5]

What can we learn from this? Riding a wave brings together an alliance of internal and external forces that produces its own rules, direction, and results. It can be creative or destructive. Creative riding requires balance, centering, cooperation, trust, timing and harmony, physical stamina, and courage. All of your attention must be devoted to the present moment, to merge with the crushing forces in order to ensure your survival and feel the joy. You cooperate with the forces at hand and look for life direction within them. Jack London, in *The Cruise of the Snark*, captured this sensation with these memorable words:

> I shall never forget the first big wave I caught out there in the deep water. I saw it coming, turned my back on it and paddled for dear life. . . . They are a mile long, these bullmouthed monsters, and they weigh a thousand tons, and they charge in to shore faster than a man can run. . . . The whole method of surf-riding and surf-fighting, I learned, is one of nonresistance. Dodge the blow that is struck at you. Dive through the wave that is trying to slap you in the face. Sink down, feet first, deep under the surface, and let the big smoker that is trying to smash you go by far overhead. Never be rigid. Relax. Yield yourself to the waters that are rippling and tearing at you. . . . If the board is going fast enough, the wave accelerates it, and the board begins its quarter-of-a-mile slide.[6]

Living with chaos requires kinetic lifestyles. You invent new, tentative organizing principles to make your life work for a while. You find your world filled with this and that, moving in various directions for various reasons, and you create a clearing. You produce the order you need for now with loose ends within the process of change: a temporary pattern that permits you to maneuver, think, and make decisions—in short, to live. Your focus is in the here and now, on the edge of tomorrow.

Living with chaos is collaging your way through time and space. You arrange and rearrange your colors and shapes as you move along. You pick and choose, search and find, wander and get lost, cut and paste—assembling and disassembling yourself and the universe around you. You are alive and you matter. You are a person and a social force.

The Human Dimensions of Chaos

We are just beginning to learn how to live with chaos—the absence of the familiar order we knew and the presence of alternative orders that we have yet to discern. What change has been to the twentieth century, chaos will be to the twenty-first. It is already happening. Change is not only accelerating in pace; it is affecting more and more aspects of global life in unanticipated ways. Change has become so extensive that we experience the world as discontinuous and unpredictable. We tend to think of chaos as a monster about to pull the rug out from under our lives. But for the most part, chaos is benign and neutral, structured and full of potential. It is— for now, at least—beyond our perception and control, and that is hard for yesterday's leaders, who were driven by their own needs for order and control, to accept. The world we experience is increasingly flexible, malleable, mobile, discontinuous, and not contained by some grand design—all characteristics of ways in which we will organize our lives from now on.[7]

The mythic consciousness of our time arises from this universal experience of chaos. Throughout the entire world, heroes search inner space, outer space, and electronic space for form and flow, focus and meaning, joy and bliss, direction and possibility. Even though our governments seem incapable of creating a world federation of nations, a world order is floating on the waters of turbulence, promoting a global populism and providing a universal prototype for life to proceed, even as wars and inflation promote the opposite. Chaos is a planetary force, representing an infinity of opportunities and threats that are within our reach but beyond our control. The whole world lives in this context, for better or worse. This is a mental picture that fits our time and frames the human prospect for the twenty-first century. It will take grown-up men and women to turn our experience of chaos into livable history far beyond today's nations and factions, rich and poor. There are at least five human dimensions of chaos within which adults have an opportunity to develop learning projects and provide new forms of leadership for the next century.

The Environment Is a Primary Reference Point for Everyone

Chaos has become a universal, operative concept for understanding our relationships with the total environment—not merely for some people or nations or corporations. Living with chaos means honoring our whole environment, becoming global citizens before there is a political structure to join. Our lives and lifestyles affect and are affected by ecological conditions and human decisions everywhere on earth. The only thing to remain "foreign" is our own inability to be responsive to the interconnectedness of life everywhere. Having a future from now on requires worldwide co-operation on the use and abuse of natural and human resources.

Like the many astronauts who have flown above the earth, we choose the whole earth as our home and find ways to live with its glory and misery. "Space travel has given us a new appreciation for the earth," confessed Apollo 15's James B. Irwin in Harry Hurt's book, *For All Mankind.* "We realize that the earth is special. We've seen it from afar, we've seen it from the distance of the moon. We realize that the earth is the only natural home for man that we know of, and that we had better protect it." Mike Collins of Apollo 11 put it differently: "The earth is one unit. You don't have the feeling that it's a fragmented place, that it's divided up into countries. You can't see any people, you can't hear any noise. It just seems like a very small, fragile, serene little sphere. It makes you wish that it really were as serene as it appears. It makes you wonder what any of us might do to make it a happier and more peaceful place."[8]

How can we live with a primary loyalty to the whole earth without being disloyal to country, state, corporate life, and family? How can we foster a healthy environment everywhere and protect it from permanent damage anywhere? What learning programs are necessary for this theme to prevail throughout the institutions of our society, including corporations and governments?

Chaos Can Be Irrational and Destructive

Chaos harbors demons, the irrational, and the unknown. In a world of chaos, there is no guarantee of safe passage through life. There are possibilities for human distortion, misuse, and harm. Chaos is a flooding process of actualities and possibilities, not a moral principle. Chaos opens the gates to adventures into the higher reaches of the mind and culture; it also feeds human meanness and self-ishness. We are all witnesses to global levels of self-interest, human neglect, and violence. Think of the issues that compromise human dignity on a global level: substance abuse, nuclear leaks, teenage suicides, oil spills, corporate cheating, murders, terrorism, white-collar crime, wars, hostages, moralistic arrogance, and endless compromises with decency and fairness. These are present realities, no matter how much we rail against them. We have watched them enter our living rooms from every corner of the world—Vietnam, Grenada, Beijing, Panama, Jonestown, Cambodia, Chile, Iraq, South Africa, Eastern Europe, Kosovo, and Bosnia. Ours is an unsure world, with high possibilities and murky subversion. All human beings fall prey to the misuse of their own finitude by overestimating the importance of their lives and possessions in relation to those of others. In a world of chaos, the gates are open to irrational thinking and destructive behavior on a global scale, particularly through corporate and governmental greed.

It will take grown-ups in a grown-up society to accept this message and to live affirming lives anyway. So far, twentieth-century Americans have not wanted to hear it; they have wanted perversity and pain to disappear through cultural progress and psychological enlightenment. Those expectations are off the mark. To face the down side of chaos takes years of experience and an acceptance of both our personal finitude and demonic qualities in ourselves. Mature adults should be able to face the down side of their own behavior and learn ways to contain it, insofar as possible. Although we cannot eradicate human arrogance and the will to destroy, adults who recognize these qualities in themselves can and will create countervailing forces to minimize their damage, and that is a leadership task in a chaotic world.

Chaos Promotes a Universal Culture

Even while demonic forces thrash about to extinguish the human prospects, intensive change has ironically created positive, universal resources for all people. For years we have been living in a global village without realizing its revolutionary impact on adult life itself. Chaos is no longer future shock; it is global transformation.

Almost all cities in the world today have electricity, television, telephones, faxes, computers, the Internet, newspapers, and radios. They have buses, trains, airplanes, and taxis. They have hotels, meeting rooms, conference centers, and restaurants. Today the entire world is furnished with the same basic tools for creating order within chaos. We are slowly learning to generate a user-friendly international system that transcends national-corporate boundaries and permits permeation from many angles and sources. These common reference points serve governments and businesspeople; they also serve the smallest universal units capable of managing order and chaos: adult human beings.

Complex change is so pervasive that it cannot be contained. Our Pandora's box of technological advances, destructive capabilities, information overload, and environmental consequences has been opened, and no one can get it closed again. Chaos extends beyond the reach of corporations, nations, presidents. As bits and pieces of information and power are increasingly available to virtually everyone, more people and agencies throughout the world have access to more and more information and power that can be used fairly rapidly. News agencies, IBM clones, software, automatic weapons, clothing, desktop publishing, explosives, ideas, VCRs, and faxes make it more and more difficult for closed societies to exist because they need to stay abreast of global change in order to stay alive, economically and otherwise. The world has been deregulated by the universal practices of commerce and governments, and a consumer-manipulated order is found almost everywhere.

Today technological change, the value of money, and the information explosion are not directly controlled by any one government or company or even by groups of governments and companies. There is a basic global order almost everywhere, with multiple sources of support but with no one ultimately in charge. Ironically, within that seeming order lie the problems of information overload, overwhelming destructive power, unpredictable events, unheralded greed, and haphazard decision making.

Living with Chaos Requires Worldwide Cooperation

Cooperative ventures such as alliances and shared responsibilities among governments, corporations, communities, and groups become the broad context for getting things accomplished. We learn to cooperate with others and with natural forces and to trust the river while looking out for alligators. In a recent study of U.S. industrial performance, a distinguished panel of experts made five recommendations for getting America moving again in the manufacturing world. Beyond the first recommendation, to improve the nation's schooling, they all had to do with transcending individualism and turf building. They promoted sharing and cooperating with others: creating employee collaboration in technological development at every level; understanding manufacturing as including planning, designing, marketing, selling, and servicing—in a global market; implementing cooperation among work teams, between companies, with research consortia, and with governments, particularly in developing a shared national goal for manufacturing strategies; and expanding our outlook beyond our own boundaries through a new set of international sensitivities. The study concluded that "Americans need to understand that the world they live in has changed. The effortless economic superiority that the U.S. enjoyed in the aftermath of World War II has gone. . . . What Americans must do is determined decreasingly by what they wish to do and increasingly by the best practices of others."[9] Cooperation is not the opposite of competition; it is the context with which competition can thrive.

Futurist Willis Harman believes that the work organizations of the world are setting the patterns for the new age we are entering:

> Leaders in world business are the first true planetary citizens. They have worldwide capability and responsibility; their domains transcend national boundaries. Their decisions affect not just economies, but societies; not just the direct concerns of business, but world problems of poverty, environment, and security. Up to now there has been no adequate guiding ethic. Although these executives and their organizations comprise a worldwide economic network, binding the planet together in a common fate, there has been within that network no tradition of and no institutionalization of a philosophy capable of wisely guiding its shaping force.[10]

That global ethic is now evolving, ever so slowly from grassroots consciousness to social morality to governmental policies and laws. Adults familiar with change in their own lives can provide learning and leadership beyond themselves by working to strengthen the bonds that now unite the planet. "Never doubt that a small group of thoughtful, committed citizens can change the world," said anthropologist Margaret Mead. "Indeed, it's the only thing that ever has." The creation of a world government while it is still possible is a planetary necessity if human cooperation is going to exceed global destruction. How could we do otherwise?

Adults Are the Primary Carriers of Culture and Consciousness

The basic unit for sustaining cultural continuities and monitoring complex change is a fully functioning person—emotionally alive and value-sensitive, rationally aware and clear, information-processing, value-driven and compassionate, adaptable and process-oriented, and uniquely capable of inventing temporary order out of inchoate experience. During a single life at this time in history, several generations now pass. For the indefinite future, adults will be the primary carriers of culture and consciousness.

As we surge along in the swirling river of our own experience, we keep organizing the resources that work for us, improving what we can, dealing with what isn't working well, and reorganizing when better options appear. It is a sloppy, unpredictable, informal process. We take on, we hold on, we let go, we move on. We attach and we detach. We make the change cycle a social process in our culture, guided by the values within us and the flow around us.

I recommend that every adult consider adopting a foreign country in order to learn what that culture is like. Within that country adopt a city, and within that city adopt a family to interface with over the years and decades. Learn the language of that country, and visit as often as you can, just to learn how the people there think, feel, and act. Exchange homes with the family you know in that country, and become as familiar as you can with the concerns, issues, and visions of the people there. If you venture in this direction, you will become a world citizen before there is a world to join, and in this fashion we can prepare ourselves for a common world beyond nations.

The scenarios for the future reside primarily in human lives that arch over the temporal swirl like bridges over troubled waters, In today's world, adults and their networks function as kinetic libraries, museums, churches, and schools. They represent memory, action, and vision; past, present, and future. The central continuity of cultural time and space is taking place within people and their temporary holding environments of personal relationships, work settings, and networks. It is not enough to have corporate or governmental visions for the future; our visions must be anchored in the lives and intimate connections of our people. As the pace of change quickens, mature adults will be particularly crucial for providing memory and future forecasting to help the large organizations of the world make intelligent, human decisions within a global context.

Chapter Twelve

The Self-Renewing Adult, the Resilient Society
Ten Qualities of Self-Renewing Persons

> *To be able to transform random events into flow, one must develop skills that stretch capacities, that make one become more than what one is. Flow drives individuals to creativity and outstanding achievement. The necessity to develop increasingly refined skills to sustain enjoyment is what lies behind the evolution of culture. It motivates both individuals and cultures to change into more complex entities. The rewards of creating order in experience provide the energy that propels evolution—they pave the way for those dimly imagined descendants of ours, more complex and wise than we are, who will soon take our place.*
> MIHALY CSIKSZENTMIHALYI, *FLOW: THE PSYCHOLOGY OF OPTIMAL EXPERIENCE*[1]

We, as today's adults, conduct our lives in the many dimensions of chaos. That is our global setting, our given space and time. When Dag Hammarskjöld was secretary general of the United Nations, he noted, "We are not permitted to choose the frame of our destiny. But what we put into it is ours. He who wills adventure will experience it—according to the measure of his courage."[2] Our destiny is to journey on the river of change, and this calls for a capacity to adventure well—at all times, in all seasons. Self-renewing adults are trained for the journey they are on. Adventure is what they seek and want.

Like good athletes, we can prepare to live fully in the world that we have—no matter what. We can learn to sustain passion, joy, and purpose throughout our years. We can find fulfillment in a world different from the one we were accustomed to. We can, when we have to, grieve our losses and find new pathways for our lives. Even when we endure transitions and losses, we can draw on resources for finding meaning in our down times. Although we may fall short on some occasions and get surprised on others, the more consistently we monitor a self-renewing process within our personal lives, the more we will ride the waves beneath us and guide our rafts down the rivers we are on. Wherever we are in the renewal cycle or in the adult life cycle, there are ways to promote a self-renewing process, with focused energy, clarity of purpose, and honest relationships.

The object of living is to live, not merely to exist or grow old. It is to live passionately, not merely to succeed or get rich. What is most crucial is that adults know how to sustain themselves in all situations throughout their lives: to draw on the crucial human skills for mastering ongoing change in their lives, even when they feel their lives are falling apart; to anchor their expectations in accurate information about their lives and times; to invent pathways for families, work organizations, and communities, even as the world churns up roadblocks and obstacles.

Ten Qualities of Self-Renewing Adults

As we race into the twenty-first century, we feel more of the earth's turbulence in our daily routines. It is in our daily lives that self-renewal is most needed. That is where our basic human competence is displayed and measured. Self-renewal means staying at our best—body, mind, and spirit—throughout life's long years, day by day. At least ten basic qualities are shared by self-renewing adults.

They Are Value Driven

Self-renewing people are committed to values and purpose. They know what they prefer. Their primary anchors are within themselves. For them, renewal is not mere responsiveness to change; it is the repeated revival of the central concerns of their lives within the changing contexts in which they find themselves. Something is always at stake, something matters, and time gets organized around those critical priorities. They are determined to make a difference. They are inspired to live their beliefs. Their commitment to life includes a more or less articulate philosophical framework within which their life experience can be interpreted and kept in perspective. They know whether they are on or off course.

Self-renewing people possess personal authority. They don't fake authority that they don't possess, nor do they refuse to use the legitimate authority they have. Their lives are firm and resilient—not limp and not authoritarian. They are definite but flexible, committed but learning. They risk and dare to fail because they believe in themselves and conduct their lives on the edge of their own growth. They trust their inner voice. The scholar Charlotte Buhler, who studied the biographies of a great many adults, concluded that having a "goal" is the most important prerequisite to feeling fulfilled during the adult years: "To live a goal-directed life means to have the desire, or even the feeling of obligation, to see one's life culminating in certain results. . . . People who live this way always seem to know where they are going and to hold only themselves responsible for their fate."[3]

They Are Connected to the World Around Them

Self-renewing people stay connected to the world around them. They seek out friends who can and will talk about whatever needs to be talked about—the whole of life experience, up and down and all around. They listen and empathize with life everywhere. They care and communicate. They stay in contact with their children and their parents, and take initiatives in sustaining relationships. They may not be joiners, but they feel that the world is there for them to enjoy, to grab on to, and to learn from. Most self-renewing people are not loners; they are profoundly connected to others and able to access the resources of their broad environment. They network information, contacts, and resources. They take advantage of art and beauty around them, visiting public gardens or libraries, traveling, and attending preferred social events. They support causes and take stands. The world belongs to them, and they belong to the world.

They Require Solitude and Quiet

Self-renewing people require times of solitude and quiet. Anthony Storr puts it simply: "Removing oneself voluntarily from one's habitual environment promotes self-understanding and contact with those inner depths of being which elude one in the hurly-burly of day-to-day life."[4] Self-renewing people know how to refill their cups before they get emptied. They plan time for introspection as well as for interaction and decision making. They have private lives that they nurture and love. They have regularly scheduled times when they withdraw from routines to spend time alone. They retreat to some "secret garden" where renewal is predictable, simple, spontaneous, wonder-full. In solitude, they look, listen, meditate, and nurture themselves. They honor their inner life and outer boundaries. For such people, solitude is a reservoir for finding more of themselves. Dag Hammarskjöld saw solitude as the source point for his personal activism: "The more faithfully you listen to the voice within you, the better you will hear what is sounding outside. Only he who listens can speak."[5]

They Pace Themselves

Our current practice is to indulge in rigorous work and maintenance schedules throughout each week, punctuated by renewal on weekends and a vacation every now and then. Occasional breaks are not enough to sustain the self-renewal process. They wash away quickly into our dominant routines. Renewal must be built into the ordinary, ongoing rhythms of our lifestyles and work styles.

Self-renewing people pace themselves. They schedule episodic breaks from their routine time, such as travel, holidays, vacations, retreats, seminars, theatre, sports activities, sabbaticals. If they misjudge and face the doldrums or a transition, they pace themselves through that space and time as well. They are not trying to sustain optimal performance at everything they do; rather, they seek to be fully present and available for all the occasions for their life course. They are more interested in quality time than in busy schedules, more concerned with effective lives than with efficient actions, more committed to integrity and style than to short-term results and applause. They do not constantly give themselves away, nor do they aspire to roles that do not fit them. They measure their resilience or energy reserves to be sure that they do not deplete themselves; they seek renewal in small or large doses as needed for the long-distance journey of their lives.

They Have Contact with Nature

Self-renewing people often find nature to be a dependable source of renewal. Throughout history, the wind, rain, sun, stars, mountains, rivers, earth, seas, and seasons have been seminal resources for the renewal of humankind. It may be hearing a wave hit the beach, seeing a leaf turning yellow in the fall, feeling a snowflake drift onto your cheek, or smelling a forest coming to life in the spring. Anne Morrow Lindbergh, in *Gift from the Sea*, which was written in her midlife years, found an oyster shell that helped her understand how to proceed:

> Yes, I believe the oyster shell is a good one to express the middle years of marriage. It suggests the struggle of life itself. The oyster has fought to have that place on the rock to which it has fitted itself perfectly and to which it clings tenaciously.
>
> Perhaps middle age is, or should be, a period of shedding shells; the shell of ambition, the shell of material accumulations and possessions, the shell of the ego. Perhaps one can shed at this stage in life as one sheds in beach-living; one's pride, one's false ambitions, one's mask, one's armor. Was that armor not put on to protect one from the competitive world? If one ceases to compete, does one need it? Perhaps one can at last in middle age, if not earlier, be completely oneself. And what a liberation that would be![6]

Much of adult life is spent away from natural forces—in buildings and settings that insulate us from powerful renewal readily available to us. Yet there are few among us who could not spend a half hour each day in some natural environment—to look and smell and listen.

They Are Creative and Playful

Self-renewing people are usually creative and playful. They are active, not passive. Rather than sitting on the sidelines to watch the world go by, they pursue ways to express themselves. Although they watch television, they are not couch potatoes. They like to exercise, explore, and experiment. They indulge in humor and are able to laugh at themselves. They become renewed when they read books, see art they like, hear their kind of music, or experience theatre events of their choosing. They stay alive by taking in life and expressing it as well.

They Adapt to Change

Self-renewing people are adaptive to change, so they keep pursuing their best options. They look for habits to give up and better ones to begin. They pay attention to what they are doing, how they are feeling, and whether they should change. They are caringly evaluative about their lives. Part of them is always looking in on the other parts and caring for the whole. They make decisions with enthusiasm and congruence and can say no as clearly as yes. Self-renewing people are competent at entering, sustaining, and letting go of emotional attachments. They feel life, and they feel loss. They seek intimacy and sustain friendships; when necessary, they start afresh. They can love and live closely with another person and can refine that love as it matures over time. They know how to adapt to new perspectives, goals, and ways of thinking. Their minds are perpetually learning new ways to distinguish what is essential from what is inessential, the enduring from the temporary. Self-renewing adults are critical thinkers who sustain the abilities to gather information, evaluate, solicit opinions of others, and make both firm decisions and firmer redecisions.

Sam, a lawyer now in his fifties, has made several changes in his adult life. As a young lawyer in his twenties, he lived on a treadmill, head down, always looking for billable hours for a large legal firm in Los Angeles. By his early thirties, his compulsive work habits and chronic complaining had all but destroyed his marriage, which included two small children. He felt that his life was draining his energy in too many directions but he didn't know what to do about it.

Sam's driving passion was to train young boys as Olympic swimmers. An avid crawl-stroke competitor, he filled his law office with trophies from his younger days. But he felt that he could not afford to live on the salary of a swimming instructor. As the years passed, he became an effective lawyer, both with legal matters and with client relationships. With his highly developed people skills, he had helped build up his legal firm, where he had become a partner. By the time Sam turned fifty, he was training Olympic swimmers at a boys' club on weekends and involved with the Olympic movement throughout California. When Sam looked back on his life, he felt some remorse about his divorce, but he felt great about the way he had achieved balance and integrity in his life.

They Learn from Down Times

Self-renewing people learn from their disappointments, necessary losses, and down times. Like the lives of most people, their lives are sometimes full of funk and disorientation. They do not live lives without stress, failures, mistakes, loss, and tragedy. Their lives are not sweet or perfect. They know that they have unresolved conflicts, limited perspectives, and impulses that sometimes overpower them. They do not deny the dilemmas of their lives or their own inevitable demise. But they know how they lived through down times earlier in their lives, and they feel confident that they can live and learn through the days ahead. They do not avoid disagreements and conflict; they know that conflict around important issues leads to deeper clarity and renewed relationships. They have a high tolerance for ambiguity and disorientation. They have learned from their own life transitions, and they have sympathy for the losses of life. They know that self-renewal is often found at the end of a grieving process. They trust the process of self-renewal. They accept the loose ends and unfinished business of their lives as part of their own future agenda.

They Are Always in Training

Self-renewing people never stop learning. When the world presents a problem, they first assume that they can master it through new training. Learning is an attitude toward facing the unknown. Self-renewing adults don't feel locked into who they were so much as alive to the people they're becoming. Learning helps them feel their pulse, measure their paths, and integrate their lives. Learning unveils more of their human competence and opens doors to new possibilities. Over the years, they experience a deepening of self-mastery and world mastery as perpetual learners. Because they remain on the cutting edge, self-renewing people often become leaders.

They Are Future Oriented

Self-renewing people are future oriented. They do not dishonor the past or the present, but they focus their lives on the "not yet" and the "what if"? They live conscious lives today, with intentionality for tomorrow. They formulate scenarios of the future and rehearse them until they are leading anticipatory lives, vitally connecting their current conditions to desired futures. They create the future in the very act of rehearsing it.

Kay Whitmore, as chairman of Eastman Kodak Company, steered his company through unchartered waters as Kodak faced a new era of photography, which will not use conventional cameras and films. Now fifty-eight, Whitmore has been with the company for thirty-four years. You might think he would be a stern defender of the old ways of doing things, but he is just the opposite. His challenge is to sustain the current market position of Kodak while pioneering in new electronic technologies that may eventually displace chemical-processed photography. "We're going to have to continually drive ourselves, push ourselves, encourage ourselves to keep at and ahead of our competition," Whitmore declares. "What people perceive as the relatively comfortable days of old are gone, and they're not going to come back."[7]

Resilience Skills

What skills do self-renewing adults need throughout their lives for finding fulfillment in today's world? What range of abilities should adults obtain to make their lives full and joyful—at their best most of the time? What would an ideal list of competencies for preparing adults to have mastery over their changing lives and environments look like? Early in this book we identified ten change cycle mastery skills. In addition to those there are life cycle mastery skills that empower adult life in all its manifestations throughout its long duration. Adults need competencies in all areas and roles of their lives—skills as human generalists. To have life cycle mastery is to sustain constancy of self throughout myriad roles and settings.[8] Adults need to monitor their own feelings, thinkings, and doings. Most adults have abiding intimate relationships and children; it is no longer satisfactory to enter into marriage or parenting without extensive training and skill development. We train extensively for career areas, often resulting in people whose specialized behavior at work is more highly developed than their basic human skills. Tom Peters talks a great deal about "high-performance organizations" that thrive on continuous skill training, but those skills are primarily work-performance-oriented, not basic skills for human empowerment.

Throughout the panorama of their experience, self-renewing people pursue human competence as consistently as they can. Adults who live creatively with global chaos are more than human doers; they are also human beings who have a singular integrity pervading all of their actions weaving together the occasions of their lives. Here is one list of comprehensive skills for sustaining resilience throughout the adult years:

Personal Mastery

Feelings

> Maintains high levels of self-confidence and self-esteem
> Imagines, wonders, and envisions
> Listens intently and objectively to others
> Empathizes with and validates others
> Expresses feelings appropriately
> Displays gratitude and appreciation

Thinkings

> Distinguishes between trivial and significant problems
> Distinguishes between situational and patterned distress
> Recognizes, accepts, and possesses legitimate personal authority
> Gives and receives criticism
> Observes and understands the conduct of self and others
> Reflects upon sense of self and its personal life course

Doings

    Discerns and clarifies personal values in self and others
    Perceives problems and evolves strategies for their solution
    Collaborates effectively and acts fairly as a team player
    Celebrates, has fun, and pursues affirmations and rituals
    Plans and feels responsible for making the future happen
    Lives own beliefs and concerns

Intimacy and Relationship Skills

Sustains intimate bonds, with an intimate partner or with others

Has parenting skills and provides an environment of love and learning for a family

Within family life, models basic skills of caring, cooperation, and conflict management

Seeks and maintains friendships that are mutually rewarding

Communication Skills

Speaks clearly and effectively in one-on-one and public meetings

Presents ideas and makes them convincing

Creates consensus through win-win strategies

Confronts and says no when necessary

Reads with both speed and comprehension

Writes factual and conceptual material clearly and persuasively

Is familiar with relevant hardware and software

Translates raw data into useful information

Accesses and networks necessary information

Team Player Skills

Fosters trust and cooperation

Motivates others toward common goals

Organizes agendas, runs meetings, and manages time

Brainstorms and problem-solves

Negotiates and compromises

Manages conflict and pursues consensus

Validates and rewards peoples' efforts

Networks—finds and establishes new resources and possibilities

Gets along with and respects diversity in men and women
from other cultures

Delegates and shares work easily; can be a follower or a
leader

Adjusts to and is curious about new conditions

Change Master Skills

Questions the status quo

Is challenged by the unknown

Is able to look at things from new perspectives

Takes risks

Is willing to make mistakes and learn from them

Is driven by personal integrity

Inspires others to be at their best

Is future oriented and cautiously optimistic

Looks for new resources and opportunities in the change
process

Pursues useful alliances and networks that enhance cooperation and results

Rehearses scenarios thoroughly before making decisions

Assumes responsibility for successes and failures

Becoming Perpetual Learners

As we become a nation of, by, and for adults, we must redesign our
learning resources to empower adults throughout their lives. Then
we will become a society of adult learners expanding and refining
their human capabilities. For today's adults, *illiteracy* refers not to
the inability to read but to the failure to learn how to learn throughout the life cycle. Three central learning questions are these: (1)
How can adults get the ongoing training they need in the life cycle
mastery skills just described? (2) Where are the adult learning centers for providing training in these skills? (3) Who can teach these
competencies?

Unfortunately, the life cycle mastery skills are not widely taught
in higher education programs in our culture, nor are they recog-

nized prerequisites for marriages, families, occupations, or leadership. Although some of the skills are taught in corporate training programs, adult education courses, seminars and workshops, retreat programs, and professional graduate schools, our society today needs institutions whose *primary* function is to educate adults to the limits of their learning abilities. Carl Jung once asked, "Are there perhaps colleges for forty-year-olds which prepare them for their coming life and its demands as the ordinary colleges introduce our young people to a knowledge of the world and of life? No, there are none. Thoroughly unprepared we take the step into the afternoon of life."[9] At this time in our cultural history, our society would benefit greatly from creating colleges or learning centers specifically for adult learning and empowerment. These would be hands-on learning programs where adults could experience, reflect on, and act on their acquired competencies.

Our most profound need for lifelong learning is to make adult life work at every level—intrapersonal, interpersonal, family, career and work, leisure, spiritual, and leadership roles. "Adult education" is learning in order to live fully and well—to develop personal power and social effectiveness. Training involves emotional, cognitive, and decisional components throughout the life cycle. Adult learning improves the physical person, inner self, and performance through the social connections of life—marriage, family, job, friendships, society. Adults are not preparing for life; they are learning how to live better and deeper. They want to understand the world in which they are living and the world within themselves. They want competence, empowerment, and newness. They want effectiveness, influence, and results. They want lucidity, consciousness, and linkage with the universe. They look for hands-on learning environments that will guide them in these directions.[10] Their main campus is the range of their own experience, and they look everywhere for learning resources. Although they want to be expert at something, they want most to be good at being themselves—to know who they are and how to live. They are less interested in knowledge than in mastery—that elusive ability to possess unconscious competence within one's life and work. They are personally drawn to simple, deep truths and to the unities of human experience.

Adult learners are reflective, not merely experiential. They think, evaluate, and look for patterns. They seek accurate information and maintain critical acumen in the service of making distinctions and informed decisions. As they age, their reservoirs get deeper, with more reference points and resources. They pay attention to their favorite words, dreams, and stories—the windows of the mind that help them see depth and beauty in their experience. They reflect as well on the world about them, forming judgments about what is taking place and what actions are called for. Attuned to emerging technologies that spray information across the globe, adult learners remain anchored in their fundamental personal resources of reading, reflecting, speaking, and writing.

Adult learning takes two forms during the life cycle—developmental and transformative. Developmental learning aims at improving human effectiveness in personal life, careers, and beyond. It focuses on evolving new competence and skills. Transformative learning aims at evoking a new consciousness and self-understanding. It promotes the unities of human experience through imaginative thinking, self-expression, and actions.

Developmental Learning

In the first half of life, adults mostly pursue developmental education to feel at home in the world. Twentysomethings, thirtysomethings, and fortysomethings seek learning that will increase proficiency in their jobs, lives, and relationships. They learn in order to get their lives into self-sustaining orbits—to complete graduate school, to progress in jobs, to prove themselves, to qualify for advancement, to gain status, to change careers, to specialize in new skills, to become managers or leaders—to make it. These learning programs are focused, practical, useful, and promote the future attainments of students. Early adult learning is competency-based and seeks to master specific fields of study, professional practice, and adult performance of roles. Although young adults may be involved in transformative learning, their ego and survival needs usually guide them to make developmental learning their priority. The central theme of adult learning for the first half of life is to gain knowledge and skills for leading secure, successful, joyous lives. Learning is for getting ahead, obtaining certification or licensure, and ensuring successful passage through careers and human systems. Although some of this learning is gained in classroom courses, much of it requires experiential settings with frontline experts or mentors as teachers. As Peter Vaill says, "Learning is a way of being in a world of permanent whitewater."

Transformative Learning

Although the learning projects of fiftysomethings, sixtysomethings, seventysomethings, eightysomethings, and ninetysomethings continue the pursuit of new skills, the overall life focus is not on practicality, effectiveness, or proficiency. The development of the self in midlife sets us forth on a pilgrimage for a new consciousness— to design life, to shape culture, to seek the future.

In the second half of life, adults feel the need for new ways of seeing and touching the world. The world is not there merely to master but becomes the container of a human adventure into internal as well as external sensibilities. Mature adults seek transformative learning because they view life as a privilege, as a pure opportunity to engage the world as creatively and fully as possible. This learning generates new ways to think and feel; it is aimed at exploring and redefining the deeper currents of human experience. In the first half of life the driving images come from history and society, to explain how to gain mastery over life in the world. In the second half of life nature becomes an equal source of driving images, suggesting a source of harmony and beauty that transcends history. The unities of life seem more available, friendly, and illuminating, and learning takes the form of a spiritual journey. The key to this learning is the integration of the inner self with its outer experience, such as environmental integrity, person-role consistency, person-system congruence, and person-transcendence discovery. This is part of the unfinished business of our culture. How do we, as a society, provide this level of adult learning? Who are the teachers, where are the learning environments, and which institutions bear primary responsibility for this kind of education?

The learning patterns of mature adults seldom mesh with the traditional divisions of knowledge or the typical course offerings of universities. These students do not seek learning in order to achieve or to make knowledge relevant. The development of passive mastery and the importance of artistic, leisure, and spiritual environments for learning are important considerations for the second half of life. Learning is much more diffuse and often more esoteric than in the first half of life, when practicality and proficiency are so important. Learning now is both intensely personal and universal, engaging a person's fullest commitment. The learning process is conceptually abstract but personally concrete. For example, mature adults might seek learning by creating an object of art, writing a biography or autobiography, producing a background document to justify the importance of a governmental task force, embarking on a vision quest, researching ways to enhance peace over violence, or elevating a hobby into a career or a job into a calling. These are not frivolous fluff for elderly creatures beyond the pale; these are conduits and vehicles for empowering the deepest currents of our civilization.

Sometimes adult learning seeks specialized, advanced knowledge in a particular field—as with reentry workers or professionals seeking to finish their highest degree during midlife—but the older we get, the more learning has to do with generalized, integrated knowledge of life itself. Older adults seeking formal learning may not want to major in a field, specialize in a profession, or conduct research on a narrow topic; they may want to explore their own thoughts and expand their consciousness. They may want to express their thoughts through art or dance. They may want to study the unities of the universe, the connections among ideas, the thoughts that unite the environment and humankind. They may seek to develop conceptual models and theories. Where are the learning environments in which they can do this? What kind of professors or mentors would and could guide them? What learning resources would they need?

Mature adults are themselves the primary mentors of the society—potential sages capable of passing on values and purpose and democratic process to those much younger than they. How can those mentors find settings where they can be guides and teachers? Who will employ them for the wisdom and mastery they possess? How can our society engage the vast educational resources of mature adults and help them "stand and deliver"? Mortimer J. Adler, chairman of the board of editors of the *Encyclopaedia Britannica,* concludes that "a culture can endure and thrive only to the extent that it is possessed by individuals, some of whom may add to it, but all of whom should be vehicles of passing it on to the next generation."[11]

Becoming Leaders

Adult learning is directly linked to the development and renewal of adult leadership. Perry Pascarella, executive editor of *Industry Week,* makes this point in his book *The New Achievers:*

> Leadership in the workplace will increasingly become dedicated to people development—not molding people to fit the organization, but enabling each individual to fulfill himself or herself. . . . A quiet revolution is taking place . . . in the business corporation. . . . Although we have been hearing more and more about corporate efforts in human resource development in recent years, we may miss the essential truth about what is happening: Individuals are awakening to the possibility of personal growth and finding opportunities to attain it. The team building we hear about is secondary to the development of the individual. . . . Management is heading toward a new state of mind—a new perception of its own role and that of the organization. It is slowly moving from seeking power to empowering others, from controlling people to enabling them to be creative. . . . As managers make a fundamental shift in values, a radical re-orientation to a greater worldview will enable the corporation to treat its human resources as *resources.*[12]

Peter Senge of MIT's Sloan School of Management portrays tomorrow's leaders as the facilitators of social learning: "Leaders are designers, teachers, and stewards. These roles require new skills: the ability to build shared vision, to bring to the surface and challenge prevailing mental models, and to foster more systemic patterns of thinking. In short, leaders in learning organizations are responsible for *building organizations* where people are continually expanding their capabilities to shape their future—that is, leaders are responsible for learning.[13]

Derek Sheane pushes this same point beyond institutional settings to include all adult networks. He describes the characteristics of a creative minority in Ulster, Ireland, illustrating how adults can lead and exert influence.

- They have overcome the "authority" problem. They can tolerate the anxiety of confronting their own power system—they will have freed themselves from slavish submission to outmoded reward and punishment systems in their own institutions.
- They are very aware people: At some critical point in their lives, they have gone through the pain barrier. They know what their mission is and what their values are.
- Although they acknowledge the need for a core structure and constitution in society, they have learned to make life up as they go along. They no longer feel threatened by a lack of structure and "disorder." They lead untidy lives.
- They have developed an open, and nondefensive, style of discussion and conversation. They can be forthright and feel comfortable with a very frank discussion. They welcome and use feedback about their behavior.
- They are aware of their own needs and motivations and know the difference between their personal needs and the needs of the situation. When they intervene, they do not work their personal agenda. They don't let ambition mock their contribution.
- They have understanding of mature leadership and help. They are concerned with helping people help themselves. They do not just give a starving man a fish. They also teach him to fish for himself. They keep their egos under control and avoid creating undue dependence in the group they lead or the people they are helping.
- They have a clear understanding of the total institutional crisis. They will be able to perceive the totality of problems. For example, they will take an interest and be able to see the interconnectedness of political, economic, and social problems.
- They are change agents in society. They are action oriented, and when they intervene they know why they intervene. They are purposeful.[14]

For the foreseeable future, formal and informal adult networks will produce vanguard leadership for all sectors of our society and beyond—inside and outside of existing governments, institutions, and careers. "This, then, is the ultimate objective of social futurism," concludes Alvin Toffler, "not merely the transcendence of technocracy and the substitution of more humane, more far-sighted, more democratic planning, but the subjection of the process of evolution itself to conscious human guidance."[15]

In my work with adults throughout the country, I have found a readiness among many graying Americans to move out of their doldrums into a new period of leadership and risk taking. Adults are finding the organizations in our society to be less stable than the adults who work in them. It used to be the other way around. Now, they often feel endangered by the structures that they thought would provide them security—governments, corporations, and even families. The smaller realms of their lives—personal life, friends, and immediate outreach—seem safer and healthier than the larger ones. We are a nation of workable parts and dysfunctional wholes. A way to proceed is to evolve a social system more congruent with the human dimensions of chaos. That is the general directive for today's leaders—to create organizations that are themselves self-renewing, that have both structures for continuity and processes for constant learning and change.

Warming up the old politics of the right and the left appeals to few. As a people, we need and deserve a new version of the old dream. We may have lost our way in the complexity of things, but we haven't lost our heritage. Many adults know the fundamental values of our society and history. They are restless for new leadership, and they are ready to provide it. I predict that the next twenty years—between 2000 and 2020—will be characterized by new sources of social energy and caring, much of which will come from mature adults, who now constitute the numerical crest of our population. A concerned, entrepreneurial social force will be led by successful, established Americans who believe they can get their act together again in a new way. While they have no blueprint at this time, they have energy, financial resources, social influence, and concern. In the past, we have expected young people or social movements to foster sweeping change. This time, it will be different. Like the main character in the movie *Stand and Deliver,* mature people are beginning to reclaim their heritage and insist that this country get moving again. This time, our dream will express itself as affirmation and consensus more than as protest and dissent.[16]

The type of leadership arising from today's adults is very likely to be what Robert K. Greenleaf calls "servant leadership"—leadership to address social needs out of stewardship and concerns, not out of charisma or power drives.[17] People who arise as leaders in midlife are driven most often by a deep desire to benefit the next

generation. Their leadership emerges from their gratitude for
their own attainments and opportunities and a wish to give something back. Compassionate leaders who arise from genuine concern for life around them have legitimate power and greatness. I
believe that there are thousands of adults now ready to become
such leaders.

Our top priority is finding leaders capable of shaping the human
dimensions of chaos. They must first know how to manage their own
lives effectively and joyously, in good times and bad. With all that has
been written about leadership, there is a dearth of material on viewing the effective management of adult life itself as a basis for creating a workable society today. As chaos etches its way into our lives,
the life structure–transition process will become the critical model
for managing social continuities and changes as well. Life-long learning will be a fundamental issue in the development and maintenance of our leaders. The leaders of tomorrow will arise from the
ranks of those who have learned how to befriend the forces of chaos
in their own lives today.

Chapter Thirteen

A New Profession of Adult Mentors and Coaches

During the past twenty years, I have watched efforts at short-term interventions in organizations prove themselves of little worth as entrenched corporate cultures struggled with the unyielding forces of global change. American work organizations have felt forced to retrench, flatten, and measure their success by short-term plans around bottom-line issues. That trend away from the long-term, human dimensions of work toward immediate financial considerations has altered most work organizations in America. A great many people are working harder than ever and enjoying it less.

In the wake of this, I have become increasingly interested in the concept of mentoring-coaching as a longitudinal resource that is readily available in most work organizations and communities and that can promote deep renewal and learning throughout organizational systems. The most profound way to learn skills, culture, and values is directly from other human beings who already possess them. As I said in Chapter Nine, sixtysomethings often feel the need to mentor—to extend their talents into the next generation. Younger adults also seek mentoring roles. What does it mean, really to mentor or to coach? How does a person go about extending talent? What, exactly, is a mentor or coach?"

A *mentor* is a trusted role model, adviser, wise person, friend, mensch, steward, or guide. A mentor-coach works with emerging human and organizational forces to tap new energy and purpose, to shape new visions and plans, and to generate desired results. A mentor-coach is someone trained and devoted to guiding others into increased competence, commitment, and confidence. Coaches play many roles to achieve future-oriented results—fostering career paths, facilitating personal and professional renewal, training high-performance teams, and providing informal leadership for transition management.

Mentoring-coaching is devoted to evoking and sustaining resilient persons and human systems. Anchored in the human reservoirs of mature people, mentoring strengths are deep, natural qualities within the mentor-coach. Mentors function not merely with skills but with personal mastery, stemming from their own self-esteem, integrity, and experience. Coaches model ways to thrive in whatever environment they are in. They connect present realities to future opportunities. More specifically, a mentor

- Models mastery in professional areas that others want to obtain
- Guides others to high performance in emerging scenarios
- Advocates, criticizes, and extends corporate culture and wisdom
- Endorses and sponsors others without having power or control over them
- Facilitates professional development and organizational system development

For the past ten to fifteen years human resource directors and organization development consultants throughout corporate America have shown considerable interest in the idea of mentoring and coaching. But I believe that most coaching efforts have lacked a conceptual framework for designing and guiding training systems for mentors and those they are mentoring. Mentoring-coaching programs are often reactions to organizational problems rather than proactive designs informed by knowledge of the art of mentoring and coaching. *Conceptually, personal and organizational coaching is derived from the knowledge of developmental psychology, adult learning theories, and human systems theories; it is applied to the practical issues facing persons within organizations throughout our culture.*[1]

For at least eight reasons, mentoring-coaching is important at this time, not only in corporate America but throughout the society. I discuss these reasons in the sections to follow.

1. To Help Adults Manage Change Effectively

We all know that change has become the most dependable reality in our lives and that people and organizations throughout the globe live with continuous uncertainty, tentativeness, and worry. Most live without long-term expectations and plans; they live intense daily and weekly schedules.

The most probable scenario for the future is that the intensity of change will increase steadily in pace and in the dimensions of our lives. Although we are not the first human beings to face the dilemmas and opportunities of constant change, the technical and universal aspects of our global situation are unique, altering human consciousness and priorities everywhere. Change diminishes our sense that we can depend on the world. Whenever change predominates over stability throughout a culture, many become angry that they have been abandoned by their society or by their work organizations. Others drop out because they see no promising future for themselves. Still others are paralyzed by fear or cynicism. Complex change often affects workers' abilities to sustain motivation and to commit to long-term projects.

In the new environment of perpetual change, workers who cannot manage the discontinuities of their own lives and work will not produce great results, no matter how great their technical skills or leadership abilities. But mentor-coaches—people who are anchored within themselves to do and accomplish what they love—search for the advantages of change, not only in work settings but wherever they can be found. Coaches are positive change agents. They motivate people around them with new hope, purpose, and concrete steps for sustaining a cautious optimism. That is a fundamental task of mentor-coaches.

The more the world around us is in flux, the more we as individuals must be certain about what matters in our lives: how we spend our time, who we are connected to, and where we are going. When the macrosystems of our lives are in considerable flux, as they are today, the microsystems rise in importance to anchor our lives. A mentor-coach is someone who can evoke passion and purpose in others, within the dissolving and reconstituting environments of our time.

The highest calling of coach-mentors today is to become guides to a transient culture, including a transient corporate culture, to grow strong persons, committed work teams, dynamic work systems, and sustainable communities that function from the grass roots up. Effective mentors model the future because they are willing to invent it, design it, and insist on it. As for change, they see change as an asset for getting the job done, not a cause for undue anxiety.

2. To Model Mastery

Much is being written about the fragmentation of our culture today, with the many self-interest groups and the culturewide anger, violence, and cynicism. Mentor-coaches cannot solve this social problem, but they represent one mature resource that can make a difference. Coaches work in small but deep ways to anchor people and human systems in a public philosophy of trust, vision, strategic thinking, conflict management, and collaboration. Effective coaches inspire those they train with a sense of self-reliance and deep-seated determination that is much needed in these uncommon times.

People need to learn how to grow themselves in our kind of world—turbulent, fast moving, unpredictable—and that requires personal maturation and mastery. Coaches facilitate the development of *radar* and of *gyroscopes* in people and in human systems so that those who are coached can master their own lives, careers, and the flow beyond.

- *Radar* is the ability to decipher your best choices within the rapidly changing environment you move through, day by day, month by month. Coaches facilitate pathways for the journey ahead, even when destinations are not clear.
- A *gyroscope* is a perpetual balancing mechanism moving through environments of constant change and unanticipated interaction; gyroscopic ability is a central capacity that coaches develop in their clients—the ability to redefine identity, ego strength, and personal commitment. Mentor-coaches enable clients—individual and organizational—to anchor themselves to their own values, confidence, compelling visions, and emerging plans.

If adults can develop dependable radar systems for guiding themselves in and out of the never-ending maze of daily life, they can sustain confidence, self-esteem, and hope. If adults can develop dependable gyroscopes for guiding themselves through the indefiniteness of their social experience, thus creating inner stability and outer constancy for living their beliefs, they will have surplus energy and courage for designing both work and communities in the kind of world we live in.

3. To Provide Ongoing Training in Technical Abilities

We live in a technocratic age in which an effective person knows how to use and learn from evolving technological systems. Because technology itself changes so swiftly, people must remain in perpetual learning systems to be at their best. Some people will pursue advanced degrees or certificates in new skill areas, but most need technical resources that are more tutorial, informal, and readily available. Mentor-coaches who specialize in technical competencies can perform these functions and transform the "technical consultant" model into that of an ongoing enabler, midwife, trainer. This is an important part of mentoring in the new environment.

4. To Elicit Core Values and Commitments

There is a great tendency today to think that technical prowess is the pioneering edge of our post-modern society. Truth is, as important as technological knowledge and skills are, they pale when compared to our need to be value-driven, bonded to others, and clear about the ultimate purposes of our lives. Technology fosters communication tools and media. But the medium is not the message. The message most people search for is about meaning, about the ultimate concerns of life. In short, the searched-for message is about values and beliefs.

Technological advancements are the province of young people whose mathematical and specialized skills are often superior to those of older people. Values and purpose, however, are the province of mature people who have been around long enough to transcend their intellectual skills and immediate personal needs and acquire trust in the flow of things. Such persons are effective generalists reaching out to a younger society of specialists. Adults in midlife and beyond are the most likely bearers of values for a culture. For that reason, many coaches—but by no means all—are in the second half of life.

5. To Renew Human Systems

In the past twenty years, corporate America has sought to transform its management styles, and one of the groups targeted for removal has been middle managers. Typically, a middle manager is a well-paid, long-term, loyal worker responsible for getting work done in some part of a business. The new management style is to train workers to manage themselves through teams, leadership training, and new rewards. This transformation has brought some astonishing improvements in the development of quality goods and services in an increasingly competitive world.

However, middle managers have often been the invisible mentors of these organizations, and without them, there is, in many organizations, a dearth of role models to foster advanced skills, management abilities, new career directions, and long-term loyalty in younger workers.

Coach-mentors can be found and trained in almost every workforce. Because they are already being paid, it is primarily a matter of allocating time to establish them as available coaches to promising, less-experienced workers seeking to grow within a work system.

6. To Sponsor Future Generations

One link in the generational chain is weak and unsure: the post-boomer groups of Americans, who at ages ranging from twenty to thirty-five go by a great variety of names: Busters, Beavis and Butt-headers, and GenXYZers. This cohort is known for its skepticism, minimalism, individualism, and social silence.

These generations challenge the assumptions of the importance of work and success. They doubt that they will have much of a future no matter what they choose to do. Of course, not everyone in this age group thinks this way, but a large number do, and it challenges the rest of us to learn how to communicate and cooperate with those who are cynical and not easily motivated by money, advancement, or recognition.

Adult coaches may be more effective than established leaders for facilitating the paths of this generation within adult roles. Coaches look for inner values as the primary source of motivation. In quiet ways, coach-mentors seek to provide cultural continuity as their fundamental legacy to the future. Coaches are committed to reaching out, bridging gaps, and finding new ways to build on what has come before. They stand and deliver. They advocate inclusion of all persons, cohorts, and identities.

7. To Model Collaboration and Consensus Building

Another way many of us experience fragmentation today is in the endless list of network niche groups, each of which has some legitimate way to define its identity. Many form around a single moral concern; others form around gender issues, illnesses, product lines, religious issues, racial or ethnic identification, or sports activities. Although these groups perform many positive functions through their special interests, they tend to pull their members away from forum discussions of the larger cultural issues that affect us all.

Where do people learn and practice democracy—government by the people—in a society made up of cul-de-sacs, that is, of isolated groups of people who are concerned about their own interests, not society's interests? The grand American rhythm of conflict and consensus has devolved into more and more conflict and less and less consensus. Whose responsibility is it to teach collaboration and consensus building? Those things used to be learned in schools, churches, town meetings, volunteer associations, even corporations. Broad debates about human concerns are certainly thriving in these settings, but in our technocratic media world, these institutions have much less impact on public concerns and opinions. Grassroots forums have been upstaged by TV and radio talk shows that focus more on alarming news and celebrity events.

Coaches can't solve this problem, but they can and will influence the human connections, alliances, and open systems. They plant the seeds of democratic process in the following ways:

• Themes that coach-mentors return to time after time with their clients are priorities, connectedness, balance, fairness, passion, purpose, vision, and planning. They show by example that living with "us" is a necessary part of living with "me." They promote a future for the whole of a system, as well as its parts.

• Coaches train clients to honor their core values, to articulate preferences, to negotiate differences, to compromise, and to manage conflict when necessary. These basic human abilities promote self-responsible behavior within interdependent contexts.

• Mentors encourage debate about the wise decisions for challenging scenarios. Coaches are concerned about making the future a developmental continuum with the past, and they promote those qualities in the persons and systems they touch.

• Mentor-coaches "coach" the organizations and environments they are in, as well as key individuals in those environments. They advocate a process of decision making in which everyone affected by a decision has some way to influence its shaping. Coaches emphasize both personal empowerment and social consensus, fostering an essential mind-set for personal, career, and organizational leadership.

8. To Tap the Genius of Older Workers

We live at a time of wasted human assets. Americans have been deluded by the myth of youthism, which is that we decline in all respects as we get older, particularly after the age of forty or so. Developmentally this is simply not true, but operationally the myth contributes greatly to the waste of corporate human assets. Corporations typically begin to divest themselves of the human potential of their older workers long before the workers retire. The graying of America will reach its zenith in the years immediately ahead of us, and with it will come a redefinition of *elderhood* that will emphasize a diversity of contributions from older workers. The smart work system will begin, in the early years of the twenty-first century, to redefine its policies and attitudes toward its older workers and to keep more of them as "seeds" for the future.

Another American myth is that of retirement. Retirement evolved as a concept in the twentieth century to force older people out of full-time work. It was the doing of corporate and labor leaders, in collusion with the federal government. It has nothing to do with optimal human development or the best use of elders as a social resource. As generation after generation of adults extend life expectancy into the eighties, nineties, and even beyond, some kind of positive engagement and recognition of elders is called for—social roles, callings, inclusions, role models.

Many if not most older workers want to leave a legacy, make a difference, and exert influence on the priorities of the environment around them. In future generations, older workers will launch new careers, assume temporary leadership assignments, engage in volunteer service, and serve as consultants and mentors.

Mentor-coaches can foster new employment challenges for older workers, both within and outside of corporate environments. Mentor-coaches can promote new challenges for older workers to find new meaning and purpose in their work. Many of these coaches will come from the ranks of older workers. Their voices will come from deep reservoirs; their actions will spring from gratitude; their joy will rise from spirit. Older workers, if prized by their companies, can help immensely to provide stability and pride in the work culture.

Coaching will not solve the perennial ills of corporate life or the American culture. Mentors simply enrich their environments with sharing, caring, and daring. Like yeast they leaven the corporate and community loaves; they roll up their sleeves to make things happen. They have that old-fashioned American spirit that says if we work hard and work together, we'll all benefit. If you have abilities that others covet and have the heart to share, make yourself available and see what happens! Coach-mentors are an enormous resource whose time has come!

Notes

Preface

1. John W. Gardner, *Self-Renewal,* rev. ed. (New York: Norton, 1981), xxi.
2. The personal case reports in Part Three are used by permission of those who wrote the material cited, and their actual names are used. However, the names, locations, and certain details of the case histories reported in the rest of this book have been deliberately changed to maintain confidentiality.
3. Robert J. Lifton, *The Broken Connection* (New York: Simon & Schuster, 1979), 88–89.
4. See Helen L. Bee, *The Journey of Adulthood,* 3rd ed. (Upper Saddle River, N.J.: 1996, 16–28). Also John Rowe and others, "Design Conduct and Analysis of Human Aging Research," in E. R. Schneider and John Rowe, eds., *Handbook of the Biology of Aging,* 3rd ed. (San Diego: Academic Press, 1996).
5. See three books that reveal this dilemma directly: Robert H. Binstock and Christine L. Day, eds., *Handbook of Aging and the Social Sciences* (New York: Van Nostrand Reinhold, 1996); Michelle F. Bellantoni and Marc R. Blackman, eds., *Handbook of the Biology of Aging* (New York: Van Nostrand Reinhold, 1997); and James E. Birren and J. F. Scroots, eds., *Handbook of the Psychology of Aging* (New York: Van Nostrand Reinhold, 1996).
6. See Carl G. Jung, *Modern Man in Search of a Soul,* trans. W. S. Dell and Carry F. Baynes (1933; reprint, New York: Harcourt Brace & World, 1983); and *The Basic Writings of C. G. Jung,* ed. Violet S. de Laszlo (New York: Bollinger Foundation, 1959).
7. Charlotte Buhler and Fred Massarik, eds., *The Course of Human Life* (New York: Springer, 1968); David C. Gutmann, "Individual Adaptation in the Middle Years: Developmental Issues in the Masculine Mid-Life Crisis," *Journal of Geriatric Psychiatry* 9, no. 1 (1976), 41–59; David C. Gutmann, "The Post-Parental Years: Clinical Problems and Developmental Possibilities," in *Mid-Life: Developmental and Clinical*

Issues, eds. William H. Norman and Thomas J. Scaramella (New York: Brunner/Mazel, 1980); Daniel J. Levinson, "A Conception of Adult Development," *American Psychologist* 41, no. 1 (1986), 3–4; Daniel J. Levinson, *The Seasons of a Man's Life* (New York: Knopf, 1978); Joseph Campbell, *The Power of Myth* (New York: Doubleday, 1988); Joseph Campbell, *The Inner Reaches of Outer Space* (New York: Van Der Marck, 1985); Robert Bly, *Iron John: A Book About Men* (Reading, Mass.: Addison-Wesley, 1990).

8. Erik H. Erikson, *Identity and the Life Cycle* (New York: International Universities Press, 1959); *Childhood and Society,* 2nd ed. (New York: Norton, 1963); *Identity: Youth and Crisis* (New York: Norton, 1968); Erik H. Erikson, Joan M. Erikson, and Helen Q. Kivnick, *Vital Involvement in Old Age* (New York: Norton, 1986).

9. Roger Gould, *Transformations* (New York: Simon & Schuster, 1978); Roger Gould, "The Phases of Adult Life: A Study in Developmental Psychology," *American Journal of Psychiatry* 129 (1972), 521–531; George E. Vaillant, *Adaptation to Life* (New York: Aronson, 1977).

10. Robert Kegan, *The Evolving Self: Problem and Process in Human Development* (Cambridge, Mass.: Harvard University Press, 1982); Robert Kegan, *In Over Our Heads: The Mental Demands of Modern Life* (Cambridge, Mass.: Harvard University Press, 1994).

Chapter One

1. Angus Campbell, *The Sense of Well-Being in America* (New York: McGraw-Hill, 1981), 9.

2. These figures are taken from the United States Census Bureau, 1996–1997.

3. Roper poll, 1998.

4. Daniel J. Boorstin, *The Image or What Happened to the American Dream* (New York: Atheneum, 1962).

5. Martin E. P. Seligman, *Helplessness: On Depression, Development and Death* (San Francisco: Freeman, 1975), 74. See also Donald L. Kanter and Philip H. Mirvis, *The Cynical Americans: Living and Working in an Age of Discontent and Disillusion* (San Francisco: Jossey-Bass, 1989).

6. *Time* 104, no. 15 (1974), 7–11.

7. See, for example, Martin E. P. Seligman, *Learned Optimism* (New York: Random House, 1990); Mihaly Csikszentmihalyi, *Flow: The Psychology of Optimal Experience—Steps Toward Enhancing the Quality of Life* (New York: Harper & Row, 1990); Mihaly Csikszentmihalyi, *Finding Flow—The Psychology of Engagement with Everyday Life* (New York: Basic Books, 1997); Robert Bly, *Iron John: A Book About Men* (Reading,

Mass.: Addison-Wesley, 1990); Ram Dass, *The Only Dance There Is* (New York: Doubleday, 1974).

8. See, for example, Peter F. Drucker, *The New Realities* (New York: Harper & Row, 1989); Charles Handy, *The Age of Unreason* (Cambridge, Mass.: Harvard Business School Press, 1989); Stanley M. Davis, *Future Perfect* (Reading, Mass.: Addison-Wesley, 1987); Richard Beckhard and Reuben T. Harris, *Organizational Transitions: Managing Complex Change,* 2nd ed. (Reading, Mass.: Addison-Wesley, 1987); Robert Tannenbaum, Newton Margulies, Fred Massarik, and Associates, *Human Systems Development: New Perspectives on People and Organizations* (San Francisco: Jossey-Bass, 1985); Joseph L. Badaracco, Jr., and Richard R. Ellsworth, *Leadership and the Quest for Integrity* (Cambridge, Mass.: Harvard Business School Press, 1989); Max DePree, *Leadership Is an Art* (New York: Doubleday, 1989).

9. John W. Gardner, *On Leadership* (New York: Free Press, 1990), 181–182.

10. Quoted in David Broder's syndicated column, *Santa Barbara News-Press,* 8, March 1990, A–12.

Chapter Two

1. Samuel Butler, *The Way of All Flesh,* quoted by Ellen Y. Siegelman, *Personal Risk: Mastering Change in Love and Work* (New York: Harper & Row, 1983), 27.

2. Roger Gould calls this "the myth of absolute safety," which is normal in childhood but for healthy adult development needs to be gradually replaced with the acceptance of the world as it is—with limits, dangers, risks, and death. See Roger Gould, *Transformations* (New York: Simon & Schuster, 1978). Judith Viorst makes a similar case in *Necessary Losses* (New York: Simon & Schuster, 1986). See Donald G. Myers, *The Pursuit of Happiness: Who Is Happy and Why* (New York: Morrow, 1992).

3. John W. Rowe and Robert L. Kahn, *Successful Aging* (New York: Pantheon, 1998); John W. Rowe and Robert L. Kahn, "Human Aging: Usual and Successful," *Science,* no. 10, July 1987. Rowe and Kahn argue that if the concept of "successful" aging is included in the research on aging, it will portray a more accurate spectrum of older people, from successful to ordinary to diseased to impaired. Similar comments are found throughout the literature on adult development, such as this one from Else Frenkel Brunswik, "Adjustments and Reorientation in the Course of the Life Span," in *Middle Age and Aging,* ed. Bernice L. Neugarten (Chicago: University of Chicago Press, 1968), 84: "Still in most lives, the reduction in vitality is not

experienced as a negative affair, since a change from a more physical to a more mental life takes place and the second half of life takes on a more positive form. The ability to transpose oneself, to take on another attitude toward life is a character trait which is almost a necessity for success in life." (See findings of the McArthur Foundation Research Network on Successful Midlife Development, to be published in 1999.)

4. Winthrop D. Jordan, "Searching for Adulthood in America," in *Adulthood*, ed. Erik H. Erikson (New York: Norton, 1978), 192.

5. Bernice L. Neugarten, "The Awareness of Middle Age," in *Middle Age and Aging* (Chicago: University of Chicago, 1968), 94. B. F. Turner and L. E. Troll, *Women Growing Older* (Thousand Oaks, Calif.: Sage, 1994).

6. Bernice Hunt and Morton Hunt, *Prime Time* (New York: Stein and Day, 1975), 19.

7. Barbara Fried, *The Middle-Age Crisis*, rev. ed. (New York: Harper & Row, 1976); Elliot Jacques, "Death and the Mid-Life Crisis," *International Journal of Psychoanalysis* 46, no. 4 (1965), 502–514; Orville G. Brim, Jr., "Theories of the Male Mid-Life Crisis," in *Counseling Adults*, eds. Nancy K. Schlossberg and Alan D. Entine (Belmont, Calif.: Wadsworth, 1977), 1–18.

8. Edmund Bergler, *The Revolt of the Middle-Aged Man* (New York: Grosset and Dunlap, 1957).

9. Daniel J. Levinson, *The Seasons of a Man's Life* (New York: Knopf, 1978); Roger Gould, "The Phases of Adult Life: A Study in Developmental Psychology," *American Journal of Psychiatry* 129, no. 5 (1972), 521–531; Lois M. Tamir, *Men in Their Forties: The Transition to Middle Age* (New York: Springer, 1982), 122–123; Marjorie Fiske Lowenthal, Majda Thurnher, David Chiriboga, and Associates, *Four Stages of Life: A Comparative Study of Women and Men Facing Transitions* (San Francisco: Jossey-Bass, 1975); Klaus Riegel, "The Dialectics of Human Development," *American Psychologist*, October 1976, 689–699; George E. Vaillant, *Adaptation to Life* (New York: Aronson, 1977); Bernice L. Neugarten, *Personality in Middle and Late Life* (New York: Atherton Press, 1964); Bernice L. Neugarten, ed., *Middle Age and Aging* (Chicago: University of Chicago Press, 1968); Bernice Neugarten, "Adult Personality: Toward a Psychology of the Life Cycle," in *The Human Life Cycle*, ed. William C. Sze (New York: Aronson, 1975); Orville G. Brim, Jr., and Jerome Kagan, eds., *Constancy and Change in Human Development* (Cambridge, Mass.: Harvard University Press, 1980); Marjorie Fiske, "Changing Hierarchies of Commitment," in *Themes of Work and Love in Adulthood*, ed. Neil J. Smelser

and Erik H. Erikson (Cambridge, Mass.: Harvard University Press, 1980); Marjorie Fiske, "Tasks and Crises in the Second Half of Life: The Interrelationship of Commitment, Coping, and Adaptation," in *Handbook of Mental Health and Aging*, eds. James E. Birren and R. Bruce Sloane (Englewood Cliffs, N.J.: Prentice Hall, 1980); Daniel Levinson, *The Seasons of a Man's Life* (New York: Knopf, 1978); Carol Gilligan, *In a Different Voice: Psychological Theory and Women's Development* (Cambridge, Mass.: Harvard University Press, 1982); Naomi Golan, *Passing Through Transitions* (New York: Free Press, 1981); Robert Kegan, *The Evolving Self: Problem and Process in Human Development* (Cambridge, Mass.: Harvard University Press, 1982); Robert Nemiroff and Calvin Colarusso, *The Race Against Time* (New York: Plenum Press, 1985).

10. Quoted by Winthrop D. Jordan in "Searching for Adulthood in America," in Erik H. Erikson, ed., *Adulthood* (New York: Norton, 1978), 198.

11. A cultural statement of the cyclical point of view can be found in Stephen Toulmin, *Cosmopolis: The Hidden Agenda of Modernity* (New York: Free Press, 1990).

Chapter Three

1. Allen Wheelis, *How People Change* (New York: Harper & Row, 1973), 105.

2. See Mandy Aftel, *The Story of Your Life* (New York: Simon & Schuster, 1996); Mary Catherine Bateson, *Composing Life* (New York: Plume, 1990).

3. Frank J. MacHovec, trans. *I Ching: The Book of Changes* (Mount Vernon, N.Y.: Peter Pauper Press, 1971), 13, 38, 46–47.

4. MacHovec, *I Ching*, 15, 25, 32–33, 35–36, 41.

5. Guess Who, "Undun," *Undun*, RCA 0195, 1965.

6. Stanley Keleman, *Living Your Dying* (New York: Random House, 1974), 51–52.

7. MacHovec, *I Ching*, 29, 33–34, 53–54.

8. The concept of "neutral zone" comes from the Dutch anthropologist Arnold Van Gennep, who wrote a classic essay on human change in the early years of the twentieth century. See Arnold Van Gennep, *The Rites of Passage*, trans. Monika B. Visedom and Gabrielle L. Chaffee (1908; reprint, Chicago: University of Chicago Press, 1960). William Bridges describes the "neutral zone" as a part of adult transitions in his book *Transitions* (Reading, Mass.: Addison-Wesley, 1980).

9. MacHovec, *I Ching*, 11, 15, 22–23, 61.

10. For further reading on the adult "life course," see Daniel J. Levinson, "A Conception of Adult Development," *American Psychologist* 41, no. 1 (1986), 3–4; Daniel J. Levinson, "Conception of the Adult Life Course," in *Themes of Work and Love in Adulthood,* eds. Neil J. Smelser and Erik H. Erikson (Cambridge, Mass.: Harvard University Press, 1980), 265–290; John A. Clausen, "The Life Course of Individuals," in *Aging and Society,* vol. 3, eds. Matilda Riley, Marilyn Johnson, and Anne Foner (New York: Russell Sage Foundation, 1972). Charlotte Buhler, in Charlotte Buhler and Fred Massarik, eds., *The Course of Human Life* (New York: Springer, 1968), 2, writes that "to live a goal-directed life means to have the desire . . . to see one's life culminating in certain results." Then, she reasons, the life course is determined by four factors: the structure of human life, genetic factors, emotional factors, and sociocultural factors. Perhaps the most important scholar to articulate the life course was Henry A. Murray, whose life work was to "study the lives" of others as living wholes. See his article "Individuality: The Meaning and Content of Individuality in Contemporary America," *Daedalus* 87 (1958), 25–47.

Chapter Four

1. Dorothy Rowe, *The Construction of Life and Death* (New York: Wiley, 1982), 208–209.
2. Judith M. Bardwick, *The Plateauing Trap* (New York: AMACOM, 1986), 126–127.
3. Bill Bridges, *Creating You & Co.: Learn to Think Like the CEO of Your Own Career* (Reading, Mass.: Addison-Wesley, 1997); Shirley Porter, Keith Porter, and Christine Bennett, *Me, Myself, & I, Inc.: 10 Steps to Career Independence* (Manassas Park, VA: Impact, 1998).
4. Allan Bloom, *The Closing of the American Mind* (New York: Simon & Schuster, 1987), 201–202.
5. Henry David Thoreau, *Walden* (New York: New American Library, 1960) (originally published in 1854).
6. Oscar Wilde, *Lady Windermere's Fan,* act 3.
7. Norman Juster, *The Phantom Tollbooth* (New York: Random House, 1961).
8. Harry Chapin, "Halfway to Heaven," *Verities & Balderdash* (Story Songs, 1973).
9. Bardwick, *The Plateauing Trap,* ix.
10. Robert Tannenbaum and Robert W. Hanna, "Holding On, Letting Go, and Moving On: Understanding a Neglected Perspective in Change," in *Human Systems Development: New Perspectives on People and*

Organizations, Robert Tannenbaum, Newton Margulies, Fred Massarik, and Associates (San Francisco: Jossey-Bass, 1985), 108–109.

11. John W. Gardner, *Self-Renewal,* rev. ed. (New York: Norton, 1981), 15.

12. Ric Masten, "Not Exactly a Command Performance," in *Stark Naked* (Carmel, Calif.: Sunflower Ink, 1980), 70. Reprinted with permission.

13. Erich Lindemann, *Beyond Grief* (New York: Aronson, 1979), 242. See also Judy Tatelbaum, *The Courage to Grieve* (New York: Harper & Row, 1980).

14. Elisabeth Kübler-Ross, *On Death and Dying* (New York: Macmillan, 1969), 2.

15. George Morrisey, *Creating Your Future: Personal Strategic Planning for Professionals* (San Francisco: Berrett-Koehler, 1992).

16. Mircea Eliade, *Myths, Dreams, and Mysteries,* trans. Philip Mairet (New York: Harper & Row, 1967), 80.

17. Arnold Van Gennep, *The Rites of Passage,* trans. Monika B. Visedom and Gabrielle L. Chaffee (1908; reprint, Chicago: University of Chicago Press, 1960).

Chapter Five

1. James Baldwin, *Nobody Knows My Name* (New York: Dial Press, 1961), 117.

2. Jimmy Carter and Rosalynn Carter, *Everything to Gain: Making the Most of the Rest of Your Life* (New York: Random House, 1987), 4, 7, 9, 26, 27, 30–34, 194. Also, see Jimmy Carter, *The Virtues of Aging* (New York: Ballantine, 1998).

3. Robert Tannenbaum first shared these ideas with me in many conversations and exchanges. See Robert Tannenbaum and Robert W. Hanna, "Holding On, Letting Go, and Moving On: Understanding a Neglected Perspective on Change," in *Human Systems Development: New Perspectives on People and Organizations,* Robert Tannenbaum, Newton Margulies, Fred Massarik, and Associates (San Francisco: Jossey-Bass, 1985), 95–121. A children's book describing this is E. B. White, *Charlotte's Web* (New York: Harper & Row, 1952); a book describing how corporate heads depart is Jeffrey Sonnenfeld, *The Hero's Farewell: What Happens When CEOs Retire* (New York: Oxford University Press, 1988).

4. Hugh Prather, *There Is a Place Where You Are Not Alone* (New York: Doubleday, 1980), 39.

5. Peter Marris, *Loss and Change,* Revised Edition (New York: Routledge & Kegan Paul, 1986).

6. Quoted by Ellen Y. Siegelman, *Personal Risk: Mastering Change in Love and Work* (New York: Harper & Row, 1983), 38.

7. Ann Kaiser Stearns, *Living Through Personal Crisis* (New York: Ballantine, 1989), 85–86.
8. Arnold R. Beisser, *A Graceful Passage: Notes on the Freedom to Live or Die* (New York: Doubleday, 1990), reported in the *Los Angeles Times,* Sunday, 8 April 1990, section E, 1, 10.
9. Robert K. Greenleaf, *Servant Leadership: A Journey into the Nature of Legitimate Power and Greatness* (Mahwah, N.J.: Paulist Press, 1977), 327.
10. Most life transitions can be managed as developmental events by the people experiencing them. Useful references for managing a life transition effectively include Nancy K. Schlossberg, *Overwhelmed: Coping with Life's Ups & Downs* (Lexington, Mass.: Heath, 1989); William Bridges, *Transitions* (Reading, Mass.: Addison-Wesley, 1980); Ann Kaiser Stearns, *Living Through Personal Crisis* (New York: Ballantine, 1989); Nancy Datan and N. Lohmann, *Transitions of Aging* (Orlando, Fla.: Academic Press, 1980); Naomi Golan, *Passing Through Transitions* (New York: Free Press, 1981); Alan B. Knox, ed., *Programming for Adults Facing Mid-Life Change* (San Francisco: Jossey-Bass, 1979); G. D. Goldman and D. S. Milman, eds., *Man and Woman in Transition* (Dubuque, Iowa: Kendall-Hunt, 1978); Nancy K. Schlossberg and Lillian Troll, *Perspectives on Counseling Adults* (College Park: Umporium, University of Maryland, 1976); Nancy Schlossberg and Alan Entine, eds., *Counseling Adults* (Monterey, Calif.: Brooks/Cole, 1977); Thomas M. Skovholt and others, eds., *Counseling Men* (Monterey, Calif.: Brooks/Cole, 1980); Lenore W. Harmon and others, eds., *Counseling Women* (Monterey, Calif.: Brooks/Cole, 1978); Ann Howard and Douglas W. Bray, *Managerial Lives in Transition* (New York: Guilford Press, 1988); Kathleen Adams, *Journal to the Self* (New York: Warner Books, 1990); Frederic Flach, *Resilience: Discovering a New Strength at Times of Stress* (New York: Fawcett, 1988); Bonnie Miller Rubin, *Time Out* (New York: Norton, 1987); G. A. Ford and Gordon L. Lippitt, *Planning Your Future: A Workbook for Personal Goal Setting* (San Diego, Calif.: University Associates, 1976); Genevieve D. Ginsburg, *To Live Again: Rebuilding Your Life After You've Become a Widow* (New York: Bantam Books, 1989); Richard E. Pearson and Albert J. Petitpas, "Transitions of Athletes: Developmental and Preventative Perspectives," *Journal of Counseling and Development* 69, no. 1 (1990), 7–10. Within a person's life cycle, some life transitions are "heavier" and more significant than others, depending on (1) the significance attributed to the life structure that one is leaving; (2) the inner strength of the present self to conduct the grieving and renewal processes and the ability of the self to manage loss and attachment to internal and external objects; (3)

the deficits of the self resulting from character formation, past personal experience, and social disempowerment; (4) available social support, friendships, and a transitional environment; (5) a healthy body and mind, free of chronic unhappiness and clinical conditions; (6) the degree of emotional resistance to risk taking and exploring the unknown; (7) financial resources for investing in the transition process; and (8) capacities in the self to imagine and facilitate a fulfilling future. Jonathan Bloom-Feshbach, Sally Bloom-Feshbach, and Associates, in *The Psychology of Separation and Loss: Perspectives on Development, Life Transitions, and Clinical Practice* (San Francisco: Jossey-Bass, 1987), conclude their recent study of separation and loss with these words: "Human development and the course of life transitions confront the individual with many experiences of separation and loss, on both the practical and the symbolic level. These experiences spur growth in the relinquishing of the familiar and habitual and in the reaching forward to new possibilities. Developmentally appropriate and emotionally manageable separation experiences are healthy and growth-promoting while unexpected, severe, and developmentally asynchronous separations are psychologically problematic" (p. 558). Most adults are capable of managing life transitions by themselves through their normal support systems. However, those who have a previous history of emotional problems or find themselves incapable of managing the transition process on a day-to-day basis may need professional help and clinical interventions. For further reading on clinical aspects of adult development, see John G. Howells, ed., *Modern Perspectives in the Psychiatry of Middle Age* (New York: Brunner/Mazel, 1981); William H. Norman and Thomas J. Scaramella, *Midlife Developmental and Clinical Issues* (New York: Brunner/Mazel, 1980); Steven H. Zarit, *Aging and Mental Disorders* (New York: Free Press, 1980); Howard L. Millman, Jack T. Huber, and Dean R. Diggins, *Therapies for Adults: Depressive, Anxiety, and Personality Disorders* (San Francisco: Jossey-Bass, 1982); Edna I. Rawlings and Dianne K. Carter, eds., *Psychotherapy for Women: Treatment Toward Equality* (Springfield, Ill.: Thomas, 1977); Robert Allan Silverberg, *Psychotherapy for Men: Transcending the Masculine Mystique* (Springfield, Ill.: Thomas, 1986).

11. Stanley Keleman, *Living Your Dying* (New York: Random House, 1974), 156.

12. Arnold J. Toynbee, *A Study of History,* vols. 1 and 2 (1946; reprint, New York: Oxford University Press, 1957).

13. Quoted in Jan Schmuckler, "Leadership and Followership in Changing Times: A Conversation with Bob Tannenbaum," *Vision/Action,* Winter 1990, 4.

14. Bridges, *Transitions*, 90–104. Also see William Bridges, *Surviving Corporate Transitions* (New York: Doubleday, 1988).

15. Mircea Eliade, *Myths, Dreams and Mysteries*, trans. Philip Mairet (New York: Harper & Row, 1967), 48.

16. Clark E. Moustakas, *Loneliness and Love* (Englewood Cliffs, N.J.: Prentice Hall, 1972), 21–22. Moustakas's main book on this topic is *Loneliness* (Englewood Cliffs, N.J.: Prentice Hall, 1961). Considerable research has been conducted on adult loneliness, and one convenient summary can be found in Benedict T. McWhirter, "Loneliness: A Review of Current Literature, with Implications for Counseling and Research," *Journal of Counseling & Development*, no. 68 (March–April 1990), 417–422.

17. Hugh Prather, *There Is a Place Where You Are Not Alone* (New York: Doubleday, 1980), 201.

18. William Wordsworth, *The Prelude: The Complete Poetical Works of William Wordsworth* (London: 1950), 261.

19. Anthony Storr, *Solitude: A Return to the Self* (New York: Free Press, 1988), 12, 21, 29, 34–35. An excellent source on the positive aspects of solitude is Jeffrey Kottler, *Private Moments, Secret Selves: Enriching Our Time Alone* (Los Angeles: Tarcher, 1990).

20. Richard E. Byrd, *Alone* (New York: Putnam, 1958), 7.

21. See Robert Kegan, *The Evolving Self: Problem and Process in Human Development* (Cambridge, Mass.: Harvard University Press, 1982); Daniel J. Levinson, *The Seasons of a Man's Life* (New York: Knopf, 1978), 209–244; John Bowlby, *Attachment and Loss*, vols. 1–3 (New York: Basic Books, 1958–1980); Erik H. Erikson, *Childhood and Society*, 2nd ed. (New York: Norton, 1963), 219–231. This "redecision" process is described in Mary McClure Goulding and Robert L. Goulding, *Changing Lives Through Redecision Therapy* (New York: Brunner/Mazel, 1979).

22. Silvano Arieti, "Creativity and Its Cultivation," in *American Handbook of Psychiatry*, 2nd ed. (New York: Basic Books, 1975), 6, 230–250. Also see Silvano Arieti, *Creativity: The Magic Synthesis* (New York: Basic Books, 1976), 6; Rollo May, "The Nature of Creativity," in *Creativity and Its Cultivation*, ed. Harold H. Anderson (New York: Harper & Row, 1959), 55–68. This entire book is a valuable resource for understanding the creative process, with key articles by Erich Fromm, Carl Rogers, Abraham Maslow, Henry Murray, Margaret Mead, and others. See also Rollo May, *The Courage to Create* (New York: Bantam Books, 1978); Richard Leider, *The Power of Purpose*, Revised Edition (San Francisco: Berrett-Koehler, 1997).

23. Ellen Y. Siegelman, *Personal Risk: Mastering Change in Love and Work* (New York: Harper & Row, 1983), 126.
24. Louis A. Zurcher, Jr., *The Mutable Self: A Self-Concept for Social Change* (Newbury Park, Calif.: Sage, 1977), 215, 234; Mihaly Csikszentmihalyi, *Flow: The Psychology of Optimal Experience—Steps Toward Enhancing the Quality of Life* (New York: Harper & Row, 1990).
25. Charles Garfield, *Peak Performance* (Los Angeles: Tarcher, 1974).

Chapter Six

1. Madeleine L'Engle, *The Summer of the Great-Grandmother* (New York: Harper & Row, 1974), 52–53.
2. Daniel N. Stern, *The Interpersonal World of the Infant* (New York: Basic Books, 1985); Donald W. Winnicott, *The Maturational Processes and the Facilitating Environment* (New York: International Universities Press, 1965); Margaret S. Mahler, Fred Pine, and Anni Bergman, *The Psychological Birth of the Human Infant* (New York: Basic Books, 1975); Erik H. Erikson, *Childhood and Society*, 2nd ed. (New York: Norton, 1963); Robert Coles, *The Spiritual Life of Children* (New York: Houghton Mifflin, 1990).
3. George E. Vaillant, *Adaptation to Life* (Boston: Little, Brown, 1977); Calvin A. Colarusso and Robert A. Nemiroff, *Adult Development* (New York: Plenum Press, 1981); William C. Sze, *Human Life Cycle* (New York: Aronson, 1975); Bernice L. Neugarten, ed., *Middle Age and Aging* (Chicago: University of Chicago Press, 1968); Carol B. Aslanian and Henry M. Brickell, *Americans in Transition: Life Changes as Reasons for Adult Learning* (Princeton, N.J.: College Entrance Examination Board, 1980).
4. Henry S. Maas and Joseph A. Kuypers, *From Thirty to Seventy: A Forty-Year Longitudinal Study of Adult Life Styles and Personality* (San Francisco: Jossey-Bass, 1974); Roger Gould, *Transformations* (New York: Simon & Schuster, 1978); Nancy Datan and N. Lohmann, eds., *Transitions of Aging* (Orlando, Fla.: Academic Press, 1980); Neil J. Smelser and Erik H. Erikson, eds., *Themes of Work and Love in Adulthood* (Cambridge, Mass.: Harvard University Press, 1980); Robert Kegan, *The Evolving Self: Problem and Process in Human Development* (Cambridge, Mass.: Harvard University Press, 1982); Daniel J. Levinson, "A Conception of Adult Development," *American Psychologist* 41, 1 (1986): 3–4; Dorothy Rowe, *The Construction of Life and Death* (New York: Wiley, 1982); Martha Storandt and Gary R. VandenBos, eds., *The Adult Years: Continuity and Change* (Washington, D.C.: American Psychological Association, 1989); Marjorie

Fiske and David A. Chiriboga, *Change and Continuity in Adult Life* (San Francisco: Jossey-Bass, 1990); Robert R. McCrae and Paul T. Costa, Jr., *Personality in Adulthood* (New York: Guilford Press, 1990).

5. For example, this book is addressed to Americans who are educated, entrenched in careers and intimacy commitments, and asking fundamental questions about their future options. Matilda White Riley, Ronald P. Abeles, and Michael S. Teitelbaum, eds., *Aging from Birth to Death*, vol. 1, *Interdisciplinary Perspectives* (Boulder, Colo.: Westview Press, 1981); Klaus F. Riegel, "Adult Life Crises: A Dialectic Interpretation of Development," in *Life Span Developmental Psychology: Normative Life Crises*, Nancy Datan and Leon H. Ginsberg, eds. (New York: Academic Press, 1975); Elizabeth J. Douvan, Jody Veroff, and R. Kulka, *A Study of Modern Living* (Ann Arbor: Institute for Social Research, University of Michigan, 1976); Andrew M. Mecca, Neil J. Smelser, and John Vasconcellos, eds., *The Social Importance of Self-Esteem* (Berkeley: University of California Press, 1989).

6. Some general references on gender issues throughout the life span include Bernice L. Neugarten, "Adult Personality: Toward a Psychology of the Life Cycle," in *Middle Age and Aging* (Chicago: University of Chicago Press, 1968); David C. Gutmann, "The Cross-Cultural Perspective: Notes Toward a Comparative Psychology of Aging," in *Handbook of the Psychology of Aging*, eds. James E. Birren and K. Warner Schaie (New York: Van Nostrand Reinhold, 1977). Carol Gilligan writes that "Conceptions of the human life cycle represent different attempts to order and make coherent the unfolding experiences and perceptions, the changing wishes and realities of everyday life. But the nature of such conceptions depends in part on the position of the observer. . . . When the observer is a woman, the perspective may be a different sort. Different judgements of the images of a man . . . to imply different ideas about human development, different ways of imagining the human condition, different notions of what is of value in life." Carol Gilligan, *In a Different Voice: Psychological Theory and Women's Development* (Cambridge, Mass.: Harvard University Press, 1982), 5. Robert Bly says much the same about how maleness relates to the male journey through life. Robert Bly, *Iron John: A Book About Men* (Reading, Mass.: Addison-Wesley, 1990). Some salient references on women's issues relating to adult development include Ruthellen Josselson, *Finding Herself: Pathways to Identity Development in Women* (San Francisco: Jossey-Bass, 1987); Mary C. Bateson, *Composing a Life* (New York: Plume, 1990); Nancy J. Chodorow, *Feminism and Psychoanalytic Theory* (New Haven, Conn.: Yale University Press, 1989); Joan J. Zilbach, "In the I: The Eye of

the Beholder: Towards a Separate Line of Development in Women,"
unpublished lecture presented at the Slavson Memorial Lecture
American Group Psychotherapy Association, 6 February 1987, in
New Orleans: Toni Bernay and Dorothy W. Cantor, eds., *The Psy-
chology of Today's Woman: New Psychoanalytic Visions* (Hillsdale, N.J.:
Analytic Press, 1986); Pamela D. McLean, "A Psycho-Social Analysis
of the Life Patterns of Five Hundred Educated Women" (Ph.D. dis-
sertation, Fielding Institute, 1980); Jean Baker Miller, *Toward a New
Psychology of Women* (Boston: Beacon Press, 1976); Lillian B. Rubin,
Women of a Certain Age: The Midlife Search for Self (New York: Harper
& Row, 1979); Martha C. McBride, "Autonomy and the Struggle for
Female Identity: Implications for Counseling Women," *Journal of
Counseling and Development* 69, no. 1 (1990), 22–27; Elise Boulding,
Women in the Twentieth Century World (New York: Halsted Press,
1977); Natalie Rogers, *Emerging Woman: A Decade of Midlife Transi-
tions* (Santa Rosa, Calif.: Personal Press, 1980); "Women at Midlife
and Beyond," *Psychology of Women Quarterly* 14, no. 4 (1990): entire
issue. Selected references on men's issues relating to adult development include Kenneth Clatterbaugh, *Contemporary Perspectives on
Masculinity: Men, Women, and Politics in Modern Society* (Boulder,
Colo.: Westview Press, 1990); Warren Farrell, *Why Men Are the Way
They Are* (New York: McGraw-Hill, 1986); Michael P. Farrell and Stanley D. Rosenberg, *Men at Midlife* (Boston: Auburn House, 1981);
Sam Keen, *Fire in the Belly: On Being a Man* (New York: Bantam,
1991); Shirley M. H. Hanson and Frederick W. Bozett, eds., *Dimen-
sions of Fatherhood* (Newbury Park, Calif.: Sage, 1985); Stanley H.
Cath, Alan Gurwitt, and Linda Gunsberg, eds., *Fathers and Their Fam-
ilies* (Hillsdale, N.J.: Analytic Press, 1989); Robert A. Lewis and
Robert E. Salt, *Men in Families* (Newbury Park, Calif.: Sage, 1986);
Samuel Osherson, *Finding Our Fathers: The Unfinished Business of
Manhood* (New York: Free Press, 1987); Samuel Osherson and
Steven Krugman, "Men, Shame, and Psychotherapy," *Psychotherapy*
27, no. 3 (1990), 327–339.

7.   Terrence E. Deal and Allen A. Kennedy, *Corporate Cultures* (Reading, Mass.: Addison-Wesley, 1982); Ichak Adizes, *Corporate Lifecycles*
(Englewood Cliffs, N.J.: Prentice Hall, 1988); Roy Lacoursiere, *The
Life Cycle of Groups* (New York: Human Sciences Press, 1980); John
R. Kimberly, Robert H. Miles, and Associates, *The Organizational
Life Cycle. Issues in the Creation, Transformation, and Decline of Organizations* (San Francisco: Jossey-Bass, 1980); Tom Peters, *Thriving
on Chaos: Handbook for a Management Revolution* (New York: Knopf,
1987); Ralph H. Kilmann, *Beyond the Quick Fix: Managing Five Tracks*

to Organizational Success (San Francisco: Jossey-Bass, 1984); Donald Super, "Career and Life Development," in *Career Choice and Development: Applying Contemporary Theories and Practice,* Duane Brown, Linda Brooks, and Associates (San Francisco: Jossey-Bass, 1984); Edgar H. Schein, *Career Dynamics: Matching Individual and Organizational Needs* (Reading, Mass.: Addison-Wesley, 1978); Duane Brown, Linda Brooks, and Associates, *Career Choice and Development: Applying Contemporary Theories and Practice,* 2nd ed. (San Francisco: Jossey-Bass, 1990); Norman C. Gysbers and Associates, *Designing Careers: Counseling to Enhance Education, Work, and Leisure* (San Francisco: Jossey-Bass, 1984); Douglas T. Hall and Associates, *Career Development in Organizations* (San Francisco: Jossey-Bass, 1986); Barbara J. Berg, *The Crisis of the Working Mother* (New York: Summit Books, 1986); Uma Sekaran, *Dual-Career Families: Contemporary Organizational and Counseling Issues* (San Francisco: Jossey-Bass, 1986).

8. Elliot Jacques, "Death and the Mid-Life Crisis," *International Journal of Psychoanalysis* 46, no. 4 (1965), 502–514; Ernest Becker, *The Denial of Death* (New York: Free Press, 1973); Judith Viorst, *Necessary Losses* (New York: Simon & Schuster, 1986); Bernice L. Neugarten, "Time, Age, and the Life Cycle," *American Journal of Psychiatry* 136 (1979), 887–894; Robert Nemiroff and Calvin Colarusso, *The Race Against Time* (New York: Plenum Press, 1985).

9. Bernice L. Neugarten, "Adult Personality: Toward a Psychology of the Life Cycle," in *Middle Age and Aging* (Chicago: University of Chicago Press, 1968); Carl G. Jung, "Individuation," in *The Basic Writings of C. G. Jung,* ed. Violet Staub de Laszlo (New York: Modern Library, 1959), 143–157; F. A. Goldberg, ed., *Advances in the Psychology of the Self* (New York: International Universities Press, 1980); Herbert Fingarette, *The Self in Transformation* (New York: Basic Books, 1963); Henry A. Murray, "Individuality: The Meaning and Content of Individuality in Contemporary America," *Daedalus* 87 (1958), 25–47.

10. J. R. Kelly, *Leisure Identities and Interactions* (London: Allen & Unwin, 1983); Rhona Rapoport and Robert N. Rapoport, *Leisure and the Family Life Cycle* (London: Routledge & Kegan Paul, 1975); John Neulinger, *The Psychology of Leisure: Research Approaches to the Study of Leisure* (Springfield, Ill.: Thomas, 1974).

11. Stephen G. Holliday and Michael J. Chandler, *Wisdom: Explorations in Adult Competence* (New York: Karger, 1986); Vivian P. Clayton and James E. Birren, "The Development of Wisdom Across the Life Span: A Reexamination of an Ancient Topic," in *Life-Span Development and Behavior,* vol. 3, eds. Paul B. Baltes and Orville G. Brim, Jr.

(New York: Academic Press, 1980), 103–135; Erik H. Erikson, *The Life Cycle Completed* (New York: Norton, 1982); David L. Norton, *Personal Destinies: A Philosophy of Ethical Individualism* (Princeton, N.J.: Princeton University Press, 1976); Eugene C. Bianchi, *Aging as a Spiritual Journey* (New York: Crossroad, 1987); John Weir Perry, *The Heart of History: Individuality in Evolution* (Albany: State University of New York Press, 1987).

12. Laurent A. Daloz, *Effective Teaching and Mentoring: Realizing the Transformational Power of Adult Learning Experiences* (San Francisco: Jossey-Bass, 1986); Robert K. Greenleaf, *Servant Leadership: A Journey into the Nature of Legitimate Power and Greatness* (Mahwah, N.J.: Paulist Press, 1977); John W. Gardner, *On Leadership* (New York: Free Press, 1990); Peter Block, *The Empowered Manager: Positive Political Skills at Work* (San Francisco: Jossey-Bass, 1987); Noel M. Tichy and Mary Anne Devanna, *The Transformational Leader* (New York: Wiley, 1986); Joseph L. Badaracco Jr., and Richard R. Ellsworth, *Leadership and the Quest for Integrity* (Boston: Harvard Business School Press, 1989).

13. See Erik H. Erikson, *Identity: Youth and Crisis* (New York: Norton, 1968); Erik H. Erikson, *Identity and the Life Cycle* (New York: Norton, 1959); Carl Rogers, *On Becoming a Person* (Boston: Houghton Mifflin, 1961); James F. Masterson, *The Search for the Real Self* (New York: Free Press, 1988); Michael Polanyi, *Personal Knowledge* (Chicago: University of Chicago Press, 1958); Leona E. Tyler, *Individuality: Human Possibilities and Personal Choice in the Psychological Development of Men and Women* (San Francisco: Jossey-Bass, 1978); William Kilpatrick, *Identity and Society* (New York: Delta Books, 1975); Kathleen Adams, *Journal to the Self* (New York: Warner Books, 1990).

14. See Charles Garfield, *Peak Performance* (Los Angeles: Tarcher, 1974); Stephen R. Covey, *The Seven Habits of Highly Effective People* (New York: Simon & Schuster, 1989); Perry Pascarella, *The New Achievers: Creating a Modern Work Ethic* (New York: Free Press, 1984); Ruth B. Kundsin, ed., *Women & Success: The Anatomy of Achievement* (New York: Morrow, 1974).

15. See Reuben Fine, *The Meaning of Love in Human Experience* (New York: Wiley, 1985); Kenneth S. Pope and Associates, *On Love and Loving: Psychological Perspectives on the Nature and Experience of Romantic Love* (San Francisco: Jossey-Bass, 1980); Willard Gaylin and Ethel Person, eds., *Passionate Attachments: Thinking About Love* (New York: Free Press, 1988); Shirley C. Luthman, *Intimacy: The Essence of Male & Female* (San Rafael, Calif.: Mehetabel, 1972); Sam Keen, *The Passionate Life: Stages of Loving* (New York: Harper & Row, 1983).

16. See Donald W. Winnicott, *Playing & Reality* (London: Tavistock,

1971); A. Reza Arasteh and Joseph D. Arasteh, *Creativity in Human Development* (New York: Schenkman, 1976); Silvano Arieti, *Creativity: The Magic Synthesis* (New York: Basic Books, 1976); Robert J. Sternberg, ed., *The Nature of Creativity* (New York: Cambridge University Press, 1988); Rollo May, *The Courage to Create* (New York: Bantam Books, 1978); Robert Grundin, *The Grace of Great Things: Creativity and Innovation* (New York: Ticknor & Fields, 1990).

17. See also Victor E. Frankl, *Man's Search for Meaning* (New York: Pocket Books, 1977); Rollo May, *The Discovery of Being* (New York: Norton, 1983); Paul Tillich, *The Courage to Be* (New Haven, Conn.: Yale University Press, 1952); Frances Vaughan, *The Inward Arc: Healing and Wholeness in Psychotherapy and Spirituality* (Boston: New Science Library, 1986); Althea Horner, *Being and Loving* (Northvale, N.J.: Jason Aronson, 1986); Stanislav Grof and Christina Grof, *The Stormy Search for the Self: A Guide to Personal Growth Through Transformational Crisis* (Los Angeles, Calif.: Teacher, 1990); Roger S. Gottlieb, *A New Creation: America's Contemporary Spiritual Voices* (New York: Crossroad, 1990).

18. Useful references for this topic are: Milton Mayeroff, *On Caring* (New York: Harper & Row, 1971); M. Scott Peck, *The Different Drum: Community Making and Peace* (New York: Touchstone, 1987); Arthur Simon, *Bread for the World* (Ramsey, N.J., and Grand Rapids, Mich.: Paulist Press and Eerdmans, 1975); Ralph E. White, ed., *Psychology and the Prevention of Nuclear War: A Book of Readings* (New York: New York University Press, 1986); Katherine Scholes, *Peace Begins with You* (Boston: Little, Brown, 1990); Joan Anzalone, ed., *Good Works* (New York: Dembner Books, 1985); Ram Dass and Paul Gorman, *How Can I Help?* (New York: Knopf, 1987).

19. See James Kavanaugh, *Search: A Guide for Those Who Dare to Ask of Life Everything Good and Beautiful* (New York: Harper & Row, 1985); Hugh Prather, *Notes to Myself: My Struggle to Become a Person* (New York: Bantam Books, 1970); Muriel James and Louis Savary, *A New Self* (Reading, Mass.: Addison-Wesley, 1977); Robert A. Johnson, *Inner Work: Using Dreams and Active Imagination for Personal Growth* (New York: Harper & Row, 1986); Ira Progoff, *At a Journal Workshop* (New York: Dialogue House, 1975); Kay Leigh Hagan, *Internal Affairs: A Journal-Keeping Workbook for Self-Intimacy* (New York: Harper & Row, 1990); Eric Shepherd and J. P. Watson, eds., *Personal Meanings: The First Guy's Hospital Symposium on the Individual Frame of Reference* (New York: Wiley, 1982).

20. See David Schnarch, *Passionate Marriage* (New York: Henry Holt, 1998); Susan M. Campbell, *The Couple's Journey: Intimacy as a Path to*

Wholeness (San Luis Obispo, Calif.: Impact, 1987); Ellyn Bader and Peter Pearson, *In Quest of the Mythical Mate* (New York: Brunner/Mazel, 1988); Augustus Y. Napier, *The Fragile Bond: In Search of an Equal, Intimate and Enduring Marriage* (New York: Harper & Row, 1988); Harville Hendrix, *Getting the Love You Want; A Guide for Couples* (New York: Holt, Rinehart & Winston, 1988); George R. Bach and Peter Wyden, *The Intimate Enemy: How to Fight Fair in Love and Marriage* (New York: Avon, 1968); Roger W. Libby and Robert N. Whitehurst, *Marriage and Alternatives: Exploring Intimate Relationships* (Glenview, Ill.: Scott, Foresman, 1977); Betty Berzon, *Permanent Partners: Building Gay and Lesbian Relationships That Last* (New York: Dutton, 1988); Robert S. Weiss, *Marital Separation* (New York: Basic Books, 1975); Florence W. Kaslow and Lita L. Schwartz, *The Dynamics of Divorce: A Life Cycle Perspective* (New York: Brunner/Mazel, 1987); Melba Colgrove, Harold H. Bloomfield, and Peter McWilliams, *How to Survive the Loss of a Love* (New York: Bantam Books, 1976); Louise Montague, *A New Life Plan: A Guide for the Divorced Woman* (New York: Doubleday, 1978); Stephen R. Schuchter, *Dimensions of Grief: Adjusting to the Death of a Spouse* (San Francisco: Jossey-Bass, 1986).

21. See Michael Popkin, *Active Parenting* (New York: Harper & Row, 1987); Ellen Galinsky, *The Six Stages of Parenthood* (Reading, Mass.: Addison-Wesley, 1987); Rudolph Schaffer, *Mothering* (Cambridge, Mass.: Harvard University Press, 1977); Michael E. Lamb, ed., *The Role of the Father in Child Development,* 2nd ed. (New York: Wiley, 1981); E. James Anthony and Therese Benedek, *Parenthood: Its Psychology and Psychopathology* (Boston: Little, Brown, 1970); Bruno Bettelheim, *A Good Enough Parent: A Book on Child-Rearing* (New York: Knopf, 1987); Alice S. Rossi, Jerome Kagan, and Tamara K. Hareven, eds., *The Family* (New York: Norton, 1978); Nicholas Hobbs and others, *Strengthening Families: Strategies for Improved Child Care and Parent Education* (San Francisco: Jossey-Bass, 1984); Elizabeth A. Carter and Monica McGoldrick, eds., *The Changing Family Life Cycle: A Framework for Family Therapy,* 2nd ed. (Boston: Allyn & Bacon, 1990); Michael Lamb and Brian Sutton-Smith, eds., *Sibling Relationships: Their Nature and Significance Across the Lifespan* (Hillsdale, N.J.: Erlbaum, 1982); Francine S. Hall and Douglas T. Hall, *The Two-Career Couple* (Reading, Mass.: Addison-Wesley, 1979); Elizabeth Einstein, *The Stepfamily: Living, Loving & Learning* (New York: Macmillan, 1982); Emily B. Visher and John S. Visher, *Stepfamilies: A Guide to Working with Stepparents and Stepchildren* (New York: Brunner/Mazel, 1979); Elizabeth B. Goldsmith, ed., *Work and Family: Theory, Research, and Applications* (Newbury Park, Calif.: Sage, 1989).

22. See Rebecca G. Adams and Rosemary Bleiszner, eds., *Older Adult Friendships* (Newbury Park: Sage, 1989); Robert Bell, *Worlds of Friendship* (Newbury Park, Calif.: Sage, 1981); Roger Fisher and Scott Brown, *Getting Together: Building Relationships as We Negotiate* (New York: Penguin, 1989); Lillian B. Rubin, *Just Friends: The Role of Friendship in Our Lives* (New York: Harper & Row, 1985).

23. See Zandy Leibowitz and Daniel Lea, eds., *Adult Career Development* (Washington, D.C.: National Career Development Association, 1986); Duane Brown, Linda Brooks, and Associates, *Career Choice and Development: Applying Contemporary Theories to Practice,* 2nd ed. (San Francisco: Jossey-Bass, 1990); Dennis T. Jaffe and Cynthia D. Scott, *Take This Job and Love It* (New York: Fireside, 1988); Stan J. Katz and Aimee E. Liu, *Success Trap* (New York: Ticknor & Fields, 1990); Diane Fassel, *Working Ourselves to Death* (New York: Harper & Row, 1990); John D. Adams, ed., *Transforming Work* (Alexandria, Va.: Miles River Press, 1984); Samuel A. Culbert and John J. McDonough, *The Invisible War: Pursuing Self-Interests at Work* (New York: Wiley, 1980); Gifford Pinchot III, *Intrapreneuring* (New York: Harper & Row, 1985); Lyman Porter and Lawrence McKibbin, *Management Education and Development: Drift or Thrust into the 21st Century* (New York: McGraw-Hill, 1988); Harrison Owen, *SPIRIT: Transformation and Development in Organizations* (Potomac, Md.: Abbott, 1987); Robert Fritz, *The Path of Least Resistance,* rev. ed. (New York: Ballantine, 1989).

24. See Carl McDaniels, *Leisure: Integrating a Neglected Component in Life Planning* (Columbus, Oh.: National Center for Research in Vocational Education, 1982); Carl McDaniels, ed., *Leisure and Career Development at Mid-Life* (Blacksburg, Va.: Virginia Polytechnic Institute and State University, 1976); John M. Whiteley, ed., special issue of *The Counseling Psychologist* 9, 3 (1981).

25. See Gordon L. Lippitt, Peter Langseth, and Jack Mossop, *Implementing Organizational Change: A Practical Guide to Managing Change Efforts* (San Francisco: Jossey-Bass, 1985); Manuel London, *Change Agents: New Roles and Innovation Strategies for Human Resource Professionals* (San Francisco: Jossey-Bass, 1988).

26. See Buckminster Fuller, *Ideas and Integrities* (New York: Collier Books, 1963); Robert Ornstein and Paul Ehrlich, *New World New Mind* (New York: Simon & Schuster, 1989); Kenneth E. Boulding, *The World as a Total System* (Newbury Park, Calif.: Sage, 1985); Urie Bronfenbrenner, *The Ecology of Human Development: Experiments by Nature and Design* (Cambridge, Mass.: Harvard University Press,

1979); Carl Friedrich von Weizsacker, *The Unity of Nature,* trans. Francis J. Zucker (New York: Farrar, Straus & Giroux, 1980).

Chapter Seven

1. Theodore Lidz, *The Person: His Development Throughout the Life Cycle* (New York: Basic Books, 1968), 363 ff.

2. Frances Horn, *I Want One Thing* (Marina del Rey, Calif.: DeVorss, 1981), 31–34.

3. "The New Teens: What Makes Them Different," *Newsweek,* special edition, Summer–Fall 1990.

4. See L. J. Bradford and C. Gains, *Twenty Something: Managing and Motivating Today's New Workforce* (New York: Mastermedia, 1992); Don Tapscott, *Growing Up Digital: The Rise of the Net Generation* (New York: McGraw-Hill, 1998).

5. Dan Brown, "Thirtynothing," *Santa Barbara Independent,* 14 December 1989, 55. See also "The New Teens: What Makes Them Different."

6. Although the names and situations here have been changed, this dialogue is based on the real-life struggle quite typical of many thirtysomethings with whom I work.

7. Carl G. Jung, "Marriage as a Psychological Relationship," in *Collected Works of C. G. Jung,* vol. 17 (London: Routledge & Kegan Paul, 1954), 193.

8. Anton P. Chekhov, *Ivanov* (New York: Everyman's Library, no. 941).

9. William Bridges, *A Year in the Life* (New York: Bantam Books, 1982), inside front cover, 5, 15–16.

10. Descriptions of the midlife transition can be found in Daniel J. Levinson, *The Seasons of a Man's Life* (New York: Knopf, 1978), 191–305; Lois M. Tamir, *Men in Their Forties: The Transition to Middle Age* (New York: Springer, 1982); Herbert J. Freudenberger and Gail North, *Women's Burnout: How to Spot It, How to Reverse It, and How to Prevent It* (New York: Doubleday, 1985); Jeanne E. Gullahorn, *Psychology and Women: In Transition* (Washington, D.C.: Winston, 1979); A. Chayes, "Disarmed at Middle Age," *Atlantic* 228 (November 1971): 72–73; Michael P. Nichols, *Turning Forty in the 80s: Personal Crisis Time for Change* (New York: Simon & Schuster, 1986), 17–32. Two Jungian contributions are Peter O'Conner, *Understanding the Mid-Life Crisis* (New York: Paulist Press, 1988), and Daryl Sharp, *The Survival Papers: Anatomy of a Midlife Crisis* (Toronto: Inner City Books, 1988). See also Solomon Cytrynbaum and others, "Midlife Development: A Personality and Social Systems Perspective," in *Aging in the 1980s: Psychological Issues,* ed.

Leonard W. Poon (Washington, D.C.: American Psychological Association, 1980), 463–474.

Chapter Eight

1. Henry David Thoreau, *Walden* (1854; reprint, New York: New American Library), 10, 66.
2. Carol Gilligan, *In a Different Voice: Psychological Theory and Women's Development* (Cambridge, Mass.: Harvard University Press, 1982), 63.
3. Erica Good, "New Study Finds Middle Age Is Prime of Life," *Santa Barbara News-Press,* February 16, 1999, A-3.
4. Marvin Banasky is a businessman and a professional working with young adults in Santa Barbara, California.
5. Marilyn Mosley is a professional educator in Ojai, California.
6. Bernice L. Neugarten, "The Awareness of Middle Age," in *Middle Age and Aging* (Chicago: University of Chicago Press, 1968), 93–98. There are a number of useful references on midlife: Janet Zollinger Giele, *Women in the Middle Years* (New York: Wiley, 1982); Ralph LaRossa and Maureen M. LaRossa, *Transition to Parenthood: How Infants Change Families* (Newbury Park, Calif.: Sage, 1981); Henry S. Maas and Joseph A. Kuypers, *From Thirty to Seventy: A Forty-Year Longitudinal Study of Adult Life Styles and Personality* (San Francisco: Jossey-Bass, 1974); Judith M. Bardwick, "Middle Age and a Sense of Future," *Merrill-Palmer Quarterly* 24, no. 2 (1978), 129–138; Stanley H. Cath, "Individual Adaptation in the Middle Years: A Testing of Faith in Self and Object Constancy," *Journal of Geriatric Psychiatry* 9 (1976), 19–40; Lillian E. Troll, *Early and Middle Adulthood* (Belmont, Calif.: Wadsworth, 1975); Lois M. Tamir, *Men in Their Forties: The Transition to Middle Age* (New York: Springer, 1982); Ross Goldstein with Diana Landau, *Fortysomething* (Los Angeles: Tarcher, 1990); Pierre Mornell, *Passive Men, Wild Women* (New York: Ballantine, 1979); Michael P. Farrell and Stanley D. Rosenberg, *Men at Midlife* (Boston: Auburn House, 1981); Lillian E. Troll, Joan Israel, and Kenneth Israel, *Looking Ahead: A Woman's Guide to the Problems and Joys of Growing Older* (Englewood Cliffs, N.J.: Prentice Hall, 1977); Marilyn R. Block, Janice L. Davidson, Jean D. Grambs, *Women over Forty* (New York: Springer, 1981).
7. Carl G. Jung, *Modern Man in Search of a Soul,* trans. W. S. Dell and Carry F. Baynes (1933; reprint, New York: Harcourt Brace & World, 1983); on "individuation" and "self," see Jolande Jacobi, "Complex/Archetype/Symbol in the Psychology of C. G. Jung" (New York: Bollingen Foundation, 1959), 113–116, 186; 65, 179, 64, 194n; and 114–115, respectively.

8. Bob Sipchen, "The Inner Warrior," *Los Angeles Times* 19 March 1991, E1, E5.

9. Herant Katchadourian, *Fifty: Midlife in Perspective* (New York: W. H. Freeman, 1987), 6. An excellent book for understanding adult development in this decade and after is Janet K. Belsky, *Here Tomorrow: Making the Most of Life After Fifty* (Baltimore: Johns Hopkins University Press, 1988).

10. Since his late twenties, Richard Haid had been an insurance executive in Hamilton, Ohio. He is now a Ph.D. student at the Union Institute and a consultant for family business executives.

11. Marie Dressler, *My Own Story* (Boston: Little, Brown, 1934), chap. 4.

12. Anne Morrow Lindbergh, *Gift from the Sea* (New York: Vintage, 1977), 84.

13. Germaine Greer, "Letting Go," *Vogue,* May 1986, 141–143.

14. David C. Gutmann, "The Post-Parental Years: Clinical Problems and Developmental Possibilities," in *Mid-Life: Developmental and Clinical Issues,* ed. William H. Norman and Thomas J. Scaramella (New York: Brunner/Mazel, 1980), 44. See also David Gutmann, *Reclaimed Powers* (New York: Basic Books, 1987).

Chapter Nine

1. Lillian E. Troll, *Early and Middle Adulthood* (Belmont, Calif.: Wadsworth, 1975), 143. See also Harry R. Moody, *Aging: Concepts and Controversies* (Thousand Oaks, Calif: Pine Forge Press, 1998); Robert Butler and Myrnia I. Lewis, *Aging and Mental Health,* 5th ed. (Needham Heights, Mass.: Allyn & Bacon, 1998); Richard Restak, *Older and Wiser* (New York: Berkley, 1997); Zalman Schachter-Shalomi, *From Age-ing to Sage-ing—A Profound New Vision of Growing Older* (New York: Warner, 1997).

2. Cathleen Rountree, *On Women Turning 60* (New York: Three Rivers, 1997), 136–137. Rachel Rosenthal, born in 1926, is a feminist, artist, and original thinker.

3. Larry L. King, "What, Me Sixty?" *Parade Magazine,* 5 November 1989, 4–9. The celebration of his sixtieth birthday in 1989 prompted author and playwright Larry L. King to reassess his attitudes about aging. Reprinted with permission from Parade, copyright © 1989.

4. "Suddenly 60," *USA WEEKEND,* 9–15 June 1989, 23.

5. See Laurent A. Daloz, *Effective Teaching and Mentoring: Realizing the Transformational Power of Adult Learning Experiences* (San Francisco: Jossey-Bass, 1986); Daniel J. Levinson, *The Seasons of a Man's Life* (New York: Knopf, 1978), 97–101.

6. Elisabeth Kübler-Ross, in Phillip L. Berman (ed.), *The Courage of*

Conviction (New York: Dodd, Mead & Company, Inc., 1985), pp. 123–124. Kübler-Ross is a major contributor to our understanding of the death and dying process.

7. Elliot L. Richardson, in Phillip L. Berman (ed.), *The Courage of Conviction* (New York: Dodd, Mead & Company, Inc., 1985), pp. 162–164. Elliot Richardson was Attorney General during the waning days of the Nixon Administration; Secretary of Defense; Secretary of Health Education and Welfare; and Secretary of Commerce.

8. Phillip L. Berman (ed.), *The Courage of Conviction* (New York: Dodd, Mead & Company, Inc., 1985), p. 211. Edward Wilson is a biologist, whose research includes a definitive and comprehensive study of insects, and author of *Sociobiology, On Human Nature,* and *Biophilia.*

9. Jimmy Carter, *The Virtues of Aging* (New York: Ballantine, 1998), pp. 51–53, 56, 65–66, 92–93, 122–123, 134. Jimmy Carter, thirty-ninth president of the United States, has written thirteen previous books.

10. Phillip L. Berman, ed., *The Courage to Grow Old* (New York: Ballantine, 1989), 72. Born in 1918, Robert Lee has coauthored some of the great contemporary classics for the American theater, including *Inherit the Wind* and *Auntie Mame.* He teaches advanced playwriting at UCLA.

11. Berman, *The Courage to Grow Old,* 187–189. Sarah McClendon operates her own news bureau in Washington, D.C. During her career, she has been a reporter, news service executive, and television and radio analyst.

12. Berman, *The Courage to Grow Old,* 260–61. Malcolm Muggeridge was a British journalist, social critic, and theologian. He died in 1990.

13. Larry Porter, "A Conversation with Bob Tannenbaum," *OD Practitioner,* September 1990, 13. See also Eugene C. Bianchi, *On Growing Older: A Personal Guide to Life after 35* (New York: Crossroad, 1986).

14. Erik H. Erikson, *Identity: Youth and Crisis* (New York: Norton, 1968), 140–141. See also Erik H. Erikson, *The Life Cycle Completed* (New York: Norton, 1982); Erik H. Erikson, Joan M. Erikson, and Helen Q. Kivnick, *Vital Involvement in Old Age* (New York: Norton, 1986); and Helen M. Luke, *Old Age* (New York: Parabola Books, 1987).

15. See Walter M. Bortz II, *We Live Too Short and Die Too Long* (New York: Bantam Books, 1991); Lissy F. Jarvik, ed., *Aging into the Twenty-First Century: Middle-Agers Today* (New York: Gardner Press, 1978); Paul Homer and Martha Holstein, eds., *A Good Old Age?* (New York: Touchstone, 1990); Leonard Hayflick, *Why and How We Age* (New York: Ballantine, 1994).

16. Jimmy Carter, *The Virtues of Aging* (New York: Ballantine, 1998), p. 19.

17. Phillip L. Berman (ed.), *The Courage of Conviction* (New York: Dodd, Mead & Company, Inc., 1985), pp. 20–21. William Barrett, born in 1913, was an editor of leading magazines and journals, including *Partisan Review.* He is a philosopher, author, and teacher.

18. Phillip L. Berman (ed.), *The Courage of Conviction* (New York: Dodd, Mead & Company, Inc., 1985), pp. 135–136. Madeleine L'Engle, born in 1918, is an author of many books, some written for children and others for adults.

19. Phillip L. Berman (ed.), *The Courage of Conviction* (New York: Dodd, Mead & Company, Inc., 1985), pp. 65–67. Hugh Downs, born in 1921, is well known as an announcer and anchorman on television.

20. Phillip L. Berman (ed.), *The Courage of Conviction* (New York: Dodd, Mead & Company, Inc., 1985), pp. 8–13. Steve Allen, born in 1921, is a comedian, musician, and author.

21. Elisabeth Kübler-Ross, *Death: The Final Stage of Growth* (Englewood Cliffs, New Jersey: Prentice-Hall, 1975); Sherwin B. Nuland, *How We Die—Reflections on Life's Final Chapter* (New York: Knopf, 1993); Ira Brock, *Dying Well—The Prospect for Growth at the End of Life* (New York: Riverhead, 1997).

Chapter Ten

1.   Further inquiry into this point of view might include a study of the writings of Sigmund Freud and Carl Jung. An easy but profound beginning point would be Donald W. Winnicott, *Human Nature* (New York: Schocken Books, 1988).

2.   See Jerry Gerber and others, *Lifetrends: The Future of Baby Boomers and Other Aging Americans* (New York: Macmillan, 1989).

3.   See Nancy Smith, "In the Shadow of the Boomers: Post-Boom," *Oregonian,* 29 July 1990, D3–D4, which suggests that the current twentysomethings can be characterized as ambivalent, indecisive, seeking to define themselves through their work. "Our lives are so open, the choices endless. We need to make decisions but don't want to leave anything out. We are grown-up children, wearing the suit but keeping the ponytail. We are migrants in search of a more perfect home. We are seriously unserious. We are confident neurotics. We are undecided, leaving the doors open. We are pending."

4.   See Bernice L. Neugarten, "The Awareness of Middle Age" and "Adult Personality: Toward a Psychology of the Life Cycle," in *Middle Age and Aging* (Chicago: University of Chicago Press, 1968). See also Robert Peck, "Psychological Developments in the Second Half of Life," in *The Human Life Cycle,* ed. William C. Sze (New York: Aronson, 1975).

5. See the Prologue to this book.

6. See, for example, Urie Bronfenbrenner, *The Ecology of Human Development* (Cambridge, Mass.: Harvard University Press, 1979); Klaus Riegel, "Adult Life Crises: A Dialectical Interpretation of Development," in *Life-span Developmental Psychology: Normative Life Crises,* eds. Nancy Datan and Leon H. Ginsberg (Orlando, Fla.: Academic Press, 1975); Matilda White Riley, Ronald P. Abeles, and Michael S. Teitelbaum, eds., *Aging from Birth to Death,* vol. 2, *Sociotemporal Perspectives* (Boulder, Colo.: Westview Press, 1981). Barry Johnson, *Polarity Management—Identifying and Managing Unsolvable Problems.* Amherst, Mass.: HRD Press, 1992.

7. See Frederick Towne Melges, *Time and the Inner Future* (New York: Wiley, 1982); Joseph E. McGrath and Janice R. Kelly, *Time and Human Interaction: Toward a Social Psychology of Time* (New York: Guilford Press, 1986); Robert Grundin, *Time and the Art of Living* (New York: Ticknor & Fields, 1982); Marilee Zdenek, *Inventing the Future* (New York: McGraw-Hill, 1987); Howard F. Didsbury, Jr., ed., *The Future: Opportunity Not Destiny* (Bethesda, Md.: World Future Society, 1989).

Chapter Eleven

1. In Robert Ornstein and Paul Ehrlich, *New World New Mind* (New York: Simon & Schuster, 1989), 200, 264–265.

2. Edward E. Sampson, "The Debate on Individualism," *American Psychologist,* 45, no. 1 (1988), 15–22.

3. Andrew M. Mecca, Neil J. Smelser, and John Vasconcellos, eds., *The Social Importance of Self-Esteem* (Berkeley: University of California Press, 1989, xi.

4. Rainer Marie Rilke, "The Ninth Elegy," *Duino Elegies,* trans. C. F. MacIntyre (Berkeley, Calif.: University of California Press, 1965), 71–73.

5. From an unpublished article, "Surfing, a Radical Yoga" (1974), by Richard Heckler, provided to me by an ardent surfer from San Diego, Mark Tourtellote.

6. Jack London, *The Cruise of the Snark* (1907; reprint, New York: Macmillan, 1939).

7. James Gleick, *Chaos: Making a New Science* (New York: Penguin Books, 1987); Gery Taubes, "The Body Chaotic, *Discover,* May 1989, 63–67.

8. Harry Hurt III, *For All Mankind* (New York: Atlantic Monthly Press, 1988), 325–326.

9. Suzanne Berger, and others, "Toward a New Industrial America,"

Scientific American 260, 6 (1989), 47. Other writings that support this way of thinking include Tom Peters, *Thriving on Chaos: Handbook for a Management Revolution* (New York: Knopf, 1987); William Bridges, *Surviving Corporate Transitions* (New York: Doubleday, 1988); Robert H. Waterman, Jr., *The Renewal Factor* (New York: Bantam Books, 1987); Donald L. Kirkpatrick, *How to Manage Change Effectively: Approaches, Methods, and Case Examples* (San Francisco: Jossey-Bass, 1985); and Burt Nanus, *The Leader's Edge: The Seven Keys to Leadership in a Turbulent World* (New York: Contemporary Books, 1989).

10. Willis Harman, *Global Mind Change: The Promise of the Last Years of the Twentieth Century* (Indianapolis, Ind.: Knowledge Systems, 1988), 132.

Chapter Twelve

1. Mihaly Csikszentmihalyi, *Flow: The Psychology of Optimal Experience—Steps Toward Enhancing the Quality of Life* (New York: Harper & Row, 1990), 213.

2. Dag Hammarskjöld, *Markings* (New York: Knopf, 1964), 55.

3. Charlotte Buhler and Fred Massarik, eds., *The Course of Human Life* (New York: Springer, 1968), 2.

4. Anthony Storr, *Solitude: A Return to the Self* (New York: Free Press, 1988), 34–35.

5. Hammarskjöld, *Markings*, 13.

6. Anne Morrow Lindbergh, *Gift from the Sea* (New York: Vintage, 1977), 80, 84–85.

7. Hilary Appelman, *Santa Barbara News-Press*, 4 February 1991, C–4.

8. See, for example, Barbara F. Okun, *Working with Adults: Individual, Family, and Career Development* (Monterey, Calif.: Brooks/Cole, 1984); David N. Ulrich and Harry P. Dunne, Jr., *To Love & Work: A Systematic Interlocking of Family, Workplace, and Career* (New York: Brunner/Mazel, 1986); John F. Nussbaum, ed., *Life-Span Communication: Normative Processes* (Hillsdale, N.J.: Erlbaum, 1989); FM–2030, *Are You A Transhuman? Monitoring and Stimulating Your Personal Rate of Growth in a Rapidly Changing World* (New York: Warner Books, 1989).

9. Carl Jung, *Modern Man in Search of a Soul*, trans. W. S. Dell and Carry F. Baynes (1933; reprint, New York: Harcourt Brace & World, 1983), 108.

10. See Morris T. Keeton and Associates, *Experiential Learning: Rationale, Characteristics, and Assessment* (San Francisco: Jossey-Bass, 1976); Malcolm S. Knowles, *Self-Directed Learning: A Guide for Learners and Teachers* (Chicago: Follett, 1975); Alan M. Thomas, *Beyond Education: A New Perspective on Society's Management of Learning* (San Francisco: Jossey-Bass, 1991); Stephen D. Brookfield, *Developing Critical*

Thinkers: Challenging Adults to Explore Alternative Ways of Thinking and Acting (San Francisco: Jossey-Bass, 1987); Trevor A. Williams, *Learning to Manage Our Futures: The Participative Redesign of Societies in Turbulent Transition* (New York: Wiley, 1982); Hugh J. Lurie, "Life Planning: An Educational Approach to Change," *American Journal of Psychiatry* 134, no. 8 (1977), 878–882.

11. Mortimer J. Adler, *Reforming Education: The Opening of the American Mind* (New York: Macmillan, 1990), 328. Adler goes on to say, "To the extent that the great books constitute the monuments of our culture, the substance of our intellectual tradition, the more individuals who in any degree actually possess some of that culture through the reading and discussion of the great books, the more favorable are the conditions for its transmission and progress."

12. Perry Pascarella, *The New Achievers: Creating a Modern Work Ethic* (New York: Free Press, 1984), 13, 110, 137, 169.

13. Peter M. Senge, "The Leader's New Work: Building Learning Organizations," *Sloan Management Review* 7 (Fall 1990), 7–23. See also Peter M. Senge, *The Fifth Discipline: The Art and Practice of the Learning Organization* (New York: Doubleday, 1990); Victoria J. Marsick and Karen E. Watkins, *Informal and Incidental Learning in the Workplace* (New York: Routledge, 1990).

14. Seymour B. Sarason and Elizabeth Lorentz, *The Challenge of the Resource Exchange Network: From Concept to Action* (San Francisco: Jossey-Bass, 1979), 226–27.

15. Alvin Toffler, *Future Shock* (New York: Random House, 1970), 429.

16. See Harry C. Boyte and Frank Riessman, eds., *The New Populism: The Politics of Empowerment* (Philadelphia: Temple University Press, 1986); Harry C. Boyte, *Citizen Action and the New American Populism* (Philadelphia: Temple University Press, 1986). The classic for understanding this model of innovation and change is John W. Gardner's *Self-Renewal*, rev. ed. (New York: Norton, 1981). Speaking in simple language, Gardner describes the personal and social renewal process with great clarity. Gardner's book *On Leadership* (New York: Free Press, 1990) expands on his earlier ideas. Also see Joseph N. Pelton, *Future Talk: Global Life in the Age of Telepower* (Boulder, Colo.: Cross Communications Press, 1990).

17. Robert K. Greenleaf, *Servant Leadership: A Journey into the Nature of Legitimate Power and Greatness* (Mahwah, N.J.: Paulist Press, 1977).

Chapter Thirteen

1. See Frederic M. Hudson, *The Handbook of Coaching*. San Francisco: Jossey-Bass, 1999.

Reading List

Ables, Ronald P., Gift, Helen C., & Ory, Marcia G. (Eds.). (1994). *Aging and the quality of life.* New York: Springer.

Adams, Paul L., Milner, Judith R., & Schrept, N. A. (1984). *Fatherless children.* New York: Wiley-Interscience.

Adams, Rebecca G., & Bleiszner, Rosemary (Eds.). (1989). *Older adult friendship.* Newbury Park, CA: Sage.

Adams-Price, C. (Ed.). (1993). *Creativity and aging: Theoretical and empirical approaches.* New York: Springer.

Adelson, J. (Ed.). (1980). *Handbook of adolescent psychology.* New York: Wiley.

Adler, Lynn Peters. (1995). *Centenarians: The bonus years.* Santa Fe, NM: Health Press.

Adlwin, Carolyn M. (1994). *Stress, coping, and development.* New York: Guilford.

Aftel, Mandy. (1996). *The story of your life: Becoming the author of your own experience.* New York: Simon & Schuster.

Alexander, Charles N., & Langer, Ellen J. (Eds.). (1990). *Higher stages of human development.* New York: Oxford University Press.

Allan, Graham. (1989). *Friendship: Developing a sociological perspective.* Boulder, CO: Westview.

Allison, Paul D., & Furstenberg, Frank F., Jr. (1989). How marital dissolution affects children. *Developmental Psychology, 25,* 540–549.

Amato, Paul R. (1996). A prospective study of divorce and parent-child relationships. *Journal of Marriage and the Family, 58,* 356–365.

American Psychiatric Association. (1994). *Diagnostic and statistical manual of mental disorders—DSM-IV.* Washington, DC: Author.

Ammerman, Robert T., & Hersen, Michel (Eds.). (1989). *Treatment of family violence.* New York: Wiley.

Anderson, B. (1989). Effects of public day care: A longitudinal study. *Child Development, 60,* 857–866.

Angel, Ronald J., & Angel, Jacqueline L. (1994). *Painful inheritance: Health and the new generation of fatherless families.* Madison: University of Wisconsin Press.

Antonucci, Toni C. (1990). Attachment, social support, and coping with negative life events. In E. M. Cummings, A. L. Greene, & H. H. Karracker (Eds.), *Life-span developmental psychology: Vol. 11. Stress and coping access the life-span.* Hillsdale, NJ: Erlbaum.

Antonucci, Toni C., & Akiyama, Hiroko. (1995). Convoys of social relations: Family and friendships within a life span context. In Rosemary Blieszner & Victoria Hilkevitch Bedford (Eds.), *Handbook of aging and the family.* Westport, CT: Greenwood Press.

Arber, Sara, & Ginn, Jay (Eds.). (1995). *Connecting gender and aging.* Buckingham, England: Open University Press.

Arendell, Terry. (1995). *Fathers and divorce.* Newbury Park, CA: Sage.

Aries, Philippe. (1981). *The hour of our death.* New York: Knopf.

Arking, Robert. (1991). *Biology of aging: Observations and principles.* Englewood Cliffs, NJ: Prentice Hall.

Aronson, Miriam K. (1994). *Reshaping dementia care.* Thousand Oaks, CA: Sage.

Astin, Alexander W. (1977). *Four critical years: Effects of college on beliefs, attitudes, and knowledge.* San Francisco: Jossey-Bass.

Astington, Janet Wilde. (1993). *The child's discovery of the mind.* Cambridge, MA: Harvard University Press.

Atchley, Robert C. (1991). Family, friends, and social support. In *Social forces and aging.* Belmont, CA: Wadsworth.

Ausman, L. M., & Russell, R. M. (1990). Nutrition in aging. In *Handbook of the biology of aging* (3rd ed.). San Diego, CA: Academic Press.

Bachrach, C. A., Clogg, C. C., & Carver, K. (1993). Outcomes of early childbearing: Summary of a conference. *Journal of Research on Adolescence, 3,* 337–348.

Baird, Robert M., & Rosenbaum, Stuart E. (Eds.). (1996). *Euthanasia—the moral issues.* New York: Prometheus.

Bakan, D. (1966). *The duality of human existence: Isolation and communion in western man.* Boston: Beacon.

Baldwin, James. (1961). *Nobody knows my name.* New York: Dial Press.

Ballard, Jack, & Ballard, Phoebe. (1993). *Beating the age game—redefining retirement.* New York: Mastermedia Limited.

Baltes, Paul B. (1993). The aging mind: Potential and limits. *The Gerontologist, 33,* 580–594.

Baltes, Paul B., & Baltes, Margaret M. (1990). Psychological perspectives on successful aging: The model of selective optimization with compensation. In Paul B. Baltes & Margret M. Baltes (Eds.), *Successful aging: Perspectives from the behavioral sciences.* Cambridge, England: Cambridge University Press.

Baltes, Paul B., & Smith, Jacqui. (1990). Toward a psychology of wisdom and its ontogenesis. In Robert J. Sternberg (Ed.), *Wisdom: Its nature, origins, and development.* Cambridge, England: Cambridge University Press.

Baltes, Paul B., Smith, J., & Staudinger, U. M. (1992). Wisdom and successful aging. In T. B. Sonderegger (Ed.), *Nebraska symposium on motivation, 1991* (pp. 123–168). Lincoln: University of Nebraska Press.

Bandura, Albert. (1995). *Self-efficacy in changing societies.* New York: Cambridge University Press.

Barber, B. K. (1994). Cultural, family, and personal contexts of parent-adolescent conflict. *Journal of Marriage and the Family, 56,* 375–386.

Barkley, R. A. (1990). Attention deficit disorders: History, definition, and diagnosis. In M. Lewis & S. M. Miller (Eds.), *Handbook of developmental psychopathology*. New York: Plenum.

Barkow, Jerome H., Cosmides, Leda, & Tooby, John (Eds.). (1992). *The adapted mind: Evolutionary psychology and the generation of culture*. New York: Oxford University Press.

Barusch, A. S. (1994). *Older women in poverty: Private lives and public policies*. New York: Springer.

Bass, S. A. (Ed.). (1995). *Older and active: How Americans over age 55 are contributing to society*. New Haven, CT: Yale University Press.

Bass, S. A., Caro, Francis G., & Chen, Yung-Ping (Eds.). (1993). *Achieving a productive aging society*. Westport, CT: Auburn House.

Bassuk, E. L. (1989). Homelessness: A growing American tragedy. *Division of Child, Youth, and Family Services Newsletter, 12,*: 1–13.

Bateson, Mary Catherine. (1990). *Composing a life*. New York: Plume.

Baumeister, Roy F. (1991). *Meanings of life*. New York: Guilford.

Bayley, Nancy, & Oden, Melita. (1955). The maintenance of intellectual ability in gifted adults. *Journal of Gerontology, 10,* Section B, (1), 91–107.

Beard, Belle Boone. (1991). *Centenarians: The new generation*. Westport, CT: Greenwood Press.

Beck, Ulrih, & Beck-Gernsheim, Elizabeth. (1995). *The normal chaos of love*. Cambridge, England: Polity Press.

Bedford, Victoria H. (1995). Sibling relationships in middle and old age. In Rosemary Blieszner & Victoria H. Bedford (Eds.), *Handbook of aging and the family*. Hillsdale, NJ: Greenwood Press.

Beizer, Judith L. (1994). Medications and the aging body: Alteration as a function of age. *Generations, 18,* 13–18.

Bell, Derrick. (1992). *Faces at the bottom of the well: The permanence of racism*. New York: Basic Books.

Bellantoni, Michele F., & Blackman, Marc R. (1996). Menopause and its consequences. In E. L. Schneider & J. W. Rowe (Eds.), *Handbook of the biology of aging*. San Diego, CA: Academic Press.

Belsky, Jay, & Kelley, John. (1994). *The Transition to parenthood*. New York: Delacorte.

Belsky, Jay, & Vondra, Joan. (1989). Lessons from child abuse: The determinants of parenting, In D. Cicchetti & V. Carlson (Eds.), *Child maltreatment: Theory and research on the causes and consequences of child abuse and neglect*. Cambridge, England: Cambridge University Press.

Bengston, Vern L., Schaie, K. Warner (Eds.). (1989). *The course of later life*. New York: Springer.

Bengston, Vern L., Schaie, K. Warner, & Burton, Linda M. (Eds.). (1995). *Adult intergenerational relations: Effects of societal change*. New York: Springer.

Bengston, Vern L., Rosenthal, Carolyn, & Burton, Linda M. (1996). Paradoxes of Families and Aging. In J. E. Birren & K. W. Schaie (Eds.), *Handbook of aging and the social sciences*. San Diego, CA: Academic Press.

Benoit, Diane, & Parker, Kevin C. (1994). Stability and transmission of attachment across three generations, *Child Development, 65*, 1444–1456.

Benson, Peter L. (1993). *The troubled journey: A portrait of 6th–12th grade youth.* Minneapolis, MN: Search Institute.

Berg, Cynthia A., & Sternberg, Robert J. (1985). A triarchic theory of intellectual development during adulthood. *Developmental Review, 5*, 334–370.

Berg, Robert L., & Cassells, Joseph E. (1990). *The second fifty years: Promoting health and preventing disability.* Washington, DC: National Academy Press.

Berger, Arthur, Badham, Paul, Kutscher, Austin H., and Associates (Eds.). (1989). *Perspectives on death and dying: Cross-cultural and multi-disciplinary views.* Philadelphia: Charles Press.

Berman, P. W., & Pedersen, F. A. (Eds.). (1987). *Men's transitions to parenthood. Longitudinal studies of early family experience.* Hillsdale, NJ: Erlbaum.

Berndt, Thomas J. (1989). Friendships in childhood and adolescence. In W. Damon (Ed.), *Child development today and tomorrow.* San Francisco: Jossey-Bass.

Berndt, Thomas J., & Perry, T. B. (1990). Distinguishing features of early adolescent friendship. In R. Montemeyer, G. R. Adams, & T. P. Gullota (Eds.), *From childhood to adolescence: A transitional period?* Newbury Park, CA: Sage.

Berndt, Thomas J., & Savin-Williams, R. C. (1992). Peer relations and friendships. In P. H. Tolan & B. J. Kohler (Eds.), *Handbook of clinical research and practice with adolescents.* New York: Wiley.

Bergquist, William H., and Associates. (1993). *In our fifties—Voices of men and women reinventing their lives.* San Francisco: Jossey-Bass.

Berry, Ruth E., & Williams, Flora L. (1987). Assessing the relationship between quality of life and marital and income satisfaction: A path analytic approach. *Journal of Marriage and the Family, 49*, 107–116.

Betancourt, Raoul Louis. (1991). *Retirement and men's physical and social health.* New York: Garland.

Bianchi, Eugene C. (1982). *Aging as a spiritual journey.* New York: Crossroad.

Bianchi, Eugene C. (1986). *On growing older: A personal guide to life after 35.* New York: Crossroad Publishing.

Bianchi, Eugene C. (1994). *Elder wisdom: crafting your own ederhood.* New York: Crossroad.

Biegel, D. E., Sales, E., & Schultz, R. (1991). *Family caregiving in chronic illness.* London: Sage.

Binstock, R. H., & George, Linda K. (Eds.). (1996). *Handbook of aging and the social sciences* (2nd ed.). New York: Van Nostrand Reinhold.

Binstock, Robert H., Post, Stephen G., & Whitehouse, Peter J. (Eds.). (1992). *Dementia and aging: Ethics, values, and policy choices.* Baltimore: Johns Hopkins University Press.

Birren, James E. (1990). *Sexuality and Aging: A Selected Bibliography.* Revised edition. Los Angeles: Andrus Gerontology Center, University of Southern California.

Birren, James E., & Bengtson, V. L. (Eds.). (1988). *Emergent theories of aging.* New York: Springer.

Birren, James E., & Sloane, R. Bruce (Eds.). (1992). *Handbook of mental health and aging* (3rd ed). Englewood Cliffs, NJ: Prentice-Hall.

Birren, James E., & Schaie, K. Warner (Eds.). (1990). *Handbook of the psychology of aging* (3rd ed.). San Diego, CA: Academic Press.

Blakely, Mary Kay. (1994). *American mom.* Chapel Hill, NC: Algonquin.

Blakemore, Ken, & Boneham, Margaret. (1994).*Age, race and ethnicity: A comparative approach.* Buckingham, England: Open University Press.

Blankenhorn, David. (1995). *Fatherless America: Confronting our most urgent social problem.* New York: Basic Books.

Blieszner, R., & Adams, R. G. (1992). *Adult friendships.* Newbury Park, CA: Sage.

Blieszner, Rosemary, & Beford, Victoria Hilkevitch (Eds.). (1995).*Handbook of aging and the family.* Westport, CT: Greenwood Press.

Bly, Robert (Ed.). (1990). *Iron John: A book about men.* Reading, Mass.: Addison-Wesley.

Blythe, Ronald. (1979). *The view in winter: Reflections on old age.* New York: Penguin.

Bolton, Frank G., Morris, Larry A., & MacEacheron, Ann E. (1989) *Males at risk: The other side of child sexual abuse.* Newbury Park, CA: Sage.

Boorstin, Daniel J. (1962). *The image or what happened to the American dream.* New York: Atheneum.

Booth, Alan (Ed.). (1991). *Contemporary families: Looking forward, looking back.* Minneapolis, MN: National Council on Family Relations.

Booth, Alan, & Edwards, John N. (1992). Starting over: Why remarriages are more unstable. *Journal of Family Issues, 13,* 179–194.

Booth, Alan, & Johnson, E. (1988). Premarital cohabitation and marital success. *Journal of Family Issues, 9,* 387–394.

Booth, Wayne (Ed.). (1992). *The Art of growing older—writers on living and aging.* New York: Poseidon Press.

Borchard, David, Kelly, John J., & Weaver, Nancy-Pat. (1998). *Your career—choices and changes* (7th Edition). Dubuque, IA: Kendall/Hunt.

Bornstein, Marc H., & Lamb, M. E. (Eds.). (1992). *Developmental psychology: An advanced textbook.* Hillsdale, NJ: Erlbaum.

Bornstein, Marc H., & Lamb, M. E. (1992). *Development in infancy* (3rd ed.). New York: McGraw-Hill.

Bowlby, John. (1969). *Attachment* (Vol. 1). New York: Basic Books.

Bradford, Lawrence J., & Raines, Claire. (1992). *Twenty-something—managing and motivating today's new work force.* New York: MasterMedia Limited.

Brandtstadter, J., & Greve, W. (1994). The aging self: Stabilizing and protective processes. *Developmental Review, 14,* 52–80.

Brayfield, April A. (1995). Juggling jobs and kids: The impact of employment schedules on fathers' caring for children. *Journal of Marriage and the Family, 57,* 321–332.

Bremner, J. Gavin. (1988). *Infancy.* Oxford, England: Blackwell.

Brent, David A., and Associates. (1994). Personality disorder, personality traits, impulsive violence, and complete suicide in adolescents. *Journal of the American Academy of Child and Adolescent Psychiatry, 33,* 1080–1086.

Bretherton, Inge. (1992). The origins of attachment theory: John Bowlby and Mary Ainsworth. *Developmental Psychology, 28,* 759–775.

Bridges, William. (1991). *Managing transitions—making the most of change.* Reading, MA: Addison-Wesley.

Briere, J. M., & Elliott, D. M. (1994). Immediate and long-term impacts of child sexual abuse. *The future of children, 4,* 54–69.

Bronstein, P., & Cowan, C.P. (Eds.). (1988). *Fatherhood today. Men's changing role in the family.* New York: Wiley.

Brookfield, Stephen D. (1987). *Developing critical thinkers—challenging adults to explore alternative ways of thinking and acting.* San Francisco: Jossey-Bass.

Brown, B. B., Lohr, Mary Jane, & McClenahan, Eben L. (1993). Early adolescents' perception of peer pressure. *Journal of Early Adolescence, 6,* 139–154.

Brown, B. B., Mounts, N., Lamborn, S. D., & Steinberg, L. (1993). Parenting practices and peer group affiliation in adolescence. *Child Development, 64,* 467–482.

Brown, Lyn Mikel, & Gilligan, Carol. (1992). *Meeting at the Crossroads—the landmark book about the turning points in girls' and women's lives.* New York: Ballantine.

Brown, Zev, McKinney, Edward A., & Williams, Michael (Eds.). (1990). *Black aged.* Newbury Park, CA: Sage.

Brownson, Ross C., Alavanja, Michael, Hock, Edward T., & Loy, Timothy S. (1992). Passive smoking and lung cancer in nonsmoking women. *American Journal of Public Health, 82,* 1525–1530.

Bruun, Ruth Dowling, & Brunn, Bertel. (1994). *A mind of its own: Tourette's syndrome—a story and a guide.* New York: Oxford University Press.

Bryan, E. (1992). *Twins, triplets, and more.* New York: St. Martin's Press.

Buckingham, Robert W. (1997). *The handbook of hospice care.* New York: Prometheus.

Buhler, Charlotte, & Massarik, Fred. (1968). *The course of human life—a study of goals in the humanistic perspective.* New York: Springer.

Burns, Ailsa, & Scott, Cath. (1994). *Mother-headed families and why they have increased.* Hillsdale, NJ: Erlbaum.

Busse, Ewald W. (1985). Normal aging: The Duke longitudinal studies. In M. Bergener, Marco Ermini, & H. B. Stahelin (Eds.), *Thresholds in Aging.* London: Academic Press.

Butler, Robert, and Brody, J.A. (Eds.). (1995). *Strategies to delay dysfunction in later life.* New York: Springer.

Butler, Robert N., Lewis, Myrna I., & Sunderland, Trey. (1998) *Aging and mental health—positive psychosocial and biomedical approaches* (5th ed.). Needham Heights, MA: Allyn & Bacon.

Byock, Ira. (1997). *Dying well—the prospect for growth at the end of life.* New York: Riverhead.

Cahalan, Don. (1991). *An ounce of prevention: Strategies for solving tobacco, alcohol, and other drug problems.* San Francisco: Jossey-Bass.

Cairns, Robert B., & Cairns, Beverly D. (1994). *Lifelines and risks: Pathways of youth in our time.* Cambridge, England: Cambridge University Press.

Campbell, Angus. (1981). *The sense of well-being in America* . New York: McGraw-Hill.

Campbell, Joseph. (1985). *The inner reaches of outer space.* New York: Van Der Marck.

Canetto, Silvia Sara. (1992). Gender and suicide in the elderly. *Suicide and Life-Threatening Behavior, 22,* 88–96.

Cappelleri, J.C., Eckenrode, J., & Powers, J.L. (1993). The epidemiology of child abuse: Findings from the second national incidence and prevalence study of child abuse and neglect. *American Journal of Public Health, 83,* 1622–1624.

Carlson, Karen J., Eisenstat, Stephanie A., & Ziporyn, Terra. (1995). *The Harvard Guide to women's health.* Cambridge, MA: Harvard University Press.

Carnegie Council on Adolescent Development. (1989). *Turning points: Preparing American youth for the 21st century.* New York: Carnegie Corporation.

Carter, Elizabeth A., & McGoldrick, Monica (Eds.). (1990). *The changing family life cycle: A framework for family therapy* (2nd Edition). Boston, MA: Allyn and Bacon.

Caruso, Richard E. (1992). *Mentoring and the business environment: Asset or liability?* Newcastle-upon-Tyne: Athenaeum Press.

Case, Robbie. (1985). *Intellectual development: Birth to adulthood.* Orlando, FL: Academic Press.

Caspi, Avshalom, Elder, Glen H., & Bem, Daryl J. (1988). Moving away from the world: Life-course patterns of shy children. *Developmental Psychology, 24,* 824–831.

Cassel, Christine K. (1996). Physician-assisted suicide: Progress or peril. In David C. Thomasma & Thomasine Kushner (Eds.), *Birth to death.* Cambridge, England: Cambridge University Press.

Cates, Willard Jr. (1995). Sexually transmitted diseases. B.P. Sachs, R. Beard, and E. Papiernik (Eds.), *Reproduction health care for women and babies.* Oxford, England: Oxford University Press.

Cattell, R. B. (1963). Theory of fluid and crystallized intelligence: A critical experiment. *Journal of Educational Psychology, 54,* 1–22.

Chen, Kevin, & Kandel, Denise. (1995). The natural history of drug use from adolescence to the mid-thirties in a general population sample. *American Journal of Public Health, 85,* 41–47.

Cherlin, A. J. (1992). *Marriage, divorce, remarriage.* Cambridge, MA: Harvard University Press.

Cherlin, Andrew, & Furstenberg, Frank F., Jr. (1986). *The new American grandparent: A place in the family, a life apart.* New York: Basic Books, 1986.

Chinen, Allan. (1989). *In the ever after: Fairy tales and the second half of life.* Wilmette, IL: Chiron.

Chiriboga, D. A., & Catron, L. A. (1992). *Divorce: Crisis, challenge or relief?* New York: NY University Press.

Cicirelli, Victor G. (1995). *Sibling relationships across the life span*. New York: Plenum Press.

Clausen, J. A. (1993). *American lives: Looking back at the children of the great depression*. New York: Free Press.

Clemens, Andra W., & Axelson, Leland J. (1985). The not-so-empty nest: The return of the fledgling adult. *Family Relations, 34*, 259–264.

Coke, Marguerite M., & Twaite, James A. (1995). *The black elderly: Satisfaction and quality of later life*. New York: Hayworth Press.

Cole, Thomas. (1992). *The journey of life: A cultural history of aging in America*. New York: Cambridge University Press.

Cole, Thomas R., & Gadow, Sally A. (Eds.). *What does it mean to grow old?* Durham, NC: Duke University Press.

Cole, Thomas R., & Winkler, Mary G. (1994). *The Oxford book of aging: Reflections on the journey of life*. New York: Oxford.

Coleman, Bing, & Coleman, Libby. (1997). *Laughter and tears: The emotional life of new mothers*. New York: Holt.

Coleman, J. C., & Hendry, L. (1990). *The nature of adolescence* (2nd ed.) London: Routledge.

Colin, Virginia L. (1996). *Human attachment*. Philadelphia: Temple University Press.

Coni, Nicholas K., Davison, William, & Webster, Stephen. (1992). *Aging: The facts*. Oxford, England: Oxford University Press.

Cosaro, W. A. (1985). *Friendship and peer culture in the early years*. Norwood, NJ: Abex.

Cowan, C. P., & Cowan, P. A. (1992). *When partners become parents*. New York: Basic Books.

Cowan, Paul E., & Hetherington, Mavis (Eds.). (1991). *Family transitions*. Hillsdale, NJ: Erlbaum.

Craik, F. I. M., & Salthouse, T. A (Eds.). (1992). *The handbook of aging and cognition*. Hillsdale, NJ: Erlbaum.

Crimmins, E. M., & Ingegneri, D. G. (1990). Interaction and living arrangements of older parents and their children: Past trends, present determinants, future implications. *Research on Aging 2*, 3–35.

Cross, W. W., Jr. (1991). *Shades of black: Diversity in African-American identity*. Philadelphia: Temple University Press.

Csikszentmihalyi, Mihaly. (1996). *Being Adolescent*. New York: Basic Books.

Csikszentmihalyi, Mihaly. (1996). *Creativity—flow and the psychology of discovery and invention*. New York: Harper/Collins.

Csikszentmihalyi, Mihaly. (1997). *Finding flow—the psychology of engagement with everyday life*. New York: Basic Books.

Cummings, E. M., & Davies, P. (1994). *Children and marital conflict: The impact of family dispute and resolution*. New York: Guilford.

Cutler, W. B., & Garcia, C. (1993). *Menopause: A guide for women and those who love them*. New York: Norton.

Daro, Deborah. (1988). *Confronting child abuse*. New York: Free Press.

Daro, Deborah. (1995). *Current trends in child abuse reporting and fatalities: Results of the 1994 annual fifty state survey.* Chicago: National Committee to Prevent Child Abuse.

Datan, Nancy, Greene, Anita, & Reese, Hayne W. (Eds.). (1986). *Life-span developmental psychology: Intergenerational relations.* Hillsdale, NJ: Erlbaum.

D'Augelli, A. R., & Hershberger, S. L. (1993). Lesbian, gay, and bisexual youth in community settings: Personal challenges and mental health problems. *American Journal of Community Psychology, 21,* 421–448.

Davidson, Christine. (1995). *Staying Home Instead—alternatives to the two-paycheck family.* San Francisco: Jossey-Bass.

Davis, John M., & Sandoval, Jonathan. (1991). *Suicidal youth.* San Francisco: Jossey-Bass.

Davis-Floyd, Robbie E. (1992). *Birth as an American rite of passage.* Berkeley: University of California Press.

Dawson, G., & Fischer, Kurt W. (Eds.). (1994). *Human behavior and the developing brain.* New York: Guilford.

DeMaris, Alfred, & Rao, Alfred. (1992). Premarital cohabitation and subsequent marital stability in the United States: A reassessment. *Journal of Marriage and the Family, 54,* 178–190.

DeSpelder, L. A., & Strickland, A. L. (1983). *The last dance: Encountering death and dying.* Palo Alto, CA: Mayfield.

Dickenson, Donna, & Johnson, Malcolm (Eds.). (1993). *Death, dying, & bereavement.* London: Sage.

Dickstein, Leah J., & Nadelson, Carol C. (Eds.). (1989). *Family violence: Emerging issues of national crisis.* Washington, DC: American Psychiatric Press.

Dixon, Roger A., & Baltes, Paul B. (1986). Toward life-span research on the functions and pragmatics of intelligence. In Robert J. Sternberg & Richard K. Wagner (Eds.), *Practical intelligence.* Cambridge, England, Cambridge University Press.

Dixon, Roger A., Kramer, Dierdre A., & Baltes, Paul B. (1985). Intelligence: A life-span developmental perspective. In Benjamin B. Wolman (Ed.), *Handbook of intelligence: Theories, measurements, and applications.* New York: Wiley.

Dreher, G., & Ash, R. (1990). A comparative study of mentoring among men and women in managerial, professional, and technical positions. *Journal of Applied Psychology, 75,* 525–35.

Dunn, Judy, & Plomin, Robert. (1990). *Separate lives: Why siblings are so different.* New York: Basic.

Dutton, Donald G. (1992). Theoretical and empirical perspectives on the etiology and prevention of wife assault. In Ray D. Peters et al (Eds.), *Aggression and violence throughout the lifespan.* Newbury Park: Sage.

Dwyer, Jeffrey W., & Coward, Raymond T. (Eds.). (1992). *Gender, families and elder care.* Newbury Park, CA: Sage.

Dychtwald, Ken. (1989). *Age wave—the challenges and opportunities of an aging America.* Los Angeles: Tarcher.

Dym, Barry, & Glenn, Michael L. (1993). *Couples—exploring and understanding the cycles of intimate relationships.* New York: HarperCollins.

Eccles, J. S., Midgley, C., Wigfield, A., Buchanan, C. M., Reuman, D., Flanagan, C., & MacIver, D. (1993). Development during adolescence: The impact of stage environment fit on young adolescents' experiences in schools and in families. *American Psychologist, 48,* 90–101.

Edelman, Marian Wright. (1992). *The measure of our success.* Boston: Beacon.

Edwards, Allen Jack. (1993). *Dementia.* New York: Plenum, 1993.

Egeland, Byron, Carlson, Elizabeth, & Sroufe, L. Alan. (1993). Resilience as process. *Development and Psychopathology, 5,* 517–528.

Elderhostel: *United States catalog.* (1998, Summer). Boston: Elderhostel, Inc.

Elkind, David. (1978). *The child's reality: Three developmental themes.* Hillsdale, NJ: Erlbaum.

Ericsson, K. Anders. (1990). Peak performance and age: An examination of peak performance in sports. In Paul B. Baltes & Margret M. Baltes (Eds.), *Successful aging: Perspectives from the behavioral sciences.* Cambridge, England: Cambridge University Press.

Erikson, Erik H. (1963). *Childhood and society (2nd ed.).* New York: Norton.

Erikson, Erik H. (1968). *Identity, youth, and crisis.* New York: Norton.

Erikson, Erik H. (1975). *Life history and the historical moment.* New York: Norton.

Erikson, Erik H., (Ed.). (1978).*Adulthood.* New York: Norton.

Erikson, Erik H., Erikson, Joan M., & Kivnick, Helen Q. (1986).*Vital involvement in old age.* New York: Norton.

Eron, Leonard D., Gentry, J., Acquelyn H., & Schlegel, Peggy (Eds.). (1994). *Reason to hope: A psychosocial perspective on violence and youth.* Washington, DC: American Psychological Association.

Everett, Craig, & Everett, Sandra. (1998). *Healthy divorce.* San Francisco: Jossey-Bass.

Fagenson, E. A. (1992). Mentoring—who needs it? Perceived career/job experiences of proteges vs. nonproteges' needs for power, achievement affiliation, and autonomy. *Journal of Vocational Behavior, 41* 48–60.

Fairburn, Christopher G., & Wilson, G. Terence (Eds.). (1993). *Binge eating: Nature, assessment and treatment.* New York: Guilford.

Falbo, T., & Polit, D. F. (1986). Quantitative review of the only-child literature: Research evidence and theory development. *Psychology Bulletin, 100,* 176–189.

Farrell, Michael P., & Rosenberg, Stanley D. (1981). *Men at midlife.* Boston: Auburn House.

Fein, Edith. (1991). Issues in foster family care: Where do we stand? *American Journal of Orthopsychiatry, 61,* 578–583.

Feldman, Shirley S., & Elliott, Glenn R. (Eds.). (1990). *At the threshold: The developing adolescent.* Cambridge, MA: Harvard University Press.

Felsenthal, G., Garrison, S. J., & Steinberg, F. U. (Eds.). (1994). *Rehabilitation of the aging patient.* Baltimore: Williams & Wilkins.

Fenwick, Elizabeth, & Smith, Tony. (1996). *Adolescence—the survival guide for parents and teenagers.* New York: Dorling Kindersley.

Field, T. M., McCabe, P. M., & Schneiderman, N. (Eds.). (1988). *Stress and coping across development*. Hillsdale, NJ: Erlbaum.

Fingerman, Karen L. (1996). Sources of tension in the aging mother and adult daughter relationship. *Psychology and Aging, 11*, 591–606.

Finkelhor, David. (1994). Current information on the scope and nature of child sexual abuse. *The Future of Children, 4*, 31–53.

Firth, Shirley. (1993). Approaches to death in Hindu and Sikh communities in Britain. In Donna Dickenson & Malcolm Johnson (Eds.), *Death, dying and bereavement*. London: Sage.

Fitch, Victoria. (1985) "The psychological tasks of old age." *Naropa Institute Journal of Psychology, V3*, 90–91.

Fivush, Robyn, & Hudson, Judith A. (Eds.). (1990). *Knowing and remembering in young children*. Cambridge, England: Cambridge University Press.

Flach, Frederic. (1988). *Resilience: Discovering a new strength at times of stress*. New York: Fawcett Columbine.

Fowler, James W. (1986). Faith and the structuring of meaning, In Craig Dykstra & Sharon Parks (Eds.), *Faith development and Fowler*. Birmingham, AL: Religious Education Press.

Fox, Margery, Gibbs, Margaret, & Auerbach, Doris. (1985). Age and gender dimensions of friendship. *Psychology of Women Quarterly, 9*, 489–502.

Fozard, James L. (1990). Vision and hearing in aging. In James E. Birren & K. Warner Schaie (Eds.), *Handbook of the psychology of aging* (3rd ed.). San Diego, CA: Academic Press.

Freeman, Ellen W., & Rickels, Karl. (1993). *Early childbearing: perspectives on black adolescents and pregnancy*. Newbury Park, CA: Sage.

Friedman, H. S., Hawley, P. H., & Tucker, J. S. (1994). Personality, health, and longevity. *Current Directions in Psychological Science, 3*, 37–41.

Fries, James F. (1994). *Living well: Taking care of your health in the middle and later years*. Reading, MA: Addison-Wesley.

Fries, James F., & Crapo, Lawrence M. (1981). *Vitality and Aging*. San Francisco: Freeman.

Fulton, Robert. (1995). The contemporary funeral: Functional or dysfunctional? In Hannelore Wass & Robert A. Neimeyer (Eds.), *Dying: Facing the facts*. Washington, DC: Taylor & Francis.

Funder, David C., Parke, Ross D., Tomlinson-Keasy, Carol, & Widaman, Keith (Eds.), (1993). *Studying lives through time*. Washington, DC: American Psychological Association.

Furstenberg, Frank F., Jr., & Cherlin, Andrew J. (1991). *Divided families: What happens to children when parents part*. Cambridge, MA: Harvard University Press.

Furstenberg, Frank F., Jr., Brooks-Gunn, Jeanne, & Morgan, Philip A. (1987). *Adolescent mothers in later life*. New York: Cambridge University Press.

Furstenberg, Frank F., Jr., & Nord, Christine Winquist. (1985). Parenting apart: Patterns of childbearing after marital disruption. *Journal of Marriage and the Family, 47*, 893–912. University Press.

Gaddis, Alan, & Brooks-Gunn, Jeanne. (1985). The male experience of pubertal change. *Journal of Youth and Adolescence, 4*, 61.

Galambos, N. L. (1992). Parent-adolescent relations. *Current Directions in Psychological Science, 1,* 146–149.

Galbraith, Michael W., & Cohen, Norman H. (1995). *Mentoring: New strategies and challenges.* San Francisco: Jossey-Bass.

Galinsky, Ellen. (1990). *The six stages of parenthood.* Reading, MA: Addison-Wesley.

Gallagher, W. (1991, May). Midlife myths. *The Atlantic Monthly,* pp. 51–68.

Galvin, Ruth Mehrtens. (1992). The nature of shyness. *Harvard Magazine, 94* (4), 40–45.

Ganong, Lawrence H., & Coleman, Marilyn. (1994). *Remarried family relationships.* Thousand Oaks: CA: Sage.

Garbarino, James, Kostelny, Kathleen, & Dubrow, Nancy. (1991). *No place to be a child: Growing up in a war zone.* New York: Lexington Books.

Garbarino, James, Kostelny, N., & Pardo, C. (1992). *Children in danger: Coping with the consequences of community violence.* San Francisco: Jossey-Bass.

Gardner, John W. (1981). *Self-renewal* (revised edition). New York: Norton.

Gardner, John W. (1990). *On leadership.* New York: Free Press.

Garrod, Andrew (Ed.). (1993). *Approaches to moral development: New research and emerging themes.* New York: Teachers College Press.

Gelles, Richard J., & Loseke, Donileen R. (Eds.). (1993). *Current controversies on family violence.* Thousand Oaks, CA: Sage.

Gelles, Richard J., & Straus, M. A. (1988). *Intimate violence.* New York: Simon & Schuster.

Genesee, Fred (Ed.). (1994). *Educating second-language children: The whole child, the whole curriculum, the whole community.* Cambridge, England: Cambridge University Press.

George, L. K. (1993). Sociological perspectives on life transition. *Annual Review of Sociology, 19,* 353–373.

Geyer, S. (1993). Life events, chronic difficulties and vulnerability factors preceding breast cancer. *Social Science and Medicine, 37,* 1545–1555.

Gibbs, G. T., & Huang, L. N. (Eds.). (1989). *Children of color.* San Francisco: Jossey-Bass.

Gibson, Rose C. (1993). The black American retirement experience. In James Jackson, Linda Chatters, & Robert Joseph Taylor (Eds.), *Aging in black America.* Newbury Park, CA: Sage.

Gilligan, Carol. (1982). *In a different voice: Psychological theory and women's development.* Cambridge, MA: Harvard University Press.

Gilligan, Carol, Murphy, John M., & Tappan, Mark B. (1990). Moral development beyond adolescence. In Charles N. Alexander & Ellen J. Langer (Eds.), *Higher stages of human development.* New York: Oxford University Press.

Gilmour, R., & Duck, S. (Eds.). (1986). *The emerging field of personal relationships.* Hillsdale, NJ: Erlbaum.

Glendenning, Frank. (1995). Education for older adults: Lifelong learning, empowerment, and social change. In Jon F. Nussbaum & Justine Coupland (Eds.), *Handbook of communication and aging research.* Mahway, NJ: Erlbaum.

Goetting, A. (1986). The developmental tasks of siblingship over the life cycle. *Journal of Marriage and the Family, 48,* 737–747.

Goldman, Connie. (1991). Late bloomers: Growing older or still growing? *Generations, 15,* 41–44.

Goldscheider, Francis K., & Goldscheider, Calvin. (1993). Leaving and returning home in 20th century America. *Population Bulletin, 48* (no. 4), 1–35.

Golub, S. (1992). *Periods: From menarche to menopause.* Newbury Park, CA: Sage.

Gomberg, Edith S., Lisansky, S., & Nirenberg, Ted D. (Eds.). (1993). *Women and substance abuse.* Norwood, NJ: Ablex.

Goncu, A. (1993). Development of intersubjectivity in social pretend play. *Human Development, 36,* 185–198.

Gonsiorek, John C., & Weinrich, James D. (Eds.). (1991). *Homosexuality: Research implications for public policy.* Newbury Park, CA: Sage.

Goodman, G. S., Hirschman, J. E., Hepps, D., & Rudy, L. (1991). Children's memory for stressful events. *Merrill-Palmer Quarterly, 37,* 109–158.

Goodman, N. C. (1987). Girls with learning disabilities and their sisters: How are they faring in adulthood? *Journal of Clinical Child Psychology, 16,* 290–300.

Goodnow, Jacqueline J., & Collins, W. Andrew. (1990). *Development according to parents: The nature, sources, and consequences of parent's ideas.* Hillsdale, NJ: Erlbaum.

Gordon, Debra Ellen. (1990). Formal operational thinking: The role of cognitive-developmental processes in adolescent decision-making about pregnancy and contraception. *American Journal of Orthopsychiatry, 60,* 346–356.

Gordon, George K., & Stryker, Ruth. (1994). *Creative long-term care administration.* Springfield, IL: Thomas.

Gottfried, Adele E., & Gottfried, Allen W. (Eds.). (1994). *Redefining families: Implications for children's development.* New York: Plenum.

Gottman, J. M., & Parker, J. G. (Eds.). (1986). *Conversations of friends. Speculations on affective development.* Cambridge, England: Cambridge University Press.

Gottman, J. M. (1994). *Why marriages succeed or fail.* New York: Simon & Schuster.

Gould, Roger. (1978). *Transformations: Growth and change in adult life.* New York: Simon & Schuster.

Government Accounting Office. (1992). *Child abuse: Prevention programs need greater emphasis.* Washington, DC: U.S. Government Printing Office.

Graebner, William. (1980). *A history of retirement—the meaning and function of an American institution, 1885–1978.* New Haven: Yale.

Gratton, Brian, & Haber, Carole. (1996). Three phases in the history of American grandparents: Authority, burden, companion. *Generations, 20,* 7–12.

Greer, Jane. (1992). *Adult sibling rivalry.* New York: Crown.

Greif, Geoffrey L., DeMaris, Alfred, & Hood, Jane C. (1993). Balancing work and single fatherhood. In Jane C. Hood (Ed.), *Men, work, and family.* Newbury Park, CA: Sage.

Grossman, Frances K., Pollack, William S., & Golding, Ellen. (1988). Fathers and children: Predicting the quality and quantity of fathering. *Developmental Psychology, 24,* 82–91.

Guillemard, A. M., & Rein, M. (1993). Comparative patterns of retirement: Recent trends in developed societies. *Annual Review of Sociology 19,* 469–503.

Gunnar, Megan R., & Collins, W. Andrew (Eds.). (1988). *Development during the transition to adolescence.* Hillsdale, NJ: Erlbaum.

Guralnik, J. M., & Simonsick, E. M. (1993). Physical disability in older Americans (Special issue). *Journals of Gerontology, 48,* 3–10.

Gutek, B. A., Stromberg, A. H., & Larwood, L. (Eds.). (1988). *Women and work. An annual review.* Newbury Park, CA: Sage.

Gutmann, David. (1987). *Reclaimed powers: Toward a new psychology of men and women in later life.* New York: Basic Books.

Hacker, Douglas J. (1994). An existential view of adolescence. *Journal of Early Adolescence, 14,* 300–327.

Hagestad, G. O. (1986). The aging society as a context for family life. *Daedalus, 115,* 119–139.

Handy, Charles. (1989). *The age of unreason.* Cambridge, MA: Harvard Business School Press.

Hanin, Israel, Yoshida, Mitsuo, & Fisher, Abraham (Eds.). (1995). *Alzheimer's and Parkinson's diseases: Recent developments.* New York: Plenum.

Hansen, L. Sunny. (1997). *Integrative life planning—critical tasks for career development and changing life patterns.* San Francisco: Jossey-Bass.

Harel, Zev, McKinney, Edward A., & Williams, Mishel (Eds.). (1990). *Black aged.* Newbury Park, CA: Sage.

Hareven, T. F. K., & Adams, K. J. (Eds.). (1982). *Aging and life course transitions: An interdisciplinary perspective.* New York: Guilford.

Hart, D. A. (1992). *Becoming men. The development of aspirations, values, and adaptational styles.* New York: Plenum.

Hartup, Willard W. (1983). Peer relations. In Paul H. Nussen (Ed.), *Handbook of child psychology: Vol. 4. Socialization, personality and social development.* New York: Wiley.

Hartup, Willard W. (1996). The company they keep: Friendships and their developmental significance. *Child Development, 67,* 1–13.

Hawkins, H. L., Kramer, A. F., & Capaldi, D. (1992). Aging, exercise, and attention. *Psychology and Aging, 7,* 643–653.

Hayflick, Leonard. (1987). Origins of longevity. *Aging* (NY), *31,* 21–34.

Hayflick, Leonard. (1994). *How and why we age.* New York: Ballantine.

Hayward, M. D., & Hardy, M. A. (1985). Early retirement processes among older men: Occupational differences. *Research on Aging, 7,* 491–518.

Hayward, Mark D. (1996). Race inequities in men's retirement. *Journals of Gerontology, 51B,* S1–S10.

Heaton, Tim, & Albrecht, Stan L. (1991). Unhappy marriages. *Journal of Marriage and the Family 53:,* 747–758.

Heikkinen, Eino, Kuusinen, Jorma, & Ruoppila, Isto (Eds.). (1995). *Preparation for aging.* New York: Plenum Press.

Heilbrun, Carolyn G. (1988). *Writing a woman's life.* New York: Ballantine

Heilbrun, Carolyn G. (1997). *The last gift of time: Life beyond 60.* New York, Dial.

Helson, Ravenna (1992). Personality change in women from the early 40s to the early 50s. *Psychology and Aging, 7,* 46–55.

Helson, Ravenna. (1995). Women's difficult times and the rewriting of the life story. *Psychology of Women Quarterly, 16,* 331–347.

Helson, Ravenna, & Moane, Geraldine. (1987). Personality change in women from college to midlife. *Journal of Personality and Social Psychology, 53,* 176–186.

Helson, Ravenna, Steward, Abigail J., & Ostrove, Joan. (1995). Identity in three cohorts of midlife women. *Journal of Personality and Social Psychology, 69,* 554–557.

Hendricks, Jon (Ed.). (1995). *The meaning of reminiscence and life review.* Amityville, NY: Baywood.

Herzog, A. R., House, J. S., & Morgan, J. N. (1991). Relation of work and retirement to health and well-being in older age. *Psychology and Aging, 6,* 202–211.

Herzog, Regula A., & House, James S. (1991). Productive activities and aging well. *Generations, 15*(1), 49–54.

Hess, Beth B., and Markson, Elizabeth W. (1995). *Growing old in America* (4th Edition). New Brunswick, NJ: Transaction.

Hetherington, E. Mavis, & Aresteh, Josephine D. (Eds.). (1988). *Impact of divorce, single parenting, and step-parenting on children.* Hillsdale, NJ: Erlbaum.

Hetherington, E. Mavis, & Clingempeel, W. Glenn. (1992). Coping with marital transitions. *Monographs of the Society for Research in Child Development, 57* (2–3, Serial No. 227).

Hetherington, E. Mavis, Reiss, David, & Plomin, Robert (Eds.). (1994). *Separate social worlds of siblings: The impact of nonshared environments on development.* Hillsdale, NJ: Erlbaum.

Hibbs, Euthymia (Ed.). (1991). *Adoption—international perspectives.* Madison, CT: International University Press.

Higgins, C., Duxbury, L., & Lee, C. (1994). Impact of life-cycle stage and gender on the ability to balance work and family responsibilities. *Family Relations, 43,* 144–150.

Hill, R. D., Storandt, M., & Malley, M. (1993). The impact of long-term exercise training on psychological function in older adults. *Journal of Gerontology: Psychological Sciences, 48,* 12–17.

Hochschild, Arlie R. (1989). *The second shift: Working parents and the revolution at home.* New York: Viking

Hochschild, Arlie R. (1997). *The time bind: When work becomes home and home becomes work.* New York: Holt.

Hodgson, J. L., & Buskirk, E. R. (1981). The role of exercise in aging. In D. Danon, N. W. Schock, & M. Marios (Eds.), *Aging: A challenge to science and society.* London: Oxford University Press.

Hoffman, Lois Wladis. (1991). Effects of maternal employment in the two-parent family: Accounting for sibling differences. *Psychological Bulletin, 110,* 187–203.

Hoffman, S. D., Foster, E. M., & Furstenberg, F. F. (1993). Reevaluating the costs of teenage childbearing. *Demography, 30,*1–13.

Holliday, Robin. (1995). *Understanding aging.* Cambridge, England: Cambridge University Press.

Hollis, James. (1993). *The middle passage—from misery to meaning in midlife.* Toronto: Inner City.

Holmes, E. R., & Holmes, L. D. (1995). *Other cultures, elder years.* Thousand Oaks, CA: Sage.

Homer, Paul, & Holstein, Martha. (1990). *A good old age?—the paradox of setting limits.* New York: Touchstone.

Horn, John L., & Hofer, Scott M. (1992). Major abilities and development in the adult period. In Robert J. Sternberg & Cynthia A. Berg (Eds.), *Intellectual development.* New York: Cambridge University Press.

Horwitz, A., Macfadyen, D. M., Nunro, H., Scrimshaw, N. S., Steen, B., & Williams, T. F. (Eds.). (1989). *Nutrition in the elderly.* Oxford, England: Oxford University Press.

Houts, Renate M., Robins, Elliot, & Huston, Ted L. (1996). Compatibility and the development of premarital relationships. *Journal of Marriage and the Family, 58,* 7–20.

Howe, Neil. (1995). Why the graying of the welfare state threatens to flatten the American dream—or worse: Age-based benefits as our downfall. *Generations, 19,* 15–19.

Howe, Neil, & Ross, H. S. (1990). Socialization, perspective-taking, and the sibling relationship. *Developmental Psychology, 26,* 160–165.

Howes, Carollee. (1987). Patterns of friendship. *Child Development, 54,* 1041–1053.

Hsu, L. K. George. (1992). *Eating disorders.* New York: Guilford.

Hudson, Frederic M. (1999). *The adult years in the twenty-first century: Mastering the art of self-renewal.* (Rev. ed.) San Francisco: Jossey-Bass.

Hudson, Frederic M., & McLean, Pamela. (1996). *LifeLaunch—a passionate guide to the rest of your life.* Santa Barbara, CA: Hudson Institute Press.

Hulbert, K. D., & Schuster, D. T. (Eds.). (1993). *Women's lives through time. Educated American women of the twentieth century.* San Francisco: Jossey-Bass.

Hunsberger, B. (1985). Religion, age, life satisfaction, and perceived sources of religiousness: A study of older persons. *Journal of Gerontology, 40,* 615–620.

Hunt, Earl. (1993). What do we need to know about aging? In John Cerella, John Rybash, William Hoyer, & Michael L. Commons (Eds.), *Adult information processing: Limits on loss.* San Diego, CA: Academic Press.

Hunter, S., & Sundel, Martin. (1989). *Midlife myths: Issues, findings and practice implications.* Newbury Park, CA: Sage.

Hyde, Kenneth E. (1990). *Religion in childhood and adolescence: A comprehensive review of the research.* Birmingham, AL: Religious Education Press.

Iber, Frank L. (1990). Alcoholism and associated malnutrition in the elderly. In Derek M. Prinsley & Harold H. Sandstread (Eds.), *Nutrition and aging.* New York: Liss.

Idler, Ellen L. (1994). *Cohesiveness and coherence: Religion and the health of the elderly*. New York: Garland.

Ingersol-Dayton, Berig, & Starrels, Marjorie E. (1996). Caregiving for parents and parents in law: Is gender important? *Gerontologist, 36*, 438–491.

Ingersoll, Barbara D., & Goldstein, Sam. (1993). *Attention deficit disorder and learning disabilities: Realities, myths and controversial treatments*. New York: Doubleday.

Jacobs, J. E., Bennett, M. A., & Flanagan, C. (1993). Decision-making in one-parent and two parent families: Influence and information selection. *Journal of Early Adolescence, 13*, 245–266.

Jacobs, Selby C., Kosten, Thomas R., Stanislav, V., Ostfeld, Adrian M., & Berkman, Lisa. (1987–1988). Attachment theory and multiple expressions of grief. *Omega, 18*, 41–52.

James, Paula. (1998). *The divorce mediation handbook—everything you need to know*. San Francisco: Jossey-Bass.

Jamison, Stephen. (1998). *Assisted suicide—a compassionate and responsible guide for helping professionals*. San Francisco: Jossey-Bass.

Jendrek, M. P. (1993). Grandparents who parent their grandchildren: Effects on lifestyle. *Journal of Marriage and the Family, 55*, 609–621.

Jessor, Richard. (1992). Risk behavior in adolescence: A psychosocial framework for understanding and action. *Developmental Review. 12*, 374–390.

Jessor, Richard, Donovan, John E., & Costa, Frances M. (1991). *Beyond adolescence: Problem behavior and young adult development*. Cambridge, England: Cambridge University Press.

John, David W., & Johnson, Roger T. (1994). *Learning together and alone: Cooperative, competitive, and individualistic learning* (4th ed.). Boston: Allyn & Bacon.

John-Steiner, Vera. (1986). *Notebooks of the mind: Explorations of thinking*. Albuquerque: University of New Mexico Press.

Johnson, Barry. (1992). *Polarity management—identifying and managing unsolvable problems*. Amherst, MA: HRD Press.

Johnson, C. I., & Bacr, B. M. (1991). Coping and a sense of control among the oldest old. *Journal of Aging Studies, 7*, 67–80.

Jones, C. J., & Meredith, W. (1996). Patterns of personality change across the life span. *Psychology of Aging, 11*,57–65.

Josselson, Ruthellen, & Lieblich, Amiz. (1993). *The narrative study of lives*. Newbury Park, CA: Sage.

Jung, C. G. (1933). *Modern man in search of a soul*. New York: Harcourt, Brace, Jovanovich.

Jung, C. G. (1959). *The basic writings of C. G. Jung*. New York: Modern Library.ung, C. G. (1961). *Memories, dreams, recollections*. New York: Vintage. (Original work published 1933)

Jung, C. G. (1972). *Man and his symbols*. New York: Dell

Kabat-Zinn, Myla, & Kabat-Zinn, Jon. (1997). *Everyday blessings: The inner work of mindful parenting*. New York: Hyperion.

Kahn, R. L., and Antonucci, T. C. (1980). Convoys over the life course: Attachment, roles, and social support. In P. B. Baltes and O. G. Brim (Eds.), *Life-Span development and behavior.* Orlando, FL: Academic Press.

Kalbfleisch, Pamela J. (Ed.). (1993). *Interpersonal communication: Evolving interpersonal relationships.* Hillsdale, NJ: Erlbaum.

Kanter, Donald L., and Mirvis, Philip H. (1989). San Francisco: Jossey-Bass.

Karen, R. (1994). *Becoming attached.* New York: Warner Books.

Karp, D. A. (1988). A decade of reminders: Changing age consciousness between fifty and sixty years old. *The Gerontologist, 28,* 727–738.

Kaslow, Florence W., & Schwartz, Lita Linzer. (1987). *The dynamics of divorce—a life cycle perspective.* New York: Brunner/Mazel.

Katchadourian, Herant. (1987). *Fifty—midlife in perspective.* New York: W. H. Freeman.

Katchadourian, Herant A., & Lunde, Donald T. (1990). *Fundamentals of human sexuality.* New York: Holt, Rinehart and Winston.

Katchaturian, Z. S., and Radebaugh, T. S. (1997). *Alzheimer's disease: Causes, diagnosis, treatment, and care.* Boca Raton, FL: CRC Press.

Kegan, Robert. (1982).*The evolving self.* San Francisco: Jossey-Bass.

Kegan, Robert. (1994).*In over our heads—the mental demands of modern life.* Cambridge, MA: Harvard University.

Kelly, J. R. (Ed.). (1993).*Activity and aging. Staying involved in late life.* Newbury Park, CA: Sage.

Killen, Melanie, & Hart, Daniel. (Eds.). (1995). *Morality in everyday life: Developmental perspectives.* Cambridge, England: Cambridge University Press.

Kitzinger, Sheila. (1997). *Becoming a grandmother: A life transition.* New York: Simon & Schuster.

Kubler-Ross, Elisabeth. (1975). *Death: The final stage of growth.* Englewood Cliffs, NJ: Prentice Hall.

Lamb, Michael E. (Ed.). (1981). *The role of the father in child development* (2nd ed.) New York: Wiley.

Lamb, Michael E. (Ed.). (1982). *Non-traditional families: Parenting and child development.* Hillsdale, NJ: Erlbaum.

Lawton, M. P. (1990). Residential environment and self-directedness among older people. *American Psychologist, 45,* 638–640.

Lederman, Ellen. (1996). *Vacations that can change your life—Adventures, retreats, and workshops for the mind, body, and spirit.* Naperville, IL: Sourcebooks.

Leenaars, Antoon (Ed.). (1991). *Lifespan perspectives on suicide.* New York: Plenum.

Leider, Richard J. (1997). *The power of purpose* (Rev. Ed.). San Francisco: Berret-Kohler.

Lentzner, Harold R., Pamuk, Elsie R., Rhodenhiser, Richard R., & Powell-Griner, Eve. (1992). The quality of life in the year before death. *American Journal of Public Health, 82,* 1093–1098.

Leong, Frederick T. L. (Ed.). (1995). *Career development and vocational behavior of racial and ethnic minorities.* Mahwah, NJ: Erlbaum.

Lerner, Harriet. (1998). *The mother dance: How children change your life.* New York: HarperCollins.

Lerner, Harriet. (1997). *The dance of anger.* New York: HarperPerrenial.

Lerner, Jacqueline V., & Galambos, Nancy L. (Eds.). (1991). *Employed mothers and their children.* New York: Garland.

Lerner, Richard M., Petersen, Ann C., & Brooks-Gunn, Jeanne (Eds.). (1991). *Encyclopedia of adolescence.* New York: Garland.

Lesnoff-Caravaglia, Gari. (1994). *The world of the older woman: conflicts & resolutions.* New York: Human Sciences.

Levenson, Robert W., Carstensen, Laura R., & Gottman, John M. (1993). Long-term marriage: Age, gender, and satisfaction. *Psychology and Aging, 8,* 301–313.

Levine, James A. (1997). *Working fathers—new strategies for balancing work and family.* Reading, MA: Addison-Wesley.

Levinson, Daniel J. (1973). *The seasons of a man's life.* New York: Knopf.

Levinson, Daniel J. (1996). *The seasons of a woman's life.* New York: Knopf.

Levinson, Ruth A., Jaccard, J., & Beamer, L. (1995). Older adolescents' engagement in casual sex: Impact of risk perception and psychosocial motivations. *Journal of Youth and Adolescence, 24,* 349–364.

Lidz, Theodore. (1968). *The person: His development throughout the life cycle.* New York: Basic Books.

Lifton, Robert J. (1979). *The broken connection.* New York: Simon & Schuster.

Lovelace, Eugene A. (Ed.). (1990). *Aging and cognition: Mental processes, self-awareness and interventions.* Amsterdam: North-Holland/Elsevier.

Lucas, A. R. (1991). Eating Disorders. In M. Lewis (Ed.), *Child and adolescent psychiatry: A comprehensive textbook.* Baltimore: Williams & Wilkins.

Ludwig, Frederick C. (Ed.). (1991). *Life span extension.* New York: Springer.

Luke, Helen M. (1987). *Old age.* New York: Parabola Books.

Mahoney, David, & Restak, Richard. (1998). *The Longevity Strategy.* New York: Wiley.

Mangen, David J., Bengston, Vern L., & Landry, Pierre H. (1998). *Measurement of intergenerational relations.* Newbury Park, CA: Sage.

Mann, L., Harmoni, R., & Power, C. (1989). Adolescent decision-making: The development of competence. *Journal of Adolescence, 12,* 265–278.

Manson, J. E., Willett, Walter C., and Associates. (1995). Body weight and mortality among women. *New England Journal of Medicine, 333,* 677–685.

Markides, K. S., & Mindel, C. H. (1987). *Aging and ethnicity.* Newbury Park, CA: Sage.

Marmot, M. G., Rose, G., Shipley, M. J., & Thomas, B. J. (1981). Alcohol and mortality: A u-shaped curve. *Lancet, 1,* 580–583.

Marris, Peter. (1986). *Loss and change* (Rev. Ed.). New York: Routledge and Kegan Paul.

Marx, Jean L. (1991). Zeroing in on individual cancer risk *Science, 252,* 612–626.

Masten, Ann S. (1992). Homeless children in the United States: Mark of a nation at risk. *Current Directions in Psychological Science, 1,* 41–43.

Masten, Ann S., Best, K. M., & Garmezy, Norman. (1990). Resilience and development: Contributions from children who overcome adversity. *Development and Psychopathology, 2,* 425–444.

Masten, Ric. (1980). Not exactly a command performance. In *Stark naked.* Carmel, CA: Sunflower Ink Press.

Masters, William H., & Johnson, Virginia E. (1981). Sex and the aging process. *Journal of the American Geriatrics Society, 29,* 385–390.

Masters, William H., Johnson, Virginia E., & Kolodny, Robert C. (1994). *Heterosexuality.* New York: HarperCollins.

Masterson, James F. (1985). *The real self—a developmental, self, and object relations approach.* New York: Brunner/Mazel.

McAdams, Dan P., de St. Aubin, Ed, & Logan, Regina L. (1993). Generativity among young, midlife, and older adults. *Psychology and Aging, 8,* 221–230.

McCabe, P. M., Schneiderman, N., Field, T. M., & Sklyer, J. S. (1991). *Stress, coping and disease.* Hillsdale, NJ: Erlbaum.

McCrae, R. R., & Costa, P. T., Jr. (1983). Psychological maturity and subjective well-being: Toward a new synthesis. *Developmental Psychology, 19,* 243–248.

McCurdy, Karen, & Daro, Deborah. (1994). *Current trends in child abuse reporting and fatalities: The results of the 1993 annual fifty-State survey.* Chicago: National Committee to Prevent Child Abuse.

McGillicuddy, A. V., & Goodnow, J. J. (Eds.). (1992). *Parental belief systems: The psychological consequences for children* (2nd ed.). Hillsdale, NJ: Erlbaum.

McIntosh, John L., and Associates. (1994). *Elder suicide—research, theory, and treatment.* San Antonio, TX: The Psychological Corporation.

McKay, Matthew, Fanning, Patrick, & Paleg, Kim. (1994). *Couple skills.* Oakland, CA: New Harbinger, Publications.

McKenry, Patrick, Julian, Teresa W., & Gavazzi, Stephen. (1995). Toward a biosocial model of domestic violence. *Journal of Marriage and the Family, 57,* 307–320.

McKenzie, Sheila C. (1989). *Aging and old age.* Glenview, IL: Scot, Foresman and Co.

McLanahan, Sara S., & Sandefur, G. (1994). *Growing up with a single parent: What hurts, what helps.* Cambridge, MA: Harvard University Press.

McLaughlin, D. K. & Jensen, L. (1993). Poverty among older Americans: The plight of nonmetropolitan elders. *Journals of Gerontology: Social Sciences, 48,* S44–S54.

McLeish, John. (1976). *The Ulyssean adult: Creativity in the middle and later years.* New York: McGraw-Hill Ryerson.

Mecca, Andrew M., Smelser, Neil J., & Vasconcellos, John. (1989). *The Social Importance of Self-Esteem.* Berkeley: University of California Press.

Mellor, Steven. (1990). How do only children differ from other children. *Journal of Genetic Psychology, 151,* 221–230.

Menken, Jane, Trussell, James, & Larsen, Ulla. (1986). Age and infertility. *Science, 233,* 1389–1394.

Midlarsky, E., & Hannah, M. E. (1989). The generous elderly: Naturalistic studies of donations across the life span. *Psychology and Aging, 4,* 346–351.

Miedzian, Miriam. (1991). *Boys will be boys: Breaking the link between masculinity and violence.* New York: Doubleday.

Miller, Craig Kenneth. (1996). *Postmoderns—the beliefs, hopes, and fears of young Americans (1965–1981).* Ithaca, NY: American Demographics.

Miller, Patricia H. (1993). *Theories of developmental psychology.* New York: Freeman.

Miller, P. M., & West, M. M. (Eds.), (1988). *Parental behavior in diverse societies.* San Francisco: Jossey-Bass.

Milne, Ann M., Myers, David E., Rosenthal, Alvin S., & Ginsburg, Alan. (1986). Single parents, working mothers, and the educational achievement of school children. *Sociology of education, 59,* 125–139.

Mindel, C. J., Haberstein, R. W., & Roosevelt, W., Jr. (1988). *Ethnic families in America* (3rd ed.). New York: Elsevier.

Minois George. (1989). *History of old age: From antiquity to the renaissance.* Cambridge, England: Polity Press.

Minuchin, Salvador, & Nichols, Michael P. (1993). *Family healing: Tales of hope and renewal from family therapy,* New York: Free Press.

Mishell, D. R., Jr. (Ed). (1987). *Menopause: Physiology and pharmacology.* Chicago: Year Book Medical Publishers.

Mitchell, John J. (1986). *The nature of adolescence.* Calgary, Alberta, Canada: Detselig.

Monk, Abraham (Ed.). (1993). *The age of aging—a reader in social gerontology.* New York: Prometheus.

Montada, L. Filipp, & Lerner, M. J. (Eds.). (1992). *Life crises and experiences of loss in adulthood.* Hillsdale, NJ: Erlbaum.

Montemayor, Raymond, Adams, Gerald R., & Gullotta, Thomas P. (Eds.). (1996). *From childhood to adolescence: A transitional period?* Newbury Park, CA, Sage.

Moody, Harry R. (1993). A strategy for productive aging: Education in later life. In Scott A. Bass, Francis G. Caro, & Jung-Ping Chen (Eds.), *Achieving a productive aging society.* Westport, CT: Auburn House.

M Moody, Harry R. (1994). *Aging—concepts and controversies.* Thousand Oaks, CA: Sage.

Moody, Harry R. (1995). Meaning and late life learning. In Eino Heikkinen, Jorma Kuusinen, & Isto Ruoppila (Eds.), *Preparation for aging.* New York: Plenum.

Moore, Susan, & Rosenthal, Doreen. (1991). Adolescent invulnerability and perceptions of AIDS risk. *Journal of Adolescent Research, 6,*164–180.

Mor, V. (1987). *Hospice care systems. Structure, process, costs, and outcome.* New York: Springer.

Morris, Edward K., & Braukmann, Curtis J. (Eds.). (1987) *Behavioral* approaches to crime and delinquency: A handbook of applications, research, and concepts. New York: Plenum.

Morris, Virginia. (1996). *How to care for aging parents*. New York: Workman.

Mortimore, Peter. (1995). The positive effects of schooling. In Michael Rutter (Ed.), *Psychological disturbances in young people: Challenges for prevention*. Cambridge, England: Cambridge University Press.

Moyer, Marth Sebastian. (1992). Sibling relationships among older adults. *Generations, 27,* (3) 55–60).

Murphy, John M., & Gilligan, Carol. (1980). Moral development in late adolescence and adulthood: A critique and reconstruction of Kohlberg's theory. *Human Development, 23,* 77–104.

Murphy, John S., & Hudson, Frederic M. (1995). *The joy of old: A guide to successful elderhood*. Altadena, CA: Geode Press.

Murphy, Patricia Ann. (1986–1987). Parental death in childhood and loneliness in young adults. *Omega 17,* 219–228.

Mussen, Paul H. (Ed.). (1983). *Handbook of child psychology: Vol. 2:Infancy and developmental psychobiology*. New York: Wiley.

Myers, David G. (1993). *The pursuit of happiness*. New York: Avon.

Nardi, P. M. (Ed.). (1992). *Gender in intimate relationships*. Belmont, CA: Wadsworth.

National Center for Injury Prevention and Control. (1993). *Injury control in the 1990s: A national plan for action*. Atlanta. GA: Centers for Disease Control and Prevention, U.S. Department of Health and Human Services.

Neisser, Ulric, Boodoo, Gwyneth, Bouchard, Thomas J., & Associates. (1996). Intelligence: Knowns and unknowns. *American Psychologist, 51,* 77–101.

Nemiroff, Robert, & Colarusso, Calvin. (1985). *The race against time*. New York: Plenum.

Neugarten, Bernice L., & Neugarten, Dail A. (1986). Changing meanings of age in the aging society. In Alan Pifer & Lynda Bronte (Eds.), *Our aging society: Paradox and promise*. New York: Norton.

Neugarten, Dail A., (Ed.) (1996). *The meanings of age—selected papers of Bernice L. Neugarten*. Chicago: University of Chicago Press.

Nordin, B. E. C., & Need, A. G. (1990). Prediction and prevention of osteoporosis. In M. Bergener, M. Ermini, & H. B. Stahelin (Eds.), *Challenges of aging*. San Diego, CA: Academic Press.

Nugent, Kevin J. (1991). Cultural and psychological influences on the father's role in infant development. *Journal of Marriage and the Family, 53,* 475–485.

Nuland, Sherwin B. (1994). *How we die*. New York: Knopf, 1994.

Nussbaum, Jon F., & Coupland, Justine. (Eds.). (1992) *Handbook of communication and aging research*. Mahwah, NJ: Erlbaum.

O'brien, Mary. (1991). Never married older women: The life experience. *Social Indicators Research, 24,* 301–315.

Offer, Daniel, & Offer, Judith. *From teenage to young manhood*. New York: Basic, 1975.

O'Hagan, Kieran. (1993). *Emotional and psychological abuse of children*. Toronto: University of Toronto Press.

O'Meara, J. J. (1989). Cross-sex friendship: Four basic challenges of an ignored relationship. *Sex-Roles, 21,* 525–543.

Ory, Marcia G., & Warner, Huber. (1990). *Gender, health, and longevity.* New York: Springer.

Osgood, Nancy J. (1992). *Suicide in later life.* Lexington, MA: Lexington Books.

Osherson, Samuel. (1992). *Wrestling with love—how men struggle with intimacy.* New York: Ballantine.

Palmore, E. B. (1990). *Ageism: Negative and positive.* New York: Springer.

Palmore, E. B. (Ed.). (1993). *Developments and research on aging. An international handbook.* Westport, CT: Greenwood Press.

Palus, C. J. (1993). Transformative experiences of adulthood: A new look at the seasons of life. In J. Demick, K. Bursik, & R. DiBiase (Eds.), *Parental development.* Hillsdale, NJ: Erlbaum.

Papernow, Patricia L. (1993). *Becoming a stepfamily: Patterns of development in remarried families.* San Francisco: Jossey-Bass.

Parcel, Toby L., & Menaghan, Elizabeth G. (1995). *Parents' jobs and children's lives.* New York: Aldine de Gruyter.

Parke, Ross D., Ornstein, Peter A., Rieser, John J., & Zahn-Waxler, Carolyn (Eds.). (1994) *A Century of Developmental Psychology.* Washington, DC: American Psychological Association.

Parkes, C. Murray, Stevenson-Hinde, J., & Marris, P. (Eds.). (1991). *Attachment across the life cycle.* London: Routledge.

Pascarella, Ernest T., & Terenzini, Patrick T. (1991). *How college affects students: Findings and insights from twenty years of research.* San Francisco: Jossey-Bass.

Perlman, D., & Duck, S. (Eds.). (1986). *Intimate relationships: Development, dynamics, and deterioration.* Hillsdale, NJ: Erlbaum.

Perun, Pamela J. (Ed.). (1982). *The undergraduate woman: Issues in educational equity.* Lexington, MA: Lexington Books.

Peters, D.L., & Pence, A.R. (1992). *Family day care: Current research for informed public policy.* New York: Teachers College Press.

Peters, R. D., McMahon, R. J. & Quincy, V. I. (Eds.). (1992). *Aggression and violence throughout the life span.* Newbury Park: Sage.

Peterson, Bill E., & Stewart, Abigail J. (1996). Antecedents and contexts of generativity motivation at midlife. *Psychology and Aging, 11,* 21–33.

Pifer, Alan, & Bronte, Lydia (Eds.) (1986). *Our aging society—paradox and promise.* New York: Norton.

Pillemer, Karl, & McCartney, Kathleen (Eds.). (1991). *Parent-child relations throughout life.* Hillsdale, NJ: Erlbaum.

Pittman, Joe F., & Blanchard, David. (1996). The effects of work history and timing of marriage on the division of household labor: A life-course perspective. *Journal of Marriage and the Family, 58,* 78–90.

Pollan, Stephen M., & Levine, Mark. (1995). The rise and fall of retirement. *Worth Magazine,* December/January, 67–74.

Pollock, George H., & Greenspan, Stanley L. (1988). *The course of life, Vol. VI: Late adulthood.* Madison, CT: International Universities Press.

Pollock, George H., & Greenspan, Stanley L. (1992). *The course of life, Vol. V: Early adulthood.* Madison, CT: International Universities Press.

Poon, Leonard W., Rubin, David C., & Wilson, Barbara A. (Eds.). (1989). *Everyday cognition in adulthood and later life*. Cambridge, England: Cambridge University Press.

Popenoe, David, Elshtain, Jean Bethke, & Blankenhorn, David (Eds.). (1996). *Promises to keep: Decline and renewal of marriage in America*. Lanham, MD: Rowman & Littlefield.

Porcino, Jane. (1988). *Growing older, getting better—a handbook for women in the second half of life*. Reading, MA: Addison-Wesley.

Posner, Richard A. (1995). *Aging and old age*. Chicago: University of Chicago Press.

Powell, Douglas. (1994). *Profiles in cognitive aging*. Cambridge, MA: Harvard University Press.

Presley, Cheryl A., Meilman, Philip, & Lyerla, Rob. (1995). *Alcohol and drugs on American college campuses*. Carbondale: Southern Illinois University Press.

Price, R. H. (1992). Psychological impact of job loss on individuals and families. *Current Directions in Psychological Science, 1*, 9–11.

Quinn, Joseph F., & Kozy, Michael. (1996). The role of bridge jobs in the retirement transition: Gender, race, and ethnicity. *Gerontologist, 36*, 363–372.

Quirk, Daniel A. (1991). The aging network: An agenda for the nineties and beyond. *Generations, 15*(3), 23–26.

Rabbitt, P. D., Donlan, C., McInnes, L., Watson, P., & Bent, N. (1995). Unique and interactive effects of depression, age, socioeconomic advantage, and gender on cognitive performance of normal healthy older people. *Psychology and Aging, 10*, 307–313.

Rafferty, Yvonne, & Shinn, Marybeth. (1991). The impact of homelessness on children. *American Psychologist, 48*, 1170–1179.

Rando, Therese A. (1994). *Grieving: How to go on living when someone you love dies*. San Francisco: Jossey-Bass.

Reese, E., & Fivush, R. (1993). Parental styles of talking about the past. *Developmental Psychology, 20*, 596–606.

Reinke, B. J., Holmes, D. S., & Harris, R. L. (1985). The timing of psychological changes in women's lives: The years 25–45. *Journal of Personality and Social Psychology, 48*, 1353–1364.

Reitzes, Donald C., Mutran, Elizabeth J., & Fernandez, Maria E. (1996). Does retirement hurt well-being? Factors influencing self-esteem and depression among retirees and workers. *Gerontologist, 26*, 649–656.

Restak, Richard M. (1997). *Older & wiser—how to maintain peak mental ability for as long as you live*. New York: Berkley.

Rich, Adrienne. (1995). *Of woman born: Motherhood as experience and institution*. New York: Norton.

Riley, Matilda White, & Riley, John W., Jr. (1994). Age integration and the lives of older people. *Gerontologist, 11*, 79–87.

Riley, Ranny, Bark, Linda, & Howard, Tracy A. (1998). *Compass: Your roadmap through menopause*. San Francisco: LifeLines Institute.

Robins, Lee N., & Rutter, Michael (Eds.). (1990). *Straight and devious pathways from childhood to adulthood.* Cambridge, England: Cambridge University Press.

Robinson, Bryan E. (1998). *Chained to the desk: A guidebook for workaholics.* New York: NY University Press.

Rodin, J., Schooler, C., & Schaie, K. W. (Eds.) (1990). *Self-directedness: Cause and effects throughout the life course.* Hillsdale, NJ: Erlbaum.

Roper Pole, (1996).

Rose, S., & Larwood, L. (Eds.). (1988). *Women's careers: Pathways and pitfalls.* New York: Praeger.

Rosen, Elliott J. (1996). *Families facing death—family dynamics of terminal illness, A guide for health-care professionals and volunteers.* San Francisco: Jossey-Bass.

Rossi, Alice S. (Ed.). (1994). *Sexuality across the life course.* Chicago: University of Chicago Press.

Rowe, Dorothy. (1982). *The construction of life and death.* New York: Wiley.

Rowe, John W., & Kahn, Robert L. (1998). *Successful aging.* New York: Pantheon.

Rubin, K. H., & Asendorf, J. B. (Eds.). (1993). *Social withdrawal, inhibition, and shyness in childhood.* Hillsdale, NJ: Erlbaum.

Rutter, Michael (Ed.). (1995). *Psychosocial disturbences in young people: Challenges for prevention.* Cambridge, England: Cambridge University Press.

Rutter, Michael, & Rutter, Marjorie. (1993). *Developing minds: Challenge and continuity across the life span.* New York: Basic Books.

Rutter, Michael, & Smith, David J. (Eds.). (1995). *Psychosocial disorders in young people: Time trends and their causes.* New York: Wiley.

Ryff, C. D., Lee, Y. H., Essex, M. J., & Pamela, A. (1994). My children and me: Midlife evaluations of grown children and of self. *Psychology and Aging, 9,* 195–205.

Sable, Pat. (1991). Attachment, loss of spouse, and grief in elderly adults. *Omega, 23,* 587–596.

Sanders, Catherine M. (1989). *Grief: The mourning after.* New York: Wiley.

Sarason, B. R., Sarason, I. G., & Pierce, G. R. (Eds.). (1990). *Social support: An interactional view.* New York: Wiley.

Sarton, M. (1993). *Encore—journal of the 80th year.* New York: W.W. Norton.

Saunders, C. M. (1978). *The management of terminal disease.* London: Edward Arnold.

Schachter-Shalomi, Zalman. (1997). *From age-ing to sage-ing—a profound new vision of growing older.* New York: Warner.

Schaie, K. Warner (1994). The course of adult intellectual development. *American Psychologist, 49,* 304–313.

Schaie, K. Warner, & Willis, Sherry L. (1996). *Adult development and aging.* New York: HarperCollins.

Schaie, K. Warner, Blazer, Dan, & House, James S. (1992). *Aging, health behaviors, and health outcomes.* Hillsdale, NJ: Erlbaum.

Schlossberg, Nancy, & Entine, Alan (Eds.). (1977). *Counseling adults.* Monterey, CA: Brooks/Cole Publishing.

Schnarch, David. (1997).*Passionate marriage: Keeping love & intimacy alive in com-mitted relationships.* New York: Holt.

Schneider, E. L., & Rowe, J. W. (Eds.). (1990). *Handbook of the biology of aging* (3rd ed.). San Diego, CA: Academic Press.

Schreiber, L. (1990). *Midstream.* New York: Viking.

Schulz, J. H. (1992). *The economics of aging* (5th ed.). Dover, MA: Auburn House.

Scott, Lucy, Schremp, Kersten, & Weiss, Barbara. (1997). *Wise choices beyond midlife: Women mapping the journey ahead.* Watsonville, CA: Papier-Mache Press.

Seltzer, Mildred M. (1995). *The impact of increased life expectancy: Beyond the gray horizon.* New York: Springer.

Shedler, Jonathan, & Block, Jack. (1990). Adolescent drug use and psycholog-ical health: A longitudinal inquiry. *American Psychologist, 45,* 612–630.

Sicherman, Barbara, & Green, Carol Hurd (Eds.). (1980). *Notable American women: The modern period.* Cambridge, MA: Belknap Press.

Sinnott, Jan D. (Ed.) (1989). *Everyday problem solving.* New York: Praeger.

Skolnick, A. (1991). *Embattled paradise: The American family in an age of uncer-tainty.* New York: Springer.

Smelser, Neil J., & Erikson, Erik H. (1980). *Themes of work and love in adulthood.* Cambridge, MA: Harvard University Press.

Smith, Robert M., & Associates. (1990). *Learning to learn across the life span.* San Francisco: Jossey-Bass.

Snarey, John R. (1993). *How fathers care for the next generation: A four-decade study.* Cambridge, MA: Harvard University Press.

Solomon, J. C., & Marx, J. (1995). *The psychology of grandparenthood: An interna-tional perspective.* London: Routledge.

Solomon, M. Z., O'Donnell, L., & Associates. (1993). Decisions near the end of life: Professional views on life-sustaining treatments. *American Journal of Public Health, 83, 14–23.*

Spanier, Graham, & Thompson, Linda. (1984). *Parting: The aftermath of separa-tion and divorce.* Beverly Hills, CA: Sage.

Spencer, Sabina A., & Adams, John D. (1990). *Life changes—growing through per-sonal transitions.* San Luis Obispo, CA: Impact.

Sperling, M. B., & Berman, W. H. (Eds.). (1994). *Attachment in adults: Clinical and developmental perspectives.* New York: Guilford.

Stanton, Annette L., & Dunkel-Schetter, Christine (Eds.). (1991). *Infertility.* New York: Plenum.

Staples, Robert, & Johnson, Leanor B. (1993). *Black families at the crossroads.* San Francisco: Jossey-Bass.

Steinmetz, Suzanne K. (Ed.). (1988). *Family and support systems across the life span.* New York: Plenum.

Sternberg, Robert J. (1988). *The triarchic mind: A new theory of human intelligence.* ___ New York: Viking.   •

Sternberg, Robert J., & Barnes, Michael L. (Eds.). (1988). *The psychology of love.* New Haven, CT: Yale University Press.

Stewart, Robert B. (1990). *The second child: Family transitions and adjustment.* Newbury Park: Sage.

Storandt, Martha, & Vandenbos, Gary R. (Eds.). (1989). *The adult years: Continuity and change.* Washington, DC: American Psychological Association.

Stroebe, M. S., Stroebe, W., & Hansson, R. O. (Eds.). (1993). *Handbook of bereavement: Theory, research, and intervention.* Cambridge, England: Cambridge University Press.

Sturdevant, Cathie Glenn. (1995). *The Movie Guide to Transitions.* San Francisco: Cognito Press.

Sze, William C. (1975). *Human life cycle.* New York: Jason Aronson.

Tatelbaum, Judy. (1980). *The courage to grieve: Creative living, recovery, and growth through grief.* New York: Harper and Row.

Thomas, Alan M. (1991). *Beyond education—a new perspective on society's management of learning.* San Francisco: Jossey-Bass.

Thomasma, David C., & Kushner, Thomasine (Eds.). (1996). *Preparation for aging.* Cambridge, England: Cambridge University Press.

Thompson, Keith (Ed.). (1991). *To be a man: In search of the deep masculine.* Los Angeles: Tarcher.

Thoreau, Henry David. (1854). *Walden* (reprint). New York: New American Library.

Thorson, J. A. (1995). *Aging in a changing society.* Belmont, CA: Wadsworth.

Timiras, Paola S. (Ed.). (1994). *Physiological basis of aging and geriatrics* (2nd ed.). Boca Raton, FL: CRC CRC Press.

Torres-Gil, Fernanda M. (1992). *The new aging.* New York: Auburn House.

Troll, Lillian E. (1975). *Early and Middle Adulthood.* Belmont, CA: Wadsworth.

Troll, Lillian E., & Skaff, Marilyn McKean. (1997). Perceived continuity of self in very old age. *Psychology and Aging, 12,* 162–169.

Tulgan, Bruce. (1995). *Managing generation X—how to bring out the best in young talent.* Santa Monica, CA: Merrit Publishing.

Turner, B. F., and Troll, Lillian E. (Eds.). (1994). *Women growing older—psychological perspectives.* Thousand Oaks: Sage Press.

Ulrich, David N., & Dunne, Harry P., Jr. (1986). *To love & work: A systemic interlocking of family, workplace, and career.* New York: Brunner/Mazel.

Umberson, Debra. (1992). Relationship between adult children and their parents: Psychological consequences for both generations. *Journal of Marriage and the Family, 54,* 366–380.

United States Census Bureau, 1996–1997.

Vaill, Peter B. (1996). *Learning as a way of being: Strategies for survival in a world of permanent white water.* San Francisco: Jossey-Bass.

Valliant, George E. (1977). *Adaptation to life.* Boston: Little, Brown.

Valliant, George E. (1993). *The wisdom of the ego.* Cambridge, MA: Harvard University Press.

Van Hasselt, V. B., & Hersen, M. (1992). *Handbook of social development. A lifespan perspective.* New York: Plenum.

Viorst, Judith. (1986). *Necessary losses.* New York: Simon and Schuster.

Walker, Barbara G. (1985). *The crone—woman of age, wisdom, and power.* New York: HarperCollins.

Wall, Ginita, & Collins, Victoria. (1997). *Your next fifty years: A completely new way to look at how, when, and if you should retire.* New York: Holt.

Wallerstein, Judith S., & Blakeslee, Sandra. (1995). *The good marriage—how and why love lasts.* New York: Warner.

Walsh, W. Bruce, & Osipow, Samuel H. (Eds.). (1995). *Handbook of vocational psychology: Theory, research, and practice* (2nd ed.). Hillsdale, NJ: Erlbaum.

Wass, Hannelore, & Neimeyer, Robert A. (Eds.). *Dying: Facing the facts.* Washington, D.C.: Taylor & Francis.

Weiss, Robert S. (1990). *Staying the course. The emotional and social lives of men who do well at work.* New York: Free Press.

Wheelis, Allen. (1973). *How people change.* New York: Harper & Row.

Whitbourne, Susan Krauss. (1985). *The aging body.* New York: Springer-Verlag.

White, Robert W. (1963). *The study of lives—essays on personality in honor of Henry A. Murray.* New York: Prentice-Hall.

Willett, W. C., & Trichopoulos, D. (1996). Nutrition and cancer: A summary of the evidence. *Cancer Causes Control, 7,* 178–180.

Winnicott, Donald W. (1965). *The maturational processes and the facilitating environment.* London: Hogarth Press; Toronto: Clarke, Irwin and CO., Ltd.

Winnicott, Donald W. (1971). *Playing and reality.* New York: Routledge.

Winnicott, Donald W. (1986). *Home is where we start from.* New York: Norton.

Winnicott, Donald W. (1993). *The family and individual development.* New York: Routledge, .

Woodruff, Diana S., & Birren, James E. (Eds.). (1990). *Aging—scientific perspectives and social issues.* New York: Van Nostrand.

Wunsch, Marie. (1994). *Mentoring revisited: Making an impact on individuals and institutions.* San Francisco: Jossey-Bass.

Wykle, May L., Kahana, Eva, & Kowal, Jerome (Eds.). *Stress and health among the elderly.* New York: Springer.

Zahn-Waxler, C., Radke-Yarrow, M., Wagner, E., & Chapman, M. (1992). *Child Development, 28,* 126–136.

Zedeck, Sheldon (Ed.). (1992). *Work, families and organizations.* San Francisco: Jossey-Bass.

Index

A

Achievement: commitment and, 84; as core value, 134, 135, 136; doers and, 105; in early adult years, 40, 155–156; in midlife years, 42

Acquisition, 32–33, 156–157

Adaptation, 130, 219, 239–240

Adler, M. J., 248–249

Adolescence, middle-age, 120, 171–172. *See also* Childhood through adolescence

Adult development: principles of, 204–219; twentieth-century concepts of, 36–39. *See also* Life cycle, adult

Adult learners, 244–249; characteristics and needs of, 244–246; developmental learning for, 246–247; transformative learning for, 247–249

Adult life cycle. *See* Life cycle, adult

Adulthood: change (renewal) cycle in, 48–49, 53–74; concepts of, in twentieth century, 36–39; cyclical view of, 30–34, 38–49; decade orientations to, 140–144; life cycle in, 48, 49, 127–144; linear view of, 30–36, 46–47; reinvention of, 9–10. *See also* Centenarian years; Early adult years; Eightysomething years; Elderhood; Fiftysomething years; Fortysomething years; Life cycle, adult; Midlife years; Ninetysomething years, Seventysomething years; Sixtysomething years; Thirtysomething years; Twentysomething years

Adult-oriented culture, 8–9

Adults: as carriers of culture and consciousness, 232–233, 248–249; decline of confidence and hope in, 13–26; dilemmas of, in changing times, 7–29; emergence of, in changing times, 7–29; as leaders, 26–29, 249–252; life span of, 10–11; as mentors and coaches, 253–261; new challenge for, 26–29, 223–261; new realities for, 8–13; self-renewing, 234–252

Adventure, for sixtysomethings, 181

Agee, J., 133

Ageism, 33–34; toward eightysomethings, 200–201; toward seventysomethings, 195; toward sixtysomethings, 186

Aging: creative, 217–219; cyclical versus linear views of, 33–34; denial of, 161; development versus, 213; diversity in patterns of, 196, 201; experience of, 80; getting old versus, 217; longevity and, 217; of population, 8–9, 10–11, 196–197; in seventies, 195–196; in sixties, 186–187. *See also* Body changes; Elderhood

Agnew, S., 22

Alcohol use, 12, 113

Allen, S., 199–200

Alzheimer's, 218

American Association of Retired Persons, 176–177, 178–179

American dream: challenge of renewing, 26–29, 224, 225, 251; decline in engagement in, 22–26

American Society on Aging, 178–179
AT&T, 7
Andretti, M., 153
Apollo 11, 228
Arieti, S., 120
As You Like It (Shakespeare), 204
Asner, E., 189
Assassinations, 22
Attachment, 84
Attitudes for healthy aging, 218
Auden, W. H., 133
Authentic self, 84
Authority, personal, 236

B

Baby boomers, 155, 208–210
Balance: in core values, 136–137; in forties, 171
Baldwin, J., 99
Banasky, M., 165–166
Bardwick, J., 80–81, 90–91
Barrett, W., 198
Beauvoir, S. de, 133
Being versus doing, 66, 97, 105, 111
Beisser, A. R., 108
Bereavement, as model for understanding change, 106. *See also* Grieving; Loss
Bergler, E., 38
Bergman, I., 133
Bergson, H., 39
Bloom, A., 84
Bly, R., 170
Body boarding, 225–226
Body care: for longevity, 218; in sixties, 182, 186–187. *See also* Health consciousness; Longevity
Body changes: in eighties, 197–198, 201; in fifties, 177; in midlife transition, 160; in seventies, 195, 196; in sixties, 186–187
Boorstin, D., 22
Boredom, 89
Boy Scouts, 36
Bradley, A. (Phase 1 case example), 58–59

Bradshaw, P., 23–24
Breaking out, in twenties, 146–153
Brecht, B., 133
Bridges, W., 160–161
Britten, B., 133
Brown, D., 152–153
Brydon, A., 23
Buber, M., 133
Buhler, C., 236
Butler, S., 30
Byrd, R. E., 116

C

Cable TV, 19
Campbell, A., 7
Campbell, J., 62
Career system, 138
Career(s): in early adult years, 40–41, 155; influence of, on adult lives, 131; linear versus cyclical views of, 47; midlife transition and, 160; in midlife years, 42, 176–177; multiple, 12–13. *See also* Work
Caring versus self-indulgence, 119
Carter Center, 100–101, 190
Carter, J., 22, 24, 99–101, 189, 190–191
Carter, R., 99–101, 189
Cassatt, M., 133
Cast of characters, 54
Catharsis, 96
Celebration: in fifties, 173, 174; in seventies, 189
Centenarian years, 201–202; aiming for, 217; core values in, 144; health in, 189; human systems in, 144; increased population in, 197, 217; life challenges in, 144; orientations in, 144; sense of purpose in, 144
Challenges: external, 28; internal, 27–28; life, by decade, 142–144; new adult, 26–29, 223–261; for twentysomethings, 152
Change, adaptability to, 239–240. *See also* Life transitions

Change agents, mentors and coaches as, 255–256

Change cycle (renewal cycle), 48–49; critical issues of, 69–71; life as a story and, 53–54; life cycle and, 127–129; overview of, 53–74; Phase 1 (Go for It) of, 56, 58–59, 75–87; Phase 2 (the Doldrums) of, 59–64, 87–95; Phase 3 (Cocooning) of, 64–67, 99–115; Phase 4 (Getting Ready for the Next Chapter) of, 67–69, 115–122; phases of, overview, 55–56, 57; skills for managing, 71–74

Change, developmental, 130; future blindness and, 206–207; generational identity and, 208–211; internal gyroscope and, 205–206; longevity and, 216–219; principles of, 204–219; trade-offs and, 211–212; visioning and, 214–216

Change master skills, 244

Change, times of: adult dilemmas in, 7–29; adult leadership in, 249–252; adult mentors and coaches in, 253–261; adults as carriers of culture and consciousness in, 232–233; American failure of nerve and, 22–26; complexity of, 19–21; cyclical versus linear views of, 30–49; decline of confidence and hope in, 13–21; global cooperation in, 230–231; human dimensions in, 226–233; information overload in, 18–19, 230; institutional chaos in, 16–18; linear view of, 36; mastering, 32–33; new adult challenges in, 26–29, 223–261; new realities for adults in, 8–13; reactions to, 19–26; resistance to, 19–26, 91–92; self-renewing adults in, 234–252; thirtysomethings in, 156; twentysomethings in, 151–152; universal culture in, 229–230; visioning in, 213–214. See also Chaos; Global change and chaos

Chaos: adult mentors and coaches in, 253–261; adults as carriers of culture and consciousness in, 232–233; challenge of, 26–29, 223–233; cyclical view of, 46; and decline in American idealism, 22–26; environment as universal reference point in, 227–228; global cooperation in, 230–231; human dimensions of, 226–233; irrational destructiveness in, 228–229; living with, 224–226; self-renewing adults in, 234–252; social, 16–18; universal culture and, 229–230. See also Change, times of; Global change and chaos

Chapin, H., 90

Chapters. See Life chapters

Chavez, C., 133

Chekhov, A., 159

Chevalier, M., 194

Childhood through adolescence: cyclical view of, 39; dreaming in, 78; influence of, on adulthood, 130; linear view of, 34; psychological distortions from, 205–206

Children, 155, 157, 158

Choices, overload of random, 18–19

Chronic ailments, 197–198

Churchill, W., 133

Claiborne, L., 189

Clark, D., 189

Clinton, B., 22

Coaches, 253–261; defined, 253–254; to elicit core values and commitments, 257–258; functions of, 254–261; to help adults manage change, 255–256; to model collaboration and consensus building, 259–260; to model mastery, 256–257; to renew human systems, 258; to sponsor future generations, 258–259; to tap the genius of older workers, 260–261; as technical consultants, 257

"Cocktail Party, The," 38

Cocooning, 107–115; in change cycle Phase 2, 61; grieving in, 65, 108, 111–113; healing in, 112, 113–114; life skill of, in change cycle Phase 3, 64–67, 74, 107–115; living with loss and, 108–111; loneliness in, 65, 113; parts of, 111; solitude in, 114–115, 116

Cocooning room, 112–113

Cohorts. See Generations

College cultures, 151

Commencement, 106

Commitment, 83–85, 235–236

Commitments: of fortysomethings, 165, 168, 172; mentoring and coaching of, 257–258

Communication skills, 243

Communications technology, historical, 209

Compassion: adult leadership and, 251–252; as core value, 136; in early adult years, 41; in midlife years, 43; in seventies, 189–191; spirituality and, 170

Competencies. See Life skills; Resilience skills; Skills, personal

Complexity: of change, 19–21; in cyclical view, 43; and decline in American idealism, 22–26

Confidence and hope: decline in adult, 13–21; decline in American, 22–26

Conflict, learning from, 240

Connection: with nature, 238; pursuit of integrity and, 123; of self-renewing adults, 236; versus separateness, 118

Consciousness, adults as carriers of, 232–233

Consensus building, modeling of, 259–260

Construction of Life and Death (Rowe), 75

Consumer choice, 18–19

Contribution: as core value, 136; in early adult years, 41; in eighties, 198–200; in midlife years, 43, 132–133; in seventies, 189–196

Control, loss of: in death, 203; information overload and, 19; intruding events and, 129, 212–213; letting go and, 219; powerlessness and, 24–25

Cooperation and collaboration: modeling of, by mentors and coaches, 259–260; worldwide, 230–231

Core values: balance in, 136–137; general human, 133–137; by life decade, 142–144; mentors and coaches for eliciting, 257–258; midlife pursuit of integrity and, 132; revision of personal, 115–119, 122–123. See also Personal mission

Couple's system, 137

Creating aging, 217–219

Creativity: in change cycle Phase 4, 67, 120; as core value, 135, 136; versus destructiveness, 118; in early adult years, 41; in midlife years, 43; of self-renewing adults, 238–239. See also Leisure life

Crisis: in general, reactions to, 21; midlife, 37–38; sense of purpose and, 129. See also Chaos; Trigger events

Critical thinking, 239

Cruise of the Snark, The (London), 226

Csikszentmihalyi, M., 121, 234

Cultural containers, change in, 16–18

Cultural diversity, 151

Cultural renewal, 110

Culture: adult-oriented, 8–9; adults as carriers of, 232–233, 248–249; American, failure of nerve in, 22–26; generational, 209; universal, 229–230; youth-oriented, 8, 9. See also Change, times of

Cyclical view, 30–31; of adult development, 38–48; characteristics of, 43–45; of development, 46; of human life cycle, 39–43; linear view versus, 30–34, 46–47; of mastering

change, 32–33; of personal life, 46–47; of positive elderhood, 33–34; of process, 31–32; of society, 46; of the world, 46. *See also* Change cycle; Life cycle, adult
Cynicism, 24

D

Dance, generational, 209
Death and dying: denial of, 95, 159; preoccupation with, in midlife and beyond, 131–132; process of, 202–203; relationship to, in eighties, 198, 201; relationship to, in seventies, 189, 195–196
Death of a Salesman, 38
Decade birthdays, 140–141
Decade orientations, 140–144. *See also* Centenarian years; Eightysomething years; Fiftysomething years; Fortysomething years; Generations; Ninetysomething years; Seventysomething years; Sixtysomething years; Thirtysomething years; Twentysomething years
Decisions, 84; of early adult years, being lost in, 14–15, 152; future blindness and, 206–207; making, in twenties, 152; reevaluating, in thirties, 157; trade-offs and, 211–212; visioning and, 214–216
Decline, sensing, 88–90
Decliners, 89
Defensiveness, 89–90
Degenerative brain diseases, 218
Deloitte Haskins & Sells, 58
Delores (planning case example), 81–82
Democracy, modeling, 259–260
Democratic institutions, 17
Demographic trends, 8–9, 10–11, 196–197
Denial: of death, 95, 159; of midlife transition, 161–162; of transitions, 102–103
Dependency, 172

Dependency, fear of, in elderhood, 195–196
Depression era, 2, 17, 208, 209
Destiny, 234
Destructiveness: versus creativity, 118; in global chaos, 228–229
Developmental change principles, 204–219
Developmental learning, 246–247
Diet, 218
Discomforted, 86
Disease, generational, 209
Disengagement, 85–86, 95, 104. *See also* Cocooning; Ending a life chapter; Self-renewal
DIS's of the self, 111–112
Divorce, 176
Doldrums: characteristics of, 87–88; feeling trapped and, 90–91; managing, 73, 88–92; resisting change and, 91–92; sensing decline and, 88–90
Doldrums (Phase 2). *See* Phase 2
Donald (case example), 13
Donna (case example), 12
Down times, learning from, 240
Downs, H., 199
Dreaming/dream: change of, in change cycle Phase 2, 62; core values embedded in, 136–137; defined, 76; life skill of, in change cycle Phase 1, 56, 58, 73, 76–79; planning and, 79–80; qualities of, 76–78, 215–216. *See also* Visioning/vision
Dressler, M., 175
Dual-career marriages, 131, 149
Dulles, J. F., 133

E

Early adult years, 145–162; cyclical view of, 40–41; decisions made in, 14–15; developmental learning in, 246–247; expectations of, 15–16, 156–157, 160; gender and, 130–131, 150; identities in, 40–41; linear

Early adult years (continued)
view of, 34. *See also* Adulthood;
Adults; Thirtysomething years;
Twentysomething years

Early and Middle Adulthood (Troll), 178

Early peakers, 150

Earth consciousness, 227–228

Eastman Kodak Company, 241

Ecclesiastes, 39

Ecology, 227–228

Eddy, M. B., 105

Edison, T., 133

Education: adult, 245; linear versus
cyclical views of, 47; seeking further, in later life, 121–122, 185. *See
also* Learning; Perpetual learning

Educational level, 130

Ehrlich, P., 224

1812 Overture, 39

Eightysomething years, 196–201; core
values in, 144; down side of, 200–
201; human systems in, 144; increased population in, 197; life
challenges in, 144; orientations in,
144; self-sufficiency in, 198; sense
of purpose in, 144; social roles in,
198–200; stellar examples of, 198–
200; up side of, 200

Einstein, A., 114

Elderescence, 120

Elderhood, 178–203; as future market
group, 188; linear view of, 33, 35;
as new frontier, 188–189; positive
view of, 33–34; race against time
and, 131–132; self-sufficiency of,
198; transformative learning in,
247–249; wisdom in, 193–195,
248–249; work in, 180–181, 185,
200–201, 260–261. *See also* Centenarian years; Eightysomething
years; Ninetysomething years; Seventysomething years; Sixtysomething years

Eliade, M., 97, 112

Eliot, T. S., 38

Emotional maturity/immaturity: in

fifties, 175–176; in forties, 120,
171–172. *See also* Feelings, management of

Empowerment: challenges for, 26–29;
new realities and, 8–13; sociocultural barriers to, 13–26

Encyclopaedia Britannica, 248

Ending a life chapter: in change cycle
Phase 2, 73, 95; in change cycle
Phase 3, 104–107; triggers of, 94

Entrepreneurship, 201, 251

Environment, as universal reference
point, 227–228

Environmental systems, 138

Erikson, E., 37–38, 194

Events beyond control, 212–213

Evolution, 223–224

Executive functions, 83

Exercise, 218

Exiting, proactive, 105–106

Exiting ritual, 122–123

Expectations: betrayal of, 15–16; and
reality, 16, 156, 158

Experimentation: in change cycle
Phase 2, 61; life skill of, in change
cycle Phase 4, 67, 74, 120–121; in
twentysomething years, 147–148

Exploration, 67, 74, 119–122

External challenge, 28

F

Family: cyclical versus linear views of,
47; investing in relationships with,
219; in sixties, 181

Family of origin, 39, 40; breaking
from, in twenties, 149–150

Family system, 138

Fathering, 155

Feeling trapped, 90–91

Feelings: management of, 91, 242;
negative, 90–91. *See also* Emotional
maturity/immaturity

Feiffer, J., 189

Fellini, F., 25

Fiftysomething years: case examples
of, 173–174; core values in, 143;

down side of, 177; human systems in, 143; interdependence in, 172–177; life challenges in, 143; orientations in, 143; sense of purpose in, 143; up side of, 174–177. *See also* Midlife years

Financial planning, retirement and, 179–180

Financial security concerns, in elderhood, 195, 196

Finch, P., 24

Flappers, 209

Flow, 121, 234

Flow: The Psychology of Optimal Experience (Czikszentmihalyi), 234

For All Mankind (Hurt), 228

Foreign country, adoption of a, 232

Forgiveness, 114

Fortysomething years: case examples of, 165–166; core values in, 142–143; developmental goals of, 167, 168; down side of, 171–172; human systems in, 142–143; individuation in, 164–172; interdependence in, 164–165; life challenges in, 142–143; orientations in, 142–143; self-reliance in, 164–172; sense of purpose in, 142–143; up side of, 167–170. *See also* Midlife years

Forty-year plan, 187

Frank and Helen (Phase 3 case example), 64, 66–67

Frankl, V., 136

Free time, retirement and, 179–180, 185

Freezing, 89

Freud, S., 37, 205

Friendship system, 138

Friendships: of fiftysomethings, 175; investing in, 219; of sixtysomethings, 181, 188

Fulfillment, human systems and, 137–138

Fuller, B., 133

Future: blindness about, 206–207; global consciousness for, 232–233; the past and, 214–215; self-renewing adult orientation to, 241; stewardship of, 189–191; visioning, 2–4, 213–216

G

Gardner, J., 28–29, 91

Garfield, C., 123

Gasoline prices, 21

Gender differences: in early adult years, 130–131, 150, 155–156, 158; in forties, 164–165; in life cycle, 130–131, 150; in midlife transition, 160; in self-reliance versus interdependence priorities, 164–165. *See also* Men; Women

Generations: baby boomer, 155, 208–210; identity and values of, 151–152, 156, 207–211; labels for, 209; mentoring and coaching, 258–259; post baby-boomer, 209, 210, 258–259

GenXers, 209, 210, 258–259

George (planning case example), 82

Gephardt, R., 29

Gerontologists, 178–179

Getting Ready for the Next Chapter (Phase 4). *See* Phase 4

Giamatti, A. B., 85

Gideon, M., 23

Gift from the Sea (Lindbergh), 238

Gigi, 194

Gilligan, C., 164

Glenn, J., 22

Global change and chaos, 17; adult leadership in, 249–252; adult mentors and coaches in, 253–261; adults as carriers of culture and consciousness in, 232–233; American reactions to, 22–26; environment as universal reference point in, 227–228; global cooperation and, 230–231; human dimensions of, 226–233; information overload and, 18, 230; irrational destructiveness in, 228–229; living with,

Global change and chaos (continued) 224–226; reactions to, 20–21; self-renewing adults in, 234–252; universal culture and, 229–230. *See also* Change, times of; Chaos

Global consciousness, 28, 229–233

Globalization: information explosion and, 19; reinvention of adulthood and, 10; universal culture and, 229–230

Go for It (Phase 1). *See* Phase 1

Goodbye, saying, 73, 95

Gould, R., 38

Graduation, 106

Gratitude, 66

Greed, corporate and governmental, 229

Greenleaf, R. K., 108–109, 251

Greer, G., 175

Grieving: in cocooning process, 65, 108, 111–113; in ending a life chapter, 95, 104–107. *See also* Loss

Group psychotherapy, 206

Guess Who, The, 60

Gyroscope, internal, 205–206, 256–257

H

Haid, R. L., 173–174

Hammarskjöld, D., 234, 237

Hanna, R. W., 91, 111

Happiness, linear view of, 32–33, 36

Harman, W., 231

Healing, 107; in cocooning process, 113–114; grieving and, 112

Health consciousness, 11–12, 202, 218–219. *See also* Body care; Longevity

Health status, of elder population, 188–189. *See also* Body changes; Physical slowdown

Heredity, 217

Heroes: generational, 209; twentieth century, 133

Heroism, 207

High-performing people, 87; twentysomething, 150

Historical marker events, 207–208, 209

Historical values, 208–211

Holding on, 59–60, 104

Hope, decline of, factors in, 13–21

Hopelessness, American, 25–26

Horn, F. (twentysomething case example), 146–147

How People Change (Wheelis), 53

Human life cycle. *See* Life cycle, human

Human systems. *See* Systems

Humanity, evolution of, 223–224

Hundred-year-olds. *See* Centenarian years

Hunt, B., 37

Hunt, M., 37

Hurt, H., 228

Hussein, S., 26

I

I Ching, 56

Identity: in change cycle, 69–70; in early adult years, 40–41; generational, 151–152, 156, 207–211; in midlife years, 42; sense of, as core value, 134. *See also* Self

Identity: Youth and Crisis (Erikson), 194

Illiteracy, 244

"I'm Glad I'm Not Young Anymore," 194

Image or What Happened to the American Dream, The (Boorstin), 22

Impeachment trial, Clinton's, 22

Income level, 130

Individuation: in forties, 164–172; in midlife years, 132; self-reliance and, 169–170

Industry Week, 249

Information explosion, 18–19, 230

Information technology, 230, 257

Inner capacities, 84

Inner self, 69–70; cocooning for renewal of, 107–115; focus on, in forties, 164–172. *See also* Self-renewal; Self-renewing adults

Institutions: for adult learning, 245;

instability of, 16–18; in linear view, 36

Integrity: midlife pursuit of, 132; seventysomething pursuit of, 189–196; transformative learning and, 247

Interconnectedness, 227–228, 236

Interdependence: as feminine priority, 164–165; in fifties, 172–177; in forties, 164–165; self-reliance and, 164–165

Internal challenge, 27–28

Internal gyroscope, 205–206, 256–257

Intimacy: choices in, 11; as core value, 135, 136; in early adult years, 40–41, 148, 149, 155, 157, 158; in midlife transition, 160; in midlife years, 42, 176; skills in, 243

Introspection, in midlife years, 132, 168–169

Ireland, 249–250

Irrationality, 228–229

Irwin, J. B., 228

Isolationism: of niche groups, 259–260; personal, 25

Ivanov (Chekhov), 159

J

Jacques, E., 38

Jeff (Phase 2 case example), 63–64

Jim (Phase 4 case example), 68–69

Job satisfaction, midlife transition and, 160

John and Monica (case example), 7–8

John (case example), 45, 48

Jordan, W. D., 36

Joy, 33, 66, 121, 135, 136

Jung, C., 37–38, 81, 133, 159, 169, 170, 205, 245

Juster, N., 87

K

Kahn, R. L., 216

Katchadourian, H., 173

Katie (case example), 15

Keleman, S., 110

Kennedy, J. F., 22

Kennedy, R., 22

Kinetic lifestyles, 226

King, L. L., 182–184, 185

King, M. L., Jr., 22

Kiwanis, 36

Kübler-Ross, E., 95, 189–190

L

Late bloomers, 176–177

Launching: commitment and, 83–85; life skill of, in change cycle Phase 1, 56, 73, 83–86; overview of, 83; personal mission and, 85–86

Leadership: adult learning and, 249; appeal of, to older adults, 251; assumption of, in later years, 132–133; challenge of, for adults, 26–29, 249–252; mentoring and, 186–187; qualities of, 250; servant, 251–252. *See also* Coaches; Mentors

Learning: continuous, 45, 218, 219, 240–241, 244–249; developmental, 246–247; from down times, 240; leadership and, 249; in sixties, 181; transformative, 247–249. *See also* Perpetual learning

Learning organizations, 249

Leave of absence, 106

Lee, R. E., 191–192

Legacy, 201, 261

Leisure ethic, 11–12

Leisure life: in early adult years, 41, 149; in eighties, 200; meaning of, 123; in midlife years, 43, 175; pacing and, 237–238; in sixties, 181. *See also* Creativity; Play and creativity

Leisure system, 138

L'Engle, M., 127, 198–199

Letting go: American resistance to, 22; grieving and, 112; holding on while, 59–60; of life chapter, 95, 104–107; for stress management, 219. *See also* Cocooning

Levinson, D., 38

Lidz, T., 145

Life challenges. *See* Challenges

Life chapters, 48–49, 75–98; in change cycle, 57; in change cycle Phase 1, 56, 58–59, 75–87; in change cycle Phase 2, 59–61, 87–95; decades as, 140–144; defined, 54–55, 70; ending, 73, 95, 104–107; life as story and, 53–54; in life cycle, 127–129; personal responsibility for, 70–71; restructuring, 60–61, 73, 96–98; skills for managing, 73, 75–98; transitioning to new, 122–123. *See also* Doldrums; Dreaming/dream; Launching; Phase 1; Phase 2; Planning/plan; Plateauing; Sorting things out

Life course, 70, 130

Life cycle, adult, 48, 49, 127–144; change cycle and, 127–129; core human values and, 133–137; decade orientations in, 140–144; gender differences in, 130–131, 150, 164–165; human systems, activities, and roles and, 137–138; key concepts of, 129–133; mastery skills for, 241–244; mastery skills learning for, 244–249; meaning and mission across, 127–144; overview of, 127–129; past, present, and future in, 214–216; principles of developmental change in, 204–219; socioeconomic differences in, 130; trade-offs in, 211–212. *See also* Centenarian years; Early adult years ; Eightysomething years; Elderhood; Fiftysomething years; Fortysomething years; Midlife years ; Ninetysomething years; Seventysomething years; Sixtysomething years; Thirtysomething years; Twentysomething years

Life cycle, human: cyclical view of, 39–44; linear view of, 34–36

Life cycle mastery skills. *See* Resilience skills

Life design, 71

Life expectancy, 10–11, 187, 217. *See also* Longevity

Life skills (of change cycle management), 71–74; for Phase 1, 73, 75–87; for Phase 2, 73, 87–95; for Phase 3, 74, 99–115; for Phase 4, 74, 115–122. *See also* Doldrums; Dreaming/dream; Ending a life chapter; Launching; Planning/plan; Plateauing; Resilience skills; Skills, personal; Sorting things out

Life themes, 44, 54

Life transitions, 48–49, 99–123; in change cycle, 57; in change cycle Phase 3, 64–67, 74, 99–115; in change cycle Phase 4, 67–69, 74, 115–122; characteristics of, 103; cocooning in, 61, 64–67, 74, 107–115; defined, 54–55, 70; exiting ritual for final phase of, 122–123; experimentation and exploration in, 67, 74, 119–122; life as story and, 53–54; minitransitions versus, 60–61, 96–97; as normal, 101–104, 110; pattern of, 102; personal responsibility for, 70–71; positive functions of, 102–104; resistance to, 62, 91–92, 102–103; self-renewal in, 67–69, 74, 115–119; triggers of, 61–62, 70, 101–102, 212–213. *See also* Cocooning; Experimentation; Midlife crisis/transition; Phase 3; Phase 4; Self-renewal

Limitations, awareness of, at midlife transition, 160

Limitations, knowledge of, 81

Linda (case example), 45, 48

Lindbergh, A. M., 175, 238

Lindemann, E., 95

Linear view, 30–31; of acquiring happiness, 32–33; of aging, 33–34; characteristics of, 36; cyclical view versus, 30–34, 46–47; of development, 46; of life cycle, 34–36; of personal life, 46–47; of progress,

31–32, 35–36; of society, 46; of the world, 46

London, J., 226

Loneliness: in cocooning process, 65, 113; in exiting, 106; managing, 113

Long-distance runners, 86–87

Longevity: practices of, 189, 202, 216–219; research on, 219. *See also* Body care; Health consciousness; Life expectancy

Loss: cocooning process and, 107–111; at end of a life chapter, 106–111; learning from, 240; living with, 108–111; at retirement, 186. *See also* Grieving

Loss and Change (Marris), 106

Louise (case example), 10

M

Mac and Gertrude (case example), 11

MacArthur Foundation Research Network on Successful Midlife Development, 165

Mahoney, D., 216

"Making it," in thirtysomething years, 153–158

Management styles, 258

Marris, P., 106

Martin (Phase 2 case example), 62–63

Mary and Derek (thirtysomething case example), 153–155

Mary (case example), 45, 48

Maslow, A., 87, 176

Massachusetts Institute of Technology (MIT) Sloan School of Management, 249

Masten, R., 93–94

Mastery, modeling of, 256–257

Maurice (planning case example), 82

McClendon, S., 192–193

McGraw-Hill, 45

Mead, M., 231

Meaning, search for: across the life cycle, 127–129; as core value, 136; in dream, 78; in early adult years, 41; in life transitions, 55, 64–67, 68–69; in midlife years, 43; in sixties, 181

Media, 22

Meeting of Minds, 199–200

Men: achievement and, 135; interdependence and, 164–165, 174–175; intimacy and, 135; life cycle of, versus women, 130–131; midlife transition of, 160; self-reliance concerns of, versus women, 164–165; thirtysomething, 155, 156, 158. *See also* Gender differences

Menopause, 177

Mental exercise, 217–218

Mentor-coaches, 253–261; defined, 253; to elicit core values and commitments, 257–258; functions of, 254–261; to help adults manage change, 255–256; to model collaboration and consensus building, 259–260; to model mastery, 256–257; to renew human systems, 258; to sponsor future generations, 258–259; to tap the genius of older workers, 260–261; as technical consultants, 257

Mentoring, 253–261; importance of, reasons for, 254–261; in sixties, 181, 185–186, 253; trend toward, in later years, 132–133; and wisdom of elderhood, 194–195, 248–249

Mentors: activities of, 254; adult, 253–261; defined, 253; to elicit core values and commitments, 257–258; functions of, 254–261; to help adults manage change, 255–256; to model collaboration and consensus building, 259–260; to model mastery, 256–257; networking to find, 121; to renew human systems, 258; to sponsor future generations, 258–259; to tap the genius of older workers, 260–261; as tech-

Mentors (continued)
   nical consultants, 257; using, in
   early adult years, 40–41, 148
Middle managers, 258
Middlescence, 120, 171–172
Midlife crisis/transition, 37–38, 158–
   162; central theme for, 160–161;
   denial of, 161–162; issues in, 160
Midlife years, 163–177; cyclical view
   of, 42–43; developmental learning
   in, 246–247; individuation in, 132;
   introspection in, 132; pursuit of
   integrity in, 132; race against time
   and, 131–132; sense of wellbeing
   in, 165; transformative learning in,
   247–249; twentieth century views
   of, 36–39. See also Adulthood;
   Adults; Fiftysomething years; Forty-
   something years
Miller, A., 38
Mills, C. W., 21
Minitransition, 60–61, 73, 96–98; indi-
   cations for, 96; life transition versus,
   60–61, 96–97. See also Restructuring
Mission, personal, 85–86. See also
   Core values
Modern Man in Search of a Soul (Jung),
   170
Mood, generational, 209
Morale, decline in, 22–26
Mosley, M., 166–167
Mother Teresa, 133, 136
Motherhood, 155
Moustakas, C., 113
Moving on, 104
Muggeridge, M., 193
Music, generational, 209

N

Nature Conservancy, 13
Nature, contact with, 238
Negative emotions, 90–91
Network niche groups, 259–260
Networking: adult leadership and,
   249–250; in change cycle Phase 4,
67, 121–122; of self-renewing adults,
   236
Neugarten, B., 37, 169
Neutral zone, 110–111
New Achievers, The (Pascarella), 249
New wealthy, 209
New World New Mind (Ornstein and
   Ehrlich), 224
New York University, 198
Newhart, B., 189
Niche groups, 259–260
Ninetysomething years, 201–202; core
   values in, 144; human systems in,
   144; life challenges in, 144; orien-
   tations in, 144; sense of purpose
   in, 144
Nixon, R., 22
Nobody Knows My Name (Baldwin), 99
Normative view of adulthood, 36
"Not Exactly a Command Perfor-
   mance," 91–92
Nuclear family, 34, 47

O

On the Waterfront, 38
Ornstein, R., 224
Others, connection versus separate-
   ness from, 118
Outer capacities, 84
Overwhelm: with information, 18–19;
   with random choices, 18–19

P

Pacing, 237–238
Palmer, A., 189
Pamela (planning case example), 82
Paralysis from polio story, 1–4
Parkinson's, 218
Partisan Review, 198
Passive activities, 186, 218, 238–239
Past, visioning and, 214–215
Perpetual learning, 45, 218, 219, 240–
   241, 244–249; adult learner needs
   and, 244–246; developmental,
   246–247; of self-renewing adults,

240–241, 244–249; transformative, 247–249

Person, The (Lidz), 145

Personal authority, 236

Personal identity: in early adult years, 40; in midlife years, 42

Personal isolationism, 25

Personal life, cyclical versus linear views of, 46–47

Personal mastery skills, 242–243

Personal mission, 85–86, 132. *See also* Core values

Personal responsibility, 69–71

Personal system, 137

Pessimism, American, 22

Phantom Tollbooth, The (Juster), 87

Phase 1 (Go for It), 56, 58–59, 75–87; characteristics of, 75–76, 77; dreaming in, 56, 58, 73, 76–79; launching in, 56, 73, 83–86; life skills for, 73, 75–87; planning in, 58, 73, 79–83; plateauing in, 58, 73, 86–87. *See also* Life chapters

Phase 2 (the Doldrums), 59–64, 87–95; characteristics of, 87–88; doldrums management in, 73, 87–92; ending a life chapter in, 73, 95; life skills out in, 73, 87–95; sorting things out in, 73, 93–95. *See also* Doldrums; Life chapters

Phase 3 (Cocooning), 61, 64–67, 99–115; letting go in, 104–107; life skill for, 74, 99–115. *See also* Cocooning; Life transitions

Phase 4 (Getting Ready for the Next Chapter), 67–69, 115–122; creativity in, 67, 120; experimentation in, 67, 74, 120–121; exploration in, 119–122; life skills for, 74, 115–122; networking in, 67, 121–122; revising core values in, 115–119, 122–123. *See also* Life transitions

Physical fitness, 218

Physical slowdown: in eighties, 197–198; in seventies, 195, 196, 201; in sixties, 186–187. *See also* Body changes

Planning/plan: case examples of, 81–82; defined, 76; dream centrality in, 79–80; dreaming and, 79; flexibility in, 82–83; life skill of, in Phase 1, 58, 73, 79–83; principles of, 79–83; in sixties, 187; strengths and weaknesses and, 80–81. *See also* Dreaming/dream; Visioning/ vision

Plateauing: early and late, 86; life skill of, in change cycle Phase 1, 58, 73, 86–87; negative, 86, 90–91; positive, 86–87

Play and creativity: in change cycle Phase 4, 67, 120; as core value, 135, 136; in early adult years, 41; meaning of, 132; in midlife years, 43; of self-renewing adults, 238–239. *See also* Leisure life

Plot, in life story, 54, 71

Polarities, perennial, 116–119

Polio, recovery from, 1–4, 213

Population aging, 8–9, 196–197

Portnoy's Complaint (Roth), 38

Poverty, 184

Powerlessness, 24–25

Prather, H., 105, 114

Present, visioning and, 215

Previn, A., 189

Primitive thought processes, 205–206

Principles of developmental change, 204–219

Private life, desire for, 168–169

Process, progress versus, 31–32

Professional psychological help, 109–110

Progress, linear view and, 31–32, 35–36

Protirement, 179, 187–188

Psychoanalytic view, 37

Psychotherapy, 206

Purpose, sense of, 133–137; by decade, 140–144

Q

Quality of life: decline in American dream and, 22–24; focus on, in fifties, 175; leisure and health ethics and, 11–12; pacing and, 237–238

R

Radar systems, for navigating change, 256–257

Random House Dictionary of the English Language, 87

Reactivity, 89–90

Reagan, R., 24, 99

Reality, expectations and, 16, 156, 158

Regressive issues, 109–110

Reintegration, 104, 119–122

Renette (Phase 2 case example), 64

Renewal cycle. *See* Change cycle

Renewal, in life transitions, 61. *See also* Self-renewal; Self-renewing adults

Repetition compulsion, 214–215

Resilience skills, 241–244; action-related, 243; change master, 244; communication, 243; feelings-related, 242; intimacy and relationship, 243; personal mastery, 242–243; team player, 243–244; thinking-related, 242

Resistance: to change in world, 19–26; to transitions, 62, 91–92, 102–103

Restak, R., 216

Restructuring, 60–61; life skill of, 73, 96–98; life transition versus, 60–61

Retirement, 9, 179, 185; issues of, 179–180; loss and, 186; myth of, 260–261; protirement and, 179, 187–188

Revolt of the Middle-Aged Man, The (Bergler), 38

Richardson, E., 190

Rilke, R. M., 224

Risk taking, 84, 120–121

Rites of Passage, The (Van Gennep), 97–98

Rituals of ending, 95

Role models. *See* Mentors

Roles: in cyclical view, 40, 42; human systems and, 137–138; in life story, 54; in linear view, 36; work, 131

Roosevelt, E., 133

Roosevelt, F. D., 17, 116

Roper poll, on work attitudes, 12–13

Rosenthal, R., 182

Rotary, 36

Roth, P., 38

Rowe, D., 75

Rowe, J. W., 216

S

Sabbaticals, 106

Sages, 193–195, 248–249

Sam (Phase 2 case example), 64

Sassoon, S., 148

School: returning to, in later life, 121–122, 185; transition from, in twenties, 148

Schweitzer, A., 38, 133, 136

Security: linear view of, 32–33; loss of, in social systems, 16–18

Self: authentic, 84; "DIS's" of, 111–112; inner, 69–70, 107–115, 164–172; new versus former, 117–118; sense of, as core value, 134, 136; "undiscovered," 81; young versus old, 118. *See also* Identity

Self-indulgence versus caring, 119

Self-reliance, 65–66; developmental goal of, 168–169; in forties, 164–172; interdependence and, 164–165, 172, 175; transformational goal of, 169–170

Self-renewal, 104; cocooning and, 107–115; life skill of, in change cycle Phase 4, 67–69, 74; revising core values for, 115–119, 122–123

Self-renewing adults, 234–252; adaptability of, 239–240; connections of, 236; creativity and play of, 238–239; future orientation of, 241; as leaders, 249–252; nature contact

of, 238; pacing of, 237–238; perpetual learning of, 240–241, 244–249; qualities of, 235–241; resilience skills for, 241–244; solitude and quiet of, 237; values commitment of, 235–236
Self-sufficiency, of the elderly, 198
Seligman, M., 24
Senge, P., 249
Sense of Well-Being in America (Campbell), 7
Sensing decline, 88–90
Separateness versus connection, 118
Servant leadership, 251–252
Seventysomething years, 189–196; case examples of, 191–193; core values in, 144, 189; diversity in, 196; down side of, 195–196; human systems in, 144; life challenges in, 144; missions of, 189; orientations in, 144; sense of purpose in, 144; stellar examples of, 189–191; up side of, 193–195. *See also* Elderhood
Sexuality: in fifties, 177; in sixties, 186. *See also* Intimacy
Shakespeare, W., 204
Shane, 38
Sheane, D., 249–250
Siegelman, E. Y., 106, 120–121
Simplicity, 112
Sixtysomething years, 179–189; case examples of, 182–184; core values in, 143; down side of, 186–189; human systems in, 143; life challenges in, 143; mentoring in, 181, 185–186, 253; orientations in, 143; retirement in, 179–180, 185, 186, 187–188; scripts for, 180–182, 187, 188; sense of purpose in, 143; up side of, 184–186; work in, 180–181, 185. *See also* Elderhood
Skills, personal: keeping up, 217–218; life, for change cycle mastery, 71–74; resilience, for life cycle mastery, 241–244; self-knowledge of,

80–81; "unconscious," 87, 176. *See also* Life skills; Resilience skills
Sloan School of Management, 249
Smoking, 12, 218
Social learning, leaders as facilitators of, 249
Social Security, 184, 195
Social status, 130, 160
Social systems: in adult life, 138; cyclical view of, 44; decline in confidence in, 22–24; decline in security of, 16–18
Society: cyclical versus linear views of, 46; making friends with, 224
Sociocultural change. *See* Change, times of; Global change and chaos
Socrates, 26
Solitude, 114–115, 116, 237
Sorting things out: life skill of, in change cycle phase 2, 73, 93–95; outcomes of, 94–95
Space travel, 228
Specialization: and generalization, in forties, 171; and generalization, mentors for, 257–258; in thirties, 158
Spirituality: of baby boomers, 208, 210; in early adult years, 41; inner self development and, 170; in midlife years, 43, 170, 175, 176; nature of, 170; search for meaning and, 136
Staking out, in twenties, 146–153
Stand and Deliver, 251
Stearns, A. K., 106–107
Stewardship of the future, 189–191
Storr, A., 115, 237
Story, life as, 53–54, 69–71. *See also* Change cycle; Life chapters; Life transitions
Strengths, knowledge of, 80–81
Stress reduction and management, 218–219
Study of History, A (Toynbee), 110
Success, 89
Succession plan, 106

Summer of the Great-Grandmother, The (L'Engle), 127
Supermarkets, 19
Surprises, 129, 212–213
Survivors, 209
Synch, feeling out of, 88. *See also* Doldrums; Phase 2
Systems: categories of human, 137–138; cyclical view of, 44; by life decade, 142–144; renewal of, by mentors and coaches, 258. *See also* Social systems

T

Taking on, 104
Tamir, L., 38
Tannenbaum, R., 91, 111, 194
Tchaikovsky, P., 39
Team player skills, 243–244
Technical consultants, mentor-coaches as, 257
Technological change, 229–230, 257
Thinking skills, 242
"Thirtynothing," 152–153
Thirtysomething years, 153–158; case example of, 153–155; core values in, 142; developmental goals of, 155; down side of, 156–158; expectations of, 156–157; human systems in, 142; life challenges in, 142; "making it" in, 153–158; midlife transition and, 37–38, 158–162; orientations in, 142; sense of purpose in, 142; transitional environments for, 151; up side of, 155–156. *See also* Early adult years
Thoreau, H. D., 84, 163
Time, perspective on: in fortysomething years, 168; in midlife and beyond, 131–132, 159; of self-renewing adults, 241; in thirtysomething years, 155; in twentysomething years, 152; visioning and, 214–216

Title of story, 54
Tocqueville, de, A., 105
Toffler, A., 250
Tom (case example), 45, 47
Touche Ross, 58
Toynbee, A., 110
Trade-offs, in life cycle, 211–212
Transformative learning, 247–249
Transitional environments, 151, 213
Transitions. *See* Life transitions; Midlife crisis/transition; Minitransitions
Trapped, feeling, 90–91
Travel, 181
Trigger events, 97–98, 101–102, 129, 212–213
Troll, L. E., 178
Trust, 219
Turning points, 54, 212–213. *See also* Life transitions
Twentieth century: evolution of adulthood in, 36–39; generational values in, 209; heroes of, 133
Twentysomething years, 146–153; breaking out and staking out in, 146–153; case example of, 146–147; core values in, 142; developmental goals of, 147; down side of, 149–153; human systems in, 142; life challenges in, 142; orientations in, 142; sense of purpose in, 142; social dilemmas in, 151–152; up side of, 147–149. *See also* Early adult years

U

Ulster, Ireland, 249–250
Unconscious competence, 87, 176
Undiscovered self, 81
UNICEF, 199
United Nations, 234
United States: aging population in, 8–9; cooperation in, 230–231; failure of nerve in, 22–26; median age in, 9; performance improvement in, 230–231

Universal culture, 229–230
University of California, Berkeley, 146
Ups and downs, 44

V

Vaill, P., 247
Values: core human, 133–137; core personal, revising, in Phase 4, 115–119, 122–123; historical/generational, 208–210; mentoring and coaching to elicit, 257–258; self-renewing adult commitment to, 235–241
Van Gennep, A., 97–98, 110–111
Vasconcellos, J., 224
Vicious circle, 22
Vietnam war, 22, 208, 209
Virtues of Aging, The (Carter), 101
Visioning/vision: in autobiographical vignette, 2–4; the future and, 215–216; global consciousness in, 232–233; the past and, 214–215; the present and, 215–216; principle of, 213–216. *See also* Dreaming/dreams
Volunteering: in seventies, 189; in sixties, 181, 185–186. *See also* Mentoring

W

Walden (Thoreau), 163
Watergate, 22
Waves, riding with, 225–226
Way of All Flesh, The (Butler), 30
Wheelis, A., 53
Whitewater, 55–56, 247
Whitmore, K., 241
Wilde, O., 86
Wilson, E. O., 190
Wilson, W., 133

Winnicott, D., 205
Winning, 85
Wisdom of elderhood, 193–195, 248–249. *See also* Mentors
Withdrawal, 106
Women: achievement and, 135; interdependency concerns of, versus men, 164–165; intimacy and, 135; life cycle of, versus men, 130–131; midlife transition of, 160; thirtysomething, 155, 156–157, 158. *See also* Gender differences
Wordsworth, W., 113
Work: cyclical view of, 40, 42, 47; in elder years, 180–181, 185, 200–201, 260–261; linear view of, 34, 35, 47. *See also* Careers
Work environments, 131
Work ethic, 11
Work system, 138
Workaholism, 131, 158
Worker morale, decline in, 22–24
Workplace, mentors and coaches in, 258, 260–261
World, cyclical versus linear views of, 46
Worldwide cooperation, 230–231
Wounds, healing of, 113–114

Y

Year in the Life, A (Bridges), 160–161
YMCA, 36, 68–69
Young versus old self, 118
Youth, clinging to, 161–162

Z

Zero-year transition, 152
Zinderman, R., 23
Zurcher, A. L., Jr., 121